"THE EARTH MOURNS"

Society of Biblical Literature

Academia Biblica

Saul M. Olyan,
Old Testament Editor

Mark Allan Powell,
New Testament Editor

Number 8

"The Earth Mourns"
Prophetic Metaphor and Oral Aesthetic

"THE EARTH MOURNS"

Prophetic Metaphor and Oral Aesthetic

Katherine M. Hayes

Society of Biblical Literature
Atlanta

"THE EARTH MOURNS"

Prophetic Metaphor and Oral Aesthetic

"Shield of Achilles," copyright © 1956 by W. H. Auden, from *W. H. Auden: The Collected Poems* by W. H. Auden. Used by permission of Random House, Inc.

Library of Congress Cataloging-in-Publication Data

Hayes, Katherine Murphey.
   The earth mourns : prophetic metaphor and oral aesthetic / by Katherine M. Hayes.
      p. cm. — (Society of Biblical Literature Academia Biblica ; 8)
Includes bibliographical references and index.
   ISBN 1-58983-034-2
   1. 1. Nature in the Bible. 2. Bible. O.T. Prophets—Language, style.
3. Metaphor in the Bible. I. Title. II. Series: Academia Biblica (Series) ; 8.
   BS1505.6.N34H39 2002
   224'.066—dc21
                                   2002010938

10 09 08 07 06 05 04 03 02   5 4 3 2 1

Printed in the United States of America
on acid-free paper

CONTENTS

ACKNOWLEDGMENTS

This study is a slightly revised version of my doctoral dissertation, which was submitted to the Department of Biblical Studies at Catholic University of America in 1997. I am grateful on many counts to those whose teaching, guidance, and support made the endeavor possible and sustained it. The careful listening and creative insights of my dissertation director, Douglas M. Gropp, shaped and pushed forward this work, and his philological expertise significantly added to it. The attention of my readers, Christopher T. Begg and Joseph J. Jensen, resulted in many refinements. Throughout the process of writing, I consistently put to use the training in textual criticism I received from Alexander A. Di Lella.

Most of the research for and writing of this study was done away from my own university library, and I am deeply appreciative of the hospitality of the Yale Divinity School Library, its Research Fellow Program, and the director of both, Paul E. Stuehrenberg. It is difficult to imagine how my work would have proceeded without this generosity, and there is no doubt that the final product greatly benefited from my access to the Yale libraries as well as from my interaction with other graduate students at the Divinity School, in particular Geraldine Dickel.

I would like to acknowledge here my appreciation of the research on traditional poetry of John Miles Foley, which gave impetus to and has informed this study. His talk at the 1994 annual meeting of the New England Region of the Society of Biblical Literature sparked in me an immediate and persistent interest. I am grateful to Susan Niditch, president of the New England region that year, for inviting him to speak, as well as for her encouragement of my work and comments on an early chapter of this study. Reaching further back in time, I owe a great deal to Joseph Brodsky (d. 1995), from whom in the span of one semester at the University of Michigan I learned so much about the critical reading and love of poetry.

Thanks go as well to Fran Brophy and Carol Breckner, librarians at the Seminary of the Immaculate Conception in Huntington, New York, for their cheerful responses to my requests for help; to Bob Buller, who expertly took over the typesetting of my manuscript, thus rescuing me from many conundrums; to Rex Matthews, Editorial Director for the Society of Biblical Literature, for patiently answering my questions; and to Saul Olyan, Hebrew Bible/Old Testament Editor for the Society of Biblical

Literature Academia Biblica series, for his close reading of my manuscript, generous help in preparing it for publication, and warm support.

Finally, my husband Thomas Hayes, to whom I dedicate this work, has truly made all things possible in the carrying through of it from beginning to end.

ABBREVIATIONS

1QIsa^a	Qumran scroll Isaiah^a
1QIsa^b	Qumran scroll Isaiah^b
4QSam^a	Qumran scroll Samuel^a
AB	Anchor Bible
ABD	*Anchor Bible Dictionary*, ed. D. N. Freedman. 6 vols. New York: Doubleday, 1992.
ABRL	Anchor Bible Reference Library
AcOr	*Acta orientalia*
AHw	Akkadisches Handwörterbuch. Wolfram von Soden. 3 vols. Wiesbaden: Harrassowitz, 1965–1981.
AnBib	Analecta biblica
ANET	*Ancient Near Eastern Texts Relating to the Old Testament.* Edited by J. B. Pritchard. 3d ed. Princeton, N.J.: Princeton University Press, 1969.
AnOr	Analecta orientalia
AS	Assyriological Studies
ATD	Das Alte Testament Deutsch
BDB	Brown, F., S. R. Driver, and C. A. Briggs, *A Hebrew and English Lexicon of the Old Testament.* Oxford: Oxford University Press, 1907.
BDF	Blass, F., A. Debrunner, and R. W. Funk. *A Greek Grammar of the New Testament and Other Early Christian Literature.* Chicago: University of Chicago Press, 1961.
BEATAJ	Beiträge zur Erforschung des Alten Testaments und des antiken Judentum
BHS	*Biblia Hebraica Stuttgartensia.* Edited by K. Elliger and W. Rudolph. Stuttgart: Deutsche Bibelgesellschaft, 1983.
BibOr	Biblica et orientalia
BJS	Brown Judaic Studies
BKAT	Biblischer Kommentar, Altes Testament. Edited by M. Noth and H. W. Wolff
BWANT	Beiträge zur Wissenschaft vom Alten und Neuen Testament
BZ	*Biblische Zeitschrift*

BZAW	Beihefte zur Zeitschrift für die alttestamentliche Wissenchaft
CAD	*Assyrian Dictionary of the Oriental Institute of the University of Chicago.* Edited by A. Leo Oppenheim et al. Chicago: University of Chicago Press, 1956–.
CAT	Commentaire de l'Ancien Testament
CBQ	*Catholic Biblical Quarterly*
CJ	*Classical Journal*
DCH	*Dictionary of Classical Hebrew.* Edited by D. J. A. Clines. Sheffield: Sheffield Academic Press, 1993–.
DBSup	*Dictionnaire de la Bible: Supplément.* Edited by L. Pirot and A. Robert. Paris: Letouzey et Ane, 1928–.
EBib	Etudes bibliques
ETL	*Ephemerides theologicae lovanienses*
Exp	*Expositor*
FB	Forschung zur Bibel
FOTL	Forms of the Old Testament Literature
GAG	*Grundriss der akkadischen Grammatik.* W. von Soden. 2d ed. AnOr 47. Rome: Pontifical Biblical Institute, 1969.
GBS	Guides to Biblical Scholarship
GKC	*Gesenius' Hebrew Grammar.* Edited by E. Kautzsch. Translated by A. E. Cowley. 2d ed. Oxford: Oxford University Press, 1910.
HAL	Koehler, L., W. Baumgartner, and J. J. Stamm. *Hebräisches und aramäisches Lexikon zum Alten Testament.* 5 vols. Leiden: Brill, 1967–1995.
HAT	Handbuch zum Alten Testament
HBT	*Horizons in Biblical Theology*
HSM	Harvard Semitic Monographs
HTR	*Harvard Theological Review*
IBC	Interpretation: A Bible Commentary for Teaching and Preaching
ICC	International Critical Commentary
IDB	*The Interpreter's Dictionary of the Bible,* ed. G. A. Buttrick. 4 vols. Nashville: Abingdon, 1962.
Int	*Interpretation*
IRT	Issues in Religion and Theology
ITC	International Theological Commentary
JANESCU	*Journal of the Ancient Near Eastern Society of Columbia University*

JBL	*Journal of Biblical Literature*
JSOT	*Journal for the Study of the Old Testament*
JSOTSup	Journal for the Study of the Old Testament: Supplement Series
JSS	*Journal of Semitic Studies*
K	Kethib
KAI	Donner, Herbert, and Wolfgang Röllig. *Kanaanäische und aramäische Inschriften.* 2d ed. Wiesbaden: Harrassowitz. 1966–1969.
KAT	Kommentar zum Alten Testament
KBL	Koehler, L., and W. Baumgartner. *Lexicon in Veteris Testamenti libros.* 2d ed. Leiden: Brill, 1958.
KHC	Kurzer Hand-Commentar zum Alten Testament
LD	Lectio divina
LSJ	Liddell, Henry G., R. Scott, and Henry S. Jones. *A Greek-English Lexicon.* 9th ed. with revised supplement. Oxford: Clarendon, 1968.
LXX	Septuagint
MS(S)	manuscript(s)
MT	Masoretic Text
NAB	New American Bible
NCB	New Century Bible
NEchtB	Neue Echter Bibel
NJBC	*The New Jerome Biblical Commentary.* Edited by Raymond E. Brown, Joseph A. Fitzmyer, and Roland E. Murphy. Englewood Cliffs, N.J.: Prentice Hall, 1990.
NRSV	New Revised Standard Version
OBO	Orbis biblicus et orientalis
OTG	Old Testament Guides
OTL	Old Testament Library
OTM	Old Testament Message
OtSt	*Oudtestamentische Studiën*
RB	*Revue biblique*
RSV	Revised Standard Version
Q	Qere
SB	Sources bibliques
SBLDS	Society of Biblical Literature Dissertation Series
SBLMS	Society of Biblical Literature Monograph Series
SBLSymS	Society of Biblical Literature Symposium Series
SBS	Stuttgarter Bibelstudien
SBT	Studies in Biblical Theology
SemeiaSt	Semeia Studies
Syr.	Syriac

TBT	*The Bible Today*
TDOT	*Theological Dictionary of the Old Testament,* ed. G. J. Botterweck and H. Ringgren, trans. J. T. Willis et al. 10 vols. Grand Rapids, Mich.: Eerdmans, 1974–.
Tg. Isa.	*Targum Isaiah*
Tg. Onq.	*Targum Onqelos*
Tg. Ps.-J.	*Targum Pseudo-Jonathan*
ThSt	Theologische Studiën
TRE	*Theologische Realenzyklopädie.* Edited by G. Krause and G. Müller. Berlin: Walter de Gruyter, 1977–
TS	Texts and Studies
TS	*Theological Studies*
TZ	*Theologische Zeitschrift*
UUÅ	Uppsala Universitetsårskrift
Vulg.	Vulgate
VT	*Vetus Testamentum*
VTSup	Supplements to Vetus Testamentum
WMANT	Wissenschaftliche Monographien zum Alten und Neuen Testament
ZAW	*Zeitschrift für die alttestamentliche Wissenschaft*

INTRODUCTION

How long will the earth mourn,
    and the grass of every field wither?
From the evil of those who dwell in it,
    the beasts and birds are swept away,
because they say, "He cannot see our end."
                        Jeremiah 12:4

Whatever cultivation was done, the ground produced no corn, because the land was ruined by such doings, and they said openly that Christ and his saints were asleep. Such things, too much for us to describe, we suffered nineteen years for our sins.
         entry for the year 1137, MS E, *The Anglo Saxon Chronicle*[1]

She looked over his shoulder
    For vines and olive trees,
Marble well-governed cities
    And ships upon untamed seas,
But there on the shining metal
    His hands had put instead
An artificial wilderness
    And a sky like lead.

A plain without a feature, bare and brown,
    No blade of grass, no sign of neighborhood,
Nothing to eat and nowhere to sit down,
    Yet, congregated on its blankness, stood
    An unintelligible multitude.
A million eyes, a million boots in line,
Without expression, waiting for a sign.
        from "The Shield of Achilles" by W. H. Auden[2]

---

[1] *The Anglo Saxon Chronicle* (ed. Dorothy Whitelock; London: Eyre & Spottiswoode, 1961), 199–200.

[2] W. H. Auden, *Collected Poems* (ed. Edward Mendelson; New York: Random House, 1976), 454.

The compelling image of the mourning earth, turned to barren wilderness because of the acts of its inhabitants, is reflected in the above verse from Jeremiah's first lament. It occurs in nine distinct prophetic passages in the Hebrew Bible: Amos 1:2; Hos 4:1–3; Jer 4:23–28; 12:1–4, 7–13; 23:9–12; Isa 24:1–20; 33:7–9; and Joel 1:5–20. That this image took hold not only in the prophetic tradition of the Hebrew Bible but also in the writings of subsequent eras can be seen in the above excerpts from the medieval *Anglo Saxon Chronicle* and the twentieth-century poet W. H. Auden. One might say that this motif has a very long literary tradition.

Even within the Hebrew Bible itself, the metaphor of earth mourning has a long run. The texts in which it occurs, it will be argued, range from the preexilic to the postexilic eras, and they demonstrate the persistence of this metaphor over a significant span of time. It is not just the metaphor itself that recurs, however. In this set of texts the mourning of the earth is linked to the state of the human community, whether Israel, Judah, the wicked, or the inhabited world as a whole. Here earth assumes a persona, responding to human distress or transgression (or to both). In creating a literary and thematic context for the metaphor, the prophetic passages in which it occurs show similarities in phraseology, motif, and theme as well as poetic technique.

Thus, in addition to the consistent recurrence of the verb *ʾābal*, "to mourn," and *ʾereṣ*, "earth" (or a related subject), in these texts, other words and phrases make multiple appearances. A close reading of the nine passages, and of related prophetic and biblical texts, discloses, further, six recurrent motifs or themes: the response of the earth, sin or punishment, social or natural disorder, the pollution of the earth, mourning as stripping, and the disintegration of the created order (decreation).[3] In addition, many of the same literary techniques and devices appear repeatedly: the use of words with both a physical or literal, and psychological or figurative, meaning; personification; metaphors that compare human and divine subjects to natural ones; and parallel structures that relate and contrast the fate or state of the human community with the fate or state of the earth. There are thus multiple lines of continuity that bind the nine passages together as a tradition.

Yet these lines of continuity are by no means unbroken. Not all of the six themes are explicitly expressed, or even suggested, in every passage. Nor are the phraseological correspondences between the passages as a whole particularly dense or exact, outside of the bicola containing the

---

[3] These themes will be discussed in detail below in relation to the passages in which they appear.

metaphor itself, and even there variation is evident. Further, the literary setting of the metaphor in each passage is distinctive.

These patterns of continuity and discontinuity raise two sets of questions about the metaphor of earth mourning in its literary contexts in the Hebrew Bible and about the interpretation of prophetic texts generally. The first set of questions concerns the way meaning is communicated and received with respect to this body of nine texts. What do the parallels between the passages say about the role of a literary tradition in shaping composition? What patterns emerge from the reading of all nine together, and how does consciousness of these patterns affect the interpretation of individual passages? On the other hand, what does the significant variation among the passages say about the flexibility of literary traditions and the role of the individual poetic and prophetic vision and style as well as of differing historical realities, including, possibly, the shift from a more oral mode of composition to one based in writing? Recent research on oral traditional poetry outside the Hebrew Bible is helpful in illumining these questions; a summary of such research and its applications to the prophetic texts of this study is presented in chapter 7.

Such questions about how to determine meaning in a group of related passages leads to a second set of questions that concern the content of the determined meaning. What is the significance of the metaphor of earth mourning in the contexts in which it occurs? How is the mourning of the earth integrally linked to wider themes: sin, punishment, and, especially, the undoing of creation? Finally, how does the metaphor, with its portrayal of earth as a persona, function to further the prophetic message?

In the discussion of these two sets of questions, synchronic and diachronic perspectives intersect. The synchronic is represented in the articulation of the metaphor in individual texts or in groups of texts from the same prophetic collection or from a similar period. The diachronic is evident in the differentiation of expression of this metaphor in texts from different periods. Yet both the synchronic and diachronic dimensions are embodied in the tradition itself. That is, the state of the tradition at a given time encompasses its previous expressions, which reach backward in time. The use of a traditional phrase or theme brings the weight of past tradition to bear on the individual instance.[4]

---

[4] See, e.g., the application of the categories of synchronic and diachronic to Homeric epic in Gregory Nagy, "Formula and Meter: The Oral Poetics of Homer," in *Greek Mythology and Poetics* (Myth and Poetics; Ithaca, N.Y.: Cornell University Press, 1990), 18–35; and to oral traditional works in general in John M. Foley, *Traditional Oral Epic: The Odyssey, Beowulf, and the Serbo-Croatian Return Song* (Berkeley and Los Angeles: University of California Press, 1990), 2–3, 10. Cf., further,

The primary thrust of biblical form-critical and traditio-historical studies has been diachronic; the study of traditional forms and themes has
been undertaken with a view toward differentiating them and tracing their
stages of growth.[5] The major goal of this study is to explore how the
diachronic dimension of a literary tradition influences and is influenced by
the synchronic meaning of particular prophetic texts, how the body of tradition, which has evolved through time, enriches and shapes the particular
instance and how that instance both evokes and contributes to shaping the
tradition as a whole.[6]

At the same time, the body of tradition is here assigned a significance
that transcends debates over the exact sequence and shape of the development of the traditions, over precisely what or who influenced whom,
and when and how. This is not to write off discussion of chronology, of
redactional changes, or of historical, social, and religious milieux. Where
lines of development are well established or can be presumed on the basis
of a preponderant weight of evidence and argument, they form an integral
part of this study. Clearly, a sense of the history of a tradition adds to the
understanding of its impact and thrust in a particular poetic context. But
the absence of agreement or clarity on the exact diachronic shaping of a
tradition should not preclude discussion of its significance, for many traditio-historical debates will never come to final closure.[7]

Albert B. Lord, *The Singer of Tales* (Harvard Studies in Comparative Literature 24;
Cambridge, Mass.: Harvard University Press, 1960), 65–66; 148. See also the discussion below in chapter 7.

[5] See the discussions of such research in Douglas A. Knight, *The Traditions of
Israel* (SBLDS 9; Missoula, Mont.: Society of Biblical Literature, 1973), 2–3; George
W. Coats, "Tradition Criticism, OT," *IDBSup* 912b–14b; Ronald E. Clements, *Prophecy
and Tradition* (Atlanta: John Knox, 1975), 5.

[6] Such an aim is, of course, not inherently contrary to form-critical work, which
began as an attempt to understand the impact of traditional forms on the meaning
of biblical texts. See the statement of Hermann Gunkel ("Fundamental Problems of
Hebrew Literary History," in *What Remains of the Old Testament* [New York:
Macmillan, 1928], 61): "To the people of Israel the laws of literary form were as
familiar as the rules of Hebrew grammar. They obeyed them unconsciously and
lived in them; it is only we who have to learn to understand them." He further
exhorted scholars of the Hebrew Bible to develop an aesthetic sense so as to
"endeavor to dissect understandingly the beauty that is there."

[7] Gunkel's assessment of the role of chronology in his proposed history of literary types provides an interesting point of reference here: "the chronology of the
writings is quite uncertain. In many cases the most that can be done is to assign
the writing in question to a period. To arrange all the books and their constituent
parts in anything like a fixed chronological order is quite impossible.... From this

This study begins in chapter 1 with a brief survey of scholarship on the relationships between the passages and a discussion of the verb *'ābal,* "to mourn," which features in all nine texts. Chapters 2 through 6 undertake a close reading of each passage in turn, proceeding in roughly chronological sequence. These discussions follow a similar pattern: (1) the Hebrew text and a translation with textual notes; (2) justification for the delimitation of the passage as it is presented; (3) a discussion of authorship and dating; (4) consideration of the metaphor in its literary context in terms of the six attendant themes mentioned above, with special attention to significant and recurrent vocabulary, phraseology, and imagery; (5) a summary of the literary techniques brought to light in the discussion of the fourth element of the study; and (6) reflections on the overall literary effect of the metaphor in the passage. As the discussion of the passages proceeds, relationships between them are pointed out, with acknowledgment of assumed chronological boundaries. Hence in general, earlier articulations of the tradition are seen as bearing on later expressions, rather than vice versa, although occasionally a later text may be considered as offering a fuller expression of a tradition found in an earlier text.[8]

The body of the study thus traces some of the strands that connect the nine passages and form the basis for a network of interrelationships between them. Chapter 7 places these interrelationships in the context of recent research on oral traditional poetry outside the Hebrew Bible, while attempting an analysis of what is distinctive about the biblical prophetic tradition. Two sets of conclusions and implications are explored in chapter 8: (1) conclusions about the interplay of common traditions and individual expression in the nine passages and the implications for reading and interpreting prophetic texts; and (2) conclusions about the overall

---

it is clear that a history of Hebrew literature, meaning an indication of the chronological order of the Old Testament writings and an exposition of each writing in the light of the personality of the author of it, cannot possibly be written. But now the question arises whether, notwithstanding this, there cannot be a history of Hebrew literature in a different sense. The lack of a definite chronology would not be an insuperable obstacle. We should have to be content with indicating the periods of literary activity and dispense with more definite statements" ("Fundamental Problems," 58).

[8] For a comparable perspective from the field of classical studies, see the comment of Jenny S. Clay in her review of Laura M. Slatkin, *The Power of Thetis: Allusion and Interpretation in the Iliad* (*CJ* 89 [1994]: 207): "We can reconstruct the mythological framework of the *Iliad* poet and his listeners with the help of the Cyclic epics, choral lyric, and the Hesiodic corpus, which constitute important sources for the traditions incorporated and presupposed by the *Iliad*. The fact that they surface at a later date is not decisive; it is simply our bad luck."

role of the metaphor of earth mourning in the nine passages and the implications for inquiry into the place of creation traditions in the Hebrew Bible,
particularly in the prophetic message. The appendix provides a chart of
words and roots that recur in three or more of the nine passages and that
can be seen as part of a configuration of such words and roots in the passages overall.

A number of relevant works have appeared in print since the initial
completion of this study. It is not possible in this revision to incorporate
discussion of the research and insights they contribute or to provide an
exhaustive list. I would like to acknowledge, however, a number of
recently published studies that bear in different ways on my analysis of a
recurrent biblical prophetic motif (metaphor) in light of patterns of traditional poetry with both oral and written dimensions. These works, listed in
the bibliography, can be grouped in three categories.

The first category consists of biblical commentaries, which include
Jörg Jeremias, *The Book of Amos;* Marvin Sweeney, *Isaiah 1–39 with an
Introduction to Prophetic Literature;* Joseph Blenkinsopp, *Isaiah 1–39;*
and Brevard S. Childs, *Isaiah.*[9] The comments of Jeremias on Amos 1:2
and of Sweeney, Blenkinsopp, and Childs on Isa 24:1–20 and 33:7–9
fill out with fine articulation many of the associations of these verses
suggested here, despite some differences in the interpretation of various details.

A second category encompasses studies that address the role of traditional language, motifs, and stylistic patterns in biblical texts and, further,
offer models for the treatment of discrete biblical motifs, image complexes,
and phraseology. Among these works are two essays on biblical prophetic
literature by Robert Culley, "Orality and Writtenness in the Prophetic
Texts"[10] and "The Confessions of Jeremiah and Traditional Discourse,"[11]
which offer general observations on oral traditional language as well as a
focus on specific biblical texts. The book-length study of Weston W. Fields,

---

[9] The full citations are: Jörg Jeremias, *The Book of Amos* (OTL; Louisville:
Westminster John Knox, 1998); Marvin A. Sweeney, *Isaiah 1–39 with an Introduc-
tion to Prophetic Literature* (FOTL 16; Grand Rapids, Mich.: Eerdmans, 1996);
Joseph Blenkinsopp, *Isaiah 1–39* (AB 19; New York: Doubleday, 2000); Brevard S.
Childs, *Isaiah* (OTL; Westminster John Knox, 2001).

[10] Robert Culley, "Orality and Writtenness in the Prophetic Texts," in *Writings and
Speech in the Israelite and Ancient Near Eastern Prophecy* (ed. Ehud Ben Zvi and
Michael H. Floyd; SBLSymS 10; Atlanta: Society of Biblical Literature, 2000), 45–64.

[11] Robert Culley, "The Confessions of Jeremiah and Traditional Discourse," in
"A Wise and Discerning Mind": Essays in Honor of Burke O. Long (ed. Saul M.
Olyan and Robert C. Culley; BJS 325; Providence, R.I.: Brown Judaic Studies,
2000), 69–81.

Sodom and Gomorrah: Story and Motif in Biblical Narrative,[12] looks at biblical narrative patterning by tracing the occurrence of a single motif and its attendant motifs. It does not refer expressly to research on oral traditional literature, but it does identify and consider the purpose of recurrent literary patterns and conventions in biblical narratives.

The third category comprises studies on the character of traditional language and the dynamic between oral and written verbal expression in both biblical and nonbiblical literature. A spate of such works has appeared in recent years, and this field of inquiry seems to be flourishing. Examples are the essays in *Poet, Public, and Performance in Ancient Greece;*[13] *Written Voices, Spoken Signs: Tradition, Performance, and the Epic Text;*[14] *Signs of Orality: The Oral Tradition and Its Influence in the Greek and Roman World;*[15] *Speaking Volumes: Orality and Literacy in the Greek and Roman World;*[16] and *Epea and Grammata: Oral and Written Communication in Ancient Greece.*[17] Some of the work represented in these volumes takes up the role of performance in the shaping and reception of texts, whether the actuality of oral performance or the implicit social context of shared associative language and interpretation. The dimension of performance is not directly addressed in my own study, but further consideration of this dimension would seem to introduce many helpful perspectives on traditional language in biblical prophetic poetry.

All translations of Hebrew, Greek, Latin, and Syriac as well as modern languages in this study are mine.

---

[12] Weston W. Fields, *Sodom and Gomorrah: Story and Motif in Biblical Narrative* (JSOTSup 231; Sheffield: Sheffield Academic Press, 1997).

[13] *Poet, Public, and Performance in Ancient Greece* (ed. Lowell Edmunds and Robert W. Wallace; Baltimore: Johns Hopkins University Press, 1997).

[14] *Written Voices, Spoken Signs: Tradition, Performance, and the Epic Text* (ed. Egbert J. Bakker and Ahuvia Kahane; Cambridge, Mass.: Harvard University Press, 1997).

[15] *Signs of Orality: The Oral Tradition and Its Influence in the Greek and Roman World* (ed. E. Anne MacKay; Mnemosyne: bibliotheca classica Batava; Supplementum 188; Leiden: Brill, 1999).

[16] *Speaking Volumes: Orality and Literacy in the Greek and Roman World* (ed. Janet Watson; Mnemosyne: bibliotheca classica Batava; Supplementum 218; Leiden: Brill, 2001).

[17] *Epea and Grammata: Oral and Written Communication in Ancient Greece* (ed. Ian Worthington and John Miles Foley; Mnemosyne: bibliotheca classica Batava; Supplementum 230; Leiden: Brill, 2002).

1

PRELIMINARY REMARKS

SUMMARY OF PREVIOUS SCHOLARSHIP
ON THE NINE PASSAGES AS A GROUP

Parallels between the nine texts in which the metaphor of earth mourning occurs are often noted in passing in discussions of individual passages, but few studies have considered at any length the relationships between all nine. The recurrent or formulaic nature of the phraseology and imagery connected with the metaphor strikes some scholars as bland, stereotypical, and even inappropriate in certain passages. For this and other reasons, they suspect that the verses in which the metaphor occurs are redactional insertions.[1]

Others attempt to elucidate the origins, development, and significance of the metaphor. Delbert R. Hillers connects the group of images associated in Lam 1:4 with seven of the nine prophetic passages of this study (Amos 1:2; Hos 4:1–3; Jer 4:23–28; 12:1–4; Isa 24:4–13; 33:7–9, Joel 1:1–20).[2] His broad concern is to illustrate by means of this set of texts how literary tradition shapes the biblical writer's perception and depiction of events, that is, how tradition is always a "third partner" in the creative process.[3]

Underlying the images of mourning and desolation in the passages he examines, Hillers discerns a literary tradition that is not immediately apparent upon reading any one text but that emerges as parallels between the nine are considered. He links this tradition to the verb *ʾābal,* "to mourn,"

---

[1] See, e.g., on the passages in Jeremiah, Paul Volz, *Der Prophet Jeremia* (2d ed.; KAT 10; Leipzig: Deicherstsche, 1928), 51 n. 1, 140–41 n. 1, 234 n. 1; and Bernhard Duhm, *Das Buch Jeremia* (KHC 11; Tübingen: Mohr, 1901), 54. On Jer 12:4 and 23:10aβ, see Wilhelm Rudolph, *Jeremia* (2d ed; HAT 12; Tübingen: Mohr, 1958), 78, 136.

[2] Delbert R. Hillers, "The Roads to Zion Mourn," *Perspective* 12/1–2 (1971): 121–34. Hillers also considers Jer 14:1–6; Isa 3:26; 16:8–10; and 19:8–10.

[3] Ibid., 121.

which can also mean "to dry up,"[4] and traces it beyond the biblical corpus to Ugaritic myth: the mourning of the goddess Anat over the rain god Baal, slain by Mot, the god of death. Hillers's aim is to reconstruct this tradition from the scattered allusions to it in biblical texts and to show how it has influenced biblical composition (although quite possibly without the consciousness of either the composers or the audiences). In this sense Hillers recognizes both the diachronic and synchronic dimensions of the literary tradition of the mourning earth.

To the extent that Hillers's major concern is to place an ancient tradition in its original setting, however, his thrust is diachronic. He does not dwell on the adoption of this tradition within the Hebrew Bible, or within the prophetic corpus in particular, although he does comment briefly on the twist given the Ugaritic *topos* by the author of Hos 4:1–3.[5] Nor does he reflect on the role consciousness of such a prophetic tradition might play in the understanding of prophetic compositions by their audiences.[6]

In his study of the first and second confessions of Jeremiah, Franz D. Hubmann explores the meaning of the metaphor as it occurs in Jer 12:4 in relation to its appearances in the other eight instances.[7] His discussion is essentially synchronic in that he reflects on the nine passages without reference to differences in historical provenance and treats the metaphor itself as a typical motif that consistently refers to a distinct theme.

Hubmann concludes that in these passages the mourning earth is a symptom of the destroyed relationship between YHWH and the people. As such it serves as a warning to the human community, a sign of the common fate of the people and the earth. Hubmann notes further that different causes are suggested for the distress of the land in different passages. This distress is linked to the transgression of the people in some instances (Hos 4:1–3; Isa 24:4–6; 33:7–9); in others it appears as a response to the theophany of YHWH (Amos 1:2; Jer 4:23–26; Joel 1:10).

---

[4] See the discussion of *'ābal,* below.

[5] That is, the cause of drought and mourning in Hos 4:1–3 is not the death of a god but the lack of faithfulness, loyalty, and knowledge of YHWH ("Roads to Zion Mourn," 133).

[6] In fact, he dismisses such reflections as irrelevant to the particular focus of his study (ibid., 130–32).

[7] Franz D. Hubmann, *Untersuchungen zu den Konfessionen Jer 11,18–12,6 und Jer 15,10–21* (FB 30; Würzburg: Echter, 1978), 139–43. Hubmann includes in his consideration Jer 14:2 and Isa 3:26, verses in which the verb *'ābal* occurs in similar contexts, as well as passages such as Jer 3:2–3 and 5:23–25, in which lack of rain is attributed to human failing, and Jer 7:20; 9:9, in which the land is laid waste.

Hubmann thus points out some of the common patterns and significant differences among the passages. He does not, however, enter into detail about how the themes and motifs associated with the metaphor of earth mourning are expressed in each text. Rather he attempts to abstract one overarching, definitive meaning for the metaphor that fits all contexts. In contradistinction to this approach is the possibility of recognizing varying dimensions of meaning in the metaphor in different instances, while still drawing conclusions about similarities in its role or function in the nine passages overall.

Hubmann's conclusions about the meaning of the metaphor rest in part on his denial of any implications of drought in the nine passages, despite the fact that the verb *ʾābal,* "to mourn," occurs in parallelism with the verb *yābēš,* "to dry up," in Jer 12:4, with which he is primarily concerned, and twice elsewhere.[8] The metaphor thus stands, he argues, not as a sign of judgment, which drought often represents in the Hebrew Bible, but rather as an expression of the destroyed relationship between God and human beings. The erosion of this relationship has, in turn, affected the order and well-being of both the human and natural realms. Hubmann's subordination of evocations of drought in the passages to either the concept of an independently activated curse (as in Isa 24:5 and Jer 23:10) or to the concept of mourning may be due to the inherent difficulties of interpretation in Jer 12:1–4. It will be argued below, contra Hubmann, that drought is an underlying nuance in all nine passages.

In his commentary on the book of Hosea, Jörg Jeremias offers a brief assessment, attributing the common imagery and phraseology in the nine passages to a cult-prophetic pronouncement that connects the disruption of the communal order with the upsetting of the created order.[9] He thus identifies the metaphor as part of a traditional complex and summarizes its common thematic associations but does not discuss its literary development in texts outside of Hos 4:1–3. In this his assessment is primarily synchronic.

Rainier Stahl's examination of the interrelationships among five of the passages considered here (Hos 4:3; Jer 4:27–28; 12:4; Isa 24:4–6; 33:9) is primarily diachronic.[10] His aim is to identify common traditions, including

---

[8] The other two instances are Amos 1:2 and Jer 23:10. Hubmann does note references to drought in Jer 3:2–3; 5:23–25; 14:2.

[9] Jörg Jeremias, *Der Prophet Hosea* (ATD 24/1; Göttingen: Vandenhoeck & Ruprecht, 1983), 62. Jeremias also includes Nah 1:4; Zeph 1:2; and Amos 8:8; 9:5 in his comparison of Hos 4:3 with related passages.

[10] "'Deshalb trocknet die Erde aus und verschmachten alle, die auf ihr wohnen…' Der Versuch einer theologiegeschichtlichen Einordnung von Hos 4, 3," in *Alttestamentlicher Glaube und Biblische Theologie: Festschrift für Horst Dietrich Preuss*

drought, theophany, and the experience of war, and to trace their transmission and development in the nine texts. His interest is more in ordering the passages in a chronological schema than in considering how the traditions he identifies play themselves out within individual passages or work together in the passages as a whole.

Stahl's conclusion that Hos 4:3, which he takes as the first full articulation of the theme of cosmic undoing among the nine, necessarily reflects the shock of the first wave of the Babylonian exile in 597 B.C.E. is open to question. Thematic considerations alone cannot be taken as a reliable basis for dating; nor is there a significant difference in scope or intensity between the vision of cosmic undoing in Jer 4:23–28, which Stahl judges to be an earlier text, and that in Hos 4:3. For that matter, the phraseology of Jer 12:4, still earlier in Stahl's schema, hints at the destruction of the created order.

All the investigations mentioned above connect the relationships between the passages in which the metaphor of earth mourning occurs with the shaping role of a tradition they attempt to identify and describe. Due to their limited scope, they are necessarily summary and do not encompass all the dimensions of the tradition as it is manifested in individual texts. Nor do they fully consider the impact of the tradition on the interpretation of passages. Their primary focus, as noted above, is either synchronic (Jeremias, Hubmann) or diachronic (Stahl, Hillers). What is further needed is an attempt to trace the interactions between the synchronic and diachronic dimensions of the nine passages, interactions in which echoes reverberate from different points yet are held together in the tradition as a whole.

THE VERB ʾĀBAL

Any discussion of the metaphor of earth mourning in the Hebrew Bible must begin with the verb ʾābal. This verb is paired with the earth, or a related subject, in all nine passages considered here.[11] When used in the Hebrew Bible with human subjects, ʾābal is translated as "to mourn." In

---

zum 65. Geburtstag (ed. Jutta Hausmann and Hans-Jürgen Zobel; Stuttgart: Kohlhammer, 1992), 166–73. Stahl also includes Amos 8:8; Jer 14:2–6; Nah 1:4–5; and Zeph 1:2–3 in his discussion.

[11] In Amos 1:2 the subject of ʾābal is nĕʾôt hārōʿîm, "the pastures of the shepherds"; in Jer 12:11, ḥelqat ḥemdātî, "my pleasant field"; and in Joel 1:10, ʾădāmâ, "the ground." In Isa 24:7 the subject of ʾābal is tîrôš, "wine," although in 24:4 it is ʾereṣ. Elsewhere in the nine passages discussed below ʾābal is paired with ʾereṣ.

Joel 1:9, for example, the priests "mourn" (*ʾābĕlû*) in an obvious context of lament; in Jer 14:2 Judah "mourns" (*ʾābĕlâ*) in a similar context; and the judgment oracle of Isa 19:1–15 announces that the fishermen of Egypt "will mourn" (*wĕʾābĕlû*, 19:8).[12] The *hitpaʿel* of the root *ʾbl* refers exclusively to human mourning, as do the noun *ʾēbel*, "mourning," and the adjective *ʾābēl*, "mourning."[13]

Even where the verb occurs with inanimate subjects, it can be read as "to mourn" in a metaphorical or figurative sense. Hence the announcement in Isa 3:26, in a judgment oracle against Jerusalem:

> And her gates will lament and mourn [*wĕʾābĕlû*]
> and, ravaged, she will sit on the ground.[14]

This metaphorical usage becomes complex, however, when the verb is paired with the subject *ʾereṣ*, "earth," or a kindred term or expression, as in the prophetic passages considered here. An Akkadian verb *abālu* means "to dry up,"[15] and *ʾābal* seems to carry associations of "drying up" in a number of the nine passages considered in this study. In three cases *ʾābal* is parallel to the unequivocal *yābēš*, "to dry up"; in Amos 1:2, for example, "the pastures of the shepherds mourn [*wĕʾābĕlû*] / and the top of Carmel withers [*wĕyābēš*]."[16] In Joel 1 *yābēš* occurs in proximity to *ʾābal*: the ground mourns (*ʾābĕlâ*) in 1:10; in 1:12 the trees of the field have withered (*yābēšû*); and in 1:20 the streams have dried up (*yābĕšû*). Further, the root *ybš* is evoked in the repetition in 1:10, 11, 12 (2x), and 17 of the homonym *hôbîš*, which can be read as the *hipʿil* of both the root *bwš*, "to be ashamed," and the root *ybš*. In other passages a background of drought and desert is apparent, as will be argued in the discussion of individual texts below. Various commentators thus assign the meaning "to dry up" to *ʾābal* in individual passages.[17]

---

[12] See also Amos 8:8; 9:5; Hos 10:5.

[13] See BDB, 5b. The *hitpaʿel* of *ʾbl* (*hitʾabbēl*) may be the prose counterpart of the *qal* (*ʾābal*), which occurs only in poetry.

[14] Cf. Lam 1:4, where the "roads to Zion mourn" (*darkê ṣiyyôn ʾăbēlôt*), and 2:8, where YHWH "has caused rampart and wall to mourn" (*wayyaʾăbel-hēl wĕhômâ*).

[15] *CAD* 1:29b–31b.

[16] See also Jer 12:4; 23:10.

[17] See, e.g., Godfrey R. Driver ("Confused Hebrew Roots," in *Occident and Orient: Being Studies in Semitic Philology and Literature, Jewish History and Philosophy and Folklore in the Widest Sense, in Honor of Haham Dr. M. Gaster's Eightieth Birthday; Gaster Anniversary Volume* [ed. Bruno Schindler with A. Marmorstein; London: Taylor, 1936], 73–74), who argues for the meaning "to dry up" in eight of the nine

Some scholars posit two separate roots for *'ābal* in Hebrew: *'bl* I, "to mourn," and *'bl* II, "to dry up";[18] others argue for one root with two meanings.[19] The possibility of a primary meaning "to mourn" and a secondary nuance "to dry up" should also be entertained. In any case, the use of *'ābal* with one meaning could easily bring to mind the other meaning or nuance in particular contexts, creating a prime opportunity for poetic wordplay.[20]

For those who propose one root with two meanings or associations, a further question arises: What might be the connection between these two senses? Driver suggests "a gradual transition from a physical meaning to its application to a mental state," implying development from a concrete meaning ("to dry up") to a figurative one ("to mourn").[21] It is interesting

---

passages. See, further, Hans W. Wolff, *Joel and Amos* (Hermeneia; Philadelphia: Fortress, 1977), 19, 116, 125; idem, *Hosea* (Hermeneia; Philadelphia: Fortress, 1974), 65; Wilhelm Rudolph, *Joel-Amos-Obadja-Jona* (KAT 13/2; Gütersloh: Mohn, 1971), 37, 38, 109; Wilhelm Rudolph, *Hosea* (KAT 13/1; Gütersloh: Mohn, 1966), 95, 96; William L. Holladay, *Jeremiah 1* (Hermeneia; Philadelphia: Fortress, 1986), 364, 378, 383, 624; Hans Wildberger, *Jesaja 13–27* (BKAT 10/2; Neukirchen-Vluyn: Neukirchener Verlag, 1978), 912; idem, *Jesaja 28–39* (BKAT 10/3; Neukirchen-Vluyn: Neukirchener Verlag, 1982), 1293.

[18] So *HAL* (6b–7a) and many of the commentators on individual passages cited in the preceding footnote.

[19] So Arnulf Baumann, "אָבַל; *'ābbal;* אָבֵל; *'ābbēl;* אֵבֶל *'ēbhel*," *TDOT* 1:44–48; Ernst Kutsch, "'Trauerbräuche' und 'Selbstminderungsriten' im Alten Testament," in *Drei Wiener Antrittsreden* (TS 78; Zürich: EVZ, 1965), 35–37; Norbert Lohfink, "Enthielten die im Alten Testament bezeugten Klageriten eine Phase des Schweigens?" *VT* 12 (1962): 267–69; and Arvid S. Kapelrud, *Joel Studies* (UUÅ 1948: 4; Uppsala: Lundequist, 1948), 37–38. Contra Baumann (*TDOT* 1:45) and David J. A. Clines ("Was There an *'BL* II 'Be Dry' in Classical Hebrew?" *VT* 42 [1992]: 1–2), I understand G. R. Driver ("Confused Hebrew Roots," 73–75) as proposing one root with two meanings, since he observes that *'ābal* resembles other verbs that are used of plants and inanimate subjects as well as of human beings. According to Clines (10 n. 20), Driver's student D. Winton Thomas, in an unpublished revision of BDB, came to a similar conclusion about his teacher's analysis of *'ābal*. Clines himself argues that there is only one root *'bl* with one meaning, "to mourn," and that the associations of drying up attached to the verb in various passages are purely contextual (6–10); cf. *DCH* 1:107b–108b.

[20] So Hillers, "Roads to Zion Mourn," 124; Holladay, *Jeremiah 1,* 167; Kapelrud, *Joel Studies,* 38.

[21] "Confused Hebrew Roots," 75. See also the discussion on the root *šmm* in Lohfink, "Enthielten," 267–68. Kutsch ("Trauerbräuche," 36) traces both meanings to a common concept of diminishment, which occurs through drying up and diminishment misfortune. This explanation does not necessarily conflict with that of G. R. Driver.

in light of this theory to note the convergence of lamenting and drying up in Ps 102:5: "My heart has been struck like grass and dried up" (*wayyībaš*). Here is an explicit example of the application of the physical meaning "to dry up" to a psychological context of grieving, a usage that points toward the internalization of an external phenomenon.[22]

At the same time mourning in the ancient world was not exclusively an internal or psychological phenomenon but itself entailed external rituals.[23] Kapelrud finds a connection between drought and mourning in a presumed performance of mourning rites over the seasonal withering of the earth, a phenomenon attributed to the death of a god (Tammuz or Baal). In this context, he argues, the verb *ʾābal*, "to dry up," could "glide into the meaning of to lament, bewail, mourn."[24]

Kapelrud's analysis of the development of one meaning of *ʾābal* out of the other is sketchy and his assumption that seasonal mourning ceremonies were performed in Israel unsubstantiated. But the possibility of a connection between ritual mourning and drought is intriguing. Ancient Near Eastern rites over the dying god aside, the mourning rituals alluded to throughout the Hebrew Bible offer a number of parallels to the state of the earth in periods of drought. In these rituals the mourner fasts, strips off clothing, shaves the head, bows down toward the ground or sits on it, and pours dust or ashes over the head and body.[25] So in a state of drought the

---

[22] Cf. the physical symptoms of mourning described in Lam 5:17, where the heart becomes faint (*dāweb*) and the eyes grow dim (*ḥāšĕkû*). According to *CAD* (3:77a), Akkadian *abālu* occurs in one attestation in a context of psychological distress. In letter 455 from the collection published by Robert F. Harper (*Assyrian and Babylonian Letters*), a correspondent of the king, defending himself against a series of complaints, declares: "How can I live? Where is my family? My blood has dried up in my heart" (*akê lablaṭ ali ni-sa(!)-ti da-me-e-a ina libbija ētablu*). See also the use of *abālu* in Gilgamesh 11:294, cited in *CAD* 1:30b: *ana mannija i-ba-li* (for *ībalu*) *da-mu libbija*, "For whom has the blood of my heart dried up?" In these contexts the drying up of the blood of the heart may convey psychological as well as physical depletion.

[23] On the ritual expression of grief (and joy) in Israelite religion, see Gary A. Anderson, *A Time to Mourn, A Time to Dance: The Expression of Grief and Joy in Israelite Religion* (University Park: Pennsylvania State University Press, 1991), esp. 3–9, 49–53.

[24] *Joel Studies,* 37–38; see also 18–30.

[25] See, e.g., Ps 35:13–14; Mic 1:8–10; Isa 15:2–3; 32:11–12; Jer 6:26; Lam 2:10; Ezek 7:18; 26:16–17; Roland de Vaux, *Ancient Israel: Social Institutions* (vol. 1 of *Ancient Israel;* New York: McGraw-Hill, 1965), 59; Delbert R. Hillers, "Dust: Some Aspects of Old Testament Imagery," in *Love and Death in the Ancient Near East: Essays in Honor of Marvin Pope* (ed. John H. Marks and Robert M. Good;

earth "fasts," or is deprived of water; plants and trees wilt and droop toward the ground; the vegetative covering withers and is shed; and dust is everywhere.[26] An image of the parallels between the two phenomena can be found in the description of the penitential ritual in Isa 58:5, a ritual that closely resembles that of mourning.[27] Here a simile compares the bowing of the head to the drooping of a plant:

> Is it like this the fast I choose,
>   a day for one to humble oneself?
> Is it to bow down one's head like a reed
>   and lay out sackcloth and ashes?

In light of the external resemblances between mourning rites and the withering of the earth, as well as of the possibility of a figurative internalization of the physical phenomenon of drought, the verb *'ābal* might be seen as functioning in Hebrew like a dead metaphor. This is a metaphor in which the distinction between vehicle and tenor has faded and the expression takes on a life of its own.[28] In the case of *'ābal* the physical signs of drought may have been applied to a psychological condition and to the human rituals associated with it. Once this figurative usage of *'ābal* became commonplace, it could be applied widely, even to inanimate subjects such as gates, roads, ramparts, and walls—entities that cannot literally be visualized as either drying up or engaging in human mourning.[29] A second stage of figurative usage would then be established.

Whatever the exact nature and history of the relationship between the meanings "to dry up" and "to mourn," however, the possibility of a relationship between them suggests a single root *'bl*. The existence of other Hebrew verbs with both a concrete or physical and figurative or psychological meaning supports this assumption. Notable among such verbs, a number of which occur in the nine passages discussed, are several connected with mourning and misfortune: *qādar,* "to turn dark" and "to

---

Guilford, Conn.: Four Quarters, 1987), 107; and Gregory R. Vall, "From Womb to Tomb: Poetic Imagery and the Book of Job" (Ph.D. diss., The Catholic University of America, 1993), 117–27.

[26] It is interesting to note that KBL (6a) translates *'bl* I in the *qal* as "observe the mourning rites," whether the reference is to people or to the earth, and assigns this meaning to *'ābal* in all the nine passages considered here, save the three in which the verb is parallel to *yābēš* (Amos 1:2; Jer 12:4; 23:10).

[27] See Kutsch, "Trauerbräuche," 25–37; Anderson, *A Time to Mourn,* 51–52.

[28] See M. H. Abrams, *A Glossary of Literary Terms* (6th ed.; Fort Worth, Tex.: Harcourt Brace, 1993), 68. The "leg of a table" is a standard example of a dead metaphor.

[29] See, as noted above, Isa 3:26; Lam 1:4; 2:8.

mourn"; *ʾumlal,* "to waste away" and "to languish"; the root *šmm,* "to be desolate" and "to be appalled"; *nābēl,* "to wilt or droop" and, at least in one context, "to be discouraged or disheartened"; *ḫānēp,* "to be polluted" and "to be ungodly"; *šiḫēt,* "to ruin" and "to corrupt"; and *ḫat,* "to be shattered" and "to be dismayed."[30] Although the precise glossing of these verbs varies, each set of meanings can be associated with one root.[31]

But whether the composers of the nine passages in which *ʾābal* occurs with the earth as subject were reviving a dead metaphor and playing with the relationship between vehicle and tenor or, rather, playing with the relationship between two homonyms, the convergence of drought and mourning apparent in these poetic texts can be seen as embodied in the verb *ʾābal.* Such a fusion of diverse concepts and levels of meaning is, of course, characteristic of poetry, and it complicates the translation of such texts into another language. Where one meaning or association underlies or stands together with another, which is primary?

The Septuagint (LXX), Syr., and Vulg. take *ʾābal* as "to mourn" in the nine passages (with two exceptions).[32] LXX represents *ʾābal* with πενθέω, "to mourn," in all nine cases; Vulg. with *lūgeō.* Syriac provides *ʾtʾbl,* "to

---

[30] These verbs will be discussed in detail below.

[31] Cf. BDB, 871a, 51ab, 369ab, 1030b–1031a, 615ab; HAL 1002ab, 61a, 1446b–1447a, 626b. Note further the comparison of the roots *ʾbl* and *šmm* by Lohfink ("Enthielten," 267–78) and the discussion of the root *qdr* by Lienhard Delekat, "Zum Hebräischen Wörterbuch," *VT* 14 (1964): 55–56. Other verbs mentioned in this study that show a similar duality include *dukkāʾ,* "to be crushed" and "to be in despair"; *ḫārēb,* "to be laid waste" and "to be desolate" (cf. Jer 2:12); *rāgaz,* "to quake" and "to be agitated"; *nābaq,* "to be emptied out," in both a physical and a psychological sense; and *nāmôg* and *hitmôgēg,* "to melt," in both a physical and a psychological sense.

[32] In Jer 12:11 LXX lacks a word corresponding to *ʾābĕlâ.* In Jer 23:10 Syr. reads *ʾtḥblt,* "has been destroyed," for *ʾābĕlâ* in MT, a reading that may reflect confusion of *ḫêt* and *ʾālep.* Critical editions of the versions used in this study include Joseph Ziegler, ed., *Duodecim prophetae* (Septuaginta; Vetus Testamentum Graecum 12; Göttingen: Vandenhoeck & Ruprecht, 1943); Joseph Ziegler, ed., *Jeremias. Baruch. Threni. Epistula Jeremiae* (Septuaginta; Vetus Testamentum Graecum 15; Göttingen: Vandenhoeck & Ruprecht, 1957); Joseph Ziegler, ed., *Isaias* (Septuaginta; Vetus Testamentum Graecum 14; Göttingen: Vandenhoeck & Ruprecht, 1967); A. Gelson, ed., *Dodekapropheton* (The Old Testament in Syriac according to the Peshiṭta Version 3/4; Peshiṭta Institute; Leiden: Brill, 1980); Sebastian P. Brock, ed., *Isaiah* (The Old Testament in Syriac according to the Peshiṭta Version 3/1; Peshiṭta Institute; Leiden: Brill, 1987); S. Lee, ed., *Vetus Testamentum Syriace* (London: British and Foreign Bible Society, 1823; repr. with the Apocrypha; Reading: United Bible Society, 1979); and Bonifatius Fischer et al., eds., *Biblia Sacra* (Iuxta Vulgatam Versionem; 3d ed.; 2 vols; Stuttgart: Deutsche Bibelgesellschaft, 1983).

mourn," in Jer 4:28; 12:4; 12:11; *'l*, "to mourn," in Isa 24:4;[33] 33:9; and *ytb b'bl*, "to sit in mourning, in Amos 1:2;[34] Hos 4:3; Isa 24:7; Joel 1:9, 10.

I have adopted "to mourn" as the primary sense of *'ābal* as well. By representing the verb this way consistently, the connection between all nine passages is underscored, in particular, the characteristic juxtaposition of the human and nonhuman realms. It should be understood, however, that whereas in certain passages the aspect of mourning seems to stand in the foreground, in others the aspect of drying up is particularly strong, and that overall, both aspects balance each other within the immediate and wider contexts of the individual passages.[35] If one takes the nine passages as a whole as indicative of traditions associated with this metaphor, signs of the interplay between drying up and mourning in individual instances become even stronger.

---

[33] In 24:4 *'ăbělâ nābělâ*, "mourns, wilts," is represented in Syr. by *'lt wytbt b'bl*, "mourns and sits in mourning."

[34] The use of the third feminine plural verb *ntbn* [*b'bl'*] with the masculine plural subject *dyr' dr'wt'*, "the dwellings of the shepherds," in Amos 1:2 is unusual. It may reflect confusion of the masculine noun *dyr'*, "sheepfold, dwelling," with the feminine noun *dr't'*, "sheepfold, enclosure," which can occur in the plural in the masculine form *dr'*. Cf. J. Payne Smith, ed., *A Compendious Syriac Dictionary* (Oxford: Clarendon, 1903), 91ab, 97a.

[35] In Jer 4:28, where *'ābal* is parallel to *qādar* (which occurs in the Hebrew Bible most often in the figurative sense of "mourn"), the sense of mourning predominates; in Amos 1:2, where *'ābal* is parallel to *yābēš*, the sense of drying up asserts itself. Yet when the image of desertification in Jer 4:25 is taken into account, as well as the reference to the scorching winds of the sirocco in Jer 4:11, the aspect of drying up in Jer 4:28 emerges as well. Similarly, when the wider context of Amos 1:2 (the judgment oracles against the nations and against Judah and Israel that follow in 1:3–2:16) is considered, the aspect of mourning in this verse is strengthened.

2

AMOS 1:2

Text, Translation, and Textual Notes

2 וַיֹּאמַר ׀

יְהוָה מִצִּיּוֹן יִשְׁאָג   וּמִירוּשָׁלַ͏ִם יִתֵּן קוֹלוֹ

וְאָבְלוּ נְאוֹת הָרֹעִים   וְיָבֵשׁ רֹאשׁ הַכַּרְמֶל:[1]

2 And he said:
YHWH roars from Zion
  and from Jerusalem gives forth his voice;
And the pastures of the shepherds mourn,
  and the top of Carmel withers.

Delimitation of the passage

This verse has traditionally been considered a "self-standing unit"[2] that functions in the present collection of Amos as a "motto" for his prophecy as a whole[3] or for the set of oracles that follow it (1:3–2:16).[4] The opening

---

[1] I have laid out the MT in each of the nine passsages so as to emphasize the division of the poetic line into cola.

[2] Meir Weiss, "Methodologisches über die Behandlung der Metapher dargelegt an Am. 1, 2," *TZ* 23 (1967): 6; see also Wilhelm Rudolph, *Joel-Amos-Obadja-Jona* (KAT 13/2; Gütersloh: Mohn, 1971), 115.

[3] See Hans W. Wolff, *Joel and Amos* (Hermeneia; Philadelphia: Fortress, 1977), 119; Theodore H. Robinson and Friedrich Horst, *Die zwölf kleinen Propheten* (HAT 1/14; Tübingen: Mohr, 1954), 75; Rudolph, *Joel-Amos-Obadja-Jona,* 117; André Neher, *Amos: Contribution à l'étude du prophétisme* (Paris: Vrin, 1950), 11; Johannes Lindblom, *Prophecy in Ancient Israel* (Philadelphia: Fortress, 1962), 116.

[4] Aage Bentzen, "The Ritual Background of Amos i 2–ii 16," *OtSt* 8 (1950): 95–96; Shalom M. Paul, *Amos* (Hermeneia; Minneapolis: Fortress, 1991), 41–45.

phrase *wayyōʾmar,* "and he said," introduces the words of the prophet. It is thus distinguished both from the biographical information provided in 1:1 and from the judgment oracles of 1:3–2:16, which are introduced with the phrase *kōh ʾāmar yhwh,* "thus says YHWH," and in which YHWH is the speaker, through Amos, rather than Amos himself.

AUTHORSHIP AND DATING

The dating of Amos 1:2 is complicated by the fact that variant forms of the verse occur in Jer 25:30 and Joel 4:16. In these verses YHWH roars and utters the divine voice: in Joel as a warning against the foreign nations opposed to Israel; in Jeremiah against all the inhabitants of the earth, including Israel (Judah).[5] Amos 1:2, then, shares not only the motif of the earth mourning with other biblical passages but also the motif of YHWH as a lion, roaring from a high place with disastrous effects.

It is possible that Amos 1:2, Jer 25:30, and Joel 4:16 each draw independently on a traditional *topos.*[6] Others argue, however, for a relationship of dependence between the three passages,[7] and a good number conclude that the verses in Jeremiah and Joel pick up on an earlier articulation in Amos, whether or not Amos 1:2 itself adapts a preexisting *topos.*[8] This last conclusion presumes an earlier date for Amos 1:2, and in fact some commentators attribute this verse, if not to Amos himself,[9] then to a preexilic Judean redaction.[10]

---

[5] See William L. Holladay, *Jeremiah 1* (Hermeneia; Philadelphia: Fortress, 1986), 678–79.

[6] See Bentzen, "Ritual Background," 95; Lindblom, *Prophecy in Ancient Israel,* 116.

[7] See the discussion in Paul, *Amos,* 41 n. 77.

[8] Wolff, *Joel and Amos,* 122; Rudolph, *Joel-Amos-Obadja-Jona,* 117–18; Paul, *Amos,* 41. On Jeremiah's citation of Amos 1:2, see Holladay, *Jeremiah 1,* 678.

[9] Rudolph, *Joel-Amos-Obadja-Jona,* 117–18; Paul, *Amos,* 36–38; Adams S. van der Woude, "Three Classical Prophets: Amos, Hosea and Micah," in *Israel's Prophetic Tradition: Essays in Honour of Peter R. Ackroyd* (ed. R. Coggins, A. Phillips, and M. A. Knibb; Cambridge: Cambridge University Press, 1982), 40; Neher, *Amos,* 11–12; Robinson and Horst, *Die zwölf kleinen Propheten,* 74–75; Francis I. Andersen and David N. Freedman, *Amos* (AB 24A; New York: Doubleday, 1989), 196–99.

[10] Wolff, *Joel and Amos,* 106–12, 120–22; Robert Martin-Achard, *Amos: L'homme, le message, l'influence* (Geneva: Labor et Fides, 1984), 57–59; Rainier Stahl, "'Deshalb trocknet die Erde aus und verschmachten alle, die auf ihr wohnen...' Der Versuch einer theologiegeschichtlichen Einordnung von Hos 4, 3," in *Alttestamentlicher Glaube und Biblische Theologie: Festschrift für Horst Dietrich Preuss zum 65. Geburtstag* (ed. Jutta Hausmann and Hans-Jürgen Zobel; Stuttgart: Kohlhammer, 1992), 169–70. Wolff dates this redaction to the time of Josiah.

Those who consider the verse original to Amos point to the lion imagery in 3:4, 8, where *šā'ag* and *nātan qôlô* recur; in 3:8 the latter phrase is used, as in 1:2, of YHWH. Together 3:4, 8 speak of the fear and destruction ensuing from the lion's roar. The saying in 3:12 is also pertinent, with its mention of shepherd and lion together: "Thus says YHWH: 'As the shepherd snatches from the mouth of the lion two legs or the piece of an ear, so the children of Israel will be snatched; those who live in Samaria with the headboard of a bed and in Damascus, with the sideboard of a couch.'"[11]

Some suggest that a Judean redactor or redactors deftly fashioned 1:2 from the material now found in Amos 3 to create a fitting motto for the book as a whole.[12] It seems also possible that Amos himself was familiar with a traditional *topos* of YHWH roaring like a lion from a high place and disturbing the earth, using it as a key image of his vision of the end of Israel (1:2) and developing its implications in further sayings (3:4, 8, 12). The metaphors of YHWH as a lion in Hos 5:14; 11:10; and 13:8 and of judgment as drought in Hos 9:16 and 13:15 support the possibility of a provenance in the preexilic period, perhaps even in the eighth century, for Amos 1:2.

THEMES AND MOTIFS

THE RESPONSE OF THE EARTH

Although Amos 1:2 can be regarded as a motto for the book as a whole, it is a discrete unit, and its connections to other compositions in the collection are not explicit. Further, although the succinct, highly figurative

---

[11] Read *ûbĕdammešeq 'āmešet 'āreś* for *ûbidmešeq 'āreś* (MT), presuming a haplography. The word *'āmešet* is interpreted here as an Akkadian loanword meaning "the sideboard of a bed"; see *CAD* 2:3a, 4a, contra Hartmut Gese ("Kleine Beiträge zum Verständnis des Amos-buches," *VT* 12 [1962]: 427–32), who glosses this word as "headboard." Wolff (*Joel and Amos*, 196) emends MT by replacing *ûbidmešeq* with *ûbĕ'āmešet* and reading "and with the sideboard of a couch." It should be acknowledged that the reading *'āmešet* poses a problem for dating the verse to the time of Amos, as Akkadian *amaštu* (as opposed to *amartu*) suggests Babylonian rather than Assyrian provenience; see *CAD* 2:3ab and *GAG* §35c. The form of the sibilant in *'āmešet* would further indicate the Babylonian rather than the Assyrian sphere; see Stephen A. Kaufmann, *The Akkadian Influence on Aramaic* (AS 19; Chicago: University of Chicago Press, 1974), 140–41. The difficulty of formulating the entire verse in poetic lines may be another indication that it is a later addition. Neither the occurrence of a prose verse nor the use of *'āmešet* can be considered definitive for dating, however.

[12] See, e.g., Wolff, *Joel and Amos*, 121–22; Martin-Achard, *Amos*, 59.

language of the verse may distill the essence of Amos's message, it gives few unequivocal clues to meaning. Discussion of the themes raised in Amos 1:2 must deal, then, with the shadings of allusion, image, and symbol and with the implicit connections of the verse with the prophecies it precedes.

The first thing to note about Amos 1:2 is its two-part structure. In the first line, YHWH acts (or, more specifically, communicates); in the second, pastures and forest react.[13] It has been frequently pointed out that this verse is reminiscent of biblical depictions of the theophany of YHWH as the divine warrior.[14] In such passages the fear, physical trembling, and devastation manifest in nature at the appearance of the divine warrior and his armies demonstrate the cosmic and unassailable power of YHWH. A number of such depictions single out the voice of YHWH as a destructive force, among them Ps 46:7:

> Nations roil, kingdoms shake;
> he gives forth his voice [*nātan běqôlô*], the earth melts.[15]

The phrase *nātan qôlô* with YHWH as subject occurs elsewhere in the Hebrew Bible as an expression for thunder—an oblique reference to the manifestation of YHWH as storm god.[16] Yet this interpretation seems to belie the apparent drought in Amos 1:2b that follows the divine action in 1:2a.

Addressing this contradiction, Weiss presumes synonymous parallelism in 1:2a and argues that the verb *šā'ag,* which appears in the first colon, sets the tone for the whole line.[17] This verb, although it occurs once in the Hebrew Bible in connection with divine thunder (Job 37:4), conveys more often the traditional image of YHWH as a lion, fearsome and destructive when aroused.[18] The implicit comparison of God and lion in the sayings

---

[13] For this pattern of action and reaction, see Wolff, *Joel and Amos,* 118; Weiss ("Methodologisches über die Behandlung der Metapher," 6) prefers the terms "propter hoc" and "post hoc"; Neher (*Amos,* 12), "before" and "after" ["de l'avant à l'après"].

[14] Wolff, *Joel and Amos,* 118–19; Paul, *Amos,* 38–41; Frank M. Cross, *Canaanite Myth and Hebrew Epic* (Cambridge, Mass.: Harvard University Press, 1973), 174; Stahl, "Deshalb trocknet," 169–70.

[15] See also Ps 29:5–8; 1 Sam 7:10; and Nah 1:4.

[16] See Ps 18:14 (= 2 Sam 22:14); Ps 68:34. See also Cross, *Canaanite Myth and Hebrew Epic,* 174.

[17] "Methodologisches über die Behandlung der Metapher," 12–13.

[18] See, e.g., Hos 11:10 (with *šā'ag*) and Isa 31:4; cf. Jer 25:30; Joel 4:16. For other portrayals of YHWH as a lion, see, e.g., Hos 5:14; 13:7–8; Jer 49:19 = 50:44.

of 3:4, 8, seems to bear out Weiss's contention that the metaphor of God as a lion dominates 1:2a and that *nātan qôlô* in the second colon echoes *yiš'āg* in the first. In Amos 3:4, as noted, the lion both roars ([*hă*]*yiš'ag*) and gives forth his voice (*yittēn qôlô*).[19] Weiss argues that the reaction to YHWH's roar or utterance in 1:2a can be seen as a psychological response of terror rather than a strictly natural phenomenon,[20] and any contradiction between the storm-theophany language of 1:2a and the drought of 1:2b is therefore muted.[21]

Yet as James L. Kugel has demonstrated, the term *synonymous parallelism* is somewhat of a misnomer, since the second colon in a line of Hebrew poetry rarely, if ever, simply mirrors the first but most often adds a new element.[22] Further, poetic words and phrases often carry more than one meaning. Thus *nātan qôlô* can retain its resonance of divine thunder while still completing the image of the lion's roar. In 1:2, then, YHWH is presented as a roaring lion, breaking into the consciousness of all in Israel with a sound reminiscent of the thunder of the divine warrior, who marshals the power of the storm against all opponents.

Within the context both of ancient Near Eastern myth and of representations of YHWH in the Hebrew Bible, there is no contradiction in the portrayal of a god who brings both storm and drought. In Sumerian literature, the laments over the destruction of cities relate the devastation of a city by a storm sent by Enlil, the air or storm god. Yet the nature of the storm may vary even within one lament. Sometimes the storm brings wind, rain, and floods,[23] and the "flood" or "flood storm" is a key image for destruction in these compositions.[24] But sometimes the storm brings intense

---

[19] In Jer 12:8 these two verbs occur together again in connection with lion imagery, although the imagery is reversed: the people of Israel are represented as a lion of the forest (*kĕ'aryēh bayya'ar*, "like a lion of the forest") lifting its voice against YHWH (*nātĕnâ 'alay bĕqôlāh*, "she has given forth her voice against me").

[20] So Weiss, "Methodòlogisches über die Behandlung der Metapher," 11–16; see also Rudolph, *Joel-Amos-Obadja-Jona*, 116–17.

[21] See, apparently, Cross, *Canaanite Myth and Hebrew Epic*, 174.

[22] *The Idea of Biblical Poetry: Parallelism and Its History* (New Haven, Conn.: Yale University Press, 1981), 1–58.

[23] "Lament over the Destruction of Ur," trans. Samuel N. Kramer (*ANET*, 455–63), lines 129–130.

[24] Ibid., lines 184, 199; "Lament over the Destruction of Sumer and Ur," trans. Samuel N. Kramer (*ANET*, 611–19), lines 2, 76, 111–112, 118; "The Curse of Agade," trans. Samuel N. Kramer (*ANET*, 646–51), lines 148–150.

heat, dust, and wind[25] along with drought and famine,[26] and sometimes earthquake as well.[27] At other times the storm represents a military invasion.[28] Exactly what actual phenomena lie behind this imagery may not be wholly clear, but the multiple forms of devastation, all emanating (either directly or indirectly) from Enlil, the storm god, are evident.[29] Mesopotamia was, of course, subject to severe flooding and heavy rains as well as to wind, dust storms, and drought.[30]

Within the Hebrew Bible, the image of YHWH as God of the storm can be equally complex. In the Elijah cycle, for example, YHWH imposes drought on Israel, then sends rain.[31] In Ps 68:8–10 YHWH the warrior brings rain, and the earth quakes at the divine presence; in Ps 18:6–16 (= 2 Sam 22:8–16) the divine weapons are darkness, lightning, hailstones, and wind. Yet the hymn in Nah 1:2–8 represents the storm of YHWH as bringing drought and earthquake.[32] Nahum 1:3b–5 states:

> In whirlwind and storm is his way,
>   and cloud is the dust of his feet,
> Who rebukes the sea and makes it dry [*wayyabběšēhû*]
>   and has dried up all the rivers [*heḥěrîb*];

---

[25] "Lament over the Destruction of Ur", lines 178–194.

[26] Ibid., lines 269–274; "Lament over the Destruction of Sumer and Ur," lines 61, 124–135, 297–318, 392–406; "The Curse of Agade," lines 170–82.

[27] "Lament over the Destruction of Ur," line 198.

[28] Ibid., lines 210–252; "Lament over the Destruction of Sumer and Ur," lines 65–117; "The Curse of Agade," lines 148–169. For the intertwining of images of storm and invasion in the Sumerian city laments and the Curse of Agade, see Frederick W. Dobbs-Allsopp, *Weep, O Daughter of Zion: A Study of the City Lament Genre in the Hebrew Bible* (BibOr 44; Rome: Pontifical Biblical Institute, 1993), 57–58.

[29] See also Delbert H. Hillers (*Treaty-Curses and the Old Testament Prophets* [BibOr 16; Rome: Pontifical Biblical Institute, 1964], 17), who points to the linking of the Assyrian god Adad, "supervisor of the waterways of heaven and earth," with curses related to "drought, flooding, and famine."

[30] Thorkild Jacobsen, "Mesopotamia: The Cosmos As a State," in *The Intellectual Adventure of Ancient Man* (ed. Henri Frankfort et al.; Chicago: University of Chicago Press, 1946; repr. with revised bibliographies, 1977), 126–26, 157–58; see also Samuel N. Kramer, *The Sumerians: Their History, Culture, and Character* (Chicago: University of Chicago Press, 1963), 151–52.

[31] 1 Kgs 17:1; 18:1, 41–45; see also Amos 4:7–8.

[32] If Amos 1:2 is dated to the time of Amos or not long after, Nah 1:2–8 represents a later prophetic text but may still be seen as drawing on phraseology associated with a traditional *topos* (as may the psalms cited).

Bashan and Carmel languish [*ʾumlal*],
    and the bud of Lebanon languishes [*ʾumlal*];
The mountains quake before him,
    and the hills melt;
The earth crashes into ruins before him,[33]
    and the world and all who live in it.

Further, in 1:6 "his wrath is poured out like fire" (*kāʾēš*); yet 1:8 states: "and with an overflowing flood [*ûbĕšetep ʿōbēr*] he will make a full end."[34]

An example of the concurrent mention of rain and drought in a poetic text occurs in Isa 25:4–5a, although YHWH's role in this instance is protective:

For you are a refuge for the poor,
    a refuge for those in want in their distress,
A shelter from the driving rain,
    shade from the parching heat.
For the spirit of the ruthless is like cold[35] driving rain,
    like the parching heat of a dry place.

Here the destructive power of the ruthless is compared both to soaking rain and searing heat. In Isa 18:4 YHWH is compared to both dry heat and dew:

For thus YHWH said to me:
    I will quietly look from my dwelling place,

---

[33] Read *wattēšeʾ* (from the root *šʾh*) for *wattiśśāʾ*, "lift up" (MT); so, probably, Syr. *zʿt*, "shakes," and Vulg., *contremuit*, "quakes." So Hermann Gunkel, *Schöpfung und Chaos in Urzeit und Endzeit* (Göttingen: Vandenhoeck & Ruprecht, 1895), 33; BDB, 671a. The verb *nāśāʾ* is transitive in the Hebrew Bible save in this and a few other contested passages (see BDB, 670b–71a). If ἀνεστάλη in the LXX is translated "lift up" (on the use of the passive for middle and deponent verbs in Hellenistic Greek, see BDF §§78, 307), it could reflect MT. It could, however, also represent the *nipʿal* form *tinnāśēʾ*, "is lifted up."

[34] See also the juxtaposed similes describing YHWH's advent in Mic 1:4b, where the mountains melt and valleys split "like wax before fire, like waters poured down a slope."

[35] Read *qōr* for *qîr*, "wall" (MT); so *BHS*. The construct *kĕzerem qōr*, in which the abstract noun *qōr*, "cold," as the *nomen rectum*, modifies *zerem*, "driving rain," is paralleled in Nah 3:17, where the feminine abstract noun *qārâ*, "cold," functions similarly: *bĕyôm qārâ*, "on a cold day" (see also Prov 25:20). MT may have resulted from a reading of *qîr* (*qîr*) for *qōr*; the shorter spelling *qîr* occurs in Isa 22:5.

Like shimmering heat upon light;
like a cloud of dew on the day[36] of harvest.[37]

In Amos 1:2a, then, YHWH sounds forth power and force, roaring like a lion and giving voice like the divine warrior of ancient myth. The reaction to this communication is presented in 1:2b and given special emphasis by the placement of the verbs (*'ābal* and *yābēš*) in first position in each colon, in contrast to the syntax of 1:2a.

In response to YHWH's roar, the pastures of the shepherds mourn (*wĕ'ābĕlû*) and the top of Carmel withers (*wĕyābēš*).[38] Although the latter verb is stative, the *qal* form of the active verb *'ābal* (*wĕ'ābĕlû*) conveys a response on the part of the earth rather than simply narrating an effect brought about by the agency of YHWH, as a passive form would do.[39]

The associations of *'ābal* with the concept of drying up are evoked here by the parallel verb *yābēš*, "to dry up," in the second colon. Yet the aspect of mourning is strengthened by the coupling of *'ābal* with the expression *nĕ'ôt hārō'îm*, "pastures of the shepherds," which introduces a human element, hinting at the impact of YHWH's roar on human beings.[40] The placement of 1:2 preceding the predictions of human disaster in the oracles against the nations (1:3–2:16) also intensifies the resonance of "mourn."[41]

---

[36] Read *bĕyôm* for *bĕhōm,* "in the heat of" (MT), with some MSS, LXX, Syr., Vulg. (so *BHS*).

[37] With these passages compare the juxtaposed metaphors in Jer 51:42–43, where both floods and drought strike Babylon.

[38] This reaction of the earth is consistent with a pattern of human mourning identified by Waldemar Janzen, *Mourning Cry and Woe Oracle* (BZAW 125; Berlin: de Gruyter, 1972), 89. He suggests "a rather regular place for anticipatory mourning within the Holy War–Day of the Lord pattern" and cites various examples of exhortations to mourn and mourning cries in the prophetic literature "because of the approaching onslaught of the Divine Warrior."

[39] Although as a stative verb *yābēš* conveys an effected state, it describes the state itself rather than the effecting act, which would clearly entail an agent.

[40] Hence a possible reason for the use of this phrase rather than the more common expression *nĕ'ôt midbār,* "pastures of the wilderness." See Weiss, "Methodologisches über die Behandlung der Metapher," 16–21; Rudolph, *Joel-Amos-Obadja-Jona,* 116; Paul, *Amos,* 40.

[41] It has been suggested that both verbs in 1:2b be read in a psychological sense by revocalizing *wĕyābēš,* "withers," to *wĕyēbōš,* "will be ashamed, confounded" (see Weiss, "Methodologisches über die Behandlung der Metapher," 8; Rudolph, *Joel-Amos-Obadja-Jona,* 117). Wordplay with the *hip'il* forms of the roots *ybš* and *bwš* occurs in Joel 1:8–20 (as does the verb *'ābal*), and it is possible that

Despite the suggestion of human society inherent in the phrase "the pastures of the shepherds," these pastures are also part of the natural world, the physical earth, as is the parallel subject, *rō'š hakkarmel,* "the top of Carmel." The two subjects together form a larger totality, a merism that can be construed as mountains and plains, woods and pastures, or north (Mount Carmel) and south (*midbār,* or desert).[42] In Jer 9:9 a similar pattern of parallelism occurs:

> For the mountains I will take up weeping and wailing,
> and for the pastures of the wilderness [*nĕ'ôt midbār*], a dirge.[43]

In each case a picture of distress throughout the natural world is presented. In Amos 1:2b the choice of Carmel as a symbol of lush fertility and the reference to the pastures of the shepherds—sheep-herding being an occupation of long standing in Israelite tradition—centers earth's response within the land of Israel.[44]

SIN OR PUNISHMENT

The earth, then, responds to the roar of YHWH by mourning and shrivelling. The verse imparts the reason for this response only by implication. A lion's roar indicates a dangerous beast on the prowl for prey, and the phrase *nātan qōlô* may allude to traditions of the divine warrior who turns the power of nature against his enemies. If the land of Israel withers on hearing this sound, then the land must be interpreting it as a sign that YHWH is threatening to ravage *it.*

That Amos 1:2 goes no further than implication is consistent with a hymnic style,[45] which proclaims the deeds and power of YHWH, as opposed to the style of a prophetic judgment oracle, which often includes

---

in Amos 1:2 *wĕyābēš* was intended to reverberate with *wĕyēbōš.* If this kind of sound play is acknowledged, the revocalization of *wĕyābēš* is unnecessary. Aside from the standard objections to an emendation of MT when it can arguably be interpreted as it stands, *'ābal* and *yābēš* are also paired in parallel cola in Jer 12:4 and 23:10.

[42] See the summary of possibilities in Paul, *Amos,* 40 n. 72.

[43] Here the natural world is lamented over rather than lamenting itself.

[44] Although Carmel may be a traditional symbol for fertility in the Hebrew Bible (see, e.g., Isa 33:9; Nah 1:4; Mic 7:14; and Weiss, "Methodologisches über die Behandlung der Metapher," 17–18), it also evokes a specific place (mountain) or area (northern Israel).

[45] Wolff, *Joel and Amos,* 118; Lindblom, *Prophecy in Ancient Israel,* 16; Freedman and Andersen, *Amos,* 219.

an indictment.[46] Whatever the genre of 1:2, however, its positioning directly before the oracles against the nations is significant. The oracles illuminate the basis and nature of the threat posed by YHWH's roar.[47] The first five oracles list the offending brutalities of the foreign nations in turn; the fire YHWH will send on them will leave their fortresses in ruins just as the raising of the divine voice results in the withering of pastures and woods in 1:2.

The oracle against Israel in 2:6–16 is yoked structurally to those that precede it, yet the indictment here is framed in the characteristic language of Israelite communal law, ritual, and history. The community of Israel has offended on many levels of its acknowledged obligations under YHWH's dominion. It may be doubted whether Amos or other eighth-century prophets prophesied within the conceptual framework of covenant as a theological *nomen* defining the relationship between YHWH and Israel.[48] Yet it seems clear from the text of Amos 2:6–8 that Amos is referring to a common tradition of law—in the sense of shared strictures and ethics—for which the Israelites are seen as accountable to YHWH.[49]

---

[46] See Claus Westermann, *Basic Forms of Prophetic Speech* (trans. Hugh Clayton White; Louisville: Westminster John Knox, 1991), 142–48; 169–86.

[47] So Bentzen, "Ritual Background," 95–96; Lindblom, *Prophecy in Ancient Israel,* 116; Cross, *Canaanite Myth and Hebrew Epic,* 174; Paul, *Amos,* 41; James L. Crenshaw, "Amos and the Theophanic Tradition," *ZAW* 80 (1968): 209; contra Wolff, *Joel and Amos,* 125; Weiss, "Methodologisches über die Behandlung der Metapher," 8, 14.

[48] On the debate over the relationship between eighth-century Israelite prophecy and the theological concept of covenant, see Lothar Perlitt, *Bundestheologie im Alten Testament* (WMANT 36; Neukirchen-Vluyn: Neukirchener Verlag, 1969), 129–55; Clements, *Prophecy and Tradition* (Atlanta: John Knox, 1975), 8–23; Robert A. Oden Jr., "The Place of Covenant in the Religion of Israel," in *Ancient Israelite Religion: Essays in Honor of Frank Moore Cross* (ed. Patrick D. Miller Jr., Paul D. Hanson, and Sean Dean McBride; Philadelphia: Fortress, 1987), 429–47; Robert Davidson, "Covenant Ideology in Ancient Israel," in *The World of Ancient Israel: Sociological, Anthropological, and Political Perspectives* (ed. Ronald E. Clements; Cambridge: Cambridge University Press, 1989), 323–47; Otto Kaiser, "The Law As Center of the Hebrew Bible," in *"Shaʿarei Talmon": Studies in the Bible, Qumran, and the Ancient Near East Presented to Shemaryahu Talmon* (ed. Michael Fishbane and Emmanuel Tov; Winona Lake, Ind.: Eisenbrauns, 1992), 93–103; Ernest W. Nicholson, *God and His People: Covenant and Theology in the Old Testament* (Oxford: Clarendon, 1986), 114–16, 179–88; see also H. W. Wolff, *Amos the Prophet: The Man and His Background* (Philadelphia: Fortress, 1973), 59–67.

[49] On the relationship between the prophets and Israelite law, see Anthony Phillips, "Prophecy and Law," in *Israel's Prophetic Tradition: Essays in Honour of Peter R. Ackroyd* (ed. Richard Coggins, Anthony Phillips, and Michael A. Knibb; Cambridge: Cambridge University Press, 1982), 217–32, esp. 220–21; Gene M.

The consequence of Israel's failure to uphold these standards is also announced in a distinctive way. Rather than using the symbol of fire for the coming disaster, as in the oracles against the foreign nations, Amos conveys in 2:13–16 a more explicit and extended picture of disaster, with specific images of military routing.

The oracles against the nations provide a historical context for the manifestation of YHWH's power in 1:2, while the extended oracle 2:6–16, to which the preceding oracles lead and for which they serve as a foil, focuses attention on the situation of the northern kingdom. Hence the adverse reaction of the land of *Israel*—the pastures of the shepherds and the top of Carmel—to the audible sign of YHWH's presence. If 1:2 is taken in conjunction with 1:3–2:16, the earth responds in 1:2b to the imminent destruction announced by YHWH in 1:2a and by the prophet in 2:13–16.[50]

As Amos 2:6–8 makes clear—especially against the background of the recurrent pattern of transgression (*pešaʿ*) and consequence (*wěšillaḥtî ʾēš*, "so I will send fire") in the preceding oracles—the coming devastation is the result of Israel's transgressions. But the direct agency of YHWH is evident, in 2:13: *hinnēh ʾānōkî mēʿîq taḥtêkem / kaʾăšer tāʿîq hāʿăgālâ / hamlēʾâ lāh ʿāmîr*, "Behold, I am about to press you down in your place, as a cart full of grain presses down."[51] In 1:2, then, the earth responds to the punishment YHWH will inflict because of the sins of the community.

Tucker, "Prophecy and the Prophetic Literature," in *The Hebrew Bible and Its Modern Interpreters* (ed. Douglas A. Knight and Gene M. Tucker; Philadelphia: Fortress, 1985), 326–31; Joseph Blenkinsopp, *A History of Prophecy in Israel* (rev. ed; Louisville: John Knox, 1996), 15–16; and Perlitt, *Bundestheologie im Alten Testament*, 133–34. On the nature and dating of early Israelite legal traditions, see Joseph Blenkinsopp, *The Pentateuch: An Introduction to the First Five Books of the Bible* (ABRL; New York: Doubleday, 1992), 200–209.

[50] The yoking of lion's roar, YHWH's speaking, and prophecy is articulated in the parallel bicola of 3:8.

[51] The translation of *mēʿîq* in the first colon and *tāʿîq* in the second is problematic. The root *ʿwq* occurs in MT only in Amos 2:13. The translation "press down" presumes a connection between *ʿwq* and *ṣwq*, which means "to constrain, press upon" in the *hipʿil* (BDB, 847b–48a), as in Syr.: *ʾn* *mʿyq* *ʾn*, "I am about to impede, even I." Yet the apparent aramaizing of the Hebrew root *ṣwq* in Amos is puzzling. LXX (κυλίω, "I am rolling") may represent a contextual interpretation, and Vulg. (*ego stridebo super vos*, "I am creaking over you"), the relation of *ʿwq* to an Arabic root meaning, "to shriek," according to Gese ("Kleine Beiträge," 418). Gese offers his own interpretation of *ʿwq* (417–24); see also Wolff's translation (*Joel and Amos*, 134). Whatever the meaning of the verb represented in MT by *mēʿîq*, it is clear from the context of 2:14–16 that some destructive action is signified, and the pronoun *ʾānōkî*, "I," in 2:13 signals that it is a direct action of YHWH.

Specifically, it mourns and withers at the prospect of the military overrunning of Israel as retribution for social practices that are understood as *pĕšāʿîm*, "transgressions," by both YHWH, speaking through Amos, and Israel, the recipient of Amos's words.

There is, in the nature of this response, an echo of the curses amassed in Deut 28 and Lev 26. These chapters list curses YHWH will impose on Israel for disobedience and transgression, among them the blighting of the land by drought and disease (Deut 28:22–24; Lev 26:19–20). That such curses were current in the ninth to seventh centuries has been argued by Hillers on the basis of Assyrian treaties of that period as well as of boundary makers (*kudurrus*) of an earlier time.[52] The sequence of punishments listed in Amos 4:6–12 reflects similar curses;[53] in 4:7–8 drought is recalled with the verb *yābēš*:

> And I also held back the rain from you
>   when there were still three months to the harvest;
> And I would send rain on one city,
>   and on another city I would not send rain;
> One field would be rained on,
>   and the field on which it did not rain would wither [*tîbāš*].

In Amos 7:4 the reference to a judgment by fire that consumes the land may also be related to the concept of drought imposed by YHWH as punishment.[54] In these passages we sense a distinct emphasis: the land mourns (or dries up) because it is plunged into mourning (or drought) by YHWH rather than because it responds itself to the oncoming horror. In Amos 1:2 both perspectives on mourning are present: the latter as the dominant view, the former as a resonance.

MOURNING AS STRIPPING

It is clear in 1:2 that the earth suffers its own kind of devastation as a result of YHWH's roar. That the verb *ʾābal* may bear a nuance of "to dry

---

[52] *Treaty-Curses and the Old Testament Prophets,* 18, 35, 41–42, 78–79, 86–87.

[53] See Wolff, *Joel and Amos,* 218; Paul, *Amos,* 144–49; and Walter Brueggemann, "Amos IV 4–13 and Israel's Covenant Worship," *VT* 15 (1965): 6–8. Some propose that this passage is later than the prophet Amos: Wolff (*Joel and Amos,* 217–18) assigns it to a Judean redaction from the time of Josiah, and Perlitt (*Bundestheologie im Alten Testament,* 135 n. 4) to the time of the composition of Deuteronomy or Leviticus. Paul (*Amos,* 141–52) and Brueggemann ("Amos IV 4–13," 1–15), however, assume that it reflects Amos's own words.

[54] It should be noted again that traces of this concept in Amos need not imply the developed notion of a covenant bolstered by the threat of curses.

up" as well as a primary meaning of "to mourn" was discussed above, as were the parallels between the physical appearance of the earth in a state of drought and the state of mourning in ancient Israel. In the mourning ritual clothes are stripped off, head shaved, sackcloth put on, and dust or ashes (*ʿāpār*) poured over the head and body; the mourner fasts and bows the head, sometimes sitting or lying down in the dust.[55] In Amos 1:2b the dual associations of *ʾābal* allow for both a psychological and a physical aspect. The overall impression in the first colon is of desolate fields stripped of herds, herders, and vegetation. The motif of stripping extends to the second colon, as the top of Carmel, presumably clothed with thick forests, withers and loses its covering. In this respect 1:2 resembles the first two of Amos's visions in Amos 7. In his first vision (7:1–2) the prophet sees locusts stripping the land of all vegetation; in the second (7:4) he sees a great fire devouring both the deep and the land.

The multiple implications of the mourning-as-stripping motif can be explored further. First, there are parallels between the rituals of mourning and repentance. Stripping, sackcloth, and ashes, as well as fasting and lowering of the head, are common to both.[56] Repentance, in fact, entails sorrow over past failings.

Second, looking at Amos 1:2 in the light of 1:3–2:16 as well as of the book of Amos as a whole, the parallel between the stripping of the land and the stripping of those defeated in battle is apparent.[57] The imagery of military defeat in 2:13–16 ends with the announcement:

The one who is strong-hearted among the valiant
    will flee naked on that day.

The prophecy concerning Samaria in 3:11 is similar, considering the semantic associations between plundering and stripping:

A foe will surround the land
    and bring down from you your might,
    and your fortresses will be plundered [*wĕnābōzzû*].

---

[55] See, e.g., Ps 35:13–14; Mic 1:8–11, 16; Isa 22:12; Jer 6:26; Lam 2:10; and the discussion above of the verb *ʾābal*. See further the depiction of stripping in the mourning over the devastation of the land in Isa 32:9–14.

[56] See, e.g., 1 Kgs 21:27; Isa 58:5; Jon 3:5–8 and Ernst Kutsch, "'Trauerbräuche' und 'Selbstminderungsriten' im Alten Testament," in *Drei Wiener Antrittsreden* (TS 78; Zürich: EVZ, 1965), 25–37, esp. 32–37.

[57] See the use of the root *pšṭ*, "to strip off," in the context of the stripping of the slain in 1 Sam 31:8; 2 Sam 23:10 and as a term for "raid" in, e.g., Hos 7:1; Judg 9:33, 44; 1 Sam 23:27; 27:8; 30:1, 14.

The effect of these overtones in the motif of mourning as stripping in Amos is to draw the mourning of the earth in 1:2 into closer connection with both the social failings and the military defeat of 2:6–16, although this is not a tightly defined connection. The motif leaves open questions about the relationship between the mourning earth and the community of Israel. Does the earth mourn in sympathy for the imminent desolation of Israel, or does it undergo a related desolation, symbolic of the destruction of the nation? The mourning-as-stripping motif fuses the two possibilities—the earth mourns for its own death as well as for the nation's and experiences both mourning and dying in the act of drying up. There is room, further, for an element of repentance in the stripping of vegetation. Again, the motif allows multiple nuances.

DECREATION

There are no hints in Amos 1:2 of creation phraseology as known, for example, in Gen 1–11, in other parts of the Hebrew Bible, or in ancient Near Eastern literature in general. There are no explicit depictions of making or unmaking by YHWH, and the naming of both Jerusalem and Carmel, as noted above, situate the verse's frame of reference within the boundaries of Judah and Israel rather than in a cosmic sphere. Parallels to biblical creation texts in this verse are considered here primarily because of the relationship of the verse to other passages within the corpus of nine texts in which creation imagery and phraseology appear to play a role.[58] Such parallels can only be spoken of in the most generic sense, however. Within these parameters, a broad correspondence between biblical creation traditions and Amos 1:2 may be suggested.[59] In this verse YHWH roars and lifts up the divine voice while the mourning earth shrivels and dries up. YHWH's roar thus forms a counterpoint to the word of God in Gen 1. Whereas in Gen 1:3 God calls creation into being through a voiced word, YHWH's utterance in Amos 1:2 brings death to the created world. Amos 1:2 evokes the elemental relationship between God and the created world—the power of God over creation that can, the verse assures us, be turned against it.

---

[58] In particular, Hos 4:1–4; Jer 4:23–28; 12:1–4; Isa 24:1–20.

[59] I do not presume here that written forms of Gen 1:1–2:4a were familiar to the author of Amos 1:2. However, the tradition of creation by divine word certainly has a long history, as may some of the phraseology found in the Priestly creation account. See Susan Niditch, *Oral World and Written Word: Ancient Israelite Literature* (Library of Ancient Israel; Louisville: Westminster John Knox, 1996), 18.

SUMMARY OF LITERARY TECHNIQUES

In Amos 1:2 *'ābal* is the only verb bearing both physical and psychological associations, although, as noted above, an implied sound play between *yābēš* and *bôš* is possible. As the subject of the verb "to mourn," the pastures of the shepherds are personified. Although there are no other metaphors or similes comparing the human and the natural in 1:2, one metaphor does compare the divine to the natural: YHWH is compared to a lion roaring (*šā'ag*). Conversely, the phrase *nātan qôlô* with YHWH as subject connects the natural (thunder) with the divine (YHWH's voice). There are no parallel structures linking the human and the natural within 1:2 itself, yet parallels emerge when the verse is taken as part of the larger unit 1:2–2:16. As noted above, the roar of YHWH parallels the speech of YHWH through the prophet, and the withering of the earth parallels the fire sent upon the foreign nations and the military disaster to fall upon Israel.

OVERALL EFFECT OF THE METAPHOR

In the extended unit 1:2–2:16, the metaphor of the pastures mourning, along with the parallel withering of Carmel, provides a backdrop to the judgment oracles against the nations that follow it. Like the natural landscape glimpsed in the distance in Renaissance paintings, the scene enacted in 1:2 introduces distance and thereby perspective on what is in the foreground: the transgressions and judgment of the nations and, above all, of Israel. In this the metaphor resembles the similes in the *Iliad,* in which the bloody events of battle are compared to natural phenomena—to falling snow or rushing flood waters. The effect of the Homeric similes can be seen as providing contrast to as well as figures for the depictions of battle by balancing a natural image against a human counterpoint.[60] Amos 1:2 can also be seen as functioning on more than one level in relation to the judgment oracles it precedes. The focus on the landscape in Amos 1:2 contrasts with the enumeration of war and social crimes in Amos 1:3–2:16. Yet the description of the ruined land also mirrors the prediction of devastation of the nations, including Israel, thus collapsing the distinction between the natural and human realms. In particular, the breakdown of the relationship

---

[60] On the role of the Homeric similes, see the discussion by Richmond Lattimore in his introduction to *The Iliad of Homer* (trans. Richmond Lattimore; Chicago: University of Chicago Press, 1951), 40–45; and by Andrew S. Becker in *The Shield of Achilles and the Poetics of Ekphrasis* (Greek Studies: Interdisciplinary Approaches; Lanham, Md.: Rowman & Littlefield, 1995), 49–50. Becker summarizes the role of the Homeric similes as a contrast to, a figure of, and a comment on the battle scenes among which they are interspersed.

between God and Israel—a breakdown based on multiple transgressions and with multiple consequences for Israel—is reflected in the single scene of YHWH's roar and the withering of the earth. The metaphor of earth mourning reduces to one image the consequences of social failing and thereby intensifies and brings them closer.

At the same time, the metaphor of mountain and pastures mourning widens the scope of the social disorder condemned in 1:3–2:16 by connecting the human sphere with the natural sphere. Not just the nations, not just the people of Israel are affected by the imminent judgment of YHWH, but also the land itself, from the pastures of the shepherds to the top of Carmel. The joining of the two spheres sets off cosmic overtones, without explicit cosmic imagery, and the echoes of divine-warrior and theophanic imagery in 1:2a deepen these overtones. What is done in Israel and in the nations surrounding it has ramifications beyond any humanly conceived concept of punishment. A primal power is unleashed that has protected, but that now destroys, both Israel and its land. An order in which YHWH, Israel, and the earth itself feature is ruptured by the lion's roar.[61]

Hartmut Gese has observed a similar juxtaposition of the natural world and the social order in Amos 8:4–8.[62] The indictment of the Israelites' commercial and monetary greed in 8:4–5[63] is followed by YHWH's avowal of retribution (8:7) and an illustration of the impact of this retribution on the earth:

> YHWH has sworn by the pride of Jacob:
>   I will never forget all their deeds!
> Because of this will not the earth shake
>   and all who dwell in it mourn [*wěʾābal*]
> And all of it rise like the Nile[64]
>   and be tossed and sink[65] like the Nile of Egypt? (8:7–8)

Although here the earth itself does not mourn, it is a major actor, suffering the consequences of the deeds of the Israelites (*ʿal zōʾt*, "because

---

[61] In this sense, even if covenant theology is a Deuteronomistic development, its roots may reach as far back as Amos.

[62] "Amos 8,4–8: Der kosmische Frevel händlerischer Habgier," in *Prophet und Prophetenbuch: Festschrift für Otto Kaiser zum 65. Geburtstag* (ed. Volkmer Fritz, Karl-Friedrich Pohlmann, and Hans-Christoph Schmitt; BZAW 185; Berlin: de Gruyter, 1989), 59–72.

[63] Gese (ibid., 62–63) considers 8:6 a later addition.

[64] Read *kayʾōr* for *kāʾōr*, "like the light" (MT), with many MSS, LXX, Syr. See Amos 9:5.

[65] Read Q, *nišqěʿâ*. See Amos 9:5.

of this")[66] and causing its inhabitants to mourn. In this passage, Gese concludes, "the natural, cosmic-physical dimension of the ruin is made clear"[67] as well as the "deep ontology of the law as the order of creation and corresponding physical order of existence."[68] The hymnic verses in Amos 4:13; 5:8; and 9:5–6 as well as in Amos 1:2 may play similar roles in their contexts.[69]

---

[66] The singular *zō᾿t*, "this," need not refer back to the plural *maʿăśêhem*, "deeds," but to the fact that YHWH will not forget the deeds. Gese ("Amos 8,4–8," 64–65) resolves this question somewhat differently.

[67] Ibid., 63 ["wird ... die naturhafte, ja kosmisch-physische Dimension des Verderbens verdeutlicht"].

[68] Ibid., 69 ["die tiefe Ontologie des Rechts als der Schöpfungsordnung und physischen Seinsordnung entsprechend"].

[69] On the relationship of these passages to the concept of YHWH as creator, see John D. W. Watts, *Vision and Prophecy in Amos* (Leiden: Brill, 1958), 64; and Karl Eberlin, *Gott der Schöpfer—Israels Gott: Eine exegetisch-hermeneutische Studie zur theologischen Function alttestamentlicher Schöpfungsaussagen* (BEATAJ 5; Frankfurt: Lang, 1986), 229–36.

3
HOSEA 4:1–3

TEXT, TRANSLATION, AND TEXTUAL NOTES

1 שִׁמְע֥וּ דְבַר־יְהוָ֖ה   בְּנֵ֣י יִשְׂרָאֵ֑ל

כִּ֣י רִ֤יב לַֽיהוָה֙   עִם־יוֹשְׁבֵ֣י הָאָ֔רֶץ

כִּ֠י אֵין־אֱמֶ֧ת וְֽאֵין־חֶ֛סֶד   וְאֵֽין־דַּ֥עַת אֱלֹהִ֖ים בָּאָֽרֶץ׃

2 אָלֹ֣ה וְכַחֵ֔שׁ וְרָצֹ֖חַ   וְגָנֹ֣ב וְנָאֹ֑ף פָּרָ֔צוּ   וְדָמִ֖ים בְּדָמִ֥ים נָגָֽעוּ׃

3 עַל־כֵּ֣ן ׀ תֶּאֱבַ֣ל הָאָ֗רֶץ   וְאֻמְלַל֙ כָּל־יוֹשֵׁ֣ב בָּ֔הּ

בְּחַיַּ֣ת הַשָּׂדֶ֔ה   וּבְע֣וֹף הַשָּׁמָ֑יִם   וְגַם־דְּגֵ֥י הַיָּ֖ם יֵאָסֵֽפוּ׃

1 Hear the word of YHWH,
    O children of Israel;
For YHWH has a dispute
    with those who dwell in the land.
For there is no trustworthiness or kindness,
    and no knowledge of God in the land.
2 Swearing and lying and murder
    and stealing and adultery break out,[a]
    and bloodshed strikes against bloodshed.
3 And so the earth [b]will mourn[b]
    and all who dwell in it languish;
[c]The animals of the field,[c]
    and the birds of the sky,
    and even the fish of the sea will be gathered up.

[a] LXX adds ἐπὶ τῆς γῆς, "upon the land." It has been suggested that Hebrew *bāʾāreṣ* was omitted from MT through *homoioteleuton* with *pārāṣû*.[1]

---

[1] So *BHS*; Hans W. Wolff, *Hosea* (Hermeneia; Philadelphia: Fortress, 1974), 65; and Wilhelm Rudolph, *Hosea* (KAT 13/1; Gütersloh: Mohn, 1966), 96.

A fourth reference to the land would reinforce its central role in this passage. However, it is also possible that the phrase has been added in LXX, or its Hebrew *Vorlage,* through attraction to the occurrences of *ʾereṣ* in 4:1 (see, e.g., the addition of καὶ εἶδεν ὁ θεὸς ὅτι καλόν, "and God saw that it was good," in LXX of Gen 1:8). The lengths of the cola in 4:2 are more balanced without the phrase *bāʾāreṣ,* although the difference is minor.

b–b So LXX (πενθήσει), Vulg. (*lugebit*); Syr. uses the circumlocution *ttb bʾblʾ.* Many commentators interpret *teʾĕbal* and the other verbs in 4:3 in an iterative or durative sense.[2] The only other instances among the nine passages considered here, however, where the *qal* of *ʾbl* occurs in the imperfect are in future contexts: in Jer 12:4, following *ʿad-mātay,* "how long?" and in Jer 4:28, as part of an announcement of divine judgment following two other imperfects (*tihyeh, ʾeʿĕšeh*). Taking this pattern of usage into consideration, I have translated the three verbs in 1:3 in the future.[3]

c–c Some commentators translate *bĕḥayyat haśśādeh* as "with the animals of the field," reading a *bĕ* of accompaniment.[4] It is more likely, however, that since this phrase initiates a list of creatures, *bĕ* indicates the parts of which the preceding phrase, "all who live in it," consists.[5] A similar construction occurs in the lists of animals in the flood narrative (see Gen 7:21; 8:17; 9:10, 16).[6] The LXX adds here καὶ σὺν τοῖς ἑρπετοῖς τῆς γῆς, "and with the crawling things of the earth," probably under the influence of Hos 2:20.

DELIMITATION OF THE PASSAGE

The first verse of Hos 4:1–3 clearly begins a new section of Hosea. The extended allegory of the marriage of Hosea to a harlot or adulteress

---

[2] So Rudolph, *Hosea,* 95; Theodore H. Robinson and Friedrich Horst, *Die zwölf kleinen Propheten* (2d ed.; HAT 14. Tübingen: Mohr, 1954), 18; Ernst Sellin, *Das Zwölfprophetenbuch* (2 vols.; 2d ed.; KAT 12/1; Leipzig: A. Deichertsche, 1929), 1:52; Jörg Jeremias, *Der Prophet Hosea* (ATD 24/1; Göttingen: Vandenhoeck & Ruprecht, 1983), 59; Francis I. Andersen and David N. Freedman, *Hosea* (AB 24; Garden City, N.Y.: Doubleday, 1980), 330.

[3] So Wolff, *Hosea,* 65. Alfons Deissler (*Zwölf Propheten* [NEchtB; Würzburg: Echter, 1981], 23) translates the three verbs as modals: "shall dry up," "shall languish," "shall perish" ["soll verdorren, soll ... verwelken, sollen zugrundegehen"]. For examples of future punishment following *ʿal-kēn,* "and so," see Jer 5:6; 20:11.

[4] So LXX; Syr.; Wolff, *Hosea,* 65; Rudolph, *Hosea,* 96.

[5] So Edmund Jacob, *Osée* (3d ed.; CAT 11a; Geneva: Labor et Fides, 1992), 39; cf. BDB, 88b.

[6] Cf. Exod 12:19 and Num 31:11, 26 for analagous uses of this construction.

concludes at the end of Hos 3, and 4:1 opens with the address: "Hear the words of YHWH, O children of Israel." In the stylistically autobiographical account of Hos 1–3, YHWH speaks only to Hosea; now the divine word is directed to all Israel, through Hosea. In the verses that follow (4:4–10), the priests of Israel are singled out for condemnation.[7]

The structure of the three verses forms a natural unit: 4:1b–2 indicts Israel for certain attitudes and acts, and 4:3 points to the consequence of those attitudes and acts. The paradigmatic character of both the accusation and the consequence, in contrast to the more focused allegations that follow, also sets this passage apart.

For these reasons, many view Hos 4:1–3 as a self-standing unit that functions as a heading or thematic introduction to the second part of the book (Hos 4–11).[8] Yet there are clearly connections between 4:1–3 and 4:4–10 that have led others to see a larger unit.[9] Most notably, 4:4 begins with the adverb *'ak,* which seems to be used here in its restrictive, rather than its asseverative, function as "but, yet," referring back to what precedes.[10] Further, the twofold repetition of the root *ryb,* "to strive, contend," in 4:4 appears to refer back to *rîb* in 4:1a, and the lack of knowledge of God that is condemned in 4:1b is mentioned again in 4:6, where it is attributed to the priests. At the same time, other passages in the rest of Hos 4–11 take up the failings and transgressions cited in 4:1–2.[11]

---

[7] In addition to the clear references to the priests in 4:6–7, read in 4:4 *wĕ'immākām rîbî kōhēn,* "for with you is my contention, O priest," for *wĕ'ammĕkā kimrîbê kōhēn,* "for your people are like those who contend with a priest" (MT); so Wolff (*Hosea,* 70) and H. Junker ("Textkritische, formkritische und traditions-geschichtliche Untersuchung zu Os 4,1–10," *BZ* NS 4 [1960]: 166). Junker proposes that *kōhēn* was originally taken as a collective noun; hence the plural suffix on the preposition *'im.* A later marginal note proposed the singular suffix *kā;* this note was incorporated into the text, and *km* became attached to the following word. It is also possible that the final *mêm* on the suffix represents an enclitic *mêm.*

[8] So Wolff, *Hosea,* 65, 68, 73; Jeremias, *Der Prophet Hosea,* 59; Freedman and Andersen, *Hosea,* 331–32; Jacob, *Osée,* 39. Heinz-Dieter Neef, *Die Heilstraditionen Israels in der Verkündigung des Propheten Hosea* (BZAW 169; Berlin: de Gruyter, 1987), 193–94.

[9] So Rudolph, *Hosea,* 98–99; Sellin, *Zwölfprophetenbuch,* 1:52; Junker, "Text-kritische, formkritische, und traditionsgeschichtliche," 168.

[10] BDB, 36b. Wolff (*Hosea,* 76), on the other hand, argues for the asseverative function of *'ak,* which, he claims, occurs elsewhere in the Hebrew Bible at the beginning of speeches.

[11] See, e.g., 4:13–15, 7:4 (adultery [*nā'ap*]); 5:7, 6:7 (deceiving, or lack of trust-worthiness [*bāgad*]); 6:6 (lack of kindness [*ḥesed*] and knowledge of God [*da'at 'ĕlōhîm*]); 6:8–9 (blood [*dām*] and murder [*riṣṣēaḥ*]); 7:1 (dealing falsely [*pā'al šeqer*]

In the present arrangement of the book, then, Hos 4:1–3 is connected with 4:4–10, the reproach of the priests, but also with the larger collection of oracles in Hos 4–11 as a whole. It serves as an introduction to both. Yet because of its distinctive character, it can also be considered as a separate unit.[12]

AUTHORSHIP AND DATING

Much of the discussion about the dating of Hos 4:1–3 centers around 4:3, the verse most pertinent to this study. Some commentators accept the whole unit, or most of it, as originating with Hosea. Others suggest that all or part of 4:3 is a later addition. Jeremias claims that 4:3 is a Judean addition that rounds off 4:1–2.[13] Sellin accepts 4:3a as Hosean but sees in 4:3b a vision of judgment over the whole earth, influenced by passages such as Jer 9:9 and 12:4; he considers this final half-verse an expansion, presumably late preexilic or exilic.[14] Rainer Stahl argues that 4:3 reflects the shock of the destruction of Judah and Jerusalem in 597 B.C.E. and is thus exilic.[15]

However, these arguments, based on stylistic or thematic suitability, are largely impressionistic. That similarities between prophetic passages (in this case, between Jeremiah and Hosea) need not indicate literary dependence is presumed in this study.[16] There is, moreover, an internal logic to the inclusion of 4:3 as part of a unified speech where consequence or judgment follows indictment (4:1–2). This pattern occurs elsewhere in Hosea in association with the root *ryb,* "to strive, contend," found here in 4:1a.[17] It seems reasonable, then, to conclude that there are no decisive

---

and stealing [*wĕgannab yābô',* "the thief enters"]); 7:3 (lying [*kāḥaš*]); 7:13 (lies [*kāzāb*]); 10:4 (swearing falsely [*'ālôt šāw'*]).

[12] See Junker ("Textkritische, formkritische, und traditionsgeschichtliche," 168), who takes 4:1–10 as a single compositional unit yet acknowledges that within it two speeches are discernible. Wolff (*Hosea,* 74), on the other hand, considers Hos 4:1–3 a separate unit but concedes that 4:4–10 may "belong to the same scene."

[13] *Der Prophet Hosea,* 60; he assigns 4:1–2 not to Hosea himself but to his school.

[14] *Zwölfprophetenbuch,* 52.

[15] "Gottesgericht oder Selbstzerstörung? Wie ist ein verbindliches Zeugnis ökumenischer Theologie angesichts der ökologischen Herausforderung zu begründen? Eine Reflexion an Hand von Hosea 4,1–3," in *Veritas et Communicatio: Ökumenische Theologie auf der Suche nach einem verbindlichen Zeugnis: Festschrift zum 60. Geburtstag von Ulrich Kühn* (ed. Heiko Franke et al.; Göttingen: Vandenhoeck & Ruprecht, 1992), 323.

[16] See further the discussion in chapter 7.

[17] See, e.g., the alternation between accusation and punishment in Hos 2:4–14; 4:4–10. See also Claus Westermann, *Basic Forms of Prophetic Speech* (trans. Hugh

grounds for treating either Hos 4:3 or 4:3b as additions significantly later than the bulk of the Hoseanic corpus.[18]

THEMES AND MOTIFS

THE RESPONSE OF THE EARTH

Hosea 4:1–3 serves as a brief thematic introduction that sets a tone for the series of judgment oracles that follow; in this way it resembles Amos 1:2. But whereas the Amos verse gives only a bare outline of the relationship between YHWH and the mourning earth, leaving the intermediary role of human action implicit, here YHWH, the people of Israel, and the land they inhabit are brought together in a concise statement of their interrelationship. The connecting phrase *'al-kēn,* "for this reason" (4:3), indicates the link between human behavior that is repudiated by YHWH (4:1–2) and the mourning of the earth (4:3).

The structure of the passage, like that of Amos 1:2, reflects a pattern of action and reaction. Here, however, the repetition of the word *'ereṣ,* "earth," reinforces the connection between actors and respondents. In 4:1a the people of Israel are addressed specifically as *yôšĕbê hā'āreṣ,* "those who dwell in the land." In 4:1b–2 their failures and crimes "in the land" (*bā'āreṣ*) are recounted.[19] And in 4:3a the response of the earth (*hā'āreṣ*) is given: it will mourn (*te'ĕbal*), "and all who dwell in it languish" (*wĕ'umlal kol-yôšēb bāh*).

The presence of the phrase *kol-yôšēb bāh,* "all who dwell in it," in 4:3a adds a twist to the basic action-reaction pattern by recalling *yôšĕbê hā'āreṣ,* "those who dwell in the land," in 4:1a, where the inhabitants of the land are the people of Israel. Those who will languish thus would seem to include not only the living creatures named in 4:3b (animals, birds, and fish) but the Israelites themselves, whose acts will rebound upon them and bring them harm.

As in Amos 1:2, the impetus for the response of the earth is presented first. In this passage, however, the focus is not solely on the decisive act of YHWH. The divine utterance here speaks of human acts, and the message consists of more than a roar, a shout, or a roll of thunder. It is a *rîb* or "case": a list of specific allegations against Israel. The list includes two levels of offense (general attributes and specific transgressions) and a

---

Clayton White; Louisville: Westminster John Knox, 1991), 199, on the resemblance of these passages to judgment oracles.

[18] So Rudolph, *Hosea,* 98, 102 n. 12. See also Neef (*Heilstraditionen Israels,* 193–94, 205–6) and Wolff (*Hosea,* 66), who excepts 4:1a as a later addition.

[19] In LXX the phrase *bā'āreṣ* also occurs in 4:2, as noted above.

culminating indictment: "bloodshed strikes against bloodshed." The order of allegations suggests a sequential development: the absence of certain habits of character or behavior (*'ĕmet, ḥesed,* and *daʿat 'ĕlōhîm* or "trustworthiness," "kindness," and "knowledge of God") leads to specific manifestations (*'ālōh wĕkaḥēš wĕrāṣōaḥ wĕgānōb wĕnā'ōp,* "swearing and lying and murder and stealing and adultery"), which result in an overall state of violence (*dāmîm,* "bloodshed").

The response of the earth to this reality is given in 4:3. The distinction between land (*'ereṣ*) as physical earth and land as a political entity is both drawn and blurred in Hos 4:1–3. In 4:1a YHWH's *rîb* is with the *yôšĕbê hā'āreṣ,* those who dwell in the land, and they are distinguished from the *'ereṣ* itself. And in 4:3a *hā'āreṣ* in the first colon is distinct from *kol-yôšēb bāh,* "all who dwell in it," in the second. No such distinction is made in 4:1b, where the prophet laments the lack of trustworthiness, kindness, and knowledge of God *bā'āreṣ,* "in the land." Here the immediate context indicates that the community of Israel is meant; at the same time, *bā'āreṣ* in this verse is echoed by *hā'āreṣ* in 4:3, where it clearly represents the physical earth.

A related blurring occurs within 4:3 itself. In 4:3a the announcement that all who dwell in the land will languish is followed by the naming of three kinds of living creatures. The phrase *kol-yôšēb bāh,* "all who dwell in it," in 4:3a echoes *yôšĕbê hā'āreṣ,* "those who dwell in it," in 4:1a, where it refers to the people of Israel, suggesting that the earth's human inhabitants languish alongside the animals. Yet the threefold naming of animals, birds, and fish that concludes the poem in 4:3b raises an image of the natural world, exclusive of human beings. The physical earth and its creatures are, then, distinguished from, and yet joined with, their human counterparts in Hos 4:1–3.

The response of the earth in 4:3 is conveyed primarily by the two verbs *'ābal* and *'umlal.* The earth itself will mourn (*te'ĕbal*), and its inhabitants, including animals and birds, languish (*wĕ'umlal*).[20] The verb *'umlal* is paired with *'ābal* in eight out of fourteen occurrences in the Hebrew Bible; this coupling occurs in four of the nine passages considered here. The word *'umlal* means "to be weak, languish" in the sense of a loss of fertility and life-bearing capability, as evident in the references to human infertility in 1 Sam 2:5 and Jer 15:9.[21] By extension it may indicate a dwindling of population.[22] The impression of the waning of nature conveyed by this use of *'umlal* draws out the nuance of "dry up" in its paired term, *'ābal.*

---

[20] Both verbs are *qal* forms, creating a focus on the active response of the subject.

[21] BDB, 51ab.

[22] See *HAL* 61a.

At the same time, *'umlal* occurs with *'ābal* almost entirely in laments or judgment oracles, in contexts of mourning or woe where the physical sense of diminishment is extended metaphorically to include a psychological meaning consonant with "mourn" or "lament."[23] In Isa 19:8–10, for example, *'umlal* is parallel to *'ābal*, "to mourn"; *'ānâ*, "to mourn"; *bôš*, "to be ashamed, confounded"; *dukkā'*, "to be crushed, in despair"; and *'agmê-nepeš*, "sad."[24] This verb, then, elicits the dual associations—physical and psychological—of *'ābal*.

The verb *ne'ĕsap*, "to be gathered, collected," is used in the last colon of 4:3b: "and even the fish of the sea will be gathered up." In the *qal* and the *pi'el*, the root *'sp* can mean, specifically, to gather or harvest crops.[25] The references to the "gathering" of the "fish of the sea" for food in Num 11:22 and the metaphor of the fishnet with which the people YHWH has made are gathered "like the fish of the sea" in Hab 1:15 suggest a link between the gathering up of the fish of the sea in Hos 4:3 and harvesting. This meaning enhances the associations of *'ābal* and *'umlal* with natural phenomena.

Finally, the noun *'ereṣ*, which is the subject of *'ābal* in 4:3, has further associations that play into the double echoes of *'ābal* and *'umlal* in that verse. Earth (*'ereṣ*) can be a term for the underworld in the Hebrew Bible. Nicholas J. Tromp asserts that when *'ereṣ* is understood not simply as the surface of the ground (*'ădāmâ*) but also as the depths of the earth, then earth can represent the underworld or realm of death. Tromp provides examples of this usage from Ugaritic texts, and he argues that *'ereṣ* was the common term for the underworld in Northwest Semitic.[26] In Hebrew the term Sheol (*šĕ'ôl*) is more frequent, but there are instances in the Hebrew Bible where the relation between *'ereṣ*, death, and the realm of the dead is clear.[27] One of the most graphic of these passages is Num 16:30–33:

---

[23] See G. R. Driver, "Confused Hebrew Roots," in *Occident and Orient: Being Studies in Semitic Philology and Literature, Jewish History and Philosophy and Folklore in the Widest Sense, in Honor of Haham Dr. M. Gaster's Eightieth Birthday; Gaster Anniversary Volume* (ed. Bruno Schindler with A. Marmorstein; London: Taylor, 1936), 75.

[24] See also Jer 14:2; Lam 2:8.

[25] BDB, 62a; see, e.g., Exod 23:10, 16; Lev 23:39; 25:3, 20; Deut 16:13; Isa 17:5; Jer 40:10, 12. The nouns *'āsîp*, "harvest," *'āsōp*, "storehouse," and *'ōsep*, "gathering," reflect this meaning.

[26] *Primitive Conceptions of Death and the Nether World in the Old Testament* (BibOr 21; Rome: Pontifical Biblical Institute, 1969), 21, 23–24.

[27] Ibid., 23–46. BDB (76a) cites Job 10:21, 22; Ps 139:15; Isa 44:23.

"But if … the ground [*hā'ădāmâ*] opens its mouth and swallows them and all who belong to them and they go down alive to Sheol, then you will know that these men despised YHWH." And when he had finished speaking all these words, the ground [*hā'ădāmâ*] split beneath them, and the earth [*hā'āreṣ*] opened its mouth and swallowed them and their households, and they and all who belonged to them went down alive to Sheol, and the earth [*hā'āreṣ*] covered them over and they died.

This passage shows that the earth as surface or ground (*'ădāmâ*) is seen as connected to the underworld. The use of *'āpār*, "dust," in references to death supports this connection, as in Ps 22:16—"You have set me in the dust of death" (*lĕ'ăpar-māwet*)—or in the well-known declaration of Gen 3:19: "For you are dust [*'āpār*] and to dust [*'āpār*] you will return."[28] This connotation of dust may explain the mourning ritual of pouring earth or dust on the head.[29] Earth and dust, then, indicate not only the surface on which the dead lie or are laid but the domain of death itself.

The interplay in Hos 4:3 between the verbs *'ābal, 'umlal,* and *ne'ĕsap* and the noun *'ereṣ* creates overlapping patterns. When associations of drying up are heard in *'ābal,* the verse raises the image of a severe drought, through which the *'ereṣ* becomes parched, and humans, animals, birds, and even fish weaken and die.[30] The hint of dwindling numbers within these groups is present in *'umlal* as well. The verb *ne'ĕsap* brings out the agricultural aspects of drought. Crops are normally gathered at the end of the growing season; harvest marks the end of that season and the beginning of winter, a state of dormancy and death. Here *ne'ĕsap* signals an abnormal harvest: the fertile season is aborted by drought, and the harvest is a harvest of death. At this point the concepts of drought and mourning come together, a confluence that is underscored by the associations of *'ereṣ* with death.

When *'ābal* is read as "mourn," the psychological sense of *'umlal,* "languish," is heightened, and 4:3 portrays a vast sorrow that touches all elements of creation. If *kol-yôšēb bāh,* "all who dwell in it," the first-named

---

[28] See BDB, 779b; Tromp, *Primitive Conceptions of Death,* 85–91; and Delbert Hillers, "Dust: Some Aspects of Old Testament Imagery," in *Love and Death in the Ancient Near East: Essays in Honor of Marvin H. Pope* (ed. John H. Marks and Robert M. Good; Guilford, Conn.: Four Quarters, 1987), 107. Hillers cites a number of ancient Near Eastern texts in which dust is part of the world of the dead. See also Gregory R. Vall, "From Womb to Tomb: Poetic Imagery and the Book of Job" (Ph.D. diss., Catholic University of America, 1993), 117–27.

[29] Tromp, *Primitive Conceptions of Death,* 91.

[30] So Wolff, *Hosea,* 68; Rudolph, *Hosea,* 101, 104; Jeremias, *Der Prophet Hosea,* 62–63.

subject of *'umlal,* is taken as including human inhabitants, the psychological connotation of languishing is strengthened.[31] At the same time, mourning and languishing imply the cessation, or curtailment, of normal activities, and the earth's figurative mourning may entail a breaking off of natural productivity and growth. Here again, images of mourning and drought conjoin.

SIN OR PUNISHMENT

That the earth exhibits a response in Hos 4:3 is evident, however complex the response. Yet the same questions arise with respect to Hos 4:1–3 as do with respect to Amos 1:2: To what, exactly, is the earth reacting? Does it mourn over YHWH's dispute (*rîb*) with its inhabitants, over the divine alienation from their behavior and attitudes? In 4:1–2 the prophet explains the basis of YHWH's complaint, intoning the failings of the Israelites toward one another and toward YHWH. The implication of a legal procedure is that judgment and punishment follow the presentation of a case. This is a pattern found elsewhere in Hosea in the context of the root *ryb,* as mentioned above. But in Hos 4:1–3, how is this pattern represented? In 4:3 there is no explicit indication, whether indirect (third person) or direct (first person), of YHWH's role in judgment or punishment.

The structure of 4:1–3, in which the depiction of the mourning earth in 4:3 follows immediately upon the catalogue of human transgressions in 4:1b–2, creates an impression of the land responding directly to the acts done in it. The choice of *'al-kēn,* "as a result, and so," rather than *lākēn,* "therefore," as the hinge between accusation (4:1b–2) and consequence (4:3) contributes to this impression. There is a fine distinction between *'al-kēn* and *lākēn,* though both may be translated "therefore."[32] The phrase *'al-kēn* generally introduces a statement of fact, designating "the (necessary) result of an action,"[33] whereas *lākēn* tends to precede a declaration, often, in prophetic texts, a divine declaration.[34] The absence of the latter conjunction in Hos 4:3 removes from the forefront of this verse the role played by the sentence of YHWH in the devastation of the earth and its creatures.[35] In fact,

---

[31] This connotation persists even if *kol-yôšēb bāh* refers only to the animal world. In this case the personification of the earth, which will mourn, is reflected in the personification of the animals dwelling in it, who will languish.

[32] BDB, 487a.

[33] Jeremias, *Der Prophet Hosea,* 62 ["die (notwendige) Folge einer Tat"]; he cites Hos 4:13 and 13:6 as examples of this usage.

[34] See, e.g., Hos 2:8, 11; 13:3.

[35] Cf. Jer 5:6. See also Jeremias, *Der Prophet Hosea,* 62–63; Rudolph, *Hosea,* 101–2; Sellin, *Zwölfprophetenbuch,* 1:54. A pattern of act followed directly by its

YHWH's indictment against Israel's human inhabitants might even seem to include the damage their acts have brought upon the earth.

In this respect Hos 4:1–3 differs from Amos 1:2, where the withering of the land is juxtaposed directly to the roar of YHWH, the premonition of divine hostility. Yet just as the crimes of the Israelites feature in the wider context of Amos 1:2, so the judgment of YHWH in Hos 1–3 and 4:4–10 forms part of the context of Hos 4:1–3. In Hos 2:4–5, YHWH uses the same language of *rîb* to threaten devastation of the land:

> Plead [*rîbû*] with your mother, plead [*rîbû*]
> for she is not my wife
> and I am not her husband,
> That she turn aside her whoring from her,
> and her adultery from between her breasts;
> Lest I strip her naked
> and show her as on the day of her birth;
> And make her like a desert,
> and turn her into a parched land,
> and kill her with thirst.

Within this broader setting, the scene of desolation in 4:3 looks back to the announcement of YHWH's *rîb* in 4:1a, and the phrase *ʿal-kēn*, which introduces the consequence of Israel's acts, seems to indicate the enactment of YHWH's judgment as well.[36]

---

consequence occurs elsewhere in Hosea; Hos 10:13–15 is a good example (see also 5:4–5; 8:7; cf. 10:12). Klaus Koch ("Is There a Doctrine of Retribution in the Old Testament?" in *Theodicy in the Old Testament* [ed. James L. Crenshaw; Philadelphia: Fortress, 1983], 64–69) argues that although this pattern does not imply, in Hosea or elsewhere in the Hebrew Bible, that YHWH stands apart from the spinning out of consequences, retribution is presented as though occurring through the vehicle of the faulted actions themselves. This may well be seen as a literary trope that emphasizes the role of human transgression in engendering harmful consequences. Patrick D. Miller (*Sin and Judgment in the Prophets: A Stylistic and Theological Analysis* [SBLMS 27; Chico, Calif.: Scholars Press, 1982], 9–11) argues, e.g. (contra Koch), that the correlation in Hos 4:1–3 between the locus of sin (the land) and the locus of punishment (the land) may be understood as a literary device underscoring the appropriateness and inevitability of punishment by YHWH. Yet the juxtaposition of the suffering earth (4:3) to the crimes of its inhabitants (4:1b–2) places a strong emphasis on the role of human transgression in the effects of punishment.

36 Note also the use of the verb *ʾāsap* (4:3b) in the context of an act of divine judgment that affects beasts, birds, and fish as well as humans in a presumably later text, Zeph 1:2–6. The relation of this text to the themes of sin and punishment inherent in the mourning of the earth is considered in greater detail in the discussion of Jer 12:1–4, below.

The passage as a whole, then, can be read as balancing two perspectives on the end of Israel. In 4:1 YHWH is the first actor on stage: YHWH initiates what will develop into a vision of total desolation in 4:3. But as the prophet continues to speak, the content of YHWH's *rîb* claims the attention, and the failings and acts that Hosea condemns draw together to a catastrophic conclusion. Hosea 4:1b–3 offers not so much a different view of divine judgment as a different emphasis, in which the connection between the transgressions of the Israelite community and the fate of its land is deliberately brought forward.[37]

Other passages in the oracles that follow 4:1–3 allude to the harm done to the earth, either literally or figuratively, as a result of the sins of the Israelites. Hosea 8:7 provides an example:

> For they sow the wind,
>   and reap the whirlwind.
> The standing grain has no growth;
>   it will not make flour.
> If it were to make it,[38]
>   foreigners would devour it.[39]

The agricultural metaphors and similes in such oracles, in which the acts of the Israelites are compared to agricultural phenomena and the state of Israel to the state of the earth, contribute to the theme of the organic connection between acts and their consequences (or the effects of punishment) throughout the book of Hosea.[40]

SOCIAL OR NATURAL DISORDER

Consistent with the connection between human failing and the suffering of the earth in Hos 4:1–3 is the vivid picture given of the community of Israel. Not only is the violation of ethical and legal standards enunciated, but

---

[37] Rainer Stahl ("'Deshalb trocknet die Erde aus und verschmachten alle, die auf ihr wohnen...' Der Versuch einer theologiegeschichtlichen Einordnung von Hos 4, 3," in *Alttestamentlicher Glaube und Biblische Theologie: Festschrift für Horst Dietrich Preuss zum 65. Geburtstag* [ed. Jutta Hausmann and Hans-Jürgen Zobel; Stuttgart: Kohlhammer, 1992], 173), concludes that the destruction announced in 4:3 is "both the consequence of human deed and the work of God" ["ist sowohl Folge menschlicher Tat, als auch Werk Gottes"]. See also Wolff, *Hosea*, 68; and Robinson and Horst, *Die zwölf kleinen Propheten*, 19.

[38] Read *ya'ăśēhû zārîm* for *ya'ăśeh zārîm* (MT), which may have resulted from haplography, due to the similarity of *wāw* and *zayin* in later scripts.

[39] See also Hos 5:7; 9:2; 10:4. Cf. Hos 10:12.

[40] See Koch, "Is There a Doctrine of Retribution?" 61, 64–65.

an overall impression of social disorder is given, summarized in the phrase "bloodshed strikes against bloodshed" (4:2b). The Decalogue-like list in 4:2a features acts that disrupt intercommunity relationships, rather than those that, like the Sabbath command, are explicitly linked to the divine-human relationship.[41] In the light of Hos 10:4, where the Israelites are reproached for *ʾālôt šāwʾ kārōt bĕrît,* "swearing falsely, making covenants," *ʾalōh,* "swearing," in 4:2a probably means swearing false oaths and alludes to the worthlessness of agreements, or covenants, between members of the community.[42] False swearing, lying, murder, stealing, and adultery all point to a lack of reliability and compassion for neighbor, qualities represented by the terms *ʾĕmet* and *ḥesed.*[43] Without these attitudes and the actions and

---

[41] Whether Hos 4:2 is actually citing a fixed form of the Decalogue is contested; that it is referencing legal and ethical norms governing the community life of Israel is clear. Neef (*Heilstraditionen Israels,* 206), Rudolph (*Hosea,* 100–101), and Junker ("Textkritische, formkritische, und traditionsgeschichtliche," 171) see connections to the Decalogue. Sellin (*Zwölfprophetenbuch,* 1:54) and Jeremias (*Der Prophet Hosea,* 61–62, esp. n. 4) conclude that collections resembling the Decalogue may have existed at the time of Hosea. Blenkinsopp (*The Pentateuch: An Introduction to the First Five Books of the Bible* [ABRL; New York: Doubleday, 1992], 209) asserts that Hos 4:2 (as well as Jer 7:9–10) refer to a common "ethical *sensus communis*" in Israel out of which the Decalogue developed "over a long period of time." Anthony Phillips ("Prophecy and Law," in *Israel's Prophetic Tradition: Essays in Honour of Peter R. Ackroyd* [ed. Richard Coggins, Anthony Phillips, and Michael A. Knibb; Cambridge: Cambridge University Press, 1982], 225) and Stahl ("Gottesgericht oder Selbstzerstörung?" 323) argue that Hos 4:2 is a later addition to Hosea. Phillips concludes that it is Deuteronomic; Stahl, only that it was added around 600 B.C.E. and is reminiscent of Jeremiah.

[42] Cf. Hos 6:7. So Robinson and Horst, *Die zwölf kleinen Propheten,* 19; Sellin, *Zwölfprophetenbuch,* 1:54; and Jeremias, *Der Prophet Hosea,* 61–62; contra Rudolph (*Hosea,* 100) and Wolff (*Hosea,* 67), who interpret *ʾālōh* as cursing another by invoking God. Rudolph looks to Judg 17:2 to support this conclusion, but the other Hosean texts offer a closer comparison.

[43] That the qualities of *ʾĕmet,* "trustworthiness, reliability," and *ḥesed,* "kindness, loyalty," refer here to interhuman relationships is borne out by the list of crimes that follows (so Wolff [*Hosea,* 67]; cf. Rudolph [*Hosea,* 99–100] and Jeremias [*Der Prophet Hosea,* 60–61]). Yet these two qualities are joined to a third—*daʿat ʾĕlōhîm,* "knowledge of God"—which is given prime position as the last named in the series. In Hos 6:6 *ḥesed* is placed in parallelism with *daʿat ʾĕlōhîm;* see Rudolph, *Hosea,* 99–100; and Jeremias, *Der Prophet Hosea,* 60–61. In terms of the specific offenses cited in 4:2, deception and adultery are treated elsewhere in Hosea in relation to the divine relationship. See, e.g., Hos 5:3–4, 7; 6:7; 7:13, 16; 8:9; and 9:1. See Jeremias (*Der Prophet Hosea,* 62) on the significance of placing adultery last in the list of transgressions.

constraints that embody them, a kind of anarchy results. The verb *pāraṣ*, with its connotations of sudden incursion, the breaching of barriers, and unchecked growth, enhances the impression of a society that has ceded its common life to random behavior.

The multiple meanings of *nāgaʿ*, "to touch, reach, strike," make the phrase *dāmîm nāgāʿû dāmîm* doubly effective in summarizing the situation. Not only does bloodshed "touch" or "reach" bloodshed, implying that it is everywhere, but bloodshed "strikes" bloodshed, illustrating the way violence breeds violence and heightening the sense of Israel as a war zone.[44] This sense is borne out in some of the oracles that follow, as in 7:1:

> Then the perversion of Ephraim is revealed
> > and the evils of Samaria;
> For they act falsely,
> > and the thief enters
> > and the gang raids outside.[45]

The placement of *dāmîm* as the culminating offense in a series that includes swearing falsely, lying, stealing, and adultery as well as murder signals the seriousness of these acts as well as the extent to which the Israelite community has turned against itself. The life of an individual

---

[44] The word *dāmîm* means both "bloodshed" and "bloodguilt" (BDB, 196b–197a). In either case the transgressions listed in 4:1b are represented as entailing or leading to violence. Wolff (*Hosea*, 68) sees only an indirect connection between these transgressions and bloodshed: all the crimes mentioned are capital offenses. Jeremias (*Der Prophet Hosea*, 62) argues that in the biblical lawcodes, not all the offenses falling under the category of "bloodguilt" involve bloodshed. Neef (*Heilstraditionen Israels*, 204) further suggests that *dāmîm*, as "bloodguilt," may indicate simply "absolute guilt" ["Schuld schlechthin"]; his proposal that the crimes of 4:1b in some way cause death seems closer to the mark. All these suggestions are unnecessary if the phrase "bloodshed strikes against bloodshed" is taken as conveying the escalation of violence and disruption by drawing on the various connotations of *dāmîm* (see also Rudolph, *Hosea*, 101).

[45] Cf. 7:6–7. There is disagreement regarding whether such passages reflect the instability and violence of the reigns of the last kings of Israel. Jeremias (*Der Prophet Hosea*, 62) concludes that they may; Wolff (*Hosea*, 68) argues that the address in 4:1 to the "people of Israel" precludes this possibility. The reference in Hos 1:4 to the blood shed in the Valley of Jezreel by Jehu (2 Kgs 9–10) shows concern with political and royal affairs, however. Thus the mourning of the land in direct response to the transgressions of the community in Hos 4:3 could fit well with both the political and social distress of the nation during the period just before the fall of Samaria and the physical effects of invasion.

inheres in its blood, according to the traditions of the Hebrew Bible, and Israel's life is seeping into the ground.[46]

POLLUTION

The image of shed blood forms part of another theme found in the nine passages of this study: the pollution of the earth. This theme is only hinted at in Hos 4:1–3. Tikva Frymer-Kensky notes that the legal codes of the Hebrew Bible single out certain acts, including some related to bloodshed, that cause pollution or defilement to the land (*'ereṣ*).[47] The concept of pollution is conveyed in these codes by the roots *ṭm'*, "to be unclean," and *ḥnp*, "to be polluted," as well as by the expression *wattāqî' hā'āreṣ*, "and the earth vomited," or a close variant.[48] Acts causing pollution include sexual transgressions[49] as well as accepting ransom for the life or freedom of a murderer[50] and letting the corpse of an executed man hang overnight.[51]

Murder, or the shedding of human blood, is seen as a fundamental act of pollution in Num 35:33a: "You shall not pollute the earth [*taḥănîpû hā'āreṣ*] in which you live, for blood [*haddām*] pollutes the earth [*yaḥănîp 'et-hā'āreṣ*]." The sanction against bloodshed is reflected in the narrative of Cain and Abel, where the blood of the slain Abel cries out to YHWH from the ground (Gen 4:10–11), and of Noah after the flood, where YHWH warns, "Whoever sheds the blood of a human being, by a human being must that one's blood be shed" (Gen 9:5–6).[52]

The relation of these traditions to Hos 4:1–3 is indirect; there is no phraseology of pollution in these verses, aside from the word *dāmîm*. But

---

[46] See Lev 17:10–11; Gen 9:4–6.

[47] "Pollution, Purification, and Purgation in Biblical Israel," in *The Word of the Lord Shall Go Forth: Essays in Honor of David Noel Freedman in Celebration of His Sixtieth Birthday* (ed. Carol L. Meyers and Michael O'Connor; Winona Lake, Ind.: Eisenbrauns, 1982), 399–414, esp. 406–9. See also Miller (*Sin and Punishment in the Prophets*, 137), who discerns a pattern of judgment as divine chastisement and purification in the Hebrew Bible.

[48] See Lev 18:25; 20:22. The root *šḥt*, "to be corrupt or corrupted," occurs outside the law codes in similar contexts (see, e.g., Jer 6:27–30; Deut 32:5; Ezek 20:43–44; Gen 6:11–12).

[49] Lev 18:24–30; Deut 24:1–4.

[50] Num 35:31–34; cf. Deut 19:10, 13.

[51] Deut 21:22–23.

[52] See also the concept of blood polluting the land in Ezek 36:16–18 and Ps 106:38–39 (cf. 2 Sam 21:1) and the discussion in Theodor H. Gaster, *Myth, Legend, and Custom in the Old Testament* (New York: Harper & Row, 1969), 65–69.

a sequential pattern is evident in 4:2–3: the bloodshed in the land, as well as the other harmful acts that break out in it, cause the earth to mourn, and this mourning is expressed as drought.[53] It is as if the blood physically alters and sickens the earth.[54] The LXX translation of 4:2 supports the connection between the crimes of Israel, blood, and the earth: ἀρὰ καὶ πσεῦδος καὶ φόνος καὶ κλοπὴ καὶ μοιχεία κέχηυται ἐπὶ τῆς γῆς, καὶ αἵματα ἐφ' αἵμασι μίσγουσι, "curse and falsehood and murder and theft and adultery have been poured out upon the earth, and bloody deeds mix with bloody deeds."

Vocabulary directly related to the theme of pollution does occur in the oracles that follow 4:1–3.[55] In 5:3 and 6:10 Israel is condemned as defiled (*niṭmā'*). In both cases the defilement is linked to the harlotry (*biznâ, zĕnût*) of Ephraim. In 6:10 the word *ša'ărûriyyâ* (Q), "horror, horrible thing," also occurs: "In the house of Israel I have seen a horrible thing."[56] In 9:4 the Israelites are associated with defilement in a reference to the coming exile: "their bread will be like mourners' bread; all who eat it will be defiled" (*yiṭṭāmā'û*).[57] Again, this pronouncement follows a condemnation of Israel's harlotry (*zānâ*) and harlot's hire (*'etnān*) in 9:1. Israel is accused of corrupting itself (*šiḥēt*) because of its sins in 9:9 and of having become a detestable and unclean thing (*šiqqûṣîm*) in 9:10.[58]

MOURNING AS STRIPPING

There are minimal verbal links to the motif of mourning as stripping within Hos 4:1–3, but these links appear stronger in light of the allegory of the harlot wife in Hos 2 and of other oracles in the Hosean collection. The

---

[53] Frymer-Kensky ("Pollution, Purification, and Purgation," 408) notes that rabbinic sources name drought as well as exile as the consequence of sins that pollute both people and land. See also Koch, "Is There a Doctrine of Retribution?" 67.

[54] See the expression "the earth vomits" (*wattāqî' hā'āreṣ*), noted above.

[55] Frymer-Kensky ("Pollution, Purification, and Purgation," 410) suggests that in Hosea we find the origins of "the concept of pollution as a historical force."

[56] In Jer 18:13 this word occurs in a context that suggests defilement: "The virgin Israel has done a very horrible thing" (*ša'ărūrît*).

[57] So many MSS; Leningradensis has *yîṭammā'û*. Further, read *laḥmām* for *lāḥem*, "to them" (MT), with *BHS*. Contact with the dead was polluting for a period of seven days, according to Israelite law (see Num 19:11–13), and mourning precluded certain cultic practices because of the potential for pollution. See James L. Mays, *Hosea* (OTL; Philadelphia: Westminster, 1969), 127.

[58] The plural form of the noun *šiqqûṣ* is translated here as a collective. The related noun *šeqeṣ* refers to what is ceremonially unclean in the Priestly law code in Leviticus (see BDB, 1054b–55a).

verb *neʾĕsap,* with its connotations of harvesting, evokes the stripping of all that the earth produces and all that covers and adorns the earth. In terms of imagery, the verbs *ʾābal* and *ʾumlal,* with their associations of drying up and wasting away, contribute to the conceptual picture of the earth stripped of plant and animal life.

The parallel here to Hos 2 is notable. In this chapter Gomer, the harlot, symbolizes Israel—not simply the community of Israel but also the land of Israel. In the frame of this allegory, Israel is condemned for deserting her husband, YHWH, and pursuing lovers—the *bĕʿālîm,* or gods of the Canaanites. In 2:4 this pursuit is labelled *zĕnûnêhā,* "her harlotry," and *naʾăpûpêhā,* "her adultery," and summarized in 2:7 with the assertion *hōbîšâ,* "she has acted shamefully." Israel seeks from foreign divinities all the fruits of the earth, as well as water: "my bread and my water," "my wool and my flax," "my oil and my drink" (2:7).

But in 2:4 YHWH charges Israel to remove (*wĕtāsēr*) her harlotry "from her face" and her adultery "from between her breasts." The image of a harlot physically stripping her shameful behavior from her body shifts to that of a dry and empty land in 2:5. If Israel does not strip herself, YHWH will do it:

> Lest I strip her [*ʾapšîṭennâ*] naked [*ʿărummâ*],
>   and exhibit her as on the day of her birth;
>   And make her like a desert [*kammidbār*],
> and set her like a dry land [*kĕʾereṣ ṣiyyâ*]
>   and kill her with thirst [*baṣṣāmāʾ*].[59]

Here, also, the the stripping of the earth is accomplished by drought.

The motif of stripping recurs in 2:11–14. In 2:11 YHWH announces the divine intent to take back grain and wine from the land and reclaim the wool and flax that were "to cover her nakedness" (*lĕkassôt ʾet-ʿerwātāh*). The noun *ʿerwâ,* "nakedness," has connotations of shame and shameful exposure that are picked up in the following verse, as YHWH declares: "I

---

[59] Hos 2:5. Delbert H. Hillers (*Treaty-Curses and the Old Testament Prophets* [BibOr 16; Rome: Pontifical Biblical Institute, 1964], 58–60) points out that the motif of the stripping of Israel and Judah as a prostitute occurs throughout the prophetic literature and may arguably be found in the curse section of one of the eighth-century Sefire treaties (Sf I A 40–41). Examples in the prophetic literature include Jer 13:26–27; Nah 3:5; Ezek 16:35–39; 23:26–30 (cf. Isa 3:18–26, where Judah is not represented as a harlot but is stripped of all finery and plunged into mourning). What is striking in Hosea is the metaphorical joining of the stripping of the earth and the stripping of Gomer, which hinges on the opposition between YHWH, the sustainer of life, and the Canaanite fertility gods.

will lay bare her shamelessness [*'ăgalleh 'et-nablūtāh*] in the sight of her lovers." The element of mourning is introduced in 2:13:

> I will make cease [*wĕhišbattî*] all her rejoicing,
>> her festival, her new moon, and her Sabbath,
>> and every appointed feast.[60]

And in 2:14 the parallel between the stripping of Gomer and the stripping of the earth resumes:

> I will lay waste [*wahăšimmōtî*] her vines and her fig trees of which she
>> said:
> These are my harlot's pay [*'etnâ*],
>> which my lovers have given me.

In these verses the stripping of the prostitute Gomer is figured in the stripping of the land. The earth must be stripped of all its "harlot's pay" (*'etnâ*), the fruit of its devotion to Baal (or, rather, of all it has understood to be its harlot's pay). Although there is no vocabulary of pollution here, the harlotry of Israel is related to defilement in the Hosean passages mentioned above. And although no explicit connection between defilement and stripping is made in these passages, the motif of the stripping of a harlot suggests that in Hos 2 the external signs of the earth's defilement will be removed forcibly through desiccation, a stripping that at the same time entails the cessation of joy (mourning).[61] The earth will become like a desert, dry and unable to support life.

The motif of stripping occurs again in Hos 13:15 in a context of drought that is similar to that of 4:3. The verse comes at the end of a series of indictments against Ephraim:

> Though he bear fruit among[62] brothers,
>> the east wind will come,
> The breath of YHWH
>> rising from the desert [*mimmidbār*].

---

[60] The removal of joyful sounds from a land represents another traditional curse seen in Aramaic and Akkadian texts from the eighth and seventh centuries as well as elsewhere in the biblical prophetic literature (Hillers, *Treaty-Curses and the Old Testament Prophets*, 57–58).

[61] A relation between harlotry, pollution, and stripping comes to full expression in Ezek 16:30–52 and 23:26–30.

[62] Read *bên* for *bēn* (MT).

And his fountain will dry up [*wĕyābēš*],[63]
  and his spring will become dry [*wĕyeḥĕrab*].
It will plunder [*yišseh*] the storehouse
  of every desirable thing.

The semantic kinship of "plunder" and "strip" is evident.[64]

This motif is also implicit in the metaphor of Hos 10:1–2, where Israel is compared to a "luxuriant vine." As the vine yields more and more fruit, Israel's pillars and altars multiply. But, Hosea proclaims,

Their heart is false,
  now they must bear punishment [*ye'šāmû*];
He will break the neck of their altars,
  and destroy [*yĕšōdēd*] their pillars.

The verb *šōdēd,* "despoil, destroy," shares the same semantic field as *hipšîṭ,* "to strip," and *šāsâ,* "to plunder," which occur in the passages discussed above. This passage, then, resumes the Hosean theme that the prosperity of Israel has become so intertwined with the proliferation of false worship and false practices that all must now be cut back.

The recurrence of the motif of stripping in the above passages reinforces the hint of this motif in 4:3. In 2:4–15; 13:15; and 10:1–2, however, the earth is clearly to be stripped and laid waste by YHWH; in 4:3 the stripping away of all forms of life from the earth can be seen as part of the mourning process. Yet the presence of the former scenario shades the dominant pattern in 4:1–3 with its own pattern of imposed mourning. Furthermore, the parallels between the stripping of the harlot Gomer and the stripping of the earth in Hos 2 suggest a connection between pollution and stripping in 4:1–3.

DECREATION

The phraseology associated with the mourning of the earth and the languishing of those who dwell in it in 4:3 seems to convey more than just

---

[63] Read *wĕyābēš* for *wĕyēbôš,* "and will be ashamed" (MT), which may be attributed to confusion of the roots *bwš* and *ybš.* Wolff (*Hosea,* 222) points out that a Qumran fragment containing this passage reads *ybš* rather than *ybwš,* a reading that is particularly informative, since the fragment shows a word with plene spelling a few verses later. The LXX (ἀναξηρανεῖ), Syr. (*wtwbš*), and Vulg. (*siccabit*) all read *wĕyôbîš,* the *hip'il* form of *ybš,* taking the east wind (or breath of YHWH) as subject. It is possible that a wordplay between *yābēš* and *bôš* is intended here; see the discussion above of the response of the earth in Amos 1:2 and the discussion below of Joel 1:5–20.

[64] Cf. the role of *nābaz,* "to be plundered," in Amos 3:11.

a massive desolation or drought and more than a stripping of the earth. The languishing of "beasts of the field," "birds of the sky," and "fish of the sea" suggests the faltering of all creation.[65] The use of these terms to constitute a merism for the totality of the created world is found in the Hebrew Bible as well as in ancient Near Eastern texts. Psalm 104:11–12, for example, praises YHWH's creation of springs:

> They give drink to every animal of the field [*kol-ḥaytô śādāy*];
>> the wild asses quench their thirst.
> By them the birds of the air [*ʿôp-haššāmayim*] dwell;
>> among the branches they give voice.

Similarities have been noted between this psalm and an Egyptian hymn that describes the world over which the sun god Aton shines, naming beasts, birds, and fish, among others:

> All beasts are content with their pasturage;
> Trees and plants are flourishing.
> The birds which fly from their nests,
> Their wings are (stretched out) in praise to thy ka.
> All beasts spring upon (their) feet.
> Whatever flies and alights,
> They live when thou hast risen (for) them.
> The ships are sailing north and south as well,
> For every way is open at thy appearance.
> The fish in the river dart before thy face;
> Thy rays are in the midst of the great green sea.[66]

The creation accounts of the Hebrew Bible reflect this phraseology. In Gen 2:4b–25, YHWH God forms out of the ground *kol-ḥayyat haśśādeh wěʾēt kol-ʿôp haššāmayim*, "every animal of the field and every bird of the sky" (2:19). In Gen 1:26 God gives men and women dominion *bidgat hayyām ûběʿôp haššāmayim ûběkol-ḥayyâ hārōmeśet ʿal-hāʾāreṣ*, "over the fish of the sea and the birds of the sky and all animals that crawl upon

---

65 So Jeremias, *Der Prophet Hosea,* 62–63; Stahl "Deshalb trocknet," 172; and Michael De Roche, "The Reversal of Creation in Hosea," *VT* 31 (1981): 400–409.

66 "The Hymn to the Aton" (trans. John A. Wilson; *ANET,* 370). Another Egyptian hymn to Aton ("Gratitude for a God's Mercy" [trans. John A. Wilson; *ANET,* 380]), is similar: "Repeat him to son and daughter, to great and small; relate him to generations of generations who have not yet come into being; relate him to fishes in the deep, to birds in the heaven." For other instances of this phraseology in ancient Near Eastern texts, see De Roche, "Reversal of Creation in Hosea," 403–4.

the earth."[67] Although both the Priestly and Yahwist narratives of Gen 1–2 may postdate Hos 4:3, the triad of land animals, birds, and fish represents traditional phraseology used in contexts of creation.[68] In Hos 4:3, then, this phraseology introduces associations of the whole created order into the vision of the desolation of Israel.

Similar phraseology is found in accounts of the flood. In the Atrahasis Epic, "the beasts of the field, the fowl of the heavens" are to be taken into the ship.[69] "The beasts of the field, the wild creatures of the field" represent the animals that board the ark in the Epic of Gilgamesh.[70] These animals are named in the flood account of Genesis as birds (*ʿôp*), beasts (*bĕhēmâ*), and crawling things of the earth (*remeś hāʾ ădāmâ*) in both the Priestly (Gen 6:20) and Yahwist (Gen 7:23) strands.

It is clear at the beginning of Gen 6 that the flood represents the undoing of creation. According to the Yahwist:

> And YHWH said, "I am going to blot out the human beings I created from the face of the ground—human beings and beasts, crawling things, and birds of the sky, for I am sorry that I made them." (Gen 6:7)

The Priestly version states:

> And God saw the earth, and behold it was corrupt [*nišḥātâ*], for all flesh had corrupted [*hišḥît*] their way on the earth. And God said to Noah: "I have decided to make an end of all flesh, for the earth is filled with violence because of them, and behold, now I am about to destroy them with the earth." (Gen 6:12–13)

The use of the root *šḥt,* "to be ruined, spoiled, corrupted," in the Priestly account (Gen 6:11, 12) links the onset of the flood to the theme of pollution. Frymer-Kensky has suggested that in its present form the biblical flood narrative is framed in terms of the divine purgation of a polluted earth and that in this form it served as a mythic paradigm for the

---

[67] Cf. Gen 1:28.

[68] On the postexilic dating of Gen 2:4b–25, see, e.g., Joseph Blenkinsopp, "P and J in Genesis 1:11–11:26: An Alternative Hypothesis," in *Fortunate the Eyes That See: Essays in Honor of David Noel Freedman in Celebration of His Seventieth Birthday* (ed. Astrid B. Beck et al; Grand Rapids, Mich.: Eerdmans, 1995), 1–15; Nicholas Wyatt, "Interpreting the Creation and Fall Story in Genesis 2–3," *ZAW* 93 (1981): 10–21; and P. E. S. Thompson, "The Yahwist Creation Story," *VT* 21 (1971): 197–208.

[69] "Atrahasis" (Middle Babylonian Version; trans. E. A. Speiser; *ANET,* 105).

[70] "The Epic of Gilgamesh" (trans. E. A. Speiser; *ANET,* 94).

Babylonian exile.[71] Certain passages in Hosea (5:3; 6:8–10), however, suggest that the desolation of the land was connected to its pollution well before the exile.[72]

The phraseology of Hos 4:3 is reminiscent of the listing of living things to be destroyed in the flood, just as the concept of total devastation in this verse is reminiscent of that described in Gen 6–7. Further, the phrase "bloodshed strikes against bloodshed" in Hos 4:2 recalls traditions concerning the pollution caused by aberrant human behavior, especially bloodshed. Hosea 4:3 may suggest, then, that the corrupt state of the community of Israel is about to ensue in a massive ablution that entails unleashing the waters of primeval chaos on the earth.[73]

Other aspects of Hos 4:3, however, do not fit the paradigm of the flood. In 4:3 even the "fish of the sea" will die; yet fish do not ordinarily perish through inundation.[74] The verb *'ābal,* with its dual associations of "mourn" and "dry up," and *'umlal,* with its connotations of the cessation of fertility, fit better with the concept of a drought—in this case a drought of such proportions that all human and animal life, including fish, expires.

In some ways the concepts of flood and drought come together in the Hebrew Bible: both represent the return to an inchoate, if not chaotic, state.[75] Mircea Eliade has observed about ancient Near Eastern mythology that the *apsū* or *tĕhōm* symbolizes both the chaos of primeval waters and the world of death, the return of the individual to the formless existence that preceded life. Yet, he suggests, these lower watery regions can "from one point of view be homologized to the unknown and desert regions that surround the inhabited territory; the underworld, over which our cosmos is firmly established, corresponds to the chaos that extends to its frontiers."[76]

Tromp summarizes these two concepts of chaos as "wet chaos" and "dry chaos."[77] Wet chaos is represented by the notion of the primeval

---

[71] On the flood as a symbol for the exile, see Blenkinsopp, *Pentateuch,* 82–83; and Walter Brueggemann, "The Kerygma of the Priestly Writers," *ZAW* 84 (1972): 403, 410, 413.

[72] Frymer-Kensky, "Pollution, Purification, and Purgation," 409–10.

[73] So Jacobs, *Osée,* 40.

[74] See Wolff (*Hosea,* 68) and Michael De Roche, "Zephaniah I:2–3: The 'Sweeping' of Creation," *VT* 30 (1980): 106.

[75] See the discussion above of the response of the earth in Amos 1:2, which evokes the image of YHWH as a diety who thunders (and thus brings rain) but who also inflicts drought.

[76] *The Sacred and the Profane* (New York: Harcourt, Brace & World, 1959), 41–42.

[77] *Primitive Conceptions of Death,* 132.

ocean in Gen 1:2 and by the flood; dry chaos, by the desert and sparsely inhabited regions on the fringes of the settled land.[78] In tracing the desert motif in the Hebrew Bible, Shemaryahu Talmon points to instances in biblical narratives and poetry where the *midbār,* "desert" or "dry wilderness," represents a region hostile to life, uncertain and dangerous, the domain of outlaws and wild animals.[79] Jeremiah 2:6 provides a vivid sketch of this region:

> Who led us in the desert [*midbār*],
>   in a land of desert [*bĕʾereṣ ʿărābâ*] and pit.
>   In a land of dryness [*bĕʾereṣ ṣiyyâ*] and the shadow of death,
> in a land [*bĕʾereṣ*] that no one crosses through
>   and where no one dwells.

The concept of a dry chaos is also evoked, Tromp asserts, "where devastation of cities or countries is portrayed as a relapse into barren conditions and cultivation ceases."[80] Passages describing the defeat of a city or state often reflect a traditional curse in which wild animals possess the wasteland created when a city or state is destroyed.[81] These

---

[78] Tromp (ibid.) notes that the word *tōhû,* "formlessness," which in combination with *bōhû* describes the watery state of the earth at the beginning of creation in Gen 1:2, is applied to the desert or wasteland in a number of biblical texts. See, e.g., Jer 4:23; Deut 32:10; Isa 34:11; Job 6:18; 12:24; Ps 107:40. He further points to Gen 2:4b–6 as illustrating the notion of "dry chaos": earth without vegetation, rain, and cultivation. (It should be noted, however, that the picture of the barren earth in 2:5 must be reconciled with the mention of the *ʾēd,* "spring," in 2:6, part of the circumstantial clause that begins in 2:5.) The dry-chaos concept might also be applied to Gen 3:17, where the earth is cursed following the disobedience of the man and woman and reverts to a semiarid condition, yielding "thorns and thistles," which thrive in poor, dry soil.

[79] "The 'Desert Motif' in the Bible and in Qumran Literature," in *Biblical Motifs: Origins and Transformations* (ed. Alexander Altmann; Cambridge, Mass.: Harvard University Press, 1966), 41–44. See also A. Penna, "Il cosmo nella letteratura profetica," in *Il cosmos nella Bibbia* (ed. Giuseppe DeGennaro; Naples: Edizioni Dehoniane, 1982), 213–17. Richard J. Clifford (*Fair Spoken and Persuading: An Interpretation of Second Isaiah* [Theological Inquiries; New York: Paulist, 1984], 22–23) compares the desert through which Israel is guided by YHWH in Second Isaiah and in, e.g., Pss 78:52–53; 136:16; Deut 32:10–13 to the hostile sea from which it is delivered in Exodus and in, e.g., Pss 77:16–20; 114; 136:13–15. Note that in Ps 136:13–16 these two motifs come together.

[80] *Primitive Conceptions of Death,* 132.

[81] See Hillers (*Treaty-Curses and the Old Testament Prophets,* 44–54), who cites Isa 13 and 34; Zeph 2:13–15; and Jer 50:39 as the best biblical examples of this curse.

animals are another sign of "the primeval state of chaos" in such areas, according to Talmon.[82] The spread of thorns, thistles, and briars over the ruins of human settlements may be a further indication of a state of dry chaos.[83]

Talmon notes the affinities of the motif of the desert as a desolate wilderness to the Ugaritic myth of Mot (death), who periodically threatens to turn the earth into an uncultivated desert,[84] just as in the other foundational Ugaritic myth Yam (sea) strives to drown the earth in swirling waters. Sigmund Mowinckel, further, links battles in the Psalms between YHWH and the powers of chaos to the myth of Mot. Despite the imagery of flood and sea in the depiction of these battles, he claims, many of them reflect the reality of a world "destroyed by the deadly powers of drought, and in danger of sinking back again into chaos."[85] In Ps 68:8–11, for example, YHWH shows power by bringing rain.

In Hos 4:3, then, the eradication of all forms of life may reflect the traditional notion of a dry chaos, in which earth becomes again a formless waste and the separation between dry land and water is erased by drought rather than by flood. The persistence of aridity and barrenness as a curse, a punishment, and a symbol of misfortune throughout the Hebrew Bible, and in the prophetic literature in particular, lends credence to the supposition of a dry-chaos motif. The connection between aridity and decreation is particularly clear in Hos 4:3 because of the phraseology of this verse.[86]

---

[82] "Desert Motif," 43.

[83] This is a frequent motif in Isaiah (see, e.g., Isa 5:6; 7:23–25; 32:13) but is also found in Hos 10:8. It occurs in the Sumerian laments over the destruction of cities (see, e.g., "Lamentation over the City of Ur" [trans. Samuel N. Kramer; *ANET,* 455–63] line 368; cf. "Lamentation over the Destruction of Sumer and Ur" [trans. Samuel N. Kramer; *ANET,* 611–19], lines 10–11, 38; and "The Curse of Agade" [trans. Samuel N. Kramer; *ANET,* 646–51], lines 262–77).

[84] "Desert Motif," 43. For further discussion of the role of Mot in Ugaritic mythology, see Umberto Cassuto, *Bible and Ancient Oriental Texts* (vol. 2 of *Biblical and Oriental Studies;* Jerusalem: Magnes, 1975), 168–77; and Theodor H. Gaster, *Thespis: Ritual, Myth, and Drama in the Ancient Near East* (New York: Henry Schuman, 1950), 124–26, esp. n. 22.

[85] *The Psalms in Israel's Worship* (2 vols.; Nashville: Abingdon, 1962), 1:152.

[86] The verb *neʾĕsap,* "to be gathered," in Hos 4:3 plays into this concept of decreation: what God has originally sown, or planted on earth, God is now gathering up. In the account of creation in Gen 2:4b–25, YHWH God plants (*wayyiṭṭaʿ*) a garden in Eden, sets (*wayyāśem*) the man there, and causes trees to sprout up (*wayyaṣmaḥ*) in it (2:8–9). In Gen 3:17–18 the land is cursed so that it grows (*taṣmîaḥ*) only inedible thorns and thistles.

This phraseology is not necessarily a sign of the dependence of the verse on either the creation or flood accounts of Genesis. As noted, similar phraseology occurs in ancient Near Eastern texts as well as elsewhere in the Hebrew Bible. More probably, Hos 4:3 reflects traditional phraseology concerning creation and the traditional myth of a cosmic "undoing" of creation by means of a great flood.[87] The freedom with which the book of Amos and other prophetic writings commingle images of wet and dry was noted above. Hosea 4:3, then, may depict the reversion of creation into a dry chaos while still drawing on the powerful tradition of the wet chaos embodied in the flood.[88]

The theme of decreation in this verse is tied within Hos 4:1–3 as a whole to the abrogation of law and ethical principles in Israel. A full discussion of the relationship between law and creation (and, obversely, transgression and decreation) in the Hebrew Bible is not possible here, but this relationship has been seen as fundamental by a number of biblical scholars. Hans H. Schmid posits a broad unity between cosmic, political, and social order in the ancient Near Eastern concept of creation; law "enacts the establishment of the order of creation seen in its juridic aspect."[89]

---

[87] Contra De Roche ("Reversal of Creation in Hosea," 407–8), who concludes that Hos 4:1–3 and 2:14, 20 allude to the Priestly creation account. Similar or even identical phraseology does not necessarily indicate literary dependence (see further the discussion in chapter 7). Even if such dependence were assumed, De Roche gives no argument for why Hosea should be dependent on P rather than vice versa. De Roche places special significance on the order in which the animal types are named in Gen 1 and in Hos 4:3. In Gen 1 the order of creation is consistently (1) fish, (2) birds, (3) animals (see Gen 1:20a, 20b, 24 and 1:26, 28). In Hos 4:3 the order is reversed, a sign, De Roche asserts, that this verse is announcing not only a massive drought but the "reversal of creation" ("Reversal of Creation in Hosea," 403). The variation in sequence does not necessarily reflect allusion to a particular literary text, however.

[88] Blenkinsopp (*Pentateuch,* 80–81) notes a similar juxtaposition within the Yahwist strand of the primeval history. Hence the account of creation from a rainless earth (Gen 2:5) is followed by the account of the flood, in which torrential rains overwhelm the earth. And whereas Mowinckel (*Psalms in Israel's Worship,* 1:143–45, 152) discerns the concept of a dry chaos in the Psalms, he also points to the frequent imagery of YHWH's battle with the primeval ocean and suggests that one concept can underlie the other. David Damrosch (*The Narrative Covenant: Transformations of Genre in the Growth of Biblical Literature* [San Francisco: Harper & Row, 1987], 273, 292–97) finds links between the biblical narratives of the flood and the wilderness (desert) wanderings. See also Clifford (*Fair Spoken,* 22–23).

[89] "Creation, Righteousness, and Salvation: 'Creation Theology' As the Broad Horizon of Biblical Theology," in *Creation in the Old Testament* (ed. Bernhard W. Anderson; Philadelphia: Fortress, 1984), 105. See also Rolf Knierim ("Cosmos and

Mowinckel stresses the connection between God as creator or ruler over creation and giver of law (or, in his words, covenant) in the psalms of YHWH's enthronement as well as in other psalms.[90] Robert Murray refers to the concept of a "cosmic covenant," reflected in the divine covenant with Noah in Gen 9:9–16: "the charter of cosmic order, between heaven and earth and between man and his fellow-creatures."[91] This concept, he claims, underlies psalms in which the king's reign is compared to the orbiting of heavenly bodies and his righteousness to abundant rain and fertile land.[92] In Ps 72, a royal psalm, the earth is even invoked to take an active part in the reign of the king:

> Let the mountains bear well-being [*šālôm*] for the people,
>   and the hills, with righteousness [*ṣĕdāqâ*]. (72:3)

The dual meaning of *šālôm,* "well-being, peace," and *ṣĕdāqâ,* "righteousness, prosperity," reinforces the link between cosmic and social order here.[93]

Hosea 4:1–3 is consistent with the perspective on the integrity of the created order implied in these texts. By rejecting a relationship with YHWH, the people of Israel are confronted with YHWH's still more fundamental relationship with all of creation. As in the flood narrative of Gen 6–9, human disregard for communal norms and constraints leads to the unravelling of the order that sustains creation itself. In a broad sense, then, Hos 4:1–3 presages the anchoring of law and human ethics in creation that is achieved in the final form of the Pentateuch.

History in Israel's Theology," *HBT* 3 [1981]: 59–123, esp. 85–101), who posits a similar relationship between cosmic order, social order, and history in the biblical literature; and Douglas A. Knight, "Cosmogony and Order in the Hebrew Tradition," in *Cosmogony and Ethical Order: New Studies in Comparative Ethics* (ed. Robin W. Lovin and Frank E. Reynolds; Chicago: University of Chicago Press, 1985), 133–57, esp. 150–51.

[90] *Psalms in Israel's Worship,* 1:106–69, esp. 143–48. See, e.g., Pss 93; 95–98 and 24; 65; 85.

[91] "Prophecy and the Cult," in *Israel's Prophetic Tradition: Essays in Honour of Peter R. Ackroyd* (ed. Richard Coggins, Anthony Phillips, and Michael A. Knibb; Cambridge: Cambridge University Press, 1982), 209.

[92] See, e.g., Pss 72:5–7, 16; 89:28–29, 36–37.

[93] BDB, 1022b–1023a, 842ab. See Mowinckel (*Psalms in Israel's Worship,* 1:164) on the unity of spiritual and material blessings in, e.g., Pss 36 and 65. On the use of *ṣedeq* and *ṣĕdāqâ* in psalms praising YHWH's presence in the cosmic order, see Knierim, "Cosmos and History in Israel's Theology," 87–88.

SUMMARY OF LITERARY TECHNIQUES

In Hos 4:1–3 the verbs *'ābal,* "to mourn," and *'umlal,* "to languish," carry both psychological and physical nuances. Personification occurs when these verbs, taken in their psychological sense, are assigned non-human subjects: in 4:3, the earth will mourn and the animals of the field and birds of the air languish. That the noun *'ereṣ,* "earth," has more than one meaning contributes to the personification of the natural world as grieving. The structure of 4:1–3 exhibits a parallel between the human and the natural, as the social dysfunction in 4:1b–2 is mirrored by the natural dysfunction in 4:3. This parallel is tightened by the repetition of the word *'ereṣ* throughout; in 4:1 the human community and its acts are located in the *'ereṣ* that will grieve in 4:3. The ambiguity of the phrase *kol-yōšēb bāh,* "all who dwell in it" (4:3a), allows a further link between what humans and animals must endure.

OVERALL EFFECT OF THE METAPHOR

In Hos 4:1–3 the metaphor of earth mourning illustrates the dynamic interaction between YHWH, the people of Israel, and the earth itself. This is the same interaction played out on a universal scale in the archetypal narratives of Gen 1–9, in both the Priestly and Yahwist strands. In the Priestly narrative, the intricate ordering by God of all creation (the heavens, the earth, the varied forms of plant and animal life, and human beings) establishes this relationship. The corruption (*nišḥat, hišḥît*) of the earth by human misdeeds and the sending of the flood disrupt it; the reordering of humans and animals and the divine commitment to preserve the earth after the flood reestablishes it.

In the Yahwist account, YHWH's creation of the first human being (*hā'ādām*) from the ground (*hā'ădāmâ*) makes the relationship inherent, and the wordplay reifies the conceptual link. This basic relationship between YHWH, *hā'ādām,* and *hā'ădāmâ* unfolds into a narrative as YHWH places the man in the garden of Eden to tend what the creator has caused to grow up from the ground (Gen 2:9, 15). When the man exceeds the limits of his appointed task, the ground is cursed: *'ărûrâ hā'ădāmâ ba'ăbûrekā,* "cursed is the ground because of you" (Gen 3:17). Although the agency of YHWH is implicit in the passive construction here, the syntax makes the ground the subject, so that it assumes a place on stage.[94]

---

[94] This placement recurs in Gen 3:18, where the ground is again a subject: *wĕqôṣ wĕdardar taṣmîaḥ lāk,* "thorn and thistle it will grow for you." The snake, who is

In Gen 4, similarly, the sin of Adam's son activates the ground, which "opens its mouth" to receive the blood of Abel (4:11). Once again the ground features in YHWH's curse, although here the man is cursed from the ground, as if the spilled blood that cries out to YHWH (4:10) transmits the curse.[95] By severing his relationship with YHWH, Cain has severed his fruitful relationship to the ground. No longer will he be a farmer, but a wanderer over the earth, vulnerable to the dangers and vagaries of life outside his own cultivated fields: "You have driven me away this day from the face of the ground, and from your face I will be hidden; I will be a fugitive and a wanderer [*nāʿ wānād*] on the earth, and whoever finds me will kill me" (4:14). In like terms Eliade describes the chaos behind the settled land in the view of primitive cultures: "no longer a cosmos but a sort of 'other world,' a foreign chaotic space peopled by ghosts, demons, 'foreigners.'"[96] In like terms is the *midbār,* the desert or wilderness, conceived in much of the Hebrew Bible. The depiction of the fate of Ephraim in Hos 9:16–17 with a metaphor of drought and sterility is reminiscent of Cain's fate:

> Ephraim is stricken,
> Their root is dried up [*yābēš*],
>> they will not yield fruit.
> Even if they give birth,
>> I will kill the desired children of their womb.
> My God will reject them,
>> because they have not listened to him,
>> and they will become fugitives [*nōdĕdîm*] among the nations.

Finally, in Gen 8:21, YHWH restores harmony between all actors:

> I will never again curse the ground [*hā'ădāmâ*] because of humankind [*hā'ādām*] ... nor will I ever again strike all living creatures as I have done. For all the days of the earth [*hā'āreṣ*], sowing and harvest, cold and heat, summer and winter, day and night, will not cease.

---

clearly an actor in Gen 3, is cursed similarly in 3:14: "Because you have done this, cursed [*'ārûr*] are you above all beasts and above all animals of the field."

95 The phrase *min-hā'ădāmâ,* "from the ground," can be interpreted in more than one way. I have translated *min* as "out of, from the site of" (BDB, 579ab), thus echoing the preceding verse: "the voice of your brother's blood is crying out to me from [*min*] the ground." The preposition *min* can also mean "by" (BDB, 579b–580a), "on account of, because of" (BDB, 580ab), or "away from" (BDB, 577b–578). The last reading implies Cain's banishment from his fields, echoing Gen 4:14.

96 *The Sacred and the Profane,* 29.

The drama of YHWH, human community, and earth spun out in the Yahwist narratives, as well as the ordering and disordering of the relationship between these three actors in the Priestly account, is evident in paradigmatic form in the three verses of Hosea considered here. In these verses earth becomes an actor in the ongoing relationship between YHWH and Israel.[97]

The parallels between Gen 1–9 and Hos 4:1–3 should not be overdrawn. Despite the metonymic naming of all creation as mourners of Israel's end, Hos 4:1–3 concerns Israel (and possibly Judah), as the address in 4:1a and the oracles that follow 4:3, with their references to Israelite institutions and practices and their invocation of Ephraim and Judah attest.[98] Hosea introduces cosmic overtones in 4:3, as Amos does in 1:2, to convey the seriousness of the bond between YHWH and Israel, the extent to which it is rooted in YHWH's purposes as ruler over all creation, and the breadth of the repercussions when this bond is sundered. In Hos 4:1–3 the land of Israel and the forms of life it nourishes mourn over and because of the degeneration of the human community of Israel, a result of its lack of knowledge of God.

---

[97] By actor is meant a *dramatis persona,* not necessarily an agent instigating an action.

[98] See the discussion of the meaning of ʾereṣ in Hosea in Wolff (*Hosea,* 51). The inclusion of Judah in some of Hosea's oracles extends the frame of reference to the whole community of the Israelite people, according to Wolff (146), although the reference to Judah in 4:15 may be secondary (89).

4

JEREMIAH

JEREMIAH 4:23–28

TEXT, TRANSLATION, AND TEXTUAL NOTES

23 רָאִ֙יתִי֙ אֶת־הָאָ֔רֶץ וְהִנֵּה־תֹ֖הוּ וָבֹ֑הוּ   וְאֶל־הַשָּׁמַ֖יִם וְאֵ֥ין אוֹרָֽם׃

24 רָאִ֙יתִי֙ הֶ֣הָרִ֔ים וְהִנֵּ֖ה רֹעֲשִׁ֑ים   וְכָל־הַגְּבָע֖וֹת הִתְקַלְקָֽלוּ׃

25 רָאִ֕יתִי וְהִנֵּ֖ה אֵ֣ין הָאָדָ֑ם   וְכָל־ע֥וֹף הַשָּׁמַ֖יִם נָדָֽדוּ׃

26 רָאִ֕יתִי וְהִנֵּ֥ה הַכַּרְמֶ֖ל הַמִּדְבָּ֑ר   וְכָל־עָרָ֗יו נִתְּצוּ֙ מִפְּנֵ֣י יְהֹוָ֔ה

מִפְּנֵ֖י חֲר֥וֹן אַפּֽוֹ׃   ס

27 כִּי־כֹה֙ אָמַ֣ר יְהֹוָ֔ה

שְׁמָמָ֥ה תִהְיֶ֖ה כָּל־הָאָ֑רֶץ   וְכָלָ֖ה לֹ֥א אֶעֱשֶֽׂה׃

28 עַל־זֹאת֙ תֶּאֱבַ֣ל הָאָ֔רֶץ   וְקָדְר֥וּ הַשָּׁמַ֖יִם מִמָּ֑עַל

עַ֤ל כִּי־דִבַּ֙רְתִּי֙ זַמֹּ֔תִי   וְלֹ֥א נִחַ֖מְתִּי וְלֹא־אָשׁ֥וּב מִמֶּֽנָּה׃

23 I looked at the earth, and behold: [a]an empty waste,[a]
and to the sky, but its light was gone.

24 I looked at the mountains, and behold, they were quaking,
and all the hills were shaking.

25 I looked, and behold there was no one,
and all the birds of the sky had fled.

26 I looked, and behold the fruitful land was desert,
and all of its cities pulled down before YHWH,
before his burning anger.

27 For thus says YHWH:
All the earth will be a desolation,
[b]yet I will not make a full end.[b]

28 Because of this the earth [c]will mourn,[c]
and the sky above turn dark,
[d]For I have spoken, I have planned;
and I have not repented nor will I turn back from it.[d]

65

ᵃ⁻ᵃ So Syr., Vulg.; ʟxx reads only οὐθέν, "nothing," which could represent a summary rendition of the hendiadys *tōhû wābōhû*[1] or, rather, an indication that part of this phrase was missing in the Hebrew *Vorlage* of ʟxx and added only later, perhaps under the influence of Gen 1:2.[2] In support of the first possibility is the fact that there is no standard translation in ʟxx of the Hebrew expression, since the words *tōhû* and *bōhû* are linked directly elsewhere only in Gen 1:2, where they are treated quite differently: ἀόρατος καὶ ἀκατασκεύαστος, "invisible and formless."[3] In support of the second possibility is the fact that the ʟxx translation of Jeremiah is, in general, fairly literal.[4] Aquila, Symmachus, and Theodotion (according to Origen) reflect the full expression literally, reading κενὴ καὶ οὐθέν, "emptiness and nothing."[5] Here κενή apparently represents *tōhû;* in Isa 45:18, in a similar context, ʟxx translates *tōhû* with κενόν. A number of those commentators who argue that ᴍᴛ is an expanded reading therefore assume that οὐθέν in ʟxx represents Hebrew *bōhû* in the *Vorlage* and that *tōhû wā* was added later.[6]

Of the two words, however, *bōhû* is the rarer, occurring only three times in ᴍᴛ and never without *tōhû*. As noted, *bōhû* is rendered in ʟxx by ἀκατασκεύαστος in Gen 1:2 and not at all in Isa 34:11. Further, in Job 26:7, in the context of physical space, ʟxx uses οὐδέν, "nothing," for *tōhû.*[7] It is

---

[1] So Brevard S. Childs, "The Enemy from the North and the Chaos Tradition," *JBL* 78 (1959): 189 n. 9; and Friedrich Giesebrecht, *Das Buch Jeremia* (HAT 3, 2/1; Göttingen: Vandenhoeck & Ruprecht, 1907), 28.

[2] So Paul Volz, *Der Prophet Jeremia* (2d ed.; KAT 10; Leipzig: Deichertsche, 1928), 51; Wilhelm Rudolph, *Jeremia* (2d ed.; HAT 12; Tübingen: Mohr, 1958), 32; Carl H. Cornill, *Das Buch Jeremia* (Leipzig: Tauchnitz, 1905), 53; Bernhard Duhm, *Das Buch Jeremia* (KHC 11; Tübingen: Mohr, 1901, 53).

[3] In Isa 34:11 *tōhû* and *bōhû* occur as a parallel pair in the same bicolon. ʟxx translates *tōhû* as ἔρημος, "desert," in the first colon but diverges widely from ᴍᴛ in the second colon.

[4] See P. Kyle McCarter Jr., *Textual Criticism: Recovering the Text of the Hebrew Bible* (GBS; Philadelphia: Fortress, 1986), 90.

[5] Aquila and Symmachus show variations in Syrohexaplaric and in an anonymous commentary; see Joseph Ziegler, ed., *Jeremias. Baruch. Threni. Epistula Jeremiae* (Septuaginta. Vetus Testamentum Graecum 15; Göttingen: Vandenhoeck & Ruprecht, 1957), 170. Both κένωμα and κενόν occur as variants for κενή in Aquila, e.g., but all variant readings reflect two terms.

[6] So Volz, *Der Prophet Jeremia,* 51; Rudolph, *Jeremia,* 32; see also Giesebrecht, *Das Buch Jeremia,* 28; and William McKane, *Jeremiah* (2 vols.; ICC; Edinburgh: T&T Clark, 1986–1996), 1:106.

[7] Giesebrecht notes the frequent translation of *tōhû* with οὐδέν (or οὐθέν) in ʟxx but does not distinguish between the concrete and figurative uses of *tōhû*, which

possible, then, that οὐθέν in LXX represents Hebrew *tōhû,* a word that naturally fits the context of a devastated landscape, since it occurs elsewhere in the Hebrew Bible in a spatial sense to represent desert, wasteland, wilderness, or untracked region (see, e.g., Deut 32:10; Ps 107[106]:40; Job 6:18; 12:24; Isa 34:11; 45:18).[8] In this sense it is translated variously by LXX: ἔρημος, "desert" (Deut 32:10, Isa 34:11); ἄβατος, "inaccessible or desolate region" (Ps 107[106]:40); κενός, "empty, fruitless place" (Isa 45:18).

In these instances the word *tōhû* bears the sense of dry chaos, or uninhabited desert, discussed above.[9] This concept of dry chaos is comparable to, if not the same as, the notion of primeval chaos conveyed by *tōhû wābōhû* in Gen 1:2. In Jer 4:23, then, the inherent sense of physical formlessness in the word *tōhû* could have been amplified at a later time by the addition of *wābōhû* in light of Gen 1:2 and of the impact of Jeremiah's powerful vision of decreation in 4:23–26 as a whole.[10]

b–b This statement appears inconsistent with what precedes in 4:27a ("All the earth will be a desolation") and with what follows in 4:28 ("I have not repented nor will I turn back from it"). Commentators have suggested various emendations of MT that would change the present amelioration of disaster in this clause to a confirmation of woe. The simplest of these include (1) excising *lō'* as a later addition influenced by Jer 5:18 and 30:11 and (2) reading *lāh,* "for it," rather than *lō',* a suggestion that has in its favor

---

can also convey moral or intellectual emptiness. In the figurative sense LXX translates *tōhû* with οὐδέν three times (1 Sam 12:21; Isa 40:17, 23).

[8] So Cornill (*Das Buch Jeremia,* 53), who sees *tōhû* here as representing a horrible waste without life, as in Isa 45:18. Helga Weippert (*Schöpfer des Himmels und der Erde: Ein Beitrag zur Theologie des Jeremiabuches* [SBS 102; Stuttgart: Katholisches Bibelwerk, 1981], 50 n. 91) also retains *tōhû* while striking *wābōhû* as secondary. Duhm (*Das Buch Jeremia,* 53) translates *tōhû* as "chaos" and assumes it is original to the Hebrew text but argues that *wābōhû wĕ'el* represents a later emendation of *ûpānōh 'el,* "and turned to," under the influence of Gen 1:2.

[9] See the discussion above of the theme of decreation in Hos 4:1–3; Weippert, *Schöpfer des Himmels und der Erde,* 51–54; and William L. Holladay, *Jeremiah 1* (Hermeneia; Philadelphia: Fortress, 1986), 165.

[10] Contra Victor Eppstein, "The Day of Yahweh in Jer 4:23–28," *JBL* 87 (1968): 96. Eppstein argues that the entire phrase *tōhû wābōhû* was added to the Hebrew text by a scribe under the influence of apocalyptic conceptions of a return to primeval chaos and that this addition occurred after the LXX translation of Jeremiah. Eppstein offers no explanation, however, as to why, if there was no phrase following *wĕhinnēh* in the Hebrew *Vorlage* of the LXX, the Greek translators supplied οὐθέν there.

the confusion of *ʾālep* and *hê* in some Hebrew scripts.[11] Considering the recurrence of the phrase "I will not make a full end," or a close variant in Jer 5:18 and 30:11, it seems likely that the negative particle *lōʾ* was added later in order to orient this prophecy of judgment toward an exilic community that had survived Judah's fall.[12] At the same time the phrase plays, in its present form, a literary role, easing the transition from 4:27 to 4:28 by anticipating the question, if the "whole earth" is to become a desolation (4:27a), what, then, of the earth will be left to mourn (*teʾĕbal*) in 4:28?

c–c So Syr. (*ttʾbl*), Vulg. (*lugebit*). LXX reflects the prefixal verb of MT but translates it as a jussive: πενθείτω, "let [the earth] mourn." The parallel verb *wĕqāděrû* is treated similarly: καὶ συσκοτασάτω, "and let [the sky] turn dark." See Amos 8:7–8 for a pattern of (1) divine announcement followed by (2) *ʿal-zōʾt*, "and so," and (3) the depiction of a future response (entailing mourning) on the part of the earth. This response is conveyed in Amos 8:8, as here, by an imperfect and a converted perfect.

d–d LXX presents these four cola in a different order, thus avoiding the unusual construction of MT, in which the first two cola are juxtaposed asyndetically and the second two are each preceded by *wāw*. Most commentators adopt the reading of LXX for its smoother and more symmetrical style,[13] but the unusual quality of the verse in MT carries its own force, and I have retained it.[14]

---

[11] On the first possibility, see McKane (*Jeremiah*, 1:109) and Volz (*Der Prophet Jeremia*, 52); on the second, see Rudolph (*Jeremia*, 32). On Hebrew scripts, see Frank M. Cross, "The Development of the Jewish Scripts," in *The Bible and the Ancient Near East: Essays in Honor of William Foxwell Albright* (ed G. Wright; Garden City, N.Y.: Doubleday, 1965), 148–49.

[12] Cf. Jer 5:10. See Cornill, *Das Buch Jeremia*, 54; and Walther Zimmerli, "Visionary Experience in Jeremiah," in *Israel's Prophetic Tradition: Essays in Honour of Peter R. Ackroyd* (ed. Richard Coggins, Anthony Phillips, and Michael A. Knibb; Cambridge: Cambridge University Press, 1982), 100. Holladay (*Jeremiah 1*, 183) considers the negative phrasing to be original in Jer 30:11 and 5:18 but secondary in 4:27 and 5:10. His revocalization of *wĕkālâ lōʾ* to *wĕkullāh lōʾ*, "and none of it," in 4:27 is possible, but his argument that *ʿāśâ* here means "to remake," a meaning it carries nowhere else in the Hebrew Bible, seems less certain. Albert Condamin (*Le Livre de Jérémie* [EBib; Paris: Gabalda, 1936], 44) argues for the authenticity of this colon on the basis of the Isaianic concept of a remnant. John Bright (*Jeremiah* [AB 21; Garden City, N.Y.: Doubleday, 1965], 33) also accepts the possibility that 4:27b is integral to the verse and "means what it says."

[13] So Holladay, *Jeremiah 1*, 144; McKane, *Jeremiah*, 1:109–10; Bright, *Jeremiah*, 31; Rudolph, *Jeremia*, 32; Cornill, *Das Buch Jeremia*, 29; Duhm, *Das Buch Jeremia*, 54; Giesebrecht, *Das Buch Jeremia*, 54.

[14] So also Volz, *Der Prophet Jeremia*, 51.

DELIMITATION OF THE PASSAGE

Jeremiah 4:23–28 can be seen as a prophetic vision (4:23–26) followed by a divine speech (4:27–28) that affirms or explains the vision.[15] The vision is set off from what precedes and follows by the fourfold repetition of *rāʾîtî,* "I looked," which occurs at the beginning of each verse. The speech is linked to the vision in two ways. The reference to the "burning anger" of YHWH at the end of 4:26 leads into the messenger formula, "For thus says YHWH," at the beginning of 4:27, and the conjunction *kî,* "for," provides a grammatical link. The phrase *ʿal-zōʾt,* "because of this," at the beginning of 4:28 extends the speech, and the final sequence of four clauses, in which YHWH voices a determination to destroy (4:28b), forms a climax and a conclusion.

Although Jer 4:23–28 can be considered a distinct unit, it also forms part of a chain of oracles concerning the military threat of the "enemy from the north" (4:6). The motif of invasion from the north runs through 4:5–6:30[16] but is concentrated in 4:5–31.[17] This collection of oracles forms the immediate context for 4:23–28 in the present book of Jeremiah.

In addition, there is a special link between 4:23–26 and the visionary speech in 4:19–22, directly preceding. As Holladay points out, the two passages share a similar structure: both begin with a speech of Jeremiah and end with a short explanatory speech of YHWH.[18] The prophet speaks in both passages out of a disturbing vision; in the first he both sees (*rāʾâ,* 4:21) and hears (*šāmaʿ,* 4:19, 21) the destruction besetting the land (*kol-hāʾāreṣ,* 4:20). In the second he looks at (*rāʾâ,* 4:23, 24, 25, 26) a land (*hāʾāreṣ,* 4:23) that is already devastated. In this context the absence of the verb *šāmaʿ* actually evokes it: there is nothing left to hear. The two passages function as a sequential pair: the prophet's focus moves from the din of battle to the unearthly silence of its aftermath. In this pairing, each vision and attached speech informs the other.

---

[15] So Giorgio R. Castellino, "Observations on the Literary Structure of Some Passages in Jeremiah," *VT* 30 (1980): 399; Holladay, *Jeremiah 1,* 148, 151; Bright, *Jeremiah,* 34; Ronald E. Clements, *Jeremiah* (IBC; Atlanta: John Knox, 1988), 40–41.

[16] See, e.g., Bright, *Jeremiah,* 33, and Clements, *Jeremiah,* 39–40; Holladay (*Jeremiah 1,* 132) extends this chain through Jer 10:25.

[17] So Holladay, *Jeremiah 1,* 133, 146; see also Rudolph, *Jeremia,* 31–32; Volz, *Der Prophet Jeremia,* 49–51.

[18] *Jeremiah 1,* 147–48. Holladay considers the two passages as a single unit with two sections.

AUTHORSHIP AND DATING

Discussion of the dating of this passage has focused largely on the core vision of 4:23–26.[19] Some commentators point to the distinctiveness of this vision in the book of Jeremiah, specifically to its cosmic and ahistorical imagery, and conclude it is a later composition influenced by apocalyptic visions of the end times.[20] Brevard S. Childs argues that the verb *rāʿaš*, "to shake," which occurs in 4:24, frequently describes the eschatological shaking of the earth in exilic and postexilic texts such as Ezek 38; Isa 13; and Joel 2 and 4. He therefore dates Jer 4:23–26 to the exilic period, while prescinding from any conclusion about its Jeremianic origins.[21] As Childs himself points out, however, the verb *rāʿaš* is associated with the theophany of YHWH, apart from notions of eschatological chaos, in early poems such as Judg 5 and Ps 18.[22]

Others concede the unique nature of the vision in 4:23–26 but claim the vision may be attributed to Jeremiah and need not be exilic. Key to these claims is the distinction between cosmic imagery, poetic style, and the extraordinary nature of the visionary experience, on the one hand, and proto-apocalyptic thinking, on the other.[23] The vision of the end of Israel in Jer 4:23–26 resembles those in Amos 1:2 and Hos 4:3: all unfold in a quasi-mythic or cosmic framework that sets them apart from the historically particularized imagery of the oracles that follow or precede them.

Whether the vision in Jer 4:23–28 is seen in its present context as the culmination of a sequence of oracles beginning with 4:5, as Zimmerli

---

[19] Those who date this vision report to the time of Jeremiah generally accept the speech of YHWH in 4:27–28 as part of an early collection of Jeremiah's prophecies, whether or not it was originally joined to 4:23–26 (4:27b is excepted; on this colon see the textual note above). Duhm (*Das Buch Jeremia*, 54) considers this divine speech a lame redactional expansion of the vision described in 4:23–26 but does not assign a late date for it, suggesting, rather, that it may derive from an "older author" ["älteren Autor"]. Contra Duhm, see Weippert, *Schöpfer des Himmels und der Erde*, 52.

[20] So Volz, *Der Prophet Jeremia*, 50–51; Giesebrecht, *Das Buch Jeremia*, 28. Eppstein ("Day of Yahweh," 93–97) posits an original vision report that was successively altered in the process of transmission until the final addition of *tōhû wābōhû* in 4:23 by a scribe influenced by apocalyptic concepts. Eppstein's account of the history of the text is elaborate and highly speculative, however.

[21] "Enemy from the North," 189–95.

[22] See also David J. Reimer, "The 'Foe' and the 'North' in Jeremiah," *ZAW* 101 (1989): 223–32.

[23] See McKane, *Jeremiah*, 1:107; Rudolph, *Jeremia*, 33; John J. Collins, "Old Testament Apocalypticism and Eschatology," *NJBC*, 298–99; Johannes Lindblom, *Prophecy in Ancient Israel* (Philadelphia: Fortress, 1962), 127; Duhm, *Das Buch Jeremia*, 54.

proposes,[24] or simply as the second part of a sequential pair, as suggested above, a natural progression can be seen from the earlier battle scenes to the surrealistic glimpse of what is left after the enemy has burst upon the land and swept away its inhabitants. The noise of battle resumes in 4:29: "From the sound of horseman and archer every city flees." The vision of 4:23–26 is thus surrounded with the immediate realities of invasion, and in this sense it does stand out. Yet it can be seen as functioning like a brief flash of insight (or foresight) in a situation of high urgency: an eye in a storm.

Further, taking the unit 4:23–28 as a whole, there are noticeable links of language and imagery between these verses and the oracles concerning the enemy from the north that precede it. In 4:7–8, at the beginning of the larger unit 4:5–31, YHWH warns:

> A lion has gone up from his thicket,
> and a destroyer of nations has set forth.
> He has gone forth from his place
> to make your land [*'arṣēk*] a waste [*lĕšammâ*];
> your cities will fall into ruins [*tiṣṣênâ*] without inhabitant.
> Because of this [*'al-zō't*], gird yourselves with sackcloth [*ḥigrû śaqqîm*],
> lament [*sipdû*] and wail [*wĕhêlîlû*];
> For the burning anger of YHWH [*ḥărôn 'ap-yhwh*]
> will not turn back [*lō'-šāb*] from it [*mimmennû*].[25]

Here the waste (*šammâ*) the lion threatens to make of the land (*'ereṣ*) can be compared to the desolation (*šĕmāmâ*) YHWH will bring upon the whole land (*kol-hā'āreṣ*) in 4:27. The prediction of ruined cities without inhabitants foreshadows the absence of people in 4:25 and the toppled cities in 4:26; the verb *tiṣṣênâ*, "will fall into ruins" (from the root *nṣḥ*), resembles the verb *nittĕṣû*, "were pulled down" (from the root *ntṣ*), phonologically as well as semantically. Because of (*'al-zō't*) this desolation, mourning will ensue: the verbs *sāpad*, "to lament," and *hêlîl*, "to wail," and the putting on of sackcloth (*ḥāgar śaqqîm*) here parallel the verbs *te'ĕbal*, "will mourn," and *wĕqādĕrû*, "will turn dark" or "will mourn," in 4:28. Similarly the reference to the "burning anger of YHWH" (*ḥărôn 'ap-yhwh*) that will not "turn back" (*lō'-šāb*) "from it" (*mimmennû*) in 4:8 corresponds to "his burning anger" (*ḥărôn 'appô*) in 4:26 as well as to his determination, "I will not turn back from it" (*wĕlō'-'āšûb mimmennāh*) in 4:28.

In 4:11, the foretelling of a "hot wind from the open spaces in the desert" (*midbār*) is consistent with the turning of fruitful land to desert

---

[24] "Visionary Experience in Jeremiah," 101–2.
[25] See also the similar passage in Jer 2:15.

(*midbār*) in 4:26. Similarly the storm imagery of the invader in 4:13 ("he comes up like clouds, his chariots like a storm wind") foreshadows the darkening of the sky in 4:23 as well as in 4:28. In 4:20, Jeremiah cries out that the whole earth (*kol-hā'āreṣ*) is ravaged (*šuddĕdâ*) along with "my tents," a symbol of human habitation, setting the scene for the wasting of the earth in 4:23, 26 and the destruction of cities in 4:26. The prophet's question, "How long must I see [*'er'eh*] the standard, must I hear [*'ešmĕ'â*] the sound of the trumpet?" in 4:21 is answered by the fourfold "I looked" (*rā'îtî*) in 4:23–26 and the absence of life that precludes hearing.[26]

The vision in Jer 4:23–28 does not, then, break suddenly into the sequence of prophecies concerning the enemy from the north that begins in 4:5 but unfolds as a climax prepared for by the speeches and visions that precede it. The links and relationships noted here cannot prove that 4:23–28 stem from Jeremiah, but they do show that this passage is not out of place in the collection of writings brought together in Jer 4. If 4:23–26 represent a visionary experience, then they would seem most appropriately dated, contra Childs, in the preexilic period, as a vision of the exile to come.[27]

THEMES AND MOTIFS

THE RESPONSE OF THE EARTH

Both Amos 1:2 and Hos 4:1–3 exhibit a two-part structure in which human or divine action is followed by the response of the earth. In Jer 4:23–28 the earth has a role throughout. What is striking about this role in the first section of the passage (4:23–26) is the absence of activity: the prophet looks out on a landscape that is for the most part stilled. The trembling of mountains and hills in 4:24 appears as the last trace of an active, if involuntary, response to disaster. The nominal clauses of 4:23, 25a, and 26a are essentially stative, describing a condition that has already been effected: the earth has turned into a formless waste; the sky has lost its light; people are absent; the fruitful land has become desert. These nominal constructions are balanced by two verbs in the perfect tense. In 4:25b

---

[26] Zimmerli ("Visionary Experience in Jeremiah," 101–3) and William L. Holladay ("Style, Irony, and Authenticity in Jeremiah," *JBL* 81 [1962]: 47–48) suggest further phraseological links between Jer 4:23–26 and Jeremiah as a whole, which they adduce in support of the composition of the passage by the prophet.

[27] Cf. Amos 7:1–2, 4–6. Holladay (*Jeremiah 1*, 133–35, 151–52), Bright (*Jeremiah*, 34), Castellino ("Observations on the Literary Structure," 399), Weippert (*Schöpfer des Himmels und der Erde*, 52 n. 99), and Stahl ("Deshalb trocknet," 169–71) also date Jer 4:23–28 to the preexilic period.

all the birds of the sky have fled (*nādādû*), and in 4:26b all the cities have been pulled down (*nittĕṣû*). The only indications of the earth's ongoing response are the participle in 4:24a, where the mountains "were quaking" (*rōʿăšîm*) and the *hitpaʿel* form in 4:24b, where all the hills "were shaking" (*hitqalqālû*).

These last two verbs apparently depict an earthquake, but it is difficult to say exactly what has brought about the conditions observed in the other verses. Some of the effects named, however, including the earthquake, resemble those created by the response of the earth to the advent of the divine warrior, a topos evoked in Amos 1:2 by the suggestion of thunder in the phrase *yittēn qôlô*.[28] The traditional signs of the presence of the divine warrior include the darkening of the sky, earthquake, the panic and presumed flight of the enemy, and the depopulation and desolation of the land.[29] Nahum 1:2–8, a hymn to the divine warrior cited above, contains a number of parallels in language and imagery to the scene in Jer 4:23–26. The declaration in Nah 1:3 that "In whirlwind and storm is his way / and cloud is the dust of his feet" corresponds to the darkness of the sky in Jer 4:23. The phraseology of Nah 1:5 is particularly close to that of Jer 4:24:

> *hārîm rāʿăšû mimmennû*
> *wĕhaggĕbāʿôt hitmōgāgû*

> Mountains quake before him,
> and the hills melt.

The verb *rāʿaš*, "to quake," occurs with the subject *hārîm*, "mountains," in both verses, while the verbs used with *gĕbāʿôt*, "hills," are *hitpaʿel* forms in each case: *hitmōgāgû* in Nah 1:5 and *hitqalqālû* in Jer 4:24.[30] In addition, the reference in Nah 1:4 to the drying up (*yibbēš* and *heḥĕrîb*) of sea and rivers and the languishing (*ʾumlal*) of Bashan, Carmel, and Lebanon corresponds to the desertification of the fruitful land (*hakkarmel*) in Jer 4:26.

Further, Nah 1:6 speaks of the anger of YHWH and its destructive effects:

> Before his wrath who can stand,
> and who can endure against his burning anger [*baḥărôn ʾappô*]?
> His rage is poured out like fire,
> and the cliffs are pulled down [*nittĕṣû*] by him.

---

[28] See the discussion above of the response of the earth in Amos 1:2.

[29] See Gerhard von Rad, "The Origin of the Concept of the Day of Yahweh," *JSS* 4 (1959): 99–100, 104, and the passages he cites (Josh 2:9; 7:5; 24:7, 12; Judg 5:4; 1 Sam 14:15 as well as Ps 18:8–16 = 2 Sam 22:8–16).

[30] These two verbs represent variant forms of the *hitpaʿel* stem.

Here YHWH's burning anger (*ḥărôn 'appô*) is connected with the pulling down (*nittaṣ*) of rocks, just as in Jer 4:26 this same anger explains the pulling down (*nittaṣ*) of cities. The close resemblance of these two passages supports a connection between the devastation described in Jer 4:23–26 and the activity of the divine warrior in battle.[31]

The oracles that precede and follow Jer 4:23–26 provide a concrete context for war as they foretell, envision, and explain the coming invasion of the foe from the north. They thus reinforce the sense of the divine warrior in 4:23–26 and center the focus of the passage on that *topos*. In these verses the devastation of the earth is not solely the effect of drought, which is the response of earth to theophany in Amos 1:2. It is also the direct result of war itself—of an invading army behind which stands YHWH.[32] Here the mythic and historic aspects of the divine warrior are brought together in a way that reflects the prophetic *topos* of the Day of Yahweh.[33]

The blending of these two aspects is played out within Jer 4:23–28 in the alternating references to human and natural realms. In 4:23–24 attention is directed to the basic structure of the cosmos: earth, sky, mountains, and hills. In 4:25 the absence of human beings is noted along with the absence of birds; in 4:26 the human element dominates: the fruitful, or cultivated land, has become desert, and its cities are in ruins.

The noun *karmel*, "fruitful land," may be related to *kerem*, "vineyard," a primary feature of the cultivation of the land of Israel and a symbol of that land as well as of the people who inhabit it.[34] The reversion of *karmel* to *midbār* clearly entails an eradication of human habitation. But these words carry additional historical associations. In Jer 2:6–7 they occur in a context that links them to the exodus from Egypt and settlement in Canaan:

---

[31] For other prophetic passages that take up the *topos* of the Day of Yahweh, see Zeph 1:7–18 (possibly preexilic) as well as Isa 13; 34; Ezek 30:1–19; Joel 2:1–11 (all probably exilic or postexilic). For a discussion of these passages, see von Rad, "Origin of the Concept," 99–103.

[32] Laurent Wisser ("La création dans le livre de Jérémie," in *La création dans l'orient ancien* [ed. Louis Derousseaux; Congrès de l'ACFEB, Lille (1985); LD 127; Paris: Cerf, 1987], 246) notes the evocation of both drought and military invasion in Jer 4:23–28; Stahl ("Deshalb trocknet," 171) points out the confluence of traditions of drought, war, and theophany. See also the juxtaposition of drought and battle in Jer 14:1–15:9 and the discussion of this passage in Holladay (*Jeremiah 1*, 421–23). Cf. the images of devastation to the earth in the context of military destruction in Isa 16:8–10; Jer 48:32–33; Nah 2:3; Deut 20:19–20.

[33] As seen, e.g., in Amos 5:6–20.

[34] See, e.g., Jer 5:10; 6:9; 12:10. On the relation of *karmel* to *kerem*, see BDB, 502a; GKC §§85, 52.

And they did not say, where is YHWH,
    who brought us up from the land of Egypt,
Who led us in the desert [*bammidbār*],
    in a land [*bĕ'ereṣ*] of desert plain ['*ărābâ*] and pit;
In a land [*bĕ'ereṣ*] of dryness and the shadow of death [*wĕṣalmāwet*];
    in a land [*bĕ'ereṣ*] no one crosses through,
    and where no one lives.
Yet I brought you to a fruitful land ['*ereṣ hakkarmel*]
    to eat its fruits and its produce.

The use of *karmel* and *midbār* together in 4:26, then, evokes the whole history of the Israelites, and the devastation of the physical earth is entwined here with the devastation both of a particular land cultivated and inhabited by generations of people and of the people themselves.[35]

In 4:27–28, the second section of the passage, the earth assumes a more active role. In these verses a speech of YHWH confirms Jeremiah's vision of the end by articulating the essence of the vision: "The whole land ['*ereṣ*] will be a desolation [*šĕmāmâ*]." The root *šmm*, "to be desolate, appalled," from which this noun derives, carries both a physical and a psychological meaning. The meaning "to be appalled," also rendered as "to be struck with horror," is clearly psychological.[36] The verb occurs with this meaning in Jer 2:12:

Be appalled [*šōmmû*], O heavens, because of this,
    and horrified [*wĕśa'ărû*], be utterly desolate [*ḥorbû*],[37]
    says YHWH.[38]

The noun *šammâ*, "waste" and "appallment," occurs frequently in both senses in Jeremiah.[39]

---

[35] So Wisser, "La création dans le livre de Jérémie," 246; see also McKane, *Jeremiah*, 1:107; Giesebrecht, *Das Buch Jeremia*, 28; and Holladay, *Jeremiah 1*, 148, 163.

[36] BDB, 1030ab–1031a; cf. *HAL*, 1446b–1447a. Note the association of the participle *mĕšômēm* with the ritual of mourning in Ezra 9:3. On the connections between the two aspects of *šmm*, see Norbert Lohfink, "Enthielten die im Alten Testament bezeugten Klageriten eine Phase des Schweigens?" *VT* 12 (1962): 267–69. Lohfink here compares the dual aspect of the root *šmm* to that of '*bl*.

[37] The verb *ḥārēb*, "to be waste, desolate," here acquires a figurative, psychological sense (so BDB, 351b), and is thus comparable to *šmm*.

[38] See also Jer 4:9, where *nāšam* occurs in parallelism with *tāmâ*, "to be astounded, dumbfounded."

[39] BDB, 1031b. For the meaning "waste" see, e.g., Jer 2:15; 4:7; 18:16; 25:38; 46:19; 48:9. For the meaning "appallment" see, e.g., Jer 5:30; 8:21; 19:8; 25:9, 18; 29:18;

With the meaning "to be desolate," the root *šmm* conveys the sense of "physically deserted" or "laid to waste," especially when applied to the land.[40] In Jer 9:10 the noun *šĕmāmâ* has this meaning:

> And I will make Jerusalem into heaps,
>   a refuge of jackals;
> And the cities of Judah I will make a desolation [*šĕmāmâ*],
>   without inhabitant.[41]

Given the dual sense of *šmm,* however, the root can convey, even in the context of physical devastation, a psychological sense of desolation or despair, as is evident in 2 Sam 13:20: "and Tamar stayed desolate [*wĕšōmēmâ*] in the house of Absalom her brother."[42] This dual sense of *šmm* is especially clear in Isa 54:1, where Zion is personified as a barren woman and urged to break into song:

> Cry out, O barren one who has not given birth,
>   break forth in a loud cry, you who have not conceived;
> For the children of the desolate one [*šômēmâ*] will be more
>   than the children of the married one, says YHWH.

Here desolate means barren, or childless, but also, in the light of the exhortation to sing, sad. In Jer 4:27, although YHWH's announcement that "the whole land shall be a desolation" is a declaration about the physical state of the earth, it also conveys a suggestion of grieving that is enhanced by the reference to mourning in 4:28.[43] The inherent play between these two nuances in *šĕmāmâ* bridges the vision of the devastated earth in 4:23–26 and the response of the earth to this devastation in 4:28.

Yet there remains an odd disjunction in 4:27–28. If the whole earth (*kol-hāʾāreṣ*) is to become a desolation, then in what sense will it mourn on this account (*ʿal-zōʾt*)? How can the earth at the same time mourn and

---

42:18; 44:12, 22; 49:13, 17; 50:23; 51:37, 41. The dual meaning of this noun is obvious in many of these contexts, and it is sometimes difficult to decide which meaning is primary.

[40] BDB, 1030b–1031a; *HAL*, 1446b. See, e.g., in the *qal*, Isa 49:8; Ezek 33:28; 35:12, 15; 36:4; Lam 5:18; cf. Lam 1:4. In the *nipʿal* see, e.g., Jer 12:11; Ezek 29:12; 30:7; 36:34, 35.

[41] Cf., e.g., Jer 6:8; 10:22; 32:43; 34:22; 49:2; 50:13.

[42] Cf. Lam 3:11; Ezek 4:17.

[43] So, possibly, in 9:10, where the word *šĕmāmâ* occurs in a context of mourning. See also the use of *šammâ,* "desolation, appallment," in connection with mourning in Jer 8:21.

be mourned over? The simplest way to understand the role of ʿal-zōʾt here is to take it as referring back not to the desolation of the earth, but to YHWH's utterance: "For thus says YHWH: the whole land shall be a desolation."[44] Because of this divine determination, earth and sky will mourn, enacting the purposed desolation.

At the same time the mourning of the earth in 4:28 is essentially a literary trope. The dual aspect of the root *šmm* associates the concept of desolation with that of stunned grief or sadness, just as drying up is associated with mourning in the verb *ʾābal*. The presentation of the earth in two capacities—as desolate (4:27) and as mourning (4:28)—expresses this latent duality, so that the announcement, "Because of this the earth shall mourn" restates, in another form, "the whole earth shall be a desolation."[45] The multiple meanings of *ʾereṣ* contribute further to the impression of enfolded phenomena. If *kol-hāʾāreṣ* in 4:27 means both the physical land and the community of Israel (as 4:26 would imply), in 4:28 *hāʾāreṣ* is paired with *haššāmayim,* "the sky," creating the image of earth in a cosmic sense grieving over the devastation of Israel.[46]

The response of earth and sky to the end of Israel is conveyed by the parallel verbs *ʾābal* and *qādar,* "to be dark." Like *ʾābal, qādar* occurs here in the *qal,* indicating a response (without indication of an agent) on the part of its subject, "sky." Like *ʾābal,* it can be understood in two senses. On a literal or physical level *qādar* means "to be dark" and is used of the sky, as here, as well as of the sun, moon, and stars[47] and, in Job 6:16, of a stream. But it occurs more frequently with the figurative meaning, "to mourn." As in the case of *ʾābal,* where the rites of mourning mimic the response of the earth to drought, so it may be that the darkening of the mourner's body with ashes and dust, heightened by the mourner's refusal to wash, parallels the darkening of the natural world, and *qādar* comes to mean "to be sad, downcast" or "to mourn."[48]

---

[44] Cf. Amos 8:8, where the earth will tremble (*tirgaz*) and mourn (*wĕʾābal*) because of (ʿal-zōʾt) YHWH's statement in 8:7: "I will never forget all their deeds!"

[45] See Holladay, *Jeremiah 1,* 168.

[46] So Eppstein, "Day of Yahweh," 96. One effect of this trope is to create the impression that in 4:28 earth, along with sky, represents what remains of creation after God's anger has left it bereft. There is a hint here that the devastation envisioned is not a final end but that there will be something left to mourn the devastation. Hence, as noted above, the relevance of the contested colon, "yet I will not make a full end."

[47] See 1 Kgs 18:45; Ezek 32:7, 8; Joel 2:10; 4:15.

[48] See BDB (871a) and the account of David's mourning for his infant son in 2 Sam 12:16–20 as well as Ps 35:14 (with the adjective *ʾābēl,* "mourning"); Pss 38:7;

This use of the verb may be particularly characteristic of Jeremiah among the prophetic collections, as *qādar* also occurs with this meaning in Jer 8:21 and 14:2 but elsewhere in the prophetic corpus only in Mic 3:6 and, in the *hipʿil,* Ezek 31:15. In Jer 4:28, the figurative sense of *qādar* strongly reinforces the aspect of mourning in *ʾābal,*[49] and both together enhance, as they are enhanced by, the nuance of grieving in *šĕmāmâ.* It would seem that the dominant picture conveyed in 4:28, then, is the mourning of earth and sky over the desolation of Israel.

Yet *ʾābal* and *qādar* work with *šĕmāmâ* on another level as well. If *qādar* is read in a literal sense, the announcement that "the sky will turn dark" implies clouds and a storm.[50] An allusion to clouds might seem incompatible with the aspect of "drying up" conveyed by *ʾābal,* yet clouds signal dust storms as well as rain storms. The reference to the sirocco, the dry desert wind that brings heat, drought, and dust, in 4:11–12 supports this interpretation: "A hot wind from the open spaces of the desert [*midbār*] toward the daughter of my people" This metaphor for the enemy is taken up again in the next verse (4:13), which links the sirocco to clouds and storm: "Behold he comes up like clouds / like the storm wind his chariots."

The verb *qādar* occurs in a context of both drought and mourning in Jer 14:2, the opening of Jeremiah's "drought liturgy." Likewise in Isa 50:2–3 the abstract noun *qadrût,* "darkness," occurs in connection with the concepts of both desert and mourning:

> Behold by my rebuke I dry up [*ʾaḥărîb*] the sea,
>   I make rivers a desert [*midbār*];
> Their fish stink from lack of water
>   and die of thirst.
> I clothe the sky with darkness [*qadrût*]
>   and make sackcloth their covering.

The first bicolon of 4:28, then, can be interpreted as a dry storm, making the earth sere (*ʾābal*) and the sky dark (*qādar*) with dust, and the desolation (*šĕmāmâ*) of the earth in 4:27 can be understood in terms of drought and, perhaps, famine. Such a perspective heightens the allusions to dryness and sterility in the vision of 4:23–26 as well: *tōhû,* "wasteland,"

42:10; 43:2. For a psychological connection between the two senses of *qādar,* see Delekat, "Zum hebräische Wörterbuch," 55–56.

[49] So Vulg., which translates *wĕqādĕrû* with *maerebunt,* "will grieve."

[50] See, e.g., 1 Kgs 18:45. Although the darkening of the sky could be the sign of an eclipse or the failure of the heavenly bodies, such phenomena are indicated by *qādar* elsewhere in conjunction with the specific naming of sun, moon, or stars. See Ezek 32:7–8; Joel 2:10; 4:15.

prevails in 4:23; the absence of both human beings and birds (and presumably all forms of life in between) in 4:25; and the repossession of the cultivated land (*hakkarmel*) by desert (*midbār*) in 4:26. The absence of light in the sky in 4:23 can also be seen in this context as a sign of the sirocco. Here mourning takes on a physical aspect.

The physical and psychological aspects of *qādar* interact with the dual aspects of *'ābal* and *šĕmāmâ* to create a complex whole in Jer 4:23–28. Whether the sky blackens in Jer 4:23–28 as a sign of the sirocco, a sign of mourning, or a sign of both, the pairing of *'ābal* with *qādar* in 4:28 underscores the motif of darkness, which functions as an inclusio: the passage begins (4:23) and ends (4:28) with allusions to a sky without light. Darkness, as noted above, is an integral element of the *topos* of the divine warrior and of the Day of Yahweh.[51] But it may also be seen as a special motif in Jeremiah. Desert, drought, and darkness are yoked in 2:6, cited above, and in 2:31:

> Have I been a desert [*midbār*] to Israel
> or a land of deep darkness [*'ereṣ ma'pēlyāh*]?

SIN OR PUNISHMENT

The devastation and subsequent mourning of the earth in Jer 4:23–28 are attributed to YHWH. This is stated explicitly in 4:26, where the cultivated land becomes desert and the cities become ruins "before YHWH, before his burning anger," and in 4:27–28, where YHWH announces the disaster to come and takes full credit for it: "I have spoken, I have resolved; I have not repented nor will I turn back from it." Allusions to the *topos* of the divine warrior contribute to the picture of a land in which human and nonhuman elements alike recoil before a God who has turned divine power against them.

Reasons for God's enmity are not given in these verses; the explanation must rather come through implication and context.[52] The parallel structuring and juxtaposition of 4:19–22 and 23–28 noted above create a wider context for the desolation of Judah. The experience of battle in 4:19–21 is followed in 4:22 by a divine speech that provides an explanation for the invasion:

---

[51] See, e.g., Amos 5:18; Zeph 1:15; cf. Jer 13:16.

[52] Holladay (*Jeremiah 1*, 167) compares the *'al-zō't*, "because of this," that begins 4:28 with the *'al-kēn*, "therefore," that begins Hos 4:3. Yet the phrase in Hos refers back to specific infractions of the community of Israel, whereas here the phrase refers back to the desolation of the land.

> For my people are foolish;
> > they do not know me [yādāʿû].
> They are foolish children
> > and have no understanding.
> They are skilled at doing evil [lĕhāraʿ]
> > but do not know [yādāʿû] how to do good [ûlĕhêṭîb].

Here the people are condemned for not knowing YHWH, just as they are faulted for lack of knowledge of God in Hos 4:1. Further, if knowledge of God implies here, as in Hosea, actual practices within the human community, then the doing of evil rather than of good may represent specific offenses like those listed in Hos 4:2. Within the wider context of Jer 1–3 and 5–6, such offenses are named, among them taking false oaths (5:2), deception (5:27), dealing falsely (6:13), failure to judge justly (5:28), taking advantage of the poor (2:34; 5:28), and worship of other gods (2:11, 20, 23, 26–28; 3:1–2).

If one views 4:19–22 and 23–28 together, the earth in 4:23–28 responds to YHWH's punishment (or announcement of punishment) of Judah for its failure as God's people. In 4:18, however, an explanation for the besieging of Judah is given from a slightly different perspective:

> Your way and your deeds
> > have done these things to you.
> This is your misfortune, for it is bitter,
> > for it has reached your heart.

Here the stress is on the connection between acts and harmful consequences without explicit mention of the punishing agency of YHWH.[53]

In the present form of Jeremiah the position of 4:18 just before the extended unit comprising 4:19–28 complements the dramatic focus on the power of divine anger in 4:23–28. Within these verses themselves, however, there is no suggestion of the earth mourning as a direct result of the misdoings of its inhabitants; rather, both are laid waste by the burning anger of YHWH.

SOCIAL OR NATURAL DISORDER

The vision of Jer 4:23–26 and the attached speech in 4:27–28 include no depiction of the realities of life in Judah before its extinction. In the parallel unit 4:19–22 there is only the hint in 4:22 of a community—"my

---

[53] For other examples within Jeremiah of an emphasis on acts engendering consequences, see Jer 2:17, 19; 3:2b–3; 5:25; 13:21. In Jer 6:19; 12:13; and 17:9–10, the role of human transgression and the role of divine retribution in bringing about misfortune are both specified.

people"—who are "skilled at doing evil." A more extensive context for the destruction announced by Jeremiah may be seen in Jer 9:9–10, however, a short speech that shows a number of similarities to Jer 4:23–28.

> For the mountains [*hehārîm*] I will take up weeping [*běkî*] and wailing [*wānehî*],
> and for the pastures of the wilderness [*ně'ôt midbār*] a dirge [*qînâ*];
> For they are in ruins [*niṣṣû*][54] so that no one crosses them,
> and the sound of cattle is not heard.
> All, from the birds of the sky [*mē'ôp haššāmayim*] to the beasts [*běhēmâ*],
> have fled [*nādědû*] and are gone.
> And I will make Jerusalem into heaps,
> the refuge of jackals;
> And the cities of Judah I will make a desolation [*šěmāmâ*],
> without inhabitant [*mibbělî yôšēb*].

The element of mourning for the ravaged earth is present in this passage, though here it is the prophet (or YHWH) who laments rather than the earth mourning for itself, as in 4:28.[55] The speech creates a picture of devastation that brings together many of the same elements found in 4:23–28. The *ně'ôt midbār,* "pastures of the wilderness," are not equivalent to *hakkarmel,* "the fruitful land" (4:26), but they speak, too, of human activity, and like the fruitful land they have become like a desert that no one crosses. The phonological similarity of the roots *nṣh* and *ntṣ* (4:26) in the *nip'al* is another link between the two passages; in 9:9 the pastures of the wilderness are ruined (*niṣṣû*); in 4:26 the cities of the fruitful land are pulled down (*nittěṣû*).[56] As in 4:25–26, the pastures in 9:9 are empty of human beings, as well as of cattle, and the "birds of the sky" have fled (*nādědû*), along with the beasts. The cities, too, are laid waste: they have been made into the desolation (*šěmāmâ*) the whole earth will become according to YHWH's words in 4:27.

---

[54] Read *niṣṣû* for *niṣṣětû* (MT), presuming a scribal corruption. So *HAL*, 410a, 675b. The verb *niṣṣû* is taken here as a *nip'al* from the root *nṣh*, "to fall into ruins," which occurs also in Jer 4:7; 2 Kgs 19:25 = Isa 37:26; and, according to *HAL* (675b), in Jer 2:15; 9:11; 46:19. In relation to *niṣṣû* in Jer 9:9 and *niṣṣětâ* in 9:11, cf. the similarities between 9:9 and 2 Kgs 19:25 = Isa 37:26, where the *nip'al* participle *niṣṣîm* occurs. BDB (428a) assigns *niṣṣětû* (MT) in 9:9 and the forms in 2:15; 9:11; 46:19 to the root *yṣt,* "to burn, kindle," proposing a secondary meaning in the *nip'al,* "to be destroyed, desolate."

[55] On the question of the speaker in Jer 9:9–10, see Holladay, *Jeremiah 1,* 303–4; Bright, *Jeremiah,* 72; and Mark S. Smith, "Jeremiah IX 9—A Divine Lament," *VT* 37 (1987): 97–99.

[56] LXX and some Hebrew MSS read *niṣṣětû* (from *yṣt,* "to burn, kindle") in Jer 4:26.

The lament over the desolation of Judah in 9:9–10 is preceded in the present form of Jeremiah by a lengthy speech decrying the failings of the Israelite community (9:1–8). Many of these accusations have to do with deception, falsehood, and lack of trust, as can be seen in the two verses immediately preceding the lament (9:7–8):

> Their tongue is a sharpened[57] arrow;
>> each speaks deceit with his mouth.
> Each speaks peace to his neighbor [rēʿēhû],
>> but within he plans his ambush.
> For these things shall I not punish them? says YHWH;
>> on a nation like this,
>> shall I not avenge myself?

These verses offer a glimpse of advanced social breakdown, where no one can trust anyone else and the term rēʿēhû, "neighbor, friend," which represents the essence of community, has become meaningless. Neighbor has in fact become adversary, as the reference to ambush, with its hint of violence, indicates.

The placement of the call in 9:9–10 to mourn over the land and cities of Judah directly after this indictment of social instability and disorder shows that at least in the view of the early interpreters of Jeremiah's prophecies, the desolation to come was connected to that kind of disorder.[58]

MOURNING AS STRIPPING; POLLUTION

As noted above, most of the action presumed in Jer 4:23–28 has already taken place. These verses present the vista of a stripped landscape: stripped of light, of human beings, of birds, of orchards and vineyards and all forms of cultivation, and of cities. Although the theme of the pollution of the land by the acts and harlotry of the people, which occurs elsewhere in Jeremiah,[59] is absent here, the present placement of 4:23–28 is suggestive. In 4:30 Jerusalem is personified as a harlot decked with various adornments, and in 4:31 her death at the hand of killers foretold. The resulting composite image of a harlot stripped of her finery and suffering death pains provides an analogue to the preceding vision of the earth stripped of all life and the subsequent mourning of earth and sky (4:23–28).

---

[57] Reading Q (*šāhût*, "sharpened") with Syr. and other Hebrew MSS; K (*šôhēṭ*) is reflected in LXX, Vulg., and a MS of Tg.

[58] Holladay (*Jeremiah 1*, 304) proposes that Jer 9:9–10 is a slightly later passage than 9:1–8, though it represents a prophetic speech of Jeremiah. He gives no reason for presuming that its present position in the book is late, however.

[59] See 2:7, 20–23; 3:1–3 (esp. in relation to Deut 24:1–4); cf. 13:26–27; 23:14–15.

DECREATION

Resonance with creation language as we know it from the Priestly creation account of Gen 1:1–2:4a has been widely noted in Jer 4:23–26.[60] This resonance can be seen as extending through 4:27–28, so that the entire passage can be viewed as an undoing of creation.[61]

Throughout 4:23–28 there is a counterbalancing of heavens (sky) and earth that recalls the fundamental structuring of creation. In 4:23 the prophet looks first at the earth and then to the sky. In 4:25 he sees that human beings, who live on the earth, are gone and that even the birds, who fill the sky, have fled.[62] And in 4:28 the earth mourns while the sky turns dark. The fourfold repetition of the verb *rā'â,* "to see," in connection with the basic elements of the created world—earth, sky, mountains, human beings, birds, fruitful land—also calls to mind the creation account of Gen 1:1–2:4a.

Individual verses of Jer 4:23–28 show parallels with this account. Even if in 4:23 one accepts only *tōhû,* rather than *tōhû wābōhû,* as original, this word expresses the sense of formless space conveyed by the full phrase in Gen 1:2. The absence of light in the sky in the second colon of 4:23 completes the correspondence to primeval chaos. The mountains and hills of 4:24 can be seen as a synecdoche for the dry land of Gen 1:9.[63] The lack of human beings (*'ādām*) and of birds in 4:25 counterbalances the creation of human beings in Gen 1:26–30 and of birds, here the sole representatives of earth's living creatures, in Gen 1:20–23. The mention of the fruitful land (*hakkarmel*) in 4:26 recalls the fruitfulness of the earth in Gen 1:12: "And the earth brought forth grass and plants yielding seed according to their kinds and trees bearing fruit with its seed in it according to their kinds." Finally, 4:28 declares that it is by the word and plan of YHWH that the elements of creation will be undone: "For I have spoken, I have planned" (*kî dibbartî zammōtî*). Just so are these elements put into place by YHWH's word and design in Gen 1:1–2:4a.

---

[60] See, in particular, Michael Fishbane, "Jeremiah IV 23–26 and Job III 3–13: A Recovered Use of the Creation Pattern," *VT* 21 (1971): 151–53; Weippert, *Schöpfer des Himmels und der Erde,* 102; and Wisser, "La création dans le livre de Jérémie," 246. As Weippert (52 n. 99) and McKane (*Jeremiah,* 1:108) stress, the phraseological parallels noted do not imply the dependence of Jer 4:23–28 on the Priestly narrative.

[61] So Weippert, *Schöpfer des Himmels und der Erde,* 50; Volz, *Der Prophet Jeremia,* 51; Stahl, "Deshalb trocknet," 170; Joseph Blenkinsopp, *A History of Prophecy in Israel* (rev. ed.; Louisville: Westminster John Knox, 1996), 239.

[62] So also Holladay, *Jeremiah 1,* 165–66.

[63] Weippert (*Schöpfer des Himmels und der Erde,* 51) suggests that they represent the foundation on which God based the world, which is now breaking apart.

Much more indirect are correspondences in Jer 4:25–26 to the creation traditions reflected in the Yahwist narrative of Gen 2:4b–25. A phrase similar to *ʾên hāʾādām*, "there was no one," in Jer 4:25 occurs also in Gen 2:5 in a description of the earth before creation: *wěʾādām ʾayin*, "and there was no human being."[64] The return of the fruitful land to desert (*midbār*) in Jer 4:26 is consistent with the rainless and barren state of the earth in this description. The image of a dry wasteland is reinforced by the noun *šěmāmâ*, "desolation," in 4:27 and by the undertones of aridity in the mourning (*ʾābal*) of earth and darkening (*qādar*) of sky in 4:28.[65] Further, if the word *tōhû* alone is read in 4:23 and interpreted as "desert, wasteland," the state of the earth there matches that of the earth in Gen 2:5.

Jeremiah 4:23–28 thus reflects creation traditions that parallel, broadly or closely, those evident in the Priestly and Yahwist narratives in Genesis, presenting the desolation of Israel at the hands of the enemy from the north as a return to primeval chaos and emptiness. Frymer-Kensky argues that underlying Jer 4:23–26 is the paradigm of the flood, in which God returns the earth to a watery chaos. Aside from the phrase *tōhû wābōhû*, which recalls Gen 1:2 but which may represent an expansion,[66] however, there is no imagery of a flood or watery chaos in this passage. On the other hand, repeated references to the desertlike condition of the earth evoke the concept of dry chaos discussed above in relation to Hos 4:3.[67]

The motif of darkness in this passage, noted above, may play a role in the recalling of this concept. Darkness is a primary feature of the watery chaos conveyed in Gen 1:2 by the phrase *tōhû wābōhû*. Yet the linking of darkness and desert in Jer 4:23–28 occurs also in Jer 2:6 and 2:31[68] and may represent a merging of variant images of primeval chaos, in which the inherent formlessness and apparent emptiness of the dark underscores the barren and desolate nature of desert regions.

---

[64] So William Holladay, "The Recovery of Poetic Passages of Jeremiah," *JBL* 85 (1966): 406; Weippert, *Schöpfer des Himmels und der Erde*, 51.

[65] I.e., if the darkening of the sky is taken as the sign of a dust storm.

[66] See the textual note above on 4:23.

[67] So Weippert (*Schöpfer des Himmels und der Erde*, 51–54) discusses the figurative or "transferred" sense of *midbār* as an utterly empty waste in Jer 2:2, 6, 31; 17:6; 22:6. She suggests that both 4:23–26 and 4:27 depict the recurrence of the chaotic conditions from the time before creation ["die chaotischen Urzustände aus der Zeit vor der Schöpfung wiederkehren"], as portrayed in Gen 2:5. This condition is described in Jer 4:26 with *midbār* and in 4:27 with *šěmāmâ*.

[68] See Weippert (ibid., 53–54) on the link of darkness and the absence of human beings to the "precreation chaos-desert" ["die vorschöpfungszeitlich Chaoswüste"].

As noted above, the terms *karmel* and *midbār* in 4:26 carry associations in Jer 2:6–7 of the wandering in the desert and settlement in the land of Canaan. These associations create another layer of interpretation through which creation traditions resound. Not only does the imminent destruction of Judah by the Babylonians raise the ghost of primeval chaos; it also recalls the tradition of the Israelite wanderings in the desert before the beginning of orderly agricultural life in Canaan. The evocation of the desert period in 4:26 follows directly the evocation of primeval disorder in 4:23–25 and is shaded by it.[69] It is into such a chaotic state of landlessness and wandering that the people of Judah are about to be thrust by the enemy from the north. The reversal of salvation history thus parallels the undoing of creation in this passage.[70]

The interpretation of the coming invasion in the framework of decreation is consistent with a traditional *topos:* the portrayal of battle against foreign enemies as a battle with the forces of chaos.[71] Here again the mythic and historic intersect. At the hands of invaders the land of Israel will become a desolation. Cities will be pulled down, people will be deported, and the cultivated fields will be abandoned to weeds. The tactics of war

---

[69] In this sense the dry chaos of the desert wanderings forms a counterpart to the passing of the Israelites through the waters of chaos in the exodus. On the wilderness (*midbār*) as "desert trek" prior to the settlement in Canaan, see Shemaryahu Talmon, "The 'Desert Motif' in the Bible and in Qumran Literature," in *Biblical Motifs: Origins and Transformations* (ed. Alexander Altmann; Cambridge, Mass.: Harvard University Press, 1966), 46–53.

[70] On the connection in Jeremiah between YHWH's power over the nations and over creation, see Wisser, "La création dans le livre de Jérémie," 259–60.

[71] Sigmund Mowinckel (*The Psalms in Israel's Worship* [2 vols.; Nashville: Abingdon, 1962], 1:51–55) finds this *topos* in psalms that praise YHWH's victory over the kings and nations of the earth; see, e.g., Pss 46; 68; 89. Fritz Stolz (*Strukturen und Figuren im Kult von Jerusalem: Studien zur altorientalischen, vor- und frühisraelitischen Religion* [BZAW 118; Berlin: de Gruyter, 1970], 78–83, 86–101) cites specific Mesopotamian as well as biblical texts in which images of war are interwoven with images of the struggle against primal chaotic forces, noting several passages in Jeremiah. These include Jer 4:13, which compares the enemy to clouds and the enemy's chariots to the storm wind, and 6:23, in which the enemy roars like the sea. See also Jer 5:15–17; Isa 5:26–30; 17:12–14. For other references to the identification of Israel's enemies with the forces of chaos, see Hans H. Schmid, "Creation, Righteousness, and Salvation: 'Creation Theology' As the Broad Horizon of Biblical Theology," in *Creation in the Old Testament* (ed. Bernhard W. Anderson; IRT 6; Philadelphia: Fortress, 1984), 103–4; Michael Fishbane, *Biblical Interpretation in Ancient Israel* (Oxford: Clarendon, 1985), 357; and Childs, "Enemy from the North," 197. Childs, however, argues that this identification occurs only in exilic and postexilic texts.

threaten both people and land, and the vision of an empty and wasted landscape in Jer 4:23–28 need not be purely symbolic.

Yet the enemy from the north is merely the instrument of God's anger in Jer 4:23–28, as 4:26, 28 make clear. More fundamental to the undoing of the created order in Israel than the onslaught of the Babylonians is the enmity of God. And this, as indicated in 4:22, has to do with the attitudes and behavior of YHWH's people (*ʿammî*, "my people"), who know neither YHWH nor how to do good but rather are skilled in the doing of evil. This summary implies that rapport is expected between YHWH and YHWH's people, a rapport defined by norms of good and evil. That this rapport is related in some way to the harmony of the created order is expressed directly in other passages in Jeremiah. In 5:22–25, for example, YHWH asks:

> Do you not fear me? says YHWH,
>   do you not tremble before me?
> Since I have made the sand a barrier for the sea,
>   an everlasting boundary [*ḥoq-ʿôlām*] that it cannot cross.
> The waves surge, but they cannot prevail;
>   though they roar, yet they do not cross over it.
> But this people has a stubborn and rebellious heart;
>   they have turned aside and gone away.
> And they do not say in their hearts,
>   "let us fear YHWH our God,"
> Who gives us rain, autumn rain and spring rain, in its time,
>   the weeks appointed [*šĕbūʿôt ḥuqqôt*] for harvest, he keeps for us.
> Your perversities have turned these away,
>   and your sins have held back what is good from you.

The dual meaning of *ḥōq*, "boundary, limit" but also "statute," is significant here, as Weippert has noted.[72] This word expresses with ultimate economy the unity of the social and natural order designed by YHWH. In Jer 5:22–25 the spatial separation of sand and sea as well as the distinction of times and seasons serve the human community,[73] and the refusal of the community to recognize its own divinely appointed ordinances throws the process out of sync.

Jeremiah 8:7 is also notable for imagery that bespeaks the unity of the social and natural orders. In this passage YHWH reflects:

> Even the stork in the sky
>   knows [*yādĕʿâ*] its appointed times;

---

[72] *Schöpfer des Himmels und der Erde,* 18–19.
[73] Ibid., 18.

And the dove and swallow[74] and crane
   keep the time of their coming.
But my people do not know [*yādĕ'û*]
   the law of YHWH [*mišpaṭ yhwh*].

In this verse the parallel syntax of all three bicola and the repetition of the verb *yāda'*, "to know," sharpen the contrast between the human and natural realms: the birds know and keep the appointed times of their movements, but the people do not know (or keep) the law (*mišpāṭ*) of YHWH. At the same time the seasons of the natural world and the laws governing interhuman relationships are linked.[75]

In the light of these passages, Jer 4:23–26 can be seen even more clearly as depicting the breakdown of the created order: a dissolution set in motion by the anger of YHWH against the people of Israel (4:26) for their failure to know their God and to respect the delineation between evil and good (4:22). Having turned to their own ways like horses plunging into battle (8:6), they have not only rejected the beneficent relationship with YHWH that protects their own social order but endangered the foundations of life itself.[76]

A question remains concerning whether the cosmic dimensions of this passage frame a vision of the end of the earth as a whole. As was true of Amos 1:2 and Hos 4:3, so here, cosmic, quasi-mythic language and imagery are brought to bear on a more particular context: the land of Israel (or Judah) and the historical circumstances that threaten its existence. The imagery of Jer 4:23–28 is impressive because it associates the specter of a cosmic end with the end of the nation.[77]

---

[74] K reads *sûs*, Q *sîs*. Both have been interpreted as words for "swallow" or "swift"; see Holladay (*Jeremiah 1*, 274); Rudolph (*Jeremia*, 52); McKane (*Jeremiah*, 1:84–85); BDB, 692a. It is possible that K reflects a confusion of *wāw* and *yôd*; alternatively, Q may represent an attempt to distinguish this term from *sûs*, "horse," in 8:6 (so Giesebrecht, *Das Buch Jeremia*, 54).

[75] See also Jer 18:13–17.

[76] See Wisser, "La création dans le livre de Jérémie," 245–46; Weippert, *Schöpfer des Himmels und der Erde*, 49–50. Both Wisser and Weippert speak of Jer 5:20–25 in terms of covenant-breaking behavior that results in natural catastrophes. There is no express mention of covenant (*bĕrît*) in the passages discussed above, however. Holladay (*Jeremiah 1*, 164) similarly refers to the "covenantal language" of Jer 4:23–26 but does not specify what this is. His association of the reference to earth and sky, mountains and hills with the traditional witnesses in a cosmic law-court scene, as in Mic 6:1–2, cannot be tied definitively into a context of covenant.

[77] Collins ("Old Testament Apocalypticism and Eschatology," 299) remarks with respect to this passage: "*national* eschatology (concern for the future of Israel) and

SUMMARY OF LITERARY TECHNIQUES

As a context for the metaphor of earth mourning, Jer 4:23–28 contains a number of words with multiple associations that create depth and complexity. These include *ʾereṣ, karmel,* and *midbār,* as well as words that have both a physical and a psychological aspect: *ʾābal, qādar, šĕmāmâ.* In addition to the personification of the earth (*hāʾāreṣ*) through its coupling with *ʾābal* is the personification of the sky (*haššāmayim*) in its pairing with *qādar,* "to mourn." Finally, the interweaving of human devastation ("there was no one," in 4:25; "all its cities pulled down," in 4:26) and natural devastation (the emptiness of earth and sky in 4:23, the trembling of mountains and hills in 4:24, and the flight of the birds in 4:25) and the joining of the two in the desertification of the cultivated land in 4:26 creates an intricate structural pattern for the passage that reflects its content.

OVERALL EFFECT OF THE METAPHOR

In Jer 4:23–28 the metaphor of earth mourning is introduced following a description of the effect on the earth of the coming invasion of Judah. It confirms the picture of desolation brought about by YHWH's anger in 4:23–26, which evokes both the undoing of creation and the undoing of Israel as a nation.

In this passage images of the earth and cosmos do not provide a separate, clarifying vision of the consequences of Israel's sin and YHWH's anger, as in Amos 1:2 and Hos 4:1–3. Rather, they intertwine with images of human devastation to create a single vision. This is a vision of exile and extinction that conveys the physical realities of military devastation yet expresses much more, as the loss of the land and

---

cosmic eschatology (concern for the future of the world) cannot be clearly separated, even in the preexilic prophets." See also Stahl, "Deshalb trocknet," 170; Zimmerli, "Visionary Experience in Jeremiah," 100–101, 103–4; and Hubmann, *Untersuchungen zu den Konfessionen,* 142. Those who assume a clear distinction between the end of the nation and cosmic devastation tend to see the character of this vision as either symbolic or "proto-apocalyptic." For the first interpretation, see Duhm (*Das Buch Jeremia,* 54); McKane (*Jeremiah,* 1:107–8); James H. Gailey ("The Sword and the Heart: Evil from the North—and within, an Exposition of Jeremiah 4:5–6:30," *Int* 9 [1955]: 300); Weippert, *Schöpfer des Himmels und der Erde,* 51–52 n. 97; Rudolph, *Jeremia,* 31; Lindblom, *Prophecy in Ancient Israel,* 127; Zimmerli, "Visionary Experience in Jeremiah," 103. Those who see a proto-apocalyptic vision in these verses include Volz (*Der Prophet Jeremia,* 50–51) and Childs ("Enemy from the North," 197), who designates the root *rʿš* (4:24) as a "technical term for the final shaking of the world at the return of chaos."

the loss of YHWH's favor are presented in terms of the relapse of the foundations and elements of life into blankness and sterility. In this way the envisioned desolation of the earth and its human inhabitants becomes a metaphor for life without YHWH. At the prospect of such a life, earth and sky—or what is left of them—will mourn.

JEREMIAH 12:1–4

TEXT, TRANSLATION, AND TEXTUAL NOTES

צַדִּיק אַתָּה יְהוָה   כִּי אָרִיב אֵלֶיךָ   אַךְ מִשְׁפָּטִים אֲדַבֵּר אוֹתָךְ   1
מַדּוּעַ דֶּרֶךְ רְשָׁעִים צָלֵחָה   שָׁלוּ כָּל־בֹּגְדֵי בָגֶד׃

נְטַעְתָּם גַּם־שֹׁרָשׁוּ   יֵלְכוּ גַּם־עָשׂוּ פֶרִי   2
קָרוֹב אַתָּה בְּפִיהֶם   וְרָחוֹק מִכִּלְיוֹתֵיהֶם׃

וְאַתָּה יְהוָה יְדַעְתָּנִי תִּרְאֵנִי   וּבָחַנְתָּ לִבִּי אִתָּךְ   3
הַתִּקֵם כְּצֹאן לְטִבְחָה   וְהַקְדִּשֵׁם לְיוֹם הֲרֵגָה׃ ס

עַד־מָתַי תֶּאֱבַל הָאָרֶץ   וְעֵשֶׂב כָּל־הַשָּׂדֶה יִיבָשׁ   4
מֵרָעַת יֹשְׁבֵי־בָהּ   סָפְתָה בְהֵמוֹת וָעוֹף
כִּי אָמְרוּ לֹא יִרְאֶה אֶת־אַחֲרִיתֵנוּ׃

1 Righteous are you, YHWH,
    when I contend with you;
    yet I will take up a case with you:
Why does the way of the wicked prosper;
    why are all those who deal treacherously at ease?
2 You have planted them, they have even taken root;
    they grow, they have even born fruit.
You are near in their mouth
    but far from their inner being.
3 But you, YHWH, you know me, you see me;
    and you have tested my heart toward you.
Pull them out like sheep for slaughter
    and set them apart for the day of killing.
4 How long will the earth mourn
    and the grass of every field wither?
From the evil of those who dwell in it,
    the beasts and birds are [a]swept away;[a]
For they say, "He cannot see [b]our end[b]."

a–a Read *suppĕtâ* (*qal* passive) for *sāpĕtâ* (MT).[78] The verb *sāpâ,* "to sweep away," is not used with the intransitive meaning "to be swept away" elsewhere in the Hebrew Bible except, possibly, in Amos 3:15.[79] Syriac (*spt,* "have perished") and Vulg. (*consumptum est,* "have been consumed") apparently read the root *swp,* "to come to an end, cease." LXX (ἠφανίσθησαν, "has disappeared") could reflect either *swp* or *sph.*

BDB (705a) suggests emending *sāpĕtâ* to *sāpâ* in Jer 12:4.[80] Holladay revocalizes MT to read *sāpîtâ,* "you [YHWH] sweep away," which accords with the direct address to YHWH in 12:3 (*wĕʾattâ*) and the second masculine singular forms there, but makes the direct agency of YHWH explicit in a way that MT does not.[81] Holladay argues that this revocalization would bring the verse into alignment with the similar verse in Zeph 1:3; on the other hand, a passive form would correspond more closely to the *nipʿal* of *ʾsp* in Hos 4:3.

b–b So Syr. (*ḥrtn,* "our end"), Vulg. (*novissima nostra,* "our last things"). LXX (ὁδοὺς ἡμῶν, "our ways") reads *ʾorḥôtēnû* for *ʾaḥărîtēnû* (MT). Metathesis of *ḥêt* and *rêš* and confusion of *wāw* and *yôd* could explain either variant. The reading of LXX makes sense, especially in light of the reference to the way of the wicked (*derek rĕšāʿîm*) in 12:1; that of MT is unusual but not necessarily problematic.

DELIMITATION OF THE PASSAGE

Jeremiah 12:1–4 is part of a larger unit, 12:1–6, which is itself considered part of the first confession of Jeremiah (11:18–12:6). The boundaries of 12:1–6 are marked by the change of speakers. The plea of Jeremiah in 11:18–20 that YHWH punish the enemies of the prophet is followed by a response from YHWH that promises punishment (11:21–23). In 12:1 Jeremiah begins a new address to YHWH, asking again for retribution. The response in 12:5–6 is not a promise to impose punishment but a riddle implying that the prophet must endure even greater suffering.[82] In 12:7–13 the lament of YHWH over the alienation and destruction of Israel clearly constitutes a new section.

---

[78] On the use of the third feminine singular verb with the plural of animals, see Paul Joüon, *Grammaire de l'Hébreu Biblique* (Rome: Pontifical Biblical Institute, 1923), §150g.

[79] So Cornill, *Das Buch Jeremia,* 157. See also *HAL,* 721a.

[80] BDB also assigns *wĕsāpû* in Amos 3:15 to the root *swp.*

[81] *Jeremiah 1,* 364, 379.

[82] So Walter Baumgartner, *Jeremiah's Poems of Lament* (trans. D. E. Orton; Sheffield: Almond, 1988), 70–71; Cornill, *Das Buch Jeremia,* 154; Volz, *Der Prophet Jeremia,* 141; Holladay, *Jeremiah 1,* 366–67.

Within the larger unit 12:1–6, 12:1–4 contains the prophet's questions and a plea to YHWH, and 12:5–6, YHWH's answer.[83] Thus although 12:1–4 is not a self-standing unit, it can be considered as a discrete section.

It should be noted that the occurrence of common vocabulary, phraseology, and imagery in the two major sections of Jeremiah's confession (11:18–23 and 12:1–6) is significant. In 11:19a the prophet compares himself to a lamb (*kebeś*) led to slaughter (*liṭbôaḥ*); in 12:3 he pleads with YHWH to treat the wicked like sheep (*kĕṣōʾn*) for slaughter (*lĕṭibḥâ*). In 11:19b the enemies of Jeremiah compare him to a tree (*ʿēṣ*) with its sap;[84] in 12:2 Jeremiah compares the wicked to plants: "you have planted them [*nĕṭaʿtām*], they have even taken root [*šōrāšû*] / they grow [*yēlĕkû*], they have even born fruit [*ʿāśû perî*]." In 11:20 Jeremiah appeals to YHWH as the one who judges righteously (*šōpēṭ ṣedeq*) and who tests (*bōḥēn*) the inner being (*kĕlāyôt*) and the heart (*wālēb*). In 12:1, in the context of court procedure, Jeremiah addresses YHWH as righteous (*ṣaddîq*) and in 12:3 as the one who tests the heart (*ûbāḥantî libbî*, "and you test my heart"). In 12:2 YHWH is far from the inmost being (*mikkilyôtêhem*) of the wicked.[85]

These links account in part for various attempts on the part of commentators to rearrange the sequence of verses in 11:18–12:6 to create a more obviously coherent unit.[86] In some cases this involves splitting 12:1–6 and inserting individual verses or pairs of verses within 11:18–23. Against such attempts it can be argued that strict logical sequence is not to be expected of poetic or prophetic utterance and that there is no way of ascertaining which, if any, of the alterations suggested are most likely to represent an earlier text. Nor, as Holladay points out, have compelling suggestions been offered for how the present text assumed its form.[87] Granted, the confession as a whole is enigmatic: it begins *in medias res* with no clear reference to a context (11:18) and ends in a riddle (12:5–6). Further, in 12:1–6 the prophet seems to circle back to, or consider from a

---

83 So Hubmann, *Untersuchungen zu den Konfessionen,* 82–83; Baumgartner, *Jeremiah's Poems of Lament,* 67; Condamin, *Le Livre de Jérémie,* 108; William Holladay, "Jeremiah's Lawsuit with God," *Int* 17 (1963): 286–87. Duhm (*Das Buch Jeremia,* 115) argues that the prophet is the speaker in 12:5–6.

84 Read *bĕlēḥô* for *bĕlaḥmô,* "with its food" (MT); cf. Deut 34:7. So BDB, 537b.

85 For further discussion of the correspondence between Jer 11:18–23 and 12:1–6, see McKane, *Jeremiah,* 1:255; Volz, *Der Prophet Jeremia,* 141–42; A. R. Diamond, *The Confessions of Jeremiah in Context: Sources of Prophetic Drama* (JSOTSup 45; Sheffield: Sheffield Academic Press, 1987), 153–54.

86 See, e.g., Bright, *Jeremiah,* 89; Cornill, *Das Buch Jeremia,* 159; Volz, *Der Prophet Jeremia,* 136, 140–41; Rudolph, *Jeremia,* 75–76; NAB.

87 *Jeremiah 1,* 365.

different angle, what he has already said in 11:18–20. But such features are typical of prophetic literature, and, as Volz notes, the sections that make up the book of Jeremiah are typically strung together loosely.[88] Thus there is no overriding reason not to consider either 12:1–6 or 12:1–4 as an integral unit.[89]

Authorship and Dating

Many of those commentators who see Jer 12:1–4 as a unit accept at least 12:1–3 as stemming from Jeremiah or from his time.[90] Questions about the dating of 12:4, which contains the lines most pertinent to this study, are more frequent, as readers have puzzled over the apparent inconsistency between this verse and 12:1–3. If in 12:1–3 Jeremiah contends with YHWH about the prosperity of the wicked, whom he compares to flourishing plants, how can the prophet in 12:4 lament the withering of the vegetation of the earth and the demise of animal life, which could not help but afflict the wicked? Further, 12:4 attributes the drought to the evil of those who dwell in it (*yōšĕbê-bāh*), a phrase with universal overtones. This phraseology stands apart from the wisdomlike references in 12:1 to the wicked and treacherous as a defined group and the plea of Jeremiah in 12:3 that YHWH drag them to slaughter. For this reason 12:4 (or at least the first two bicola) has been seen as an interpolation, though not necessarily from a time later than Jeremiah.[91]

---

[88] *Jeremia,* 141.

[89] Of all the explanations of redactional alteration, that of McKane (*Jeremiah,* 1:255) is the most plausible, in my opinion. He proposes that Jer 11:21–23 is a secondary commentary on 11:18–19 and that 12:6 is a secondary gloss on 12:1–5. Both these additions identify Jeremiah's opponents as relatives (12:6) or neighbors in Anathoth (11:21–23). The proposal of Holladay (*Jeremiah 1,* 365), following Hubmann, that 11:21; 12:6; and the phrase "men of Anathoth" in 11:23 are redactional is similar. These explanations do not not alter the integrity of the units of the present text. McKane's further suggestion that 11:20 is a secondary expansion added to parallel 12:3 is less convincing.

[90] One exception is Duhm (*Das Buch Jeremia,* 114), who considers Jer 12:1–4 to be thematically incompatible with the vision of total destruction elsewhere in Jeremiah, since in these verses the prophet pleads for punishment for the wicked alone. The question of the prosperity of the wicked, Duhm argues, is a primary postexilic concern, and 12:1–4 should be dated to that period. Cornill (*Das Buch Jeremia,* 156) strikes 12:3 as a later addition on similar grounds. Against attempts to establish thematic uniformity in Jeremiah, see Baumgartner, *Jeremiah's Poems of Lament,* 66.

[91] Bright (*Jeremiah,* 87), Cornill (*Das Buch Jeremia,* 156–57), and Rudolph (*Jeremia,* 75–76) consider 12:4ab to be derived from Jeremiah but foreign to this context; see also Giesebrecht, *Das Buch Jeremia,* 74. Volz (*Der Prophet Jeremia,*

That 12:4 shows a shift in focus, however, does not mean it is redactional. This shift will be discussed further below, but McKane's conclusion functions as a reasonable summation: "There is no textual evidence to support the deletion of the whole or part of 12:4, and it represents a kind of unevenness which should be tolerated."[92] On the positive side, the question posed in 12:4 creates a structural parallel to the question in 12:1.[93] Further, the allusion to the mourning (*ʾābal*) of the earth and the withering of the grass in 12:4 plays on the imagery of planting and growth introduced in 12:2, while the sweeping away of beasts and birds in 12:4b echoes the pulling away of sheep for slaughter in 12:3. These unifying details of structure and imagery speak against the simple insertion of 12:4 into an extant text.

The difficulties of laying out 12:4 in poetic cola may reflect, however, additions to this verse: notably, the explanatory phrases *mērāʿat yōšĕbê-bāh,* "from the evil of those who dwell in it," and *kî ʾāmĕrû lōʾ yirʾeh ʾet-ʾaḥărîtēnû,* "for they say, 'He cannot see our end.'"[94] These phrases look back to the "wicked" (*rĕšāʿîm*) and "treacherous" (*bōgĕdê bāged*) of 12:1–3 and make explicit the implicit connection between the two sections of the poem.[95] If these are additions, they do not alter the essential thrust of 12:1–4 as a whole, nor do they necessarily represent late redactional work. I consider Jer 12:1–4, then, overall, as an integral unit that probably dates to the time of Jeremiah or not long afterward.

---

140 n. 1) deems it an addition (though not necessarily a late one), arguing that it is a stereotypical [formelhafter] formulation, similar to Amos 1:2.

[92] *Jeremiah,* 1:263. By "no textual evidence" McKane means no grammatical irregularities within 12:4 itself. See, further, the resolution of the discrepancy between 12:3 and 12:4 in Baumgartner, *Jeremiah's Poems of Lament,* 107. It might also be noted that the use of traditional phrases may entail a certain lack of compositional smoothness on the surface but still reflect a coherent conceptual schema. See the discussion on oral traditional poetry in chapter 7 and the works cited there, esp. John M. Foley, "Word-Power, Performance, and Tradition" (*Journal of American Folklore* 105 [1992]: 282–85).

[93] So Hubmann (*Untersuchungen zu den Konfessionen,* 82–86, 139), who points out that both questions show a two-part chiastic pattern and are followed by a further elaboration (12:2, 4b) and a reference to relationship with YHWH (12:3, 4c).

[94] It should be noted, however, that the phrase *mērāʿat yōšĕbê-bāh* is likely poetic, since a noun in construct to a preposition is typically a poetic construction (see, e.g., Hos 4:3; Ps 107:34). I am indebted to Douglas M. Gropp for this point.

[95] The connection is even tighter, of course, if one reads *ʾorḥōtēnû,* "our ways," in 12:4 with LXX, since it would then balance *derek,* "way," in 12:1.

THEMES AND MOTIFS

THE RESPONSE OF THE EARTH

The two questions posed in 12:1–4 divide this unit in two, juxtaposing the actions of the wicked, the subject of 12:1–3, with the condition of the earth, the subject of 12:4.[96] The "Why?" of 12:1 is echoed by the "How long?" of 12:4, ironically yoking the planting and flowering of the wicked to the mourning and drying up of the land. The structure and imagery of this passage, then, appear to confirm what is stated explicitly in 12:4: the response of the earth is tied to human evil (*rā'â*).

This response is conveyed in 12:4a, as in Amos 1:2, by the pairing of the verb *'ābal* with the verb *yābēš*, "to dry up, wither." The use of *yābēš* brings out the associations of drying up in *'ābal*, and Jer 12:4 has been related to the lament over a drought in Jer 14:1–10, in which the verb *'ābal* occurs with Judah as subject.[97] Both verbs are *qal*, as opposed to passive, forms, suggesting a response on the part of the earth rather than simply the effect of an agent. The sweeping away of beasts and birds in 12:4b elaborates this response, implying that the drought is extensive enough to affect not just "the grass of every field" but those who feed on it and live above it. The pairing of beasts and birds (*běhēmôt wā'ôp*) functions as a merism for all living creatures.[98] The phonological and even semantic similarities of the roots *sph*, "to sweep away," and *'sp*, "to gather up," which occurs in an almost identical context in Hos 4:3, create an echo of harvesting that adds to the impression of an aberrant agricultural cycle.

In the response of the earth in 12:4 there is no mention of the effect on human beings: the earth mourns; the grass withers; beasts and birds are swept away. This is a picture of the natural world separate from human realities. Yet the suffering of the earth and its creatures is attributed to "the evil of those who dwell in it" (*mērā'at yōsĕbê-bāh*). MT groups this phrase with the sweeping away of beasts and birds; *BHS* brackets it with the mourning of the earth and drying up of the grass. Placed as it is between the two, it looks back to the withering of the grass

---

[96] Hubmann (*Untersuchungen zu den Konfessionen,* 82–86) and Condamin (*Le Livre de Jérémie,* 104) see these questions as dividing the passage into two sections: 12:1–2 and 12:3–4. It is possible to acknowledge the validity of this division while still noting the shift in focus from the fate of the wicked in 12:1–3 to the fate of the earth in 12:4.

[97] So Cornill, *Das Buch Jeremia,* 157; Giesebrecht, *Das Buch Jeremia,* 74; Rudolph, *Jeremia,* 75–76.

[98] See also Jer 9:9 and Stahl, "Deshalb trocknet," 169.

and forward to the perishing of living creatures, offering an explanation for both.

Despite the explicit link between the mourning earth and the actions or attitudes of its inhabitants in 12:4, the relation of this verse to the prophet's contemplation of the wicked in 12:1–3 is not wholly clear. In 12:4 the evil of those who dwell in the land has brought mourning and drought upon it. The phrase *yōšĕbê-bāh,* "those who dwell in it," seems to refer to the people of Judah as a whole, as the phrase *yôšĕbê hā'āreṣ,* "those who dwell in the land," in Hos 4:1 refers to the people of Israel. Yet in Jer 12:1, the wicked and treacherous are named as a group in potential contrast to those who are not wicked and in explicit contrast to the prophet himself (12:3a). This sense is bolstered by the similarities of 12:1–3 to 11:18–20, in which the prophet refers to a specific group of evildoers who have plotted to destroy him. Hence some commentators, as noted above, discern inconsistencies between 12:1–3 and 12:4. What is the relationship between the wicked or treacherous of 12:1–3 and the evil of those who dwell in the land (12:4)? If the activities of the wicked have brought on a massive drought affecting every field and all living creatures (12:4), how can these same people be represented as thriving like fruit-bearing plants in 12:2? Finally, since the prophet appeals to YHWH to punish the wicked in 12:3, what role does the drying up of the earth in 12:4 play?

Clearly there is a shift in focus from 11:18–20[99] to 12:1–3 to 12:4, as the scope of the lament widens. In 11:18–20 the prophet recounts the evil acts of his opponents and pleads his case to YHWH. In 12:1 he poses questions about the fate of the wicked as a generic group in a style consistent with wisdom sayings, albeit with a challenge to traditional expectations of retribution.[100] The prophet demands that this group be pulled away and set aside for punishment in 12:3b, yet he is still speaking of the wicked in general terms.[101] In 12:4 the prophet's focus enlarges again, as he considers the state of the community as a whole and the impact of the evil done within it (*mērā'at yōšĕbê-bāh,* "from the evil of those who dwell in it").

---

[99] Or Jer 11:18–23.

[100] On the shift of reference to a generalized group of the wicked, see McKane (*Jeremiah,* 1:261), Volz (*Der Prophet Jeremia,* 141), Cornill (*Das Buch Jeremia,* 155–56), Rudolph (*Jeremia,* 79); contra Hubmann (*Untersuchungen zu den Konfessionen,* 144) and Condamin (*Le Livre de Jérémie,* 108), who claim that the wicked (*rĕšā'îm*) here represent Jeremiah's personal enemies.

[101] Cornill (*Das Buch Jeremia,* 154) characterizes the tone of 12:1–4, in contrast to that of Jer 11:18–20, as "calm … almost academic" ["ruhige, ich möchte fast sagen akademische"].

The phrase *mērāʿat yōšĕbê-bāh* conveys a sense of significant collective wrong but, despite its universal overtones, does not preclude the characterization of the bulk of the land's inhabitants as a wicked and treacherous group.[102] The question in 12:4 can be seen as the obverse of the question posed in 12:1 about why the wicked thrive: How long must the land suffer from their wickedness?[103]

The apparent contradiction between the prosperity of the wicked in 12:1–2 and the pervasive drought of 12:4 has given rise to various explanations. Hubmann concludes that the imagery of drought is not primary; rather, it represents a traditional motif that functions as a "symptom" and "warning" of the broken relationship between YHWH and Israel.[104] He thus interprets 12:4 on a figurative level and does not consider fully the imagery and vocabulary of drought that dominates the verse and seems to contradict the images of fertility in 12:2. Duhm's interpretation, on the other hand, is quite literal: in his view a drought would scarcely affect the wicked in Israel who, he asserts, would belong to an urban, well-to-do class.[105] No such details are given about the material circumstances of the *rĕšāʿîm* in 12:1–3, however.

It is possible to avoid either a wholly symbolic or a wholly literal interpretation of 12:4 by not presuming an immediate connection between the thriving of the wicked in 12:1–3 and the mourning of the earth in 12:4. That misdeeds and defiant attitudes on the part of the wicked bring drought and mourning to the earth is assumed here as a pattern, and the prophet asks how long that pattern will continue. But the deeds of the wicked need not have an immediate impact on the land. It may be that in 12:1–4 the prophetic speaker attributes the periodic bouts of aridity and famine suffered in Judah to the failings of its inhabitants, as elsewhere in Jeremiah.[106] The reference to a particular drought in Jer 14:1–10 testifies to an experience of drought by both the prophet and his audience. But it cannot supply a specific historical reference for 12:1–4.[107] In this passage the

---

[102] Baumgartner (*Jeremiah's Poems of Lament*, 67) asserts: "It makes little difference whether the whole population has participated in the wickedness or a portion. Even the sin of an individual can result in a general punishment (Joshua 7)." This assertion may be an overstatement, however, since the phrase *yōšĕbê-bāh*, "those who dwell in it," suggests a comprehensive frame of reference.

[103] See Hubmann, *Untersuchungen zu den Konfessionen*, 144.

[104] Ibid., 139, 142–43.

[105] Duhm, *Das Buch Jeremia*, 115.

[106] See Jer 3:1–3; 5:24–25; cf. 14:1–10.

[107] Cornill (*Das Buch Jeremia*, 157) disputes attempts to find an original setting for 12:4 within Jer 14; so also Hubmann, *Untersuchungen zu den Konfessionen*, 139.

author may be using traditional phraseology with concrete associations to figure the harm done by the wicked to the world around them, inflicting a blight that has not yet developed to the point of eradicating them from the land.

SIN OR PUNISHMENT

In this poem, as in Hos 4:1–3, the role of human misdeeds in the mourning of the earth is central. The rampant flourishing of the wicked and treacherous in 12:1–3 and the withering of the earth in 12:4 are linked in Jeremiah's two questions: "Why does the way of the wicked prosper?" (12:1) and "How long will the earth mourn?" (12:4) The explanatory phrases in 12:4, which may be redactional,[108] make explicit this connection: the grass of the field is dry "from the evil [*mērāᶜat*] of those who dwell in it," and the beasts and birds of the earth perish "because [*kî*] they say, 'He cannot see our end.'"[109] The depiction of human evil in 12:1–4 does not cite specific transgressions or legal norms but is framed in the terminology of wisdom writings: *ṣaddîq*, "righteous"; *derek*, "way"; *rěšāᶜîm*, "wicked ones"; *rāᶜâ*, "evil." This poem points to a lack of ethical qualities and of the proper posture toward YHWH. The concluding statement "for they say, 'He cannot see [*yir'eh*] our end,'" points to the attitude underlying the evil deeds of the inhabitants of Judah: a disbelief in the power of YHWH over them. It stands in contrast to Jeremiah's affirmation of trust in 12:3a—"But you, YHWH, know me, you see [*tir'ēnî*] me / and you test my heart toward you"—and his appeal for retribution in 12:3b. At the same time it reflects the assertion in 12:2 that the wicked speak facilely of YHWH ("You are near in their mouth") but disregard him inwardly ("but far from their inner being").

Further, the legal associations of *ṣaddîq*, "righteous," *rîb*, "to dispute, contend," and *mišpāṭîm*, "case, judgment," all of which occur in 12:1, imply an established standard behind the prophet's complaint. The evil cited as a cause in 12:4 shows itself both in a defiant attitude toward YHWH and in habits of behavior that contradict acknowledged norms.

The link between the evil of the wicked and the withering of the earth in 12:4 does not preclude a role for the punitive power of YHWH, however. The prophet appeals to YHWH directly in 12:3b to punish the wicked, to "pull them out like sheep for slaughtering." The second colon of 12:3b is reminiscent of the language and imagery of the Day of YHWH:

---

[108] See the discussion above of the authorship and dating of this passage.

[109] *lō' yir'eh 'et-'aḥărîtēnû*. I assume here, as do most commentators, that the subject of the third masculine singular verb *yireh* in this colon is YHWH; contra Condamin (*Le Livre de Jérémie*, 107), who holds that the prophet is the subject.

"and set them apart [*wĕhaqdīšēm*] for the day of killing." The reference to a day of punishment evokes this concept, and the verb *hiqdîš*, "to set apart, consecrate," is consistent with the image of this day as a sacrifice in which all spoils are dedicated to YHWH.[110]

Within 12:4 itself, the verb *sāpâ*, used to describe the disappearance of beasts and birds, occurs elsewhere in connection with human sin and divine punishment. The story of Sodom and Gomorrah in Gen 19 provides an example. Here the angels urge Lot to flee with his wife and daughters *pen-tissāpeh baʿăwôn hāʿîr* (Gen 19:15). This clause can be translated either, "lest you be swept away in the punishment of the city" or "lest you be swept away with the iniquity of the city." In either case the context of the phrase is YHWH's raining of punishment on the two cities.[111]

The semantic and phonological similarities of the roots *sph* and *ʾsp* create strong associations between Jer 12:4 and Hos 4:3, in which the verb *ʾāsap* occurs in the context of the destruction of all living creatures. They also recall what is possibly a more contemporary text, Zeph 1:2–6, generally dated to late seventh-century Judah.[112] This oracle introduces a sequence of pronouncements about the imminent Day of YHWH. In 1:3 YHWH declares an intention to gather up (*ʾāsap*)[113] human beings (*ʾādām*), beasts (*ûbĕhēmâ*), the birds of the sky (*ʿôp-haššāmayim*), and the fish of the sea (*ûdĕgê hayyām*). The sweeping away of beasts and birds (*bĕhēmôt wāʿôp*) in Jer 12:4 may thus suggest the punitive force of YHWH.

Finally, in Ps 107:33–34 the phrase *mērāʿat yōšĕbê bāh* occurs as an explanation for why YHWH dries up the earth:

---

[110] See, e.g., Zeph 1:7–9 and von Rad, "Origin of the Concept," 102–3.

[111] It is interesting to note that this traditional story of all-consuming punishment is associated in Gen 18:16–33 both with the verb *sāpâ* (18:23, 24) and the impact of the wicked on the community as a whole (and, in 18:25, with the assumption that YHWH is a righteous judge). For other examples of the root *sph* in connection with sin and punishment, see Deut 29:18; Num 16:26; 1 Sam 12:25.

[112] Holladay (*Jeremiah 1*, 379) and Stahl ("Deshalb trocknet," 171) connect Jer 12:1–4 and Zeph 1:2–6. On the dating of Zeph 1:2–6 to the seventh century see, e.g., Blenkinsopp, *History of Prophecy in Israel*, 113–15. For a critical analysis of the possibility of an exilic or postexilic dating for the composition of Zephaniah as a whole, see Adele Berlin, *Zephaniah* (AB 25a; New York: Doubleday, 1994), 33–43; on the historical setting of Zeph 1:2–6, see pp. 80–84.

[113] Read *ʾāsōp ʾōsēp*, "I will surely gather up," for *ʾāsōp ʾāsēp* (MT) in Zeph 1:2, and read *ʾōsēp*, "I will gather up," for *ʾāsēp* (MT) in Zeph 1:3. For discussion of these forms and this emendation, see BDB, 62b; GKC §72aa; Holladay, *Jeremiah 1*, 284; J. J. M. Roberts, *Nahum, Habakkuk, and Zephaniah* (OTL; Louisville: Westminster John Knox, 1991), 167, 169. Cf. Jer 8:13.

He makes rivers into desert [*midbār*],
    and springs of water into thirsty ground [*lĕṣimmā'ôn*];
Fruitful earth ['*ereṣ pĕrî*] into a salty waste [*limlēḥâ*]
    because of the evil of those who dwell in it [*mērā'at yōšĕbê bāh*].

Here the turning of earth to desert is attributed again to the execution of divine power in response to human evil.

In Jer 12:4, however, the role of the wickedness of the inhabitants in the suffering of the land is stressed above the punitive power of YHWH. Such an emphasis on the direct connection between the failings of the people of Judah and disaster is found elsewhere in Jeremiah,[114] and in two cases the sins of the community are linked directly to lack of rain. Jeremiah 3:2b–3 speaks of the effects of human sin on the earth:

So you have polluted [*wattaḥănîpî*] the earth ['*ereṣ*]
    with your harlotry [*biznûtayik*] and your evil [*ûbĕrā'ātēk*];
And so the showers have been held back [*wayyimmānĕ'û*],[115]
    and the spring rain has not fallen.

Similarly in 5:25 iniquity ('*āwôn*) and sin (*ḥaṭṭā'*) turn away rain and hold back (*mānĕ'û*) the good things that rain brings. In 5:24, as in 12:4c, this iniquity is related to an inner disregard for YHWH: "they do not say in their heart: let us fear YHWH our God, who gives rain, autumn rain and spring rain, in its time."[116]

As noted above, there is a discrepancy in 12:1–4 that prevents a simple equation of the mourning of the earth with the punishment of evildoers.

---

[114] See the discussion above of the theme of sin or punishment in Jer 4:23–28.

[115] Translated as a passive, "have been held back," the verb *wayyimmānĕ'û* implies an unspecified agent (YHWH), who speaks through the prophet. Yet the juxtaposition of harlotry, evil, and drought in this verse places in the foreground the connection between the acts of the people and the condition of the earth, while the role of YHWH remains implicit. Note also that it is possible to translate the *nip'al* of *mn'* as a reflexive: "have held themselves back."

[116] Mic 7:13, generally thought to date from the postexilic period, provides another articulation of the same theme: "But the earth [*hā'āreṣ*] will become a desolation [*lišmāmâ*] / because of its inhabitants ['*al-yōšĕbêhā*], / from the fruit [*mippĕrî*] of their deeds." Here the inhabitants of the earth are presented as the cause of desolation, as in 12:4. Further, the "fruit" of their deeds, which is reminiscent of the "fruit" borne by the wicked in Jer 12:2, creates a similar sense of ironic contrast: "fruit" and "desolation" in Mic 7:13 and "fruit" and "withering" in Jer 12:2, 4.

Hubmann denies that the mourning can be understood as punishment, since the wicked, according to 12:4c, do not understand it that way: they do not believe YHWH will inflict punishment on them.[117] Further, the prophet's appeal in 12:3 for divine judgment on the wicked implies that judgment is still unrealized and therefore not wholly manifest in the drying up of the earth in 12:4. It is possible, however, to separate the plea for punishment of the wicked from the prophet's reflections on the general cycle of human evil and drought in 12:4.[118] The question "How long?" posed in 12:4 raises the further question of whether Jeremiah is calling for a decisive reckoning and thereby hinting at an ultimate destruction to come. In this sense Hubmann's characterization of the mourning of the earth as symptom and warning is appropriate.[119]

SOCIAL OR NATURAL DISORDER

Because this passage speaks of human evil in terms of qualities and attitudes rather than specific acts, no details of social disorder are given. In 12:1 the phrase *bōgĕdê bāged,* literally "those who deal treacherously in treachery," which is parallel to the *derek rĕšā'îm,* "the way of the wicked," hints at a breakdown in trust and relationships. This breakdown is exemplified in 12:6, part of YHWH's answer to the prophet's complaint in 12:1–4:[120]

> For even your brothers and the house of your father,
>   even they have dealt treacherously [*bāgĕdû*] with you,
>   even they have called loudly after you.
> Do not believe them,
>   though they speak pleasingly to you.

---

[117] *Untersuchungen zu den Konfessionen,* 142–43. Cf. 12:11, where the land is desolate, yet "no man lays it to heart."

[118] See Baumgartner, *Jeremiah's Poems of Lament,* 66.

[119] *Untersuchungen zu den Konfessionen,* 142. In Hubmann's words: "so it appears to be according to most texts, as if Nature senses the destruction essentially earlier, and its reaction—active and/or passive—constitutes both symptom and warning for people" ["so scheint es nach den meisten Texten so zu sein, als spürte die Natur die Störung wesentlich früher und ihre Reaction—activ und/oder passiv—bildet für die Menschen Symptom und Warnung zugleich"].

[120] Even if 12:6 is redactional (so McKane, *Jeremiah,* 1:265; Holladay, *Jeremiah 1,* 365), it shows the interpretation given to the situation described in 12:1–4. If 12:6 belongs with 11:18–23 (so Volz, *Der Prophet Jeremia,* 136; Rudolph, *Jeremia,* 77), it is still part of the immediate context of the plea in 12:1–4.

Further, the metaphor of the wicked and treacherous as plants, shooting up unhindered and bearing fruit, conveys an image of abundant but noxious growth, contributing to the impression of an order that has gone awry.[121]

MOURNING AS STRIPPING

There are hints of this motif in Jer 12:1–4. The withering grass and the sweeping away of living creatures in 12:4 creates an image of the earth stripped and barren. The verb *sāpâ*, "to sweep away," itself conveys a particular physical motion consistent with stripping. The links between the roots *sph* and *'sp*, "to gather," contribute to this imagery by adding the connotation of harvesting, where the earth is stripped of its fruit.

The imagery of 12:4 is reminiscent of that in other passages in Jeremiah where allusions to harvesting and stripping are stronger. In 5:10–11, for example, YHWH commands:

> Go up among her vine rows[122] and destroy,
> > but do not make a full end;
> Remove [*hāsîrû*] her tendrils,
> > for they are not YHWH's;
> For they have been utterly treacherous [*bāgôd bāgĕdû*] with me,
> > the house of Israel and the house of Judah.[123]

The use of the root *bgd*, "to act treacherously," here, as in 12:1, provides another link between the two passages and is a sign of the connection between the breakdown of social order and the stripping away of that order.

Although, as noted above, Jeremiah's plea for punishment of the wicked in 12:3 is not directly linked to the drying up of the earth in 12:4, the two verses are bound together by the overall structure and common

---

[121] Cf. the comparison of different types of people to plants in Jer 17:5–10, although in that passage the wicked wither and the righteous flourish.

[122] Revocalize *bĕšārôtêhā* (MT) to *bĕšūrôtêhā*. MT is a *hapax legomenon*. The noun *šûrâ*, "row" (of olives or vines; see BDB, 1004b), occurs only once elsewhere in MT (*šûrōtām* in Job 24:11), but context argues for the appropriateness of this word here.

[123] See also Jer 6:9; 11:16–17. YHWH's call to Jeremiah in 1:10 to "pluck up [*lintôš*] and pull down [*wĕlintôs*], to destroy [*ûlĕha'ăbîd*] and throw down [*wĕlaharôs*]" may arguably be seen in this light (the *nip'al* of *ntṣ* occurs in Jer 4:23–28 as well and is related to the motif of mourning as stripping in the discussion of that passage above).

imagery of 12:1–4. In 12:3 the verb *hittîq*, "to pull off or away," describes the stripping of the herd: "pull them away like sheep to slaughter."[124] The imagery created here is consonant with the sweeping away of beasts and birds in 12:4. Further, since the wicked who are to be slaughtered as sheep have already been compared to plants in 12:2, the appeal to "pull them away" can also be heard as the uprooting of plants, complementing the shrivelling of the grass in 12:4. The overlapping images of 12:2–3, then, influence the reading of 12:4, creating a continuity in imagery despite the discontinuity in frame of reference.

DECREATION

The phraseology of creation traditions is present in 12:4 in the merism *bĕhēmôt wā*ʿ*ôp*, "beasts and birds," which represents the entire animal world. The expression *wĕ*ʿ*ēśeb kol-haśśādeh*, "and the grass of every field," also reflects traditional phraseology. The phrase ʿ*ēśeb haśśādeh*, "the grass of the field," and the related ʿ*ēśeb hā*ʾ*āreṣ*, "the grass of the earth," frequently stand for the vegetation of the earth,[125] and *wĕkol-*ʿ*ēśeb haśśādeh* occurs in the Yahwist narrative of creation in Gen 2:5.[126] The noun ʿ*ēśeb* occurs apart from this phrase in various contexts of creation, including Ps 104:14; Gen 1:11, 12, 29, 30; 9:3.

With these traditional phrases Jer 12:4 opens up a broad scenario of decreation that goes beyond the cessation of rain. The parallels between this verse and the vision of decreation in Zeph 1:2–3 have already been mentioned. A similar scenario, with similar phraseology, is conveyed in Jer 7:20:

> Therefore thus says the Lord, YHWH: Behold my anger and my wrath are about to be poured out on this place, upon humankind [*hā*ʾ*ādām*] and upon the beasts [*habbĕhēmâ*] and upon the trees of the field [ʿ*ēṣ haśśādeh*] and upon the fruit of the ground [*pĕrî hā*ʾ*ădāmâ*], and it will burn and not be quenched.

---

[124] The root *ntq* is also used in the *nip*ʿ*al* in Jer 6:29 in the context of the refining (*ṣārap*) of the people of Judah; the refining is in vain because the wicked are not stripped away (*nittāqû*).

[125] See, e.g., ʿ*ēśeb haśśādeh* in Gen 3:18; Exod 9:22, 25; Amos 7:2 and ʿ*ēśeb hā*ʾ*āreṣ* in Exod 10:12; Ps 72:16.

[126] Holladay (*Jeremiah 1*, 378) notes the connection between *wĕkol-*ʿ*ēśeb haśśādeh* in Gen 2:5 and *wĕ*ʿ*ēśeb kol-haśśādeh* in Jer 12:4. If the Yahwist narrative of Gen 3 is seen as a reordering by YHWH of the creation described in Gen 2:4b–25, then ʿ*ēśeb haśśādeh* in Gen 3:18 likewise occurs in a context of creation.

In 12:4, the pairing of *'ābal* with *yābēš,* "to dry up," summons, in its own way, the picture of an arid wasteland.[127] Taking Jer 12:1–4 as a whole, the denial by the wicked of a divinely monitored order has threatened the existence of fundamental elements of that order and prefigured the unravelling of creation itself.

SUMMARY OF LITERARY TECHNIQUES

Words with a dual meaning in Jer 12:1–4 include *'ābal* and *'ereṣ.* Nature is personified in the mourning of the earth in 12:4, and humans are compared to plants in 12:2 and to sheep in 12:3. The interchange of natural and human references in this passage is a unifying formal element that witnesses to the contiguity of the natural and the human expressed in the metaphor of earth mourning. The structure of the poem demonstrates this contiguity as well by creating a parallel between the human realm (12:1–3) and the natural realm (12:4) that demonstrates the impact of the one upon the other.

OVERALL EFFECT OF THE METAPHOR

In Jer 12:1–4 the metaphor of earth mourning broadens the scope of Jeremiah's outcry against the wicked. It moves the poem beyond the prophet's personal indignation and beyond his reflection on the individual fates of the wicked (they are planted, they grow, they bear fruit) to their impact on a lateral world—the earth itself. In contrast to the passages considered to this point, there is no hint in Jer 12:4 of the human beings who may be caught up in the response of the earth. Rather, the mourning and withering of the earth and sweeping away of beast and bird serve as a chorus from another realm to heighten Jeremiah's lament.

This chorus is revelatory because the two realms are not entirely separate. The imagery of plants, growth, and animals in 12:1–3 leads the hearer from the immediate focus of these verses to the broader vista of 12:4, where associations of creation as a whole recall the fundamental basis of the relationship between YHWH and humankind. Here the earth sees and responds to the treachery of human beings: a sign that YHWH, who sends rain in its season and stands behind creation, sees and responds. The wordless testimony of the earth reveals that it is the wicked themselves who are blind in their confidence that "he will not see our end." At the same time, the juxtaposition of the metaphor of earth mourning with the metaphor of the wicked as plants shows the wicked to be as vulnerable as the grass they blight.

---

[127] Holladay (*Jeremiah 1,* 378) connects these two verbs in 12:4 (as well as the phrase *wĕ'ēśeb kol-haśśādeh*) with the "pre-creation chaos" depicted in Gen 2:5, before the sending of rain on the earth.

JEREMIAH 12:7–13

TEXT, TRANSLATION, AND TEXTUAL NOTES

עָזַ֙בְתִּי֙ אֶת־בֵּיתִ֔י 7
נָטַ֖שְׁתִּי אֶת־נַחֲלָתִ֑י
נָתַ֛תִּי אֶת־יְדִד֥וּת נַפְשִׁ֖י
בְּכַ֥ף אֹיְבֶֽיהָ׃

הָיְתָה־לִּ֥י נַחֲלָתִ֖י 8
כְּאַרְיֵ֣ה בַיָּ֑עַר
נָתְנָ֥ה עָלַ֖י בְּקוֹלָ֑הּ
עַל־כֵּ֖ן שְׂנֵאתִֽיהָ׃

הַעַ֨יִט צָב֤וּעַ נַחֲלָתִי֙ לִ֔י 9
הַעַ֖יִט סָבִ֣יב עָלֶ֑יהָ
לְכ֗וּ אִסְפ֛וּ כָּל־חַיַּ֥ת הַשָּׂדֶ֖ה
הֵתָ֥יוּ לְאָכְלָֽה׃

רֹעִ֤ים רַבִּים֙ שִֽׁחֲת֣וּ כַרְמִ֔י 10
בֹּסְס֖וּ אֶת־חֶלְקָתִ֑י
נָֽתְנ֛וּ אֶת־חֶלְקַ֥ת חֶמְדָּתִ֖י
לְמִדְבַּ֥ר שְׁמָמָֽה׃

שָׂמָהּ֙ לִשְׁמָמָ֔ה 11
אָבְלָ֥ה עָלַ֖י שְׁמֵמָ֑ה
נָשַׁ֖מָּה כָּל־הָאָ֑רֶץ
כִּ֛י אֵ֥ין אִ֖ישׁ שָׂ֥ם עַל־לֵֽב׃

עַֽל־כָּל־שְׁפָיִ֣ם בַּמִּדְבָּ֗ר 12
בָּ֖אוּ שֹׁדְדִ֑ים
כִּ֣י חֶ֤רֶב לַֽיהוָה֙ אֹֽכְלָ֔ה
מִקְצֵה־אֶ֖רֶץ וְעַד־קְצֵ֣ה הָאָ֑רֶץ
אֵ֥ין שָׁל֖וֹם לְכָל־בָּשָֽׂר׃ ס

זָרְע֤וּ חִטִּים֙ וְקֹצִ֣ים קָצָ֔רוּ 13
נֶחְל֖וּ לֹ֣א יוֹעִ֑לוּ
וּבֹ֕שׁוּ מִתְּבוּאֹֽתֵיכֶ֑ם
מֵחֲר֖וֹן אַף־יְהוָֽה׃ ס

7 I have abandoned my house;
    I have forsaken my possession.
  I have given the love of my being
    into the hands of her enemies.
8 My possession has become to me
    like a lion in the forest.
  She has given forth her voice against me,
    and so I hate her.
9 [a]Is my possession a hyena's den to me;[a]
    are birds of prey circling over her?
  Go, gather together all animals of the field;
    bring them to devour!
10 Many shepherds have ruined my vineyard;
    they have trampled my field.
  They have made the field of my delight
    into a desolate desert.

11 ᵇIt has been madeᵇ a desolation;
    ᶜit mournsᶜ ᵈto my sorrow,ᵈ desolate.
All the earth is desolate,
    yet no man lays it to heart.
12 Upon all the bare tracks in the desert
    destroyers have come.
For the sword of YHWH is devouring
    from the end of ᵉthe earthᵉ to the end of the earth;
    there is peace for no flesh.
13 They have sown wheat but reaped thorns;
    they have made themselves sick, they have not profited.
And they are ashamed of ᶠtheir yields,ᶠ
    because of the burning anger of YHWH.

---

a–a So LXX, μὴ σπήλαιον ὑαίνης ἡ κληρονομία μου ἐμοί, "is my inheritance a hyena's cave to me?" The word *ṣābûaʿ* is a *hapax legomenon* in MT but occurs in Sir 13:18 with the meaning "hyena," as well as in Aramaic in *Genesis Rabbah* and in the Palestinian and Babylonian Talmuds.[128] If this meaning is accepted, it is difficult to read the preceding word, *haʿayiṭ*, as "bird(s) of prey," according to its attested meaning elsewhere (see BDB, 743a). Hence John A. Emerton proposes relating *ʿayiṭ* in this verse to an Arabic noun, *ǵawṭun,* meaning "hollow cavity, pit."[129]

In this reading, the imagery of 12:9a is consistent: the den represents the land of Judah, and the hyena, those who inhabit it and whose violent acts attract birds of prey, as described in the following colon.[130] This fits well with the comparison of Judah to a lion in 12:8 and with the summoning of devouring animals in 12:9b. A similar configuration of images occurs in Ezek 39:4 in a prophecy against Gog, who is to be given to birds of prey (*lĕʿêṭ ṣippôr*) and the animals of the field (*wĕḥayyat haśśādeh*) for devouring (*lĕʾoklâ*).

---

[128] For the reference to Sir 13:18, see BDB, 840b; *HAL* (936ab); Holladay, *Jeremiah 1,* 387. For the Aramaic noun, see Marcus Jastrow, *A Dictionary of the Targumim, the Talmud Babli and Yerushalmi, and the Midrashic Literature* (New York: Judaica, 1971), 1257b. See also Wolf Leslau, *Comparative Dictionary of Geʿez* (Wiesbaden: Harrassowitz, 1991), 147b, 542a.

[129] "Notes on Jeremiah 12 9 and on Some Suggestions of J. D. Michaelis about the Hebrew Words *naḥā, ʿaebrā,* and *jadăʿ,*" *ZAW* 81 (1969): 187–88. Emerton here takes up a suggestion first proffered by Johann D. Michaelis and subsequently adopted by Godfrey R. Driver, both of whom Emerton cites. A Hebrew noun *ʿāweṭ* (construct *ʿôṭ*) might be presumed on the basis of this hypothesis.

[130] See the explanation by G. R. Driver (cited in Emerton, "Notes on Jeremiah 12 9," 187) of the imagery in this bicolon.

This reading presumes either wordplay or a play on similar sounds in the first and second cola of 12:9a, since in the first colon *ʿayiṭ* (or *ʿôṭ*) is read as "den," but in the second colon *ʿayiṭ* is taken as "bird(s) of prey." LXX reads "cave" (or "den") in both instances; hence the second colon of 12:9a becomes ἢ σπήλαιον κύκλῳ αὐτῆς, "is a cave surrounding her?" This creates a puzzling shift in imagery.

Syriac (*mzyrtʾ*, "speckled") and Vulg. (*discolor*, "variegated") have interpreted *ṣābûaʿ* as an adjective related to the noun *ṣebaʿ*, "dye, dyed stuff," found in Judg 5:30, and to the root *ṣbʿ*, "to dye," which is not attested in classical biblical Hebrew but occurs in rabbinic Hebrew; in the Aramaic of *Targum Onkelos*, the *Targum of Canticles*, and the Palestinian and Babylonian Talmuds; and in Syriac.[131] The major problem with the readings of Syr. and Vulg. is that the role of the adjective "speckled" or "variegated" in the verse is enigmatic. Further, considering 12:9a as a whole, do birds of prey ordinarily circle over another bird of prey?

There is no doubt that 12:9a is a difficult text, and the variety of proposed readings testifies to its obscurity.[132]

b–b So LXX (ἐτέθη, "it has been made"), which reflects the impersonal use of the third masculine singular form *śāmāh:* "one has made it" or "it has been made."[133] Syriac and Vulg. have third masculine plural forms here, but such forms can also express an unspecified or indefinite subject, and it is unnecessary to revocalize MT to *śammûhā*, as do many commentators.

c–c So Syr. (*ʾtʾblt*), Vulg. (*luxitque*). LXX reads 12:11a and the first half of 11b together, without a corresponding word for "mourn": ἐτέθη εἰς ἀφανισμὸν ἀπωλείας, δι' ἐμὲ ἀφανισμῷ ἠφανίσθη πᾶσα ἡ γῆ, "It has been made an utter destruction; because of me all the earth has been utterly destroyed." The genitive noun ἀπωλείας may represent a reading of *ʾobdâ*, the infinitive construct of *ʾābad*, "to perish, be destroyed," rather than of *ʾābĕlâ*, "it mourns" (MT).[134] Since *ʾobdâ* and *ʾābĕlâ* share three out of four consonants, a scribal error is possible, especially considering the references to destruction and desolation throughout 12:11.

d–d A literal translation would read: "over me"; so Vulg. (*super me*, "over me" or "upon me"). This phrase has been interpreted as conveying the effect

---

[131] See Jastrow, *Dictionary*, 1259a; and J. Payne Smith, ed., *A Compendious Syriac Dictionary* (Oxford: Clarendon, 1903), 472b.

[132] See, e.g., Holladay, *Jeremiah 1*, 387; McKane, *Jeremiah*, 1:268; NAB. For a summary of such proposals, see McKane, *Jeremiah*, 1:272–73; and Emerton, "Notes on Jeremiah 12 9," 182–88.

[133] See Joüon, *Grammaire de l'Hébreu Biblique*, §155d.

[134] Volz (*Der Prophet Jeremia*, 144) suggests that LXX has read *ʾibbĕdûhā*, "they have destroyed it."

of the earth's mourning on YHWH: "it mourns to my sorrow" or "it makes me mourn." Samuel R. Driver cites a similar phrase in Gen 48:7: *mētâ ʿālay rāḥēl*, which he translates, "Rachel died to my sorrow."[135] LXX reads δι᾽ ἐμέ, "because of me," which jars with the imagery of the shepherds trampling YHWH's vineyard and field in the preceding verse.

e–e Read *miqṣēh-hāʾāreṣ* for *miqṣēh-ʾereṣ* (MT); *hē* omitted before *ʾereṣ* through haplography.

f–f Read *mittĕbûʾōtêhem* for *mittĕbûʾōtêkem*, "your yields" (MT). The preceding verb *ûbōʾšû*, "and they are ashamed," is taken by LXX as an imperative (αἰσχύνθητε, "be ashamed"). Such an interpretation could have resulted in a second masculine plural suffix on the following noun in MT. LXX also supplies a different noun here: ἀπὸ καυχήσεως ὑμῶν, "of your boasting," a reading that may reflect *mittipʾartĕkem* in its Hebrew *Vorlage*. Note also that in the following colon LXX (ἀπὸ ὀνειδισμοῦ ἔναντι κυρίου, "because of reproach before the Lord") has read *mēḥerpâ* for *mēḥărôn* (MT).

DELIMITATION OF THE PASSAGE

Jeremiah 12:7–13 is YHWH's lament over the destruction willed for the people and their land. YHWH is also the presumed speaker in 12:5–6, but these two verses constitute the response to Jeremiah's questions in 12:1–4. In 12:7 YHWH begins a soliloquy on the fate of Judah. The phrase *kōh ʾāmar yhwh*, "thus says YHWH," introduces a new section in 12:14.

AUTHORSHIP AND DATING

The poem is generally considered to be a composition of Jeremiah, although questions have been raised about particular verses. The apparent shift in subject, style, and imagery in 12:13 and the reference there to YHWH in the third person has led some commentators to view this verse as a separate saying of Jeremiah, added as a concluding reflection.[136] The shift in focus in 12:13, like that in 12:4, does not preclude seeing 12:7–13 as an integral unit, however.[137] Nor is a reference to YHWH in the third person inconceivable in a speech of YHWH.[138] The

---

[135] *The Book of the Prophet Jeremiah* (New York: Scribner's, 1907), 74. See also the discussion in McKane, *Jeremiah,* 1:268, 274; cf. Cornill, *Das Buch Jeremia,* 164.

[136] So Cornill, *Das Buch Jeremia,* 164; Condamin, *Le Livre de Jérémie,* 111–12; McKane, *Jeremiah,* 1:275; Holladay, *Jeremiah 1,* 385. Duhm (*Das Buch Jeremia,* 117–18) considers 12:13 a later gloss, either on 12:7–12 or on 12:14.

[137] Cornill (*Das Buch Jeremia,* 165) in fact connects the imagery of the failed harvest in 12:13 to that of the withering earth in 12:4.

[138] McKane (*Jeremiah,* 1:275) speaks of the "convention that Yahweh refers to himself in the third person," and Holladay (*Jeremiah 1,* 384) cites Jer 2:3 as an example.

name occurs here in a set phrase, "the burning anger of YHWH," which can be seen as formulaic.

For similar or the same reasons the phrase "the sword of YHWH" in 12:12 need not mark this verse as an addition.[139] Nor, considering the extent of figurative language throughout the poem, is the full expression "the sword of YHWH is devouring from the end of the earth to the end of the earth" necessarily indicative of late conceptions of eschatological warfare and punishment, as Volz and Rudolph assert.[140] Yet as McKane points out, 12:12 is difficult to set out in poetic lines and may represent a secondary prose expansion that develops the images of chaos and disorder that precede it.[141]

THEMES AND MOTIFS

THE RESPONSE OF THE EARTH

The passage is replete with wordplay, metaphors, and figurative language that bring to mind both the land and its human inhabitants. Only in 12:10–11 does the imagery differentiate even in part between the two so as to depict the response of the earth to human actions. These verses, which describe the desolation of the land of Judah, form a central vision that the preceding verses lead up to and the succeeding verses develop, ending in 12:13 with the reverse image of the people responding in shame to the ruin of the land.

In 12:7, at the beginning of the lament, YHWH declares that he has abandoned *bêtî*, "my house," *naḥălātî*, "my possession," and *yĕdîdût napšî*, "the love of my being." All are expressions that can refer both to the land and the people of YHWH, and all are linked in this verse by the syntactic parallelism of the three cola in which they occur. Each colon begins with a first common singular transitive verb in the perfect tense, followed by a marked direct object. The noun *naḥălâ* means "possession, inheritance" in the sense of both the land and the people of Israel.[142] The pairing

---

[139] Duhm (*Das Buch Jeremia,* 117) and Cornill (*Das Buch Jeremia,* 164) strike this phrase as secondary.

[140] Volz, *Der Prophet Jeremia,* 144; Rudolph, *Jeremia,* 78. Cf. the battle cry in Judg 7:20: "A sword for YHWH and for Gideon!" See further the discussion of the figurative and mythological coloring of Hebrew poetry in Lindblom, *Prophecy in Ancient Israel,* 293.

[141] *Jeremiah,* 1:275.

[142] See BDB, 635a. For the meaning "people" see, e.g., 1 Sam 10:1; 1 Kgs 8:51, 53; Pss 28:9; 78:62, 71. In these instances *naḥălâ* is found in conjunction with or parallel to *ʿam,* "people."

of *naḥălātî* with *bêtî* brings out two similar dimensions in the latter. The phrase *bêtî* carries tribal or kinship associations and thus probably stands primarily for the people of Israel. Yet in Hos 9:15 it seems to refer to the land of Israel: "I will drive them from my house" (*mibbêtî*).[143] The additional association of the house of YHWH with the temple adds further resonance to the coupling of *naḥălātî* and *bêtî*. These two terms are yoked with the expression *yĕdîdût napšî*, which conveys a strong sense of human relationship. Taken with *bêtî* and *naḥălātî*, it could be heard as another expression for the land of Judah,[144] but it also amplifies the sense of *naḥălātî* and *bêtî* as the people of YHWH.[145] Some commentators choose between a reference to the land of Judah or to the people of Judah for the three terms, but it is possible to hear both meanings at once,[146] although the latter may be primary.

In 12:8 the *naḥălâ* of YHWH assumes an active role; it raises its voice against him. Here the possession of YHWH is compared to a "lion in the forest," a creature of the earth that has turned in rebellion as have the people of Judah. Figurative language continues in 12:9 with the metaphor of YHWH's *naḥălâ* as a hyena's den, an image that incorporates the dual associations of *naḥălâ* as a place and as the people that inhabit that place. Both have become dangerous. The den is surrounded by birds of prey, presumably the enemies of Judah. These enemies are also represented by the wild animals summoned by YHWH to devour in 12:9b.

In 12:10–11, the center of the lament, the consequences of YHWH's abandonment of the land and people of Judah are revealed and the imagery shifts again. The birds of prey and wild animals of 12:9 become shepherds who have destroyed YHWH's vineyard (*karmî*), trampled his field (*ḥelqātî*), and made his pleasant field (*ḥelqat ḥemdātî*) into a desolate desert (*lĕmidbar šĕmāmâ*). Here the land ("my vineyard" and "my field") is distinguished from the human actors ("shepherds") who destroy, trample, and turn it to desert.[147] This distinction is continued in 12:11, where all the land (*kol-hā'āreṣ*) is made desolate, yet no one (*kî 'ên 'îš*) lays it to heart.

---

[143] Cf. Hos 8:1. Note also in Hos 9:15 and Jer 12:8 the common use of the verb *śānā'*.

[144] So Volz, *Der Prophet Jeremia*, 145.

[145] So Rudolph (*Jeremia*, 82), who asserts that both *naḥălātî* and *bêtî* refer to the people or family of YHWH.

[146] So Holladay, *Jeremiah 1*, 384.

[147] Holladay (ibid., 386) claims that the focus of the poem from 12:10 on is the land that the people of Israel inhabit.

In this metaphor for the destruction of Judah, "shepherds" can be taken literally, as the owners of flocks and herds that overrun the land, destroying plants and crops so that fields revert to a desertlike condition.[148] Or the shepherds can be interpreted figuratively, as foreign rulers who invade the land.[149] The latter interpretation is borne out by the imagery of 12:12: "Upon all the bare tracks of the desert destroyers have come." The images of predators in 12:9 support this interpretation as well. In either case, human agents eradicate the agricultural base of the land, leaving it like a desert.[150]

At the same time *kerem,* "vineyard," often serves as a symbol for the people of Israel,[151] and *karmî* and *ḥelqātî,* both nouns with a first singular suffix, recall the similar appellations *bêtî, naḥălātî,* and *yĕdîdût napšî* in 12:7, with their dual associations of both "people" and "land."[152]

The dual resonance in 12:10 influences the reading of 12:11, which describes the response of the land to devastation.[153] This response is conveyed solely by the verb *'ābĕlâ.* The *qal* stem indicates an active response, which stands out particularly here. The earth not only mourns; its desolation impresses itself on YHWH: literally, "it mourns upon me." Yet, as in Amos 1:2 and Jer 4:23–28, the imposed state and active response of the earth are the same: the land has been made into a desolate desert (*lĕmidbar šemāmâ*), and so it is dry and mourns.

Although in a concrete sense *'ābal* may be associated with the drying up of the earth, the aspect of mourning is strong in this setting. Since "my

---

[148] Duhm (*Das Buch Jeremia,* 117), Cornill (*Das Buch Jeremia,* 163), and Volz (*Der Prophet Jeremia,* 146) point to the ongoing tension between herders and farmers in Israelite history as a basis for the imagery of this verse.

[149] See the discussion in McKane (*Jeremiah,* 1:316) of the destruction of the land by military invasion in Jer 14:15, 18. Cf. the imagery in Isa 16:8–10; Jer 48:32–33; and Nah 2:3, where the verb *šiḥēt* also occurs.

[150] The image of the vineyard is particularly apt here, since the roots of grapevines retain water in the ground throughout the dry season.

[151] Within Jeremiah, see, e.g., the metonymy in 5:10 and the simile in 6:9.

[152] Note that *ḥelqâ,* "field," can also be translated as "portion (of ground)," creating a strong parallel to *naḥălâ,* "possession or inheritance." See BDB, 324b.

[153] The connection of these two verses is marked formally by the repetition of the root *šmm* in a refrainlike pattern. The conclusion of 12:10, "they have made the field of my delight into a desolate desert" (*lĕmidbar šĕmāmâ*), is not only restated in the first colon of 12:11a but underscored by internal rhyme: *šāmāh lišmāmâ,* "it has been made a desolation." In the second colon of 12:11a the response of the land is given: *'ābĕlâ 'ālay šĕmēmâ,* literally "it mourns upon me, desolate." The first colon of 12:11b echoes again the end of 12:10: *nāšammâ kol-hā'āreṣ,* "the whole land has become desolate," and the second colon provides a last trace of rhyme in the verb *śām: kî 'ên 'îš śām 'al-lēb,* "but no man lays it to heart."

vineyard" and "my field" in 12:10 can be heard on a figurative level as allusions to the people of Israel, a human context is created that enhances the inherent sense of *'ābal* as "to mourn." The root *šmm*, "to be desolate" and "to be appalled," which occurs three times in 12:11, implies psychological as well as physical devastation. Further, the phrase *kol-hā'āreṣ*, "all the land," in 12:11b can refer to the nation of Israel as well as to the land on which it lives.

In addition, the structure of 12:11, in which the first colon of 12:11a, "it has been made a desolation," is echoed by the first colon of 12:11b, "the whole land is made desolate," places the second cola of the two lines in parallelism. Hence *'ābĕlâ 'ālay šĕmēmâ*, "it mourns upon me, desolate," is parallel (antithetically) to *kî 'ên 'îš śām 'al-lēb*, "yet no man lays it to heart." In this yoking of the response of the land with the lack of human feeling, the mourning aspect of *'ābal* dominates.

In light of the fusion of natural and human imagery throughout the poem to this point, the existence of both literal and figurative dimensions in 12:10–11 does not mean these verses need be interpreted uniformly on one or the other plane. The metaphor of the shepherds in 12:10 provides a concrete scenario of the ravaging and subsequent drying up of the land, but the response of the earth to being ravaged (whether by herders or military leaders) can also be seen as mourning, whether *karmî*, *ḥelqātî*, and *'ereṣ* are understood as the people of Judah or the physical land of Judah.

In 12:12 images of military invasion dominate, but the language of 12:13 draws out further the ambiguities of 12:10–11. On a concrete level the sequence of sowing wheat and reaping thorns mirrors the turning of pleasant field into desolate desert in 12:10 and is consistent with the drying up of the land latent in the expression "it mourns upon me, desolate" in 12:11.[154] At the same time, the verb *neḥĕlâ* in 12:13a ("they have made themselves sick [*neḥlû*], they have not profited") carries connotations of suffering and grief that fit the context of mourning.[155] The *nipʿal* participle *naḥlâ*, "serious, grievous," modifies *makkâ*, "wound, blow," in contexts of woe and weeping in Jer 10:19 and 14:17.[156] In Amos 6:7 the psychological aspect of *neḥĕlâ* is fully evident:

---

[154] Commentators who suggest that 12:13 speaks on a literal level of crop failure include Volz, *Der Prophet Jeremia*, 146; Rudolph, *Jeremia*, 82; and Holladay, *Jeremiah 1*, 388. Cf., e.g., the curses in Deut 28:30b, 38–40. Cornill (*Das Buch Jeremia*, 164) sees a figurative speech of gnomic character in this verse, which he compares to Hos 8:7.

[155] Cf. the connection between mourning (*'ēbel*) and sickness or faintness (*dāweh*) in Lam 5:15–17.

[156] See also Jer 30:12 in the context of 30:12–15.

[Woe to those …] who drink wine in bowls
and anoint themselves with the best oils,
But are not sickened [*neḥlû*] over the ruin of Jacob.

The response of the people of Judah to their failed harvest ("they will be ashamed [*ûbōšû*] of their yields") in 12:13b corresponds to the response of the earth to devastation in 12:11a. The root *bwš*, "to be ashamed," occurs in the Hebrew Bible, and in Jeremiah in particular, in the sense of guilt but also in contexts of defeat, failure, and disaster.[157] In Jer 9:16–18, for example, shame and mourning come together in a communal lament, as seen in 9:18:

For a sound of wailing [*nĕhî*]
is heard from Zion.
How we have been destroyed [*šuddādnû*];
we are utterly ashamed [*bōšnû*].
For we have abandoned the land [*'ereṣ*],
because they have thrown down our dwellings.

In Jer 12:13b the verb *bôš* brings out the aspect of mourning in the response of the earth in 12:11. Further, *bôš* occurs in Jer 14:1–10 in a particular context of drought. In this communal lament, drought, mourning, and shame interact as the responses of the earth and of the people of Judah interweave. In 14:2–4:

Judah mourns [*'ābĕlâ*],
and her gates languish [*'umlĕlû*];
They mourn [*qāderû*] on the ground,
and the cry of Jerusalem goes up.
And her leading men have sent their servants[158] for water;
they have come to cisterns.
They have not found water;
they return, their vessels empty;
they are ashamed [*bōšû*] and confounded [*wĕhoklĕmû*] and have covered their heads;
The ground [*hā'ădāmâ*] is dismayed [*ḥattâ*] by its yield,[159]
because no rain has come on the earth [*bā'āreṣ*].

---

157 See Meir Weiss, "Methodologisches über die Behandlung der Metapher dargelegt an Am. 1,2," *TZ* 23 (1967): 8; and the discussions in Frederick W. Dobbs-Allsopp, *Weep, O Daughter of Zion: A Study of the City Lament Genre in the Hebrew Bible* (BibOr 44; Rome: Pontifical Biblical Institute, 1993), 119–20; and Holladay, *Jeremiah 1*, 431. Cf. BDB, 101b.

158 Read *ṣĕʿîrêhem* (Q) for *ṣĕʿôrêhem* (K).

159 Read *baʿăbûrāh 'ădāmâ* for *baʿăbûr hā'ădāmâ* (MT). So Holladay, *Jeremiah 1*, 419, 431; Condamin, *Le Livre de Jérémie*, 124.

The farmers are ashamed [*bōšû*];
    they have covered their heads.

The association of shame and drought in this passage suggests that *bôš* in 12:13 fits the context of the drying up of the earth as well as the more general context of mourning over disaster. The human response to the degrading of the land in 12:13 and the land's response to its own degredation in 12:11 thus echo each other.

SIN OR PUNISHMENT

In Jer 12:7–13 the mourning of the earth is presented as a response to punishment inflicted by YHWH through human agents. That this punishment stems from the rebellion of the people is made clear in 12:8. In a reversal of the metaphor of Amos 1:2, the *naḥălâ,* "possession," of YHWH has become like a hostile predator. This hostility has turned Judah from an object of love (*yĕdīdût napšî,* "the love of my being") into an object of hate: "so I hate her" (*ʿal-kēn śĕnēʾtîhā*).

In 12:9 the poem deftly links sin and punishment by shifting the frame of reference of a single image. In 12:9a the hyena's den (if that is the correct reading) represents the violence of Judah, which has attracted birds of prey; in 12:9b this violence turns back in force against the nation, and the animals of the field (wild animals) are summoned by YHWH to devour it.[160]

This last image yields to another: the "many shepherds" of 12:10 do not simply menace the land; they have entered and devastated it. That both images suggest military invasion bears out what is stated explicitly in the opening verse of the poem: "I have given the love of my being into the hands of her enemies" (12:7b). YHWH does not act directly here, then, as seems to be the case in Amos 1:2 and even in Jer 4:23–28, passages that strongly evoke the *topos* of YHWH as the divine warrior.

Yet there are hints of this *topos* in Jer 12:7–13. The devouring "sword of YHWH" in 12:12 is a metonymic symbol of the divine warrior.[161] Moreover, the attribution in 12:13 of the disastrous harvest to the "burning anger of YHWH" parallels the attribution of the ruin of the land and its cities in Jer 4:26 to "his burning anger."[162]

---

[160] Cf. 12:7. According to Delbert H. Hillers (*Treaty-Curses and the Old Testament Prophets* [BibOr 16; Rome: Pontifical Biblical Institute, 1964], 54–56), the *topos* of the devouring of an enemy (or Israel itself) by wild animals, which occurs throughout the prophetic literature as well as in Deut 28:16 and Lev 26:22, reflects a traditional ancient Near Eastern treaty curse.

[161] See, e.g., Judg 7:20.

[162] See also the figurative language in Jer 25:36–37, where the destroying (*šōdēd*) of the shepherds' pasture is linked to the "burning anger" (*ḥărôn ʾap*) of YHWH.

The sequence of images of disaster in 12:7–13 (the devouring of wild animals and of the sword and the failed harvest) reflect curses like those found in Deut 28 and Lev 26,[163] curses incurred through divine disfavor. The behavior that has brought down divine punishment on Judah in 12:7–13 is not specified. As in 12:1–4, it is primarily the attitude of Judah toward YHWH that is faulted. This is clear not only in the introductory image of the lion but also in the statement in 12:11 that, despite the desolation of the land, "no one lays it to heart": the people's attitude toward YHWH is unchanged.

The juxtaposition of Jer 12:7–13, in which the effect on the earth of punishment commissioned by YHWH is primary, with 12:1–4, in which the effect of human evil on the earth is stressed, is noteworthy. Each passage shows the reverse side of its mate, so that together they present a more complete view of the mourning of the earth than would each taken alone.

It should also be noted that the devastation and mourning of the earth in 12:7–13, as in 12:4, does not represent a final or definitive punishment. In 12:11, witnesses to the devastation remain who do not lay it to heart; in 12:13 the people survive their disastrous harvest, though they are ashamed of it.

SOCIAL OR NATURAL DISORDER

Figurative language prevails in this lament, and it contains no explicit reference to social disorder. On the figurative level, however, a scene of aberration is created through imagery and ironic wordplay. The image of Judah as a hyena's den conveys a state of violence and fear that is consistent with condemnations of the social order elsewhere in Jeremiah.[164] The elaboration of this image with the depiction of birds of prey hovering over the den and wild animals gathering to

---

The imagery of sowing and reaping in 12:13 has been associated with the concept of acts begetting consequences (see, e.g., Prov 11:18, 30; 22:8; Hos 8:7; 10:13–14; Jer 4:3); so Klaus Koch ("Is There a Doctrine of Retribution in the Old Testament?" in *Theodicy in the Old Testament* [ed. James L. Crenshaw; Philadelphia: Fortress, 1983], 61, 64–65). In Jer 12:13 this imagery might suggest that the people of Judah have produced a thorny harvest through their own misdoings. Yet the verse concludes with explicit reference to the punitive role of divine anger, and that is where the emphasis rests. See the use of similar imagery and phraseology in the context of divine judgment in Mic 6:15 and the divine curses articulated in Deut 28:39; Lev 26:20.

[163] See, esp. Lev 26:20–26. Cf. the images of both drought and military invasion in Jer 4:23–28.

[164] See, e.g., Jer 2:34–35; 5:1–5, 7–8, 26–28.

devour it builds a picture of violence begetting violence and ensuing in final destruction.

Yet the disorder implied here pertains not so much to the state of the nation before the coming of disaster as to the state induced by the disaster itself. In 12:9 the animals of the field are summoned to devour or eat (*lĕʾoklâ*), and in 12:12 the sword of YHWH devours or eats (*ʾōkĕlâ*) from one end of the earth (*ʾereṣ*) to the other. By putting these images of eating together with the devastation of the earth in 12:10–11, the impression of a distorted harvest is formed: not a natural scene of harvesting, eating, and rejoicing but a devouring that leaves the earth a desert, incapable of producing food. The almost perfect rhyme between *ʾoklâ* and *ʾōkĕlâ* and the close rhyme between these two forms and the verb *ʾābĕlâ,* "it mourns," which occurs between them in 12:11, drive home the fusion of eating, death, invasion, and mourning that constitute this harvest. The use of the verb *ʾāsap,* "to gather, harvest," in the call to devour in 12:9 ("Come, gather together [*ʾispû*], all wild animals of the field") adds another note of irony. The final verse of the poem features explicit imagery of an abnormal harvest: wheat is planted, but thorns are reaped; the people have made themselves sick but have nothing to show for their pains.[165]

POLLUTION

Traces of the theme of the pollution of the earth are evident in this passage but are, again, primarily bound up with the experience of devastation itself. The description of the destruction of vineyard and field in 12:10 recalls this theme:

> Many shepherds have destroyed [*šiḥătû*] my vineyard;
>   they have trampled [*bōsĕsû*] my field.

That the two verbs used here both carry associations of pollution is reflected in the translation of LXX: "Many shepherds have destroyed [διέφθειραν] my vineyard; they have defiled [ἐμόλυναν] my portion." The Greek verb διαφθείρω, which means "to corrupt, ruin" in a moral sense as well as "to destroy" in a physical sense, reflects the dual aspect of the Hebrew root *šḥt,* which means both to "destroy" and to "pervert, corrupt" in the *piʿel* and *hipʿil* and "to be destroyed" and "to be corrupt" in the *nipʿal.*[166]

---

[165] Sickness itself is a mark of abnormality and disorder.

[166] The corresponding root in Syriac (*ḥbl*) also bears the dual meaning "to destroy" and "to corrupt." See Payne Smith, *Compendious Syriac Dictionary,* 123b–124a.

In Jer 6:28 the root occurs in the context of the refining of base metals. The dual resonance of *šḥt* as "corrupt" and "destroyed" may also be at play in Jer 13:7 in the allegory of the ruined loincloth, a symbol of the inner corruption as well the external destruction of Israel, and in 18:4 in the allegory of the ruined pot, where it probably expresses both these meanings as well.[167]

The root *bws*, "to tread down, trample," is almost always used in the Hebrew Bible in a literal or a concrete sense. However, in one postexilic context it acquires the extended sense "desecrate." In Isa 63:18 the *po‘el* verb occurs in the context of the overrunning of the sanctuary:

> For a little while your holy people had possession;
> our enemies have trampled [*bôsĕsû*] your holy place.

Clearly Isa 63:18 and Jer 12:10 represent very different times and settings; still, the verse from Third Isaiah provides another context in which the *po‘el* of *bws* is associated with desecration and defilement. Whether because those responsible for Jer 12:10 LXX understood the verb in this way or because they were influenced by the possible associations of *siḥătû* in the preceding colon, they rendered *bôsĕsû* with the verb μολύνω, "to defile."

The impression of pollution in Jer 12:10 is linked to the experience of devastation. It is the invaders who have defiled Judah rather than the people of Judah themselves. At the same time, associations with the use of *šḥt* elsewhere in Jeremiah suggest that in this instance the invaders are making into a physical actuality what is an internal reality within the vineyard or field of YHWH.

MOURNING AS STRIPPING

This motif is evoked in Jer 12:7–13 more by imagery than by vocabulary. Birds of prey (12:9a) strip the flesh off the bones of their victims; wild animals (12:9b) devour all that moves on the ground. Similarly the shepherds who overrun the land destroy and trample what is growing in its vineyards and fields, stripping it down to desert land (12:10). The motif is manifest more precisely in the destroyers (*šōdĕdîm*) who swoop in from the desert (12:12); the verb *šad*, "to despoil, devastate," implies stripping and plundering as well as destruction. The conceptualization of this motif in terms of military invasion is continued in the subsequent image of the

---

[167] As noted in the discussion above on the theme of decreation in Hos 4:1–3, *šḥt* conveys the moral corruption of the earth in the Priestly account of the flood in Gen 6:11–12.

sword of YHWH devouring from one end of the land to the other, consuming all life (12:12).

SUMMARY OF LITERARY TECHNIQUES

The concentration of literary techniques and devices and the constant shifting of imagery in this lament are striking. Throughout the poem wordplay bolsters the central personification of the earth as mourning by drawing out the dual meanings of *bêtî*, "my house," and *naḥălātî*, "my possession," in the sense of both "land" and "people"; *šiḥēt*, "to destroy" and "to corrupt"; *bōsēs*, "to trample" and "to desecrate"; the root *šmm*, "to be desolate" and "to be appalled"; *neḥĕlâ*, "to be sick" and "to be grieved"; *'ereṣ*, "earth" and "political territory." The blending of natural and human spheres is also effected by the sequence of metaphors and similes that speak of human phenomena in terms of natural ones: the people of Judah are like a lion, a hyena's den, a vineyard, and a field; the invaders of Judah are like birds of prey and animals of the field. The intertwining of human and natural imagery persists throughout the poem, and there is no overall structural separation between human actions and the response of the earth. The internal rhymes formed by *lĕ'oklâ* (12:9), *'ōkĕlâ* (12:12), and *'ābĕlâ* (12:11) bind together human and natural images, as does the echo created by the phrases *kol-hā'āreṣ* (12:11) and *kol-bāśār* (12:12).

OVERALL EFFECT OF THE METAPHOR

In this passage, the mourning of the earth adds a note of dissonance or, rather, a dissenting presence. This is a presence that impresses itself upon YHWH but that the human community does not heed ("no man ['ên 'îš] lays it to heart"). The relationship of the earth to YHWH contrasts with the hostility and indifference that characterize the attitude of Judah to YHWH, creating a strong impression of earth as a persona. In this poem the people of Judah are identified with wild and vicious animals, while the earth becomes almost human.

The mourning of the earth in 12:7–13 does not bespeak total destruction but serves as a warning—another prophetic voice, as it were, albeit a silent witness—to those who still do not hear the voice of YHWH. These are those whom YHWH laments in 8:6:

> I have listened closely,
> but they have not spoken what is right.
> No man ['ên 'îš] repents of his wickedness [rā'ātô]
> saying, "What have I done?"

JEREMIAH 23:9–12

TEXT, TRANSLATION, AND TEXTUAL NOTES

9 לַנְּבִאִ֒ים

רָחֲפוּ֙ כָּל־עַצְמוֹתַ֔י   נִשְׁבַּ֤ר לִבִּ֣י בְקִרְבִּ֗י

וּכְגֶ֖בֶר עֲבָ֣רוֹ יָ֑יִן   הָיִ֙יתִי֙ כְּאִ֣ישׁ שִׁכּ֔וֹר

וּמִפְּנֵ֖י דִּבְרֵ֥י קָדְשֽׁוֹ׃   מִפְּנֵ֣י יְהֹוָ֔ה

10 כִּ֤י מִפְּנֵ֤י אָלָה֙ אָבְלָ֣ה הָאָ֔רֶץ   כִּ֤י מְנָֽאֲפִים֙ מָלְאָ֣ה הָאָ֔רֶץ

יָבְשׁ֖וּ נְא֣וֹת מִדְבָּ֑ר

וּגְבוּרָתָ֖ם לֹא־כֵֽן׃   וַתְּהִ֤י מְרֽוּצָתָם֙ רָעָ֔ה

11 גַּם־בְּבֵיתִ֛י מָצָ֥אתִי רָעָתָ֖ם נְאֻם־יְהֹוָֽה׃   כִּֽי־גַם־נָבִ֥יא גַם־כֹּהֵ֖ן חָנֵ֑פוּ

12 בָּאֲפֵלָה֙ יִדַּ֣חוּ וְנָ֣פְלוּ בָ֔הּ   לָכֵן֩ יִֽהְיֶ֨ה דַרְכָּ֜ם לָהֶ֗ם כַּחֲלַקְלַקּוֹת֙

שְׁנַ֥ת פְּקֻדָּתָ֖ם נְאֻם־יְהֹוָֽה׃   כִּֽי־אָבִ֧יא עֲלֵיהֶ֛ם רָעָ֖ה

9 ᵃConcerning the prophets:ᵃ
   My heart is broken within me;
      all my bones grow soft.
   I have become like a drunken man,
      and like a man overcome by wine,
   Because of YHWH
      and because of his holy words.
10 For the earth is full of adulterers,
      for because of ᵇa curseᵇ the earth mourns,ᶜ
      the pastures of the wilderness dry up.
   And their course is evil,
      and their power is not right.
11 For even the prophet, even the priest is impure;
      even in my house I have found their evil, says YHWH.
12 ᵈTherefore their way shall be to them
      like slippery ground
      in the darkness they will be thrust down and fall in it.ᵈ
   For I will bring evil upon them:
      the year of their punishment, says YHWH.

ᵃ⁻ᵃ Read (with Vulg. and most modern commentators) as a superscription for the longer section 23:9–40. Jeremiah's distress in 23:9 and the
indictment and announcement of judgment that follow in 23:10–12 do not
concern the prophets exclusively.

b–b So also Vulg. LXX (τούτων) and Syr. (*hlyn*) read *'ēlleh,* "these." The pronoun *'ēlleh* is much more common in MT than the noun *'ālâ,* "curse," and the reading "because of these" is also smoother. Hence *'ālâ* represents *lectio difficilior.* The noun *'ālâ* occurs in prose passages elsewhere in Jeremiah in a sequence of threats directed by YHWH against Israel. Jeremiah 42:18, for example, reads, "they shall become an execration, a horror, a curse, and a taunt" (cf. 44:12 and 29:18). For a connection between *'ālâ,* "curse," and the drying up of the land, see Deut 29:18–24.

c So LXX (ἐπένθησεν) and Vulg. (*luxit*). Syriac reads *'thblt,* "has become corrupt," which may represent a confusion of *ḥêt* for *'ālep.*

d–d So *BHS.* MT divides 23:12a as follows: "Therefore their way shall be to them like slippery ground in the darkness / they will be thrust down and fall in it."

DELIMITATION OF THE PASSAGE

The phrase *lannĕbī'îm,* "concerning the prophets," at the head of 23:9 marks the beginning of a new section. The phrase *nĕ'ūm-yhwh,* "says YHWH," which occurs at the end of 23:11, often concludes an oracle. But since 23:12 begins with *lākēn,* "therefore," referring back to the preceding verses, the passage continues through the end of 23:12. There a second *nĕ'ūm-yhwh* brings the unit to a close.

That the passage as a whole, as well as its heading, *lannĕbī'îm,* functions as a general introduction to the larger unit 23:9–40 is clear from the content of 23:9–12. These three verses address the evil rampant among the people of Judah, beginning with *mĕnā'ăpîm,* "adulterers," and then naming both prophet and priest specifically. The oracles that follow, beginning with 23:13–15, focus on the prophets alone.[168]

AUTHORSHIP AND DATING

Once again, discussion of the dating of this passage centers on the reference to the mourning earth in 23:10. Although most commentators consider 23:9–12 to be a speech stemming from Jeremiah, many strike

---

[168] On Jer 23:9–12 as addressing moral failure in Judah as a whole, see Duhm, *Das Buch Jeremia,* 181; Cornill, *Das Buch Jeremia,* 267; Volz, *Der Prophet Jeremia,* 234; Rudolph, *Jeremiah,* 138; McKane, *Jeremiah,* 1:570. It should be noted, however, that 23:13–15 shares a fair amount of vocabulary with 23:9–12 (the verb *nā'ap,* "to committ adultery"; the roots *nb',* "to prophesy," and *ḥnp,* "to be polluted, ungodly"; and the noun *rā'â,* "evil"). Holladay (*Jeremiah 1,* 624) points out that both sets of verses at least touch on the corruption of the prophets and that both exhibit a similar structure: an indictment followed by a judgment speech beginning with *lākēn* (23:12, 15).

the second two cola of 23:10a, which describe the earth mourning and withering under a curse, for a variety of reasons.[169] First, these cola are seen as interrupting the sequence of thought in 23:10–11: the condemnation of evil in the land (*'ereṣ*) that has penetrated even into the temple (*bĕbêtî*, "my house," [23:11]).[170] Yet the word *'ereṣ*, "land," is a connecting verbal and conceptual link between the first colon of 23:10a and the second two cola, and the flow of thought in this tricolon and in 23:10–11 as a whole is not foreign to Jeremiah. Jeremiah 3:1–3, for example, connects the violation of marriage vows, harlotry (*zānâ, zĕnût*), evil (*rā'â*), pollution (*ḥānēp, beḥĕnîp*), and the drying up of the land (*'ereṣ*); 3:8–9, harlotry (*zānâ, zĕnût*), adultery (*ni'ēp*), and the pollution (*beḥĕnîp*)[171] of the land (*'ereṣ*). Admittedly there is a break between the first colon and the second and third cola of 23:10a, as the prophet segues into a reflection on the impact of the adultery he sees around him. But the break is not wholly anomalous.[172]

Second, the last two cola of 23:10a, in which the earth mourns and dries up, are seen as out of place because the rest of 23:10–11 do not mention punishment but simply present the case against Judah. Only in 23:12 is judgment announced, and there it is imminent rather than in progress.[173] This objection resembles that raised against 12:4: If the wicked have to date escaped punishment, why is the land now suffering drought? The same objection could be posed with respect to 12:11, where the land mourns yet is ignored by an unrepentant remnant. Jeremiah 23:10 offers another instance where the sins of the people have induced a response from YHWH in the form of punishment, or from the earth itself, but a final reckoning still looms. In these passages the distinction between the two types

---

[169] So Driver, *Book of the Prophet Jeremiah,* 135; Cornill, *Das Buch Jeremia,* 167; Condamin, *Le Livre de Jérémie,* 181; Bright, *Jeremiah,* 151; Volz, *Der Prophet Jeremia,* 234; Rudolph, *Jeremia,* 136. Duhm (*Das Buch Jeremia,* 183) considers the present tricolon in 23:10a a later variant of an original bicolon of which only the first colon (23:10aɑ) remains.

[170] The reference to prophet and priest in connection with *bêtî* in 23:11 suggests that "my house" should be taken here as an allusion to the temple rather than, as in Jer 12:7, to the land of Judah.

[171] Read *wattaḥănēp,* the second masculine singular *hip'il* of *ḥnp,* for *watteḥĕnap* (MT), the second masculine singular *qal.* Cf. BDB, 338a; Holladay, *Jeremiah 1,* 59.

[172] Holladay (*Jeremiah 1,* 626–27) suggests moving the first colon of 23:10 so that it directly precedes 23:10b, assuming that this colon originally dropped out of the verse (so LXX) through *homoioarchton* and was restored in a different place. This emendation creates a logical text but is unnecessary.

[173] So Condamin, *Le Livre de Jérémie,* 180; Rudolph, *Jeremia,* 136.

of punishment (or consequence) can be noted without concluding that the text has been expanded.

Third, the resemblance of 23:10aβ to 12:4 has led some commentators to assume some form of redactional dependence of the former on the latter.[174] It is possible, however, that similar thoughts were expressed in similar ways on different occasions. Volz further notes the similarities shared by these two cola and cola in other of the nine passages considered in this study. He judges 23:10aβ inauthentic precisely because of its stereotypical ("formelhaften") content and bland ("blasse") character.[175] Yet the echoing of the metaphor of earth mourning like a refrain through these passages does not mean that this metaphor was not actually taken up independently by individual prophetic voices.[176] Finally, it should be noted that none of those who consider the second two cola of Jer 23:10 as secondary argue for a late date for their addition.

Themes and Motifs

The Response of the Earth

Images of the earth are concentrated in 23:10 in this passage. Here the earth responds to, or through the agency of, a curse (*'ālâ*):

> For because of the curse, the earth mourns [*'ābĕlâ*]
> and the pastures of the wilderness wither [*yābĕšû*].

As in Amos 1:2 and Jer 12:4, *'ābal* is paired here with a verb that clearly signals drought (*yābēš*). The phrase "the pastures of the wilderness" (*nĕ'ôt*

---

[174] Giesebrecht, *Das Buch Jeremia,* 129; Duhm, *Das Buch Jeremia,* 182; Cornill, *Das Buch Jeremia,* 267; Rudolph, *Jeremia,* 136. These commentators assume, as Giesebrecht first proposed, that the second colon of 23:10 (*kî mippĕnê 'ālâ 'ābĕlâ hā'āreṣ*) represents a dittography or textual variant of the first colon (*kî mĕnā'ăpîm mālĕ'â hā'āreṣ*). This second colon was then expanded into a full bicolon on the pattern of 12:4. A dittography seems unlikely, however. Although the two cola share many consonants, they are sufficiently different to suggest the deliberate use of alliteration, consonance, assonance, and internal rhyme rather than duplication.

[175] *Jeremia,* 234. His assessment of Jer 12:4 is on similar lines.

[176] As noted in the discussion above of Jer 12:1–4, that such phrases possess a certain integrity and stand out to some extent from their surrounding contexts may be characteristic of traditional poetry and does not mean they do not participate fully in the thematic development of a passage. See, e.g., John M. Foley, *Immanent Art: From Structure to Meaning in Traditional Oral Epic* (Bloomington: University of Indiana Press, 1991), 252. See further the discussion in chapter 7 and the sources cited there.

midbār) is reminiscent of the "pastures of the shepherds" (*nĕʾôt bārōʿîm*) in Amos 1:2, but whereas in Amos the mention of shepherds introduces a human element, in Jer 23:10 that element is only implicit. The "pastures of the wilderness" represent a marginal region mentioned to illustrate the extent of the drought.[177] The association of curse with drought strengthens the aspect of drying up in the verb *ʾābal* in this passage.[178] From this perspective, the response of the earth is seen as a state of dryness induced by the curse. The stative quality of *yābēš*, "to be dry" as well as "to dry up," strengthens this impression. Yet the dominant meaning of *ʾābal* as "to mourn" conveys the impression that the earth is actively responding.[179]

SIN OR PUNISHMENT

The mourning and drying up of the earth is attributed in the second and third cola of 23:10a to a curse (*ʾālâ*). But are the curse and the response of the earth to it connected to the statement in the preceding colon that "the earth is full of adulterers"? The first two cola are bound together by the key word "earth" (*ʾereṣ*), which occurs in both; by formal similarities, since both begin with *kî* and end with *hāʾāreṣ;* and by phonological similarities, since together they exhibit a high degree of consonance and assonance (*kî mĕnāʾăpîm mālĕʾâ hāʾāreṣ / kî mippĕnê ʾālâ ʾābĕlâ hāʾāreṣ*). These formal links suggest a connection between the adultery of the people, the curse, and the mourning of the earth.

Curses were deployed in the ancient world by one hostile party against another, but it is clear from ancient Near Eastern treaties and boundary-stone markers (*kudurrus*) as well as from the Hebrew Bible itself that curses were also used as threats against *potentially* hostile parties. Such curses were latent, only becoming activated if an agreement were broken or a boundary line transgressed.

In Jer 23:10 the word *ʾālâ*, "curse," recalls the curses with which YHWH threatens Israel in Deut 28 and Lev 26.[180] In Deut 29:19–20 *ʾālâ* occurs in the context of a warning to the Israelite who turns away from YHWH:

---

[177] See Jer 9:9, where the "mountains" (*hehārîm*) and the "pastures of the wilderness" (*nĕʾôt midbār*) serve as a merism for the land of Judah.

[178] See, e.g., Deut 28:22–24; 29:21–26.

[179] Note also that the phrase *nĕʾôt midbār* occurs in Jer 9:9 in a context of weeping and wailing (*bĕkî wānehî*) over the devastation of the land and the desolation of the cities of Judah.

[180] Jer 23:10 articulates the concept of curse explicitly, but the resonance of curse language and imagery has been noted repeatedly in the passages considered above.

YHWH would not be willing to pardon him, but rather the anger of YHWH and his jealousy would smoke against that man, and every curse [*'ālâ*] written in this book would cleave[181] to him. And YHWH would blot out his name from beneath the sky. And YHWH would separate him out for evil from all the tribes of Israel according to all the curses [*'ālôt*] of the covenant [*bĕrît*] written in this book of the law.[182]

The next three verses (29:21–23) link these curses with the drying up of the earth:

And the next generation, your children who will rise up after you, and the foreigner who comes from a distant land will say when they see the wounds of that land [*'ereṣ*] and the diseases with which YHWH had made it sick—brimstone and salt, all of its land [*'arṣāh*] burning; it will not be sown nor will it let anything grow, and no plants will come up in it, like the overthrow of Sodom and Gomorrah, Admah and Zeboim, which YHWH overthrew in his anger and his wrath—and all the nations will say: "Why has YHWH done this to this land [*'ereṣ*]?"

If the context of *'ālâ* in Deut 29:19–20 is considered along with the curse list of Deut 28, the adulterers of Jer 23:10 can be seen as representative of those who transgress YHWH's known commandments or laws or, in a figurative sense, of those who worship foreign gods (Deut 29:17).[183] Such an offense incurs a divine anger that is expressed in a curse desiccating the earth (the second and third cola of 23:10a).

---

[181] Read *wĕdābĕqâ* for *wĕrābĕṣâ* (MT). LXX (κολληθήσονται, "will cleave") reads the third plural form of *dābēq*; cf. Tg. and Deut 28:21, 60. See also Samuel R. Driver, *Deuteronomy* (3d ed; ICC: Edinburgh: T&T Clark, 1901), 326. As a verb, *rābaṣ*, "to stretch out, lie down," is used elsewhere in the Hebrew Bible of animals and only figuratively of human beings. Driver considers the metaphor implied in MT here "forced."

[182] In Deuteronomistic fashion the curses threatening Israel are tied here not just to law and commandment but to the whole concept of covenant (*bĕrît*). Such a connection cannot be assumed for *'ālâ* in Jer 23:10, though it cannot be ruled out, either.

[183] Such a relationship between these passages is more probable if the early stages of the composition of Deuteronomy are dated to the seventh century, preceding or contemporaneous with Jeremiah (see, e.g., Joseph Blenkinsopp, *The Pentateuch: An Introduction to the First Five Books of the Bible* [ABRL; New York: Doubleday, 1992], 214–17). The reference to adulterers here may be taken literally (cf. Jer 5:7–8; so Condamin, *Le Livre de Jérémie*, 181; Volz, *Der Prophet Jeremia*, 235; Rudolph, *Jeremia*, 138), though perhaps at the same time as standing for other infractions of Israelite law. It can also be taken in a figurative sense (so Duhm, *Das Buch Jeremia*, 181) as a breaking away from YHWH (see, e.g., Jer 3:8–9, 20; 13:27; Hos 2:4).

At the same time the curses recorded in Deuteronomy are potential threats enacted only when triggered by the acts of the people themselves. When an Israelite disregards the laws or covenant of YHWH, "every curse written in this book will cleave to him" (Deut 29:19). The language gives the curses a dynamic of their own.[184]

Such a perspective is consonant with the view that evil acts beget evil consequences. It is reinforced by the reference to the evil course (*mĕrûṣâ*) of the adulterers in Jer 23:10b and by the judgment speech in 23:12:

> Therefore [*lākēn*] their way [*darkām*] shall be to them
> like slippery ground in the darkness;
> they will be thrust down and fall in it.

The nouns "course" (*mĕrûṣâ*) and "way" (*derek*), as elsewhere in the Hebrew Bible, represent patterns of behavior, patterns that here will lead the wicked into trouble.[185]

The conjunction *lākēn*, which begins 23:12, however, often precedes an announcement of divine judgment, and the ultimate agency of YHWH is affirmed in the concluding bicolon:

> For I will bring evil [*rāʿâ*] upon them
> in the year of their punishment [*pĕquddātām*].

At the same time the wordplay that juxtaposes the "evil" of the course of the adulterers (23:10) and the "evil" found in YHWH's house (23:11) with the "evil" YHWH will bring upon those who do wrong points to the connection between act and consequence.[186]

---

[184] Hubmann (*Untersuchungen zu den Konfessionen,* 142 n. 31) reflects this view of the curse when he refers to the "somehow independent working of the curse" ["das irgendwie selbständige Wirken des Fluches"] in Jer 23:10 and Isa 24:4.

[185] See the reference to the way (*derek*) of the wicked in Jer 12:1. On the metaphor of the path in Proverbs, see Koch ("Is There a Doctrine of Retribution?" 61–62). Holladay (*Jeremiah 1,* 628) notes the similarities between this verse and Prov 4:19. See also McKane, *Jeremiah,* 1:572. It is interesting to note that in Deut 28:29 the curses that will befall the Israelites if they turn away from YHWH entail darkness ([*bā*]*ʾăpēlâ*), confusion, and failure to prosper "in your ways" (*dĕrākêkā*).

[186] Cf. the discussion in McKane (*Jeremiah,* 1:572–73) on the alternative perspectives of self-destructive behavior and divine punishment in 23:12. The linking of act and consequence in this verse does not diverge from traditional notions of divine justice in the Hebrew Bible, but can be seen as a special emphasis in 23:12, as in Hos 4:1–3.

Just as in Jer 12:1–4 and 12:7–13, the interplay of perspectives in Jer 23:9–12 creates a dual vision of punishment. In 23:10 the land mourns and dries up in response to a curse set off by its adulterous inhabitants, yet the adulterers apparently persevere ("their course is evil, and their power is not right"). Furthermore, despite the withering of the land, both prophet and priest remain corrupt (23:11). In 23:12 the future tenses of the verbs indicate that the overthrow of the evildoers (or the return of evil upon the evildoers) is still to be accomplished in the decisive "year of punishment" brought about by YHWH.

SOCIAL DISORDER

That "the land [*hā'āreṣ*] is full [*mālē'â*] of adulterers" (23:10) is a sign of social disorder, as on a literal level adultery embodies a lack of commitment to promises.[187] Another symptom of this disorder is the impurity (*ḥānēp*) and evil (*rā'â*) of prophets and priests (23:11), the supposed moral leaders of the community.

POLLUTION

An explicit verbal link to the theme of pollution occurs in 23:11: *gam-nābî' gam-kōhēn ḥānēpû*, "even the prophet, even the priest is impure." The verb *ḥānēp*, "to be polluted," when applied to human beings, is often interpreted as meaning "to be profane, godless."[188] On the literal or physical level this root describes the pollution of the earth by bloodshed in Num 35:33 and Ps 106:38. In Jer 23:11 it refers to the prophets and priests of Judah: they, too, are polluted in their godlessness or disregard of YHWH, even within the temple, YHWH's house.

The association of the religious leaders of Israel with defilement and pollution continues in the related passage that follows (Jer 23:13–15). In 23:13–14 YHWH reveals that he has seen among the prophets of Samaria *tiplâ*, "unseemliness," and among the prophets of Jerusalem *ša'ărûrâ*, "a horrible thing."[189] The Jerusalem prophets "commit adultery" (*nā'ōp*) and have made the inhabitants of Jerusalem like Sodom and Gomorrah in YHWH's eyes. These denunciations point to utter degeneracy and the kind

---

[187] So in Gen 6:11 the utter corruption of the earth is represented by the statement: "the earth [*hā'āreṣ*] was filled [*wattimmālē'*] with violence."

[188] BDB, 337b–338a. Cf. the adjective *ḥānēp*, "profane, godless." LXX translates *ḥānēpû* here with ἐμολύνθησαν, "are defiled"; Vulg. with *polluti sunt,* "are polluted."

[189] Note the connection between the related noun *ša'ărûrît*, "horrible thing," and defilement in Jer 18:13: "The virgin Israel has done a very horrible thing" (*ša'ărūrīt*).

of sexual offenses said to cause pollution in the Levitical and Deuteronomic law codes.[190] They are summed up in 23:15:

> For from the prophets of Jerusalem
> pollution [ḥănuppâ] has gone forth to all the earth [lĕkol-hā'āreṣ].

Similarly, the impurity of priest and prophet in the first colon of 23:11 parallels the adultery of the inhabitants of the land in the first colon of 23:10. The reference to the evil (rā'â) of both adulterers (23:10b) and religious leaders (23:11b) further links these two groups. The brief description in 23:10aβ of the mourning and withering earth, which interrupts the condemnation of these groups, can be seen as a sign of the pollution caused by the sin of both. Adultery is tied to the pollution of the earth in Jer 3:1–3 as well:

> If a man sends away his wife
> and she goes from him
> And belongs to another man,
> will he return to her again?
> Will not that land
> be utterly polluted [ḥānôp teḥĕnap]?
> But you have been a harlot with many companions,
> yet you return to me? says YHWH.
> Raise your eyes to the open spaces, and see:
> Where have you not been ravished?
> Beside pathways you have lingered for them
> like an Arab in the desert.
> So you have polluted [wattaḥănîpî] the earth ['ereṣ]
> with your harlotry and your wickedness [ûbĕrā'ātēk].
> And so the showers have been withheld [wayyimmānĕ'û],[191]
> and the spring rain has not fallen.
> But you have the forehead of a harlot:
> you refuse to be ashamed.[192]

The pollution of the earth is manifest as lack of rain in this passage. In Jer 23:10, too, the drying up of the earth triggered by the adultery of its inhabitants can be seen as a sign of pollution, an association that is strengthened by the condemnation of the religious leaders of Judah as profane (ḥānēpû), or, literally, "polluted," in 23:11.

---

[190] See esp. Deut 24:1–4 and Lev 18:24–30. See, further, the discussion of the theme of pollution in Hos 4:1–3, above.

[191] Or "have held themselves back."

[192] See also Jer 3:8–9.

MOURNING AS STRIPPING

The motif of mourning as stripping is not developed here beyond the image of shrivelled pastures bereft of vegetation in 23:10.

SUMMARY OF LITERARY TECHNIQUES

In this passage the dual meaning of *ḥānēp*, "to be polluted" and "to be ungodly," creates an association between the withering of the earth and the corruption of prophet and priest as well as the adultery of the people. The formal and phonological similarities of the first two cola of 23:10a also tie the pervasive adultery cited in the first colon to the mourning and drying up of the earth in the second and third. The personification of the earth is represented only in the pairing of *ʾābal*, "to mourn," with *hāʾāreṣ*, "the earth."

OVERALL EFFECT OF THE METAPHOR

The metaphor of the earth mourning in Jer 23:9–12 illustrates the impact of the acts of the inhabitants of Judah on the earth through a curse that desiccates it. The full elaboration of such a curse in passages such as Deut 28:22–24 and 29:18–24 suggests that in Jer 23:10 the people themselves bring on the death of their existence. They cannot live indefinitely on a land that continues to mourn and dry up; hence their course is "evil" (*rāʿâ*) in two ways: it is both morally and literally no good.

The two cola that describe the mourning earth in this passage thus capture in a single image the essence of the exile to come, when the people of Judah will leave the land altogether and YHWH will bring evil (*rāʿâ*) upon them "in the year of their punishment" (23:12). The mourning of the earth in this passage both reflects the corruption of its inhabitants and foreshadows their final devastation.

5
ISAIAH

ISAIAH 24:1–20

TEXT, TRANSLATION, AND TEXTUAL NOTES

1   הִנֵּה יְהוָה בּוֹקֵק הָאָרֶץ וּבוֹלְקָהּ   וְעִוָּה פָנֶיהָ וְהֵפִיץ יֹשְׁבֶיהָ׃

2   וְהָיָה כָעָם כַּכֹּהֵן   כַּעֶבֶד כַּאדֹנָיו   כַּשִּׁפְחָה כַּגְּבִרְתָּהּ

    כַּקּוֹנֶה כַּמּוֹכֵר   כַּמַּלְוֶה כַּלֹּוֶה   כַּנֹּשֶׁה כַּאֲשֶׁר נֹשֶׁא בוֹ׃

3   הִבּוֹק ׀ תִּבּוֹק הָאָרֶץ   וְהִבּוֹז ׀ תִּבּוֹז

     כִּי יְהוָה דִּבֶּר אֶת־הַדָּבָר הַזֶּה׃

4   אָבְלָה נָבְלָה הָאָרֶץ   אֻמְלְלָה נָבְלָה תֵּבֵל   אֻמְלָלוּ מְרוֹם עַם־הָאָרֶץ׃

5   וְהָאָרֶץ חָנְפָה תַּחַת יֹשְׁבֶיהָ   כִּי־עָבְרוּ תוֹרֹת חָלְפוּ חֹק

     הֵפֵרוּ בְּרִית עוֹלָם׃

6   עַל־כֵּן אָלָה אָכְלָה אֶרֶץ   וַיֶּאְשְׁמוּ יֹשְׁבֵי בָהּ

    עַל־כֵּן חָרוּ יֹשְׁבֵי אֶרֶץ   וְנִשְׁאַר אֱנוֹשׁ מִזְעָר׃

7   אָבַל תִּירוֹשׁ אֻמְלְלָה־גָּפֶן   נֶאֶנְחוּ כָּל־שִׂמְחֵי־לֵב׃

8   שָׁבַת מְשׂוֹשׂ תֻּפִּים   חָדַל שְׁאוֹן עַלִּיזִים   שָׁבַת מְשׂוֹשׂ כִּנּוֹר׃

9   בַּשִּׁיר לֹא יִשְׁתּוּ־יָיִן   יֵמַר שֵׁכָר לְשֹׁתָיו׃

10   נִשְׁבְּרָה קִרְיַת־תֹּהוּ   סֻגַּר כָּל־בַּיִת מִבּוֹא׃

11   צְוָחָה עַל־הַיַּיִן בַּחוּצוֹת   עָרְבָה כָּל־שִׂמְחָה   גָּלָה מְשׂוֹשׂ הָאָרֶץ׃

12   נִשְׁאַר בָּעִיר שַׁמָּה   וּשְׁאִיָּה יֻכַּת־שָׁעַר׃

13   כִּי כֹה יִהְיֶה בְּקֶרֶב הָאָרֶץ   בְּתוֹךְ הָעַמִּים

     כְּנֹקֶף זַיִת   כְּעוֹלֵלֹת אִם־כָּלָה בָצִיר׃

14   הֵמָּה יִשְׂאוּ קוֹלָם יָרֹנּוּ בִּגְאוֹן יְהוָה צָהֲלוּ מִיָּם׃   15   עַל־כֵּן

     בָּאֻרִים כַּבְּדוּ יְהוָה בְּאִיֵּי הַיָּם שֵׁם יְהוָה אֱלֹהֵי יִשְׂרָאֵל׃

16 מִכְּנַ֨ף הָאָ֜רֶץ זְמִרֹ֤ת שָׁמַ֙עְנוּ֙ צְבִ֣י לַצַּדִּ֔יק וָאֹמַ֛ר רָזִי־לִ֥י רָֽזִי־לִ֖י
אֹ֣וי לִ֑י בֹּגְדִ֤ים בָּגָ֙דוּ֙ וּבֶ֥גֶד בֹּוגְדִ֖ים בָּגָֽדוּ׃

17 פַּ֥חַד וָפַ֖חַת וָפָ֑ח   עָלֶ֖יךָ יֹושֵׁ֥ב הָאָֽרֶץ׃

18 וְֽ֠הָיָה הַנָּ֞ס מִקֹּ֤ול הַפַּ֙חַד֙   יִפֹּ֣ל אֶל־הַפַּ֔חַת
וְהָֽעֹולֶה֙ מִתֹּ֣וךְ הַפַּ֔חַת   יִלָּכֵ֖ד בַּפָּ֑ח
כִּֽי־אֲרֻבֹּ֤ות מִמָּרֹום֙ נִפְתָּ֔חוּ   וַֽיִּרְעֲשׁ֖וּ מֹ֥וסְדֵי אָֽרֶץ׃

19 רֹ֥עָה הִֽתְרֹעֲעָ֖ה הָאָ֑רֶץ   פֹּ֤ור הִֽתְפֹּורְרָה֙ אֶ֔רֶץ   מֹ֥וט הִֽתְמֹוטְטָ֖ה אָֽרֶץ׃

20 נֹ֣ועַ תָּנֹ֤ועַ אֶ֙רֶץ֙ כַּשִּׁכֹּ֔ור   וְהִֽתְנֹודְדָ֖ה כַּמְּלוּנָ֑ה
וְכָבַ֤ד עָלֶ֙יהָ֙ פִּשְׁעָ֔הּ   וְנָפְלָ֖ה וְלֹא־תֹסִ֥יף קֽוּם׃ ס

1 Behold YHWH is about to empty out the earth and lay it waste,
   and twist its surface and scatter its inhabitants.
2 And as the people, so will the priest be;
   as the servant, so his master,
   as the maidservant, so her mistress,
As the buyer, so the seller,
   as the lender, so the borrower,
   as the creditor, so the debtor.
3 The earth will be utterly emptied
   and utterly plundered,
For YHWH has spoken this word.

4 The earth mourns, wilts;
   the world languishes, wilts;
   ᵃthe height of heaven languishes with the earth.ᵃ
5 And the earth lies polluted under its inhabitants,
   for they have transgressed the laws, overstepped the decree,
   broken the eternal covenant.
6 And so a curse devours the earth,
   and its inhabitants bear their guilt.
And so the inhabitants of the earth ᵇhave dwindled,ᵇ
   and few are left.
7 The new wine mourns, the vine languishes,
   all the glad of heart sigh.
8 The joy of the timbrel has ceased,
   the noise of the jubilant has died down,
   the joy of the lyre has ceased.
9 They do not drink wine with singing;
   beer tastes bitter to those who drink it.

10 The empty city is broken,
    every house is shut up so none can enter.
11 There is an outcry for wine in the streets;
    all gladness has ᶜpassed on,ᶜ
    the joy of the earth has gone into exile.
12 Desolation is left in the city,
    and the gate is beaten to a ruin.
13 For thus it will be in the midst of the earth,
    among the peoples,
  Like the beating of the olive tree,
    like the gleaning when the vintage is complete.

14 They lift up their voices, they sing for joy; over the exaltation of YHWH they cry out from the west. 15 And so ᵈin the coastlandsᵈ give glory to YHWH, in the coastlands of the west, to the name of YHWH, God of Israel. 16 From the end of the earth we have heard songs, "Glory to the righteous one!" But I say, "ᵉLeanness to me! Leanness to me!ᵉ Woe to me! The treacherous have dealt treacherously, and with treachery the treacherous have dealt treacherously."

17 Dread and the pit and the trap
    are upon you, O inhabitant of the earth!
18 And the one who flees from the sound of the terror
    will fall into the pit,
  And the one who climbs up from the midst of the pit
    will be seized by the trap.
  For the ᶠwindows of the heightᶠ are opened,
    and the foundations of the earth quake.
19 The earth ᵍbreaks into piecesᵍ,
    the earth splits apart,
    the earth shakes violently.
20 The earth staggers like a drunkard
    and sways like a shack.
  And heavy upon it is its transgression,
    and it falls and cannot rise again.

a–a Read *'umlal mārôm 'im-hā'āreṣ* for *'umlālû mĕrôm 'am-hā'āreṣ*, "the lofty of the earth languish" (MT);[1] so *BHS*. LXX (ἐπένθησαν οἱ ὑπσηλοὶ

---

[1] Hans Wildberger (*Jesaja 13–27* [BKAT 10/2; Neukirchen-Vluyn: Neukirchener Verlag, 1978], 914) reads MT's consonantal text differently; he revocalizes *mĕrôm* as *mārôm* and takes it as an adverbial accusative: "In the height the people of the earth languish."

τῆς γῆς, "the exalted ones of the earth mourn") and Vulg. (*infirmata est altitudo populi terrae*, "the height of the people of the earth has become weak") reflect MT, although Vulg. may be reading a singular verb. Syriac reads *ʾlʾ rwmh dʾrʿ*, "the height of the earth laments," perhaps in an attempt to simplify MT. A reference to the "lofty" among the people of the earth seems out of place in the context of the following verses (24:5–6), which refer to the inhabitants of the earth as a whole, as well as in the context of 24:2, in which all classes of people are assigned the same fate. The word *mārôm* recurs with the meaning "height of heaven" or "sky" in 24:18, in tandem with references to *ʾereṣ*, "earth," in 24:19. Earth, the world, and the heavenly heights form a natural group in 24:4; the related pair earth (*ʾereṣ*) and sky (*šāmayim*) occurs in a similar context in Jer 4:28, where both mourn the devastation of Judah.[2] The vocalization of the consonantal text as *mĕrôm ʿam-hāʾāreṣ*, "the lofty of the earth" (MT), may have been influenced by Isa 26:5 (*kî hēšaḥ yōšĕbê mārôm*, "for he has brought low the inhabitants of the height") and other Isaian passages that stress judgment upon the arrogant and lofty.[3] This reading could have prompted a subsequent adjustment of the verb *ʾumlal* to the plural form *ʾumlĕlû*.

b–b The verb *ḥārû* is interpreted as derived from a hypothetical hollow root *ḥwr* and assigned the meaning "decrease, diminish," on the basis of Arabic *ḥāra*.[4] 1QIsaᵃ reads *ḥāwĕrû*, "grow pale" (cf. Isa 29:22); LXX, πτωχοὶ ἔσονται, "will become poor."

c–c The verb *ʿārĕbâ* is translated here on the basis of an Arabic cognate *ġariba*, "go away, depart, absent oneself";[5] it is also possible to assume metathesis of *bêt* and *rêš* and read *ʿābĕrâ*, with essentially the same meaning: "has passed on."[6] LXX has a bicolon in 24:11 rather than a tricolon and reads the last two cola of MT as πέπαυται πᾶσα εὐφροσύνη τῆς γῆς, "all

---

[2] Ronald E. Clements (*Isaiah 1–39* [NCB; Grand Rapids, Mich.: Eerdmans, 1987], 201) and George B. Gray (*A Critical and Exegetical Commentary on the Book of Isaiah* [ICC; New York: Charles Scribner's, 1912], 410–11) argue that the heavens are not caught up in the world judgment described in Isa 24 and discount the figurative aspect of the merism "earth and sky." Otto Kaiser (*Isaiah 1–39* [OTL; Philadelphia: Westminster, 1974], 183) finds a literal meaning in the languishing of the heavens: the drought that besets the earth is seen as affecting the heavens, the source of rain, as well.

[3] See, e.g., Isa 2:12 and 13:11. Isaiah 26:5 is, of course, part of the same larger unit as 24:4 (Isa 24–27, the Isaiah Apocalypse).

[4] See Hans Wehr, *A Dictionary of Modern Written Arabic* (ed. J. Milton Cowan; 3d ed.; Ithaca, N.Y.: Spoken Language Series, 1976), 212b.

[5] Ibid., 668a.

[6] So Wildberger, *Jesaja 13–27*, 915.

the joy of the earth has ceased," which looks like a conflation. The verb πέπαυται, "has ceased," could reflect either ʿārĕbâ, with the meaning suggested above, or ʿābĕrâ.[7] Syriac reads the last two cola *bṭlt klh ḥdwtʾ wʿbr dyṣḥ dʾrʿ*, "all gladness has ceased, and the joy of the earth has passed away." Here *bṭlt*, "has ceased," may be a reading of ʿābĕrâ, "has passed away," in MT even though *wʿbr* follows in Syr.; see 24:4, where *ʾlt* corresponds to ʾābĕlâ in MT and *wytb bʾblʾ* to nābĕlâ. Vulgate reads *deserta est omnis laetitia*, "all joy has been abandoned," which could also reflect a reading of either ʿārĕbâ or ʿābĕrâ, since a passive construction recurs in the following phrase: *translatum est gaudium terrae*, "the joy of the earth has been carried away."

d–d Read bĕʾîyîm for bāʾūrîm (MT), often translated "in the east." There is no corresponding word or phrase in LXX or Syr.; Vulg. reads *in doctrinis*, "according to the teaching," which reflects Hebrew ʾûrîm, one of the objects used in giving oracles. The word ʾūrîm is a *hapax legomenon*, and the translation "east" is uncertain.[8] The phrase bĕʾîyê hayyām, "the coastlands of the sea," occurs later in 24:15 and in Isa 11:11; the word ʾîyîm, "coastlands," appears frequently in Second and Third Isaiah (see BDB, 16a). A broad resemblance between *yôd* and *rêš* could explain the reading ʾūrîm in MT.[9]

e–e The literal translation "Leanness to me! Leanness to me!" shows the contrasting parallelism between this phrase and ṣĕbî laṣṣaddîq, "Glory to the righteous one!" which precedes it. Syriac (*rʾz ly rʾz ly*, "it is a mystery to me, it is a mystery to me") and Vulg. (*secretum meum mihi, secretum meum mihi*, "my secret is mine, my secret is mine") have interpreted rozî in MT as the noun rāz, "mystery," with a first singular suffix. This noun occurs in Sir 8:18, and its Aramaic counterpart rāzâ/rāzāʾ, in Dan 2.[10] LXX lacks a corresponding phrase, although Symmachus, Theodotion, and the

---

[7] Theodotion adds απεσχισθη χαρα, "joy will be taken away." This reading may reflect the last colon of MT, since απεσχισθη could stand for gālâ, "has gone into exile." On the use of the verb ἀποσχίζω to represent the separation of a tribe, see LSJ, 221b. Wildberger (*Jesaja 13–27*, 915) and others read with LXX, emending MT to ʿābĕrâ.

[8] Kaiser (*Isaiah 1–39*, 186), citing Marcus Jastrow, notes the use of the noun ʾôr, "light," with the meaning "daybreak" in talmudic literature. Yet according to Jastrow (*A Dictionary of the Targumim, the Talmud Babli and Yerushalmi, and the Midrashic Literature* [New York: Judaica, 1971], 32b), ʾôr can also mean "sunset, twilight, evening."

[9] See, e.g., the examples in Frank M. Cross, "The Development of the Jewish Scripts," in *The Bible and the Ancient Near East: Essays in Honor of William Foxwell Albright* (ed. G. Ernest Wright; Garden City, N.Y.: Doubleday, 1965), 149.

[10] See Dan 2:18–19, 27–30; cf. KBL, 1123b.

Syrohexaplaric text interpret *rozî* as "my mystery." The noun *rozî* is a *hapax legomenon* but is related to the root *rzh,* "to be lean" (Zeph 2:11; Isa 17:4), and the adjective *rāzeh,* "lean" (Num 13:20; Ezek 34:20).[11] Gray argues that the expected vocalization of a noun from a third-*hê* root would be *rĕzî,*[12] but *rozî* conforms to the pattern of a *qutl* noun that conveys an abstract quality, in this case "leanness."

f–f Read *ʾărubbôt mārôm* for *ʾărubbôt mimmārôm* (MT). Either a dittography has occurred, or the initial *mêm* in *mimmārôm* represents an enclitic *mêm* that was once attached to *ʾărubbôt,* here in a construct state.

g–g Read *rōaʿ hitrōʿăʿâ* for *rōʿâ hitrōʿăʿâ* (MT); the form *rōʿâ* probably resulted through dittography of the initial *hê* of the following *hitpaʿel* form. 1QIsa^b and one Hebrew MS read the first form as *rôaʿ* (see *BHS*).

DELIMITATION OF THE PASSAGE

Although discrete sections are evident within Isa 24:1–20, this passage may be considered as an integrated composition united by the theme of world judgment. The introductory *hinnēh* in 24:1 marks the beginning of a new section; the focus of this oracle on the earth as a whole sets it apart from the oracles against the nations that precede it (Isa 13–23).[13] The last colon of 24:20 sounds a final note: "and it [the earth] falls and cannot rise again." At the same time the phrase *wĕhāyâ bayyôm hahûʾ,* "and on that day," which begins 24:21, indicates a new oracle.[14] The following verses concern the punishment of the "host of heaven" along with the "kings of the earth" and hence differ in content from 24:1–20, which focus on the earth and its inhabitants.[15]

The verses within 24:1–20 that stand out most distinctly from the rest are 24:14–16.[16] In terms of form, these verses are difficult to arrange in

---

[11] See BDB, 981a.

[12] Gray, *Critical and Exegetical Commentary,* 419.

[13] That the judgment described in Isa 24:1–20 befalls the whole earth is suggested in part by the lack of any proper name associated with the devastation; see further the discussion below.

[14] See Jacques Vermeylen, *Du Prophète Isaïe à l'apocalyptique* (2 vols; EBib; Paris: Gabalda, 1977), 1:352, 360; Otto Plöger, *Theocracy and Eschatology* (Oxford: Basil Blackwell, 1968), 58.

[15] These verses may be a later addition to Isa 24. On the phrase "on that day" as indicative of redactional insertion, see Joseph Blenkinsopp, *A History of Prophecy in Israel* (rev. ed.; Louisville: Westminster John Knox, 1996), 233–34.

[16] So Gray, *Critical and Exegetical Commentary,* 414–19; and Wilhelm Rudolph, *Jesaja 24–27* (BWANT 4/10; Stuttgart: Kohlhammer, 1933), 31–32. Other commentators define this section as comprising either 24:14–16a or 24:14–18a. In support

poetic lines and read more like poetic prose than poetry.[17] They relate the raising up of joyful songs of praise to YHWH from far away (24:14–16aα), followed by a negative response on the part of the narrator (24:16aβ–16b), who appears to be the speaker of 24:1–20 as a whole. The jubilant tone of 24:14–16aα jars with the account of disaster that precedes these verses. The echoing of the phrase *ṣĕbî laṣṣaddîq*, "Glory to the righteous one!" in 24:16aα by the phrase *rozî-lî*, "Leanness to me!" in 24:16aβ, however, formally links the lines of praise to the negative response. The change of tone in 24:14–16aα thus does not effect a breaking off of the passage as a whole, and in 24:17–20 the description of impending judgment continues.[18] Isaiah 24:14–16, then, can be heard as an interlude that strengthens the sense of inexorable judgment by providing a contrasting voice, after which the theme of catastrophe is resumed with greater intensity.[19]

---

of the former unit are Wildberger, *Jesaja 13–27*, 904, 931, 933; Rémi Lack, *La Symbolique du Livre d'Isaïe: Essai sur l'image littéraire comme élément de structuration* (AnBib 59; Rome: Pontifical Biblical Institute, 1973), 68–69; and Kaiser, *Isaiah 1–39*, 185–86, 189. In support of the latter unit are Plöger, *Theocracy and Eschatology*, 57; and Vermeylen, *Du Prophète Isaïe à l'apocalyptique*, 1:352, 356–60.

[17] See Gray (*Critical and Exegetical Commentary*, 415) on the irregularity of the meter and parallelism in 24:14–16 and the resemblance of this section (especially its latter half) to prose. It should also be noted that 24:13, 17, and 18a show similar irregularities.

[18] Vermeylen (*Du Prophète Isaïe à l'apocalyptique*, 1:353 n. 1) points out phraseological and syntactic parallels between 24:1–13 and 24:18b–20 that connect these two sections. These include the noun *mārôm*, "height of heaven" (24:4, 18); the verbs *hēpēr*, "to break" (24:5), and *hitpôrēr*, "to split" (24:19); the coupling of the infinitive absolute with a finite verb of the same root (24:3, 19, 20); and the marked repetition of the word *'ereṣ*, "earth" (24:1–6, 18b–20), which binds the entire composition together. In addition to these parallels, the overstepping of legal boundaries in 24:5 corresponds to the *peša'*, "transgression," mentioned in 24:20. On the resumption of the themes begun in 24:1–13 in the concluding section of the composition, see also Kaiser, *Isaiah 1–39*, 189; Gray, *Critical and Exegetical Commentary*, 419; Rudolph, *Jesaja 24–27*, 33; Wildberger, *Jesaja 13–27*, 898, 933.

[19] So Wildberger (*Jesaja 13–27*, 933–34), who interprets the songs of praise in 24:14–16a as an inappropriate response to the prospect of world judgment by the Israelites, who do not realize that they, too, are subject to judgment. See also Paul Auvray, *Isaïe 1–39* (SB; Paris: Gabalda, 1972), 227. Clements (*Isaiah 1–39*, 203–4) notes the stress on judgment in 24:16aβ–16b but interprets 24:14–16a as a hymnic affirmation by the nations of the glory of this judgment. It should be noted that although 24:14–16 are taken as an integral part of 24:1–20 in the discussion below, they are tangential to the question of the role of the earth in this passage and are not examined at length.

Isaiah 24:1–20 as a whole may be divided into four connected sections: an introductory announcement of coming devastation (24:1–3); the elaboration of this announcement with a sequence of different motifs (24:4–13); a contrasting report of rejoicing followed by a comment from the narrator (24:14–16); and a conclusion reiterating and intensifying the initial announcement of judgment (24:17–20). Other interpreters divide these verses differently, but most affirm that the individual units within 24:1–20 have been integrated into an overall unity.[20]

AUTHORSHIP AND DATING

Both Isa 24:1–20 and the longer composition Isa 24–27 (the Isaiah Apocalypse), of which it forms the introduction, are difficult to date with precision because they lack explicit historical references. A number of the literary features of Isa 24–27 may, however, be seen as characteristic of late prophetic literature.[21] These include the paucity of historical references, the eschatological focus on final judgment and ultimate restoration, the persistence of cosmic and mythological imagery and language,[22] and the prevalence of apparent allusions to previous prophetic collections.[23]

----

[20] See, e.g., Wildberger, *Jesaja 13–27*, 904, 925–29; Vermeylen, *Du Prophète Isaïe à l'apocalyptique*, 1:353–54; Rudolph, *Jesaja 24–27*, 29, 32–33; Plöger, *Theocracy and Eschatology*, 56–57.

[21] On the characteristics of late prophecy in Israel, see, e.g., David L. Petersen, *Late Israelite Prophecy: Studies in Deutero-Prophetic Literature and in Chronicles* (SBLMS 23; Chico, Calif.: Scholars Press, 1977), 14–15; Ronald E. Clements, "Patterns in the Prophetic Canon," in *Canon and Authority* (ed. George W. Coats and Burke O. Long; Philadelphia: Fortress, 1977), 54; idem, "Prophecy As Literature: A Re-appraisal," in *The Hermeneutical Quest: Essays in Honor of James Luther Mays on His Sixty-Fifth Birthday* (ed. D. G. Miller; Allison Park, Pa.: Pickwick, 1986), 73; and Blenkinsopp, *History of Prophecy*, 226–39.

[22] For a summation of such motifs in Isa 24–27, see Collins, "Old Testament Apocalypticism and Eschatology," *NJBC*, 302; and Wildberger, *Jesaja 13–27*, 909. On the relation of mythological *topoi* to late prophecy, see William R. Millar, *Isaiah 24–27 and the Origin of Apocalyptic* (HSM 11; Missoula, Mont.: Scholars Press, 1976), 118–19; and Frank M. Cross, *Canaanite Myth and Hebrew Epic* (Cambridge, Mass.: Harvard University Press, 1973), 345.

[23] Within Isa 24:1–20, see Isa 24:2 and Hos 4:9; Isa 24:6 and Jer 23:10; Isa 24:7–9 and 16:8–10; Isa 24:8–9 and Ezek 26:13; Isa 24:13 and 17:6 (cf. Mic 7:1); Isa 24:14–15 and 42:10–12; Isa 24:16 and 21:2 (cf. Jer 12:1); Isa 24:17–18a and Jer 48:43–44; Isa 24:18b and Gen 7:11; Isa 24:20 and Amos 5:2. Note also the similarities between Isa 24:5 and 33:8, and 24:16b and 33:1. The parallels between Isa 24:4 and the passages considered in this study are evident. The distinction between textual allusions and traditional phraseology is often blurry, but it is significant that

The elaborate style of Isa 24:1–20, which distinguishes it from many of the passages examined in this study, may also indicate a later date, as complexity of style is often associated with composition in writing.[24] The marks of this style in Isa 24:1–20 include the extended development of imagery as opposed to the brief reference[25] and the concentration of literary devices such as alliteration, assonance, paronomasia, rhyme, and repetition.

There are a few specific verbal hints of a late date for Isa 24:1–20. The reference to a *bĕrît ʿôlām,* "eternal covenant," in 24:5 suggests the concept and terminology of covenant that is a key element of the Priestly

---

here a number of the parallels are almost literal citations of one other passage. The density of such allusions within the text of Isa 24:1–20 is also significant. On the growth of innerbiblical exegesis in postexilic prophecy, see Brevard S. Childs, *Introduction to the Old Testament As Scripture* (Philadelphia: Fortress, 1979), 65. Kaiser (*Isaiah 1–39,* 177) makes this feature a key element in his dating of the earliest version of the Isaiah Apocalypse to the fourth century. For a full discussion of the literary citations in Isa 24–27, see Marvin A. Sweeney, "Textual Citations in Isaiah 24–27: Toward an Understanding of the Redactional Function of Chapters 24–27 in the Book of Isaiah," *JBL* 107 (1988): 39–52. See also the lists in Wildberger, *Jesaja 13–27,* 910; and Vermeylen, *Du Prophète Isaïe à l'apocalyptique,* 1:356.

[24] On the relation of the use of writing to compositional style, see Albert B. Lord (*The Singer of Tales* [Harvard Studies in Comparative Literature 24; Cambridge, Mass.: Harvard University Press, 1960], 128–32), who concludes that works composed primarily in writing are often more elaborate and polished than those composed orally. See also the observation of Jack Goody (*The Interface between the Written and the Oral* [Cambridge: Cambridge University Press, 1987], 95) that compositions oriented to the written word are simultaneously more elaborate, or longer, and more deliberate, or "tighter." For further discussion of the influence of writing on composition, see Ellen F. Davis, *Swallowing the Scroll: Textuality and the Dynamics of Discourse in Ezekiel's Prophecy* (Bible and Literature 21; Sheffield: Almond, 1989), 30–37. She cites Margaret Rader's comment on the tendency of written language toward "syntactic complexity and lexical elaboration" and notes that writing "elicits more writing; it invites amplification, exegesis, commentary" as well as promoting "greater sensitivity to words and their usage, to various possibilities for the flow of speech." Many commentators have noted the distinct style of Isa 24:1–20: see, e.g., Wildberger (*Jesaja 13–27,* 916), whom it strikes as occasionally "artificial" ["gekünselt"]; Gray, *Critical and Exegetical Commentary,* 401, 464–65; and Millar, *Isaiah 24–27,* 103–4, 117–19. On the basis of language and style alone Gray would date Isa 24–27 to around 400 B.C.E. Millar sees a close affinity between the style of Isa 24 and that of Second Isaiah and dates the former in the exilic period.

[25] See, e.g., the extension of the theme of mourning and languishing throughout the sequence of motifs in Isa 24:4–13.

writings,[26] especially in the context of the image of the opening up of the *ʾărubbôt*, "windows," of heaven in 24:18. This phrase is reminiscent of the Priestly account of the flood.[27] Both the concept and terminology of the "eternal covenant" may predate the Priestly composition in Gen 1–11,[28] but the term *bĕrît ʿôlām* appears in prophetic contexts for the most part in works generally considered to be exilic or postexilic.[29] Wildberger also points to the word *tôrōt*, "laws," in 24:5. The plural of *tôrâ* occurs elsewhere in the prophetic literature only in Ezek 43 and 44.[30]

The placement of Isa 24–27 within the book of Isaiah as a kind of finale to the oracles against the foreign nations (Isa 13–23) does not prove, yet is consistent with, a late dating for the Isaiah Apocalypse. Clearly some of the oracles against the nations are post-Isaianic, notably the introductory oracles against Babylon (Isa 13 and 14:1–23). The Isaiah Apocalypse takes the oracles in this collection a step further into an expanded vision of both profound desolation and fundamental reordering and restoration.[31]

For these reasons, among others, most commentators date Isa 24–27 as a whole, and 24:1–20 in particular, to the postexilic period. One exception is the study of Dan G. Johnson on Isa 24–27.[32] Johnson claims to

---

[26] See e.g., Gen 9:16; 17:7, 13, 19; Exod 31:16; Lev 24:8; Num 18:19. Wildberger (*Jesaja 13–27*, 922) notes that the phrase *bĕrît ʿôlām* is also used of the Davidic covenant in 2 Sam 23:5 and Isa 55:3, but such a reference does not fit as well the context of Isa 24:5. See further the discussion below.

[27] The phrase *ʾărubbōt haššāmayim*, "windows of the heavens," occurs in Gen 7:11 and 8:2. It is possible that P has taken over preexisting phraseology; note the poetic form of Gen 7:11, which may indicate an old poetic bicolon.

[28] See the discussion in Wildberger, *Jesaja 13–27*, 910–11.

[29] This term occurs in Jer 32:40; 50:5; Ezek 16:60; 37:26; Isa 55:3; 61:8. On Jer 32:40, see William L. Holladay, *Jeremiah 2* (Hermeneia; Philadelphia: Fortress, 1989), 208; on Ezek 16:60, see Walther Zimmerli, *Ezekiel 1* (Hermeneia; Philadelphia: Fortress, 1983), 349, 352–53; and Joseph Blenkinsopp, *Ezekiel* (IBC; Louisville: John Knox, 1990), 79.

[30] Ezek 43:11; 44:5, 24; see also Neh 9:13 and Dan 9:10. Wildberger (*Jesaja 13–27*, 922) argues that few, if any, of the other passages in which *tôrōt* (or *tôrôt*) occurs (Exod 16:28; 18:20; Lev 26:46; Gen 26:5; Ps 105:45) can be considered preexilic. Note, however, that LXX and Syr. have read *tôrōtāy*, "my laws," for *tôrātî*, "my law" (MT) in Hos 8:12; so *BHS*. Cf. BDB, 914a.

[31] Clements, *Isaiah 1–39*, 197; Wildberger, *Jesaja 13–27*, 892–93; Plöger, *Theocracy and Eschatology*, 53–54; Peter R. Ackroyd, "The Book of Isaiah," in *The Interpreter's One-Volume Commentary on the Bible* (ed. Charles M. Laymon; Nashville: Abingdon, 1971), 331.

[32] *From Chaos to Restoration: An Integrative Reading of Isaiah 24–27* (JSOTSup 61; Sheffield: Sheffield Academic Press, 1988).

discern a number of allusions to Jerusalem or to Judah (or Israel) within 24:1–20, and he interprets the passage as a late preexilic prophecy about the imminent destruction of Jerusalem by the Babylonians in 587 B.C.E. None of the allusions he cites is explicit, however, and he concedes that some of them are ambiguous.[33] Many of his arguments for the central role of Judah or Jerusalem in this passage rest on the fact that similar vocabulary is used to portray the judgment against Israel in earlier prophetic passages. Yet neither the recurrence of motifs and phraseology nor actual textual citations need imply precisely the same context in each instance. Motifs such as the cessation of joy and of mourning over the ruined vine, which occur in Isa 24:7–9, are found in the oracle against Moab, a foreign nation, in Isa 16:8–11 as well as in the oracle against Israel in Hos 2:13–14. The yoking of the verbs *ʾābal*, "to mourn," and *ʾumlal*, "to languish," found in Isa 24:4, 7, occurs not only in the oracle against Israel in Hos 4:3 and in the lament of Judah in Jer 14:2, but also in the oracle against Egypt in Isa 19:8.[34]

It seems more likely that in Isa 24:1–20 motifs, images, vocabulary, and phraseology associated with divine judgment against Judah or other nations in previous prophetic speeches are used to describe a judgment of wider proportions. In the light of Isa 24–27 as a whole, it is no longer just Judah, the dwelling place of God's people, nor Babylon, the world power whose defeat stirs heaven and earth in Isa 13, that must face judgment, but all who set themselves above or apart from the will of Yahweh.[35] At the

---

[33] E.g., *měśôś hāʾāreṣ*, "the joy of the earth," in 24:11 and *běqereb hāʾāreṣ*, "in the midst of the earth," in 24:13 (ibid., 30–33).

[34] Sweeney ("Textual Citations in Isaiah 24–27," 50) concludes that the use of texts from First Isaiah by the authors of Isa 24–27 shows that they "did not necessarily employ them according to their meanings in their prior Isaianic contexts." On the occurrence of traditional motifs and images in new contexts in Isa 24–27, see Clements, *Isaiah 1–39*, 198–99; Wildberger, *Jesaja 13–27*, 929–30; and Plöger, *Theocracy and Eschatology*, 59.

[35] See, e.g., 26:7–21. On the universal scope of Isa 24–27 as a whole and of 24:1–20 in particular, see, among others, Wildberger, *Jesaja 13–27*, 892–93, 929–30; Clements, *Isaiah 1–39*, 196–99, 200; Plöger, *Theocracy and Eschatology*, 53–59; Vermeylen, *Du Prophète Isaïe à l'apocalyptique*, 1:352–56; Gray, *Critical and Exegetical Commentary*, 397; Kaiser, *Isaiah 1–39*, 173; Rudolph, *Jesaja 24–27*, 27; Sweeney, "Textual Citations in Isaiah 24–27," 39–52. Christopher R. Seitz (*Isaiah 1–39* [IBC; Louisville: John Knox, 1993], 175–79) acknowledges the perspective of world judgment in Isa 24–27 but, in light of the parallels between these chapters and the oracles against Babylon in Isa 13 and 14, considers Babylon both the immediate agent of judgment and the future object of judgment in Isa 24. He thus dates Isa 24–27 to the exilic period, before the fall of Babylon. Against this view it

same time, echoes of the desolation of Jerusalem and Judah (Israel) in Isa 24:1–20 recall the special significance of the community of Israel.

The postexilic dating of Isa 24–27 encompasses a wide range of proposals for more specific settings, from the early postexilic period to late Maccabean times.[36] Wildberger presents a convincing case, on the basis of word usage, the nature of the eschatological motifs, and the allusions to other biblical texts in Isa 24, for dating the first stage of composition to the early postexilic period (fifth century).[37]

That Wildberger and others discern stages of growth within Isa 24:1–20 is not of major concern in this study. Fine distinctions of dating are almost impossible to determine in this passage, and it can easily be read as an integrated unit, despite the possibility of an extended period of composition.[38] Isaiah 24:14–16 stand out from the surrounding text, and they are held by some commentators to represent a later addition. Yet these verses can be read in terms of the portrayal of judgment in the preceding and following verses, and they add force to the thrust of the passage as a whole.[39] Although some consider 24:7–13 either an addition or an independent unit,[40] these verses fit almost seamlessly into the context of the devastation of the earth established in 24:1–6. Inconsistencies between the imagery of

should be noted that the closest parallels to Isa 24:1–20 in Isa 13 and 14 occur in Isa 13:9–16 and that these verses are considered by Clements (*Isaiah 1–39*, 135) to be a later eschatological reinterpretation. Further, the imagery of world judgment in Isa 13–14 and 24–27 is not necessarily evidence of the same historical setting (there is, e.g., similar imagery in Jer 4:23–28 and Isa 18:3).

[36] For a dating in the Maccabean period, see Bernhard Duhm, *Das Buch Jesaia* (HAT 3/1; Göttingen: Vandenhoeck & Ruprecht, 1902), 143–44.

[37] *Jesaja 13–27*, 911. Wildberger includes Isa 24:1–6, 14–20 in this earliest stage of composition and concludes that Isa 24–27 developed over time between 500 and 300 B.C.E. Rudolph (*Jesaja 24–27*, 61–63) and Kaiser (*Isaiah 1–39*, 178–79) also presume an ongoing process of composition but date the earliest stage (to which they assign much of Isa 24:1–20) to the fourth century.

[38] On this approach to reading Isa 24–27, see also Wildberger, *Jesaja 13–27*, 896–97; and Plöger, *Theocracy and Eschatology*, 56–57.

[39] Kaiser (*Isaiah 1–39*, 178) and Vermeylen (*Du Prophète Isaïe à l'apocalyptique*, 1:356) consider these verses as part of a secondary stage of composition; Wildberger (*Jesaja 13–27*, 898) does not; Rudolph (*Jesaja 24–27*, 32) sees them as secondary but not necessarily by a different author.

[40] Wildberger (*Jesaja 13–27*, 904, 925–29) considers 24:7–9, 10–12, and 13 as separate additions; Rudolph (*Jesaja 24–27*, 32) suggests that 24:7b–12 may have been added later by the same author; Plöger (*Theocracy and Eschatology*, 56) claims that 24:8–12 represent an independent unit integrated into the final composition with the transitional verses 24:7 and 13.

24:1–6 and that of 24:7–13 may simply represent the characteristic juxta-position of motifs found in many biblical poetic passages.[41]

THEMES AND MOTIFS

THE RESPONSE OF THE EARTH

The central role of the earth in this passage is immediately apparent in the persistent recurrence of the word *'ereṣ*, "earth," throughout. The word itself appears fourteen times in Isa 24:1–20; it is indicated by suffixes (*-āh* or *-êhā*) seven times. The opening section of the poem (24:1–3) begins and closes with a pronouncement about the coming desolation of the earth. Subsequent occurrences of *'ereṣ* are concentrated in 24:4–6 (5x) and in the concluding verses (5x), where the constant repetition of the word falls like a hammer on the ear.

The earth is sometimes represented as distinct from its inhabitants (24:1b, 4–5, 6, 17, 18–19, 20a); at other times it seems to include them (24:1a, 13, 20b). In like fashion, human images and images of the earth alternate throughout the poem, balancing each other in varying propor-tions. Further, images that show the earth in an active role (24:4, 18b–20) interweave with those that convey the devastation of the earth by an agent (24:1, 3, 6, 13).

In 24:1 the earth is the object of devastation: YHWH is about to act upon it, to "empty it" (*bôqēq*) and to "lay it waste" (*ûbôlĕqāh*). The author does not rely here on the vocabulary of destruction encountered in the passages discussed above: *nāšam, šĕmāmâ, šammâ, šiḥēt, ne'ĕsap, sāpâ,* and *midbār* do not appear. Rather, he chooses the less common roots *bqq*, "to empty out," and *blq*, "to lay waste."[42] YHWH will accomplish this emp-tying and laying waste by "twisting" (*wĕ'iwwâ*) the surface of the earth so that those who dwell on it are scattered. The impression of an earthquake is formed here, but this earthquake is not portrayed as an active response of the earth, as in Jer 4:24. Instead, the surface of the earth is twisted by the hands of YHWH.

The inhabitants of earth, who are distinguished from the earth itself in 24:1, are described in 24:2. The listing of the various classes and types of human beings who will be affected by the twisting of the earth influ-ences, in turn, the reading of 24:3. This verse recapitulates 24:1, with

---

[41] See further the discussion below.

[42] The former occurs elsewhere in the Hebrew Bible in Isa 19:3; Jer 19:7; Nah 2:3. The latter occurs elsewhere only in Nah 2:11, where it is linked to the nouns *bûqâ*, "emptiness," and *mĕbûqâ*, "emptiness," both of which BDB (101b) attributes to *bwq*, a bi-form of *bqq*.

minor variation, but the referent of "earth" in 24:3 now expands to include both the natural and the human realms visualized in 24:1–2.

This introduction sets the stage for a closer look at the coming devastation (24:4–13). The future orientation of the verbs in 24:1–3 (converted perfects, imperfects, and participles) shifts in 24:4, where a series of perfect forms (and a *wayyiqtol*) begins. That most of the perfect tenses of 24:4–12 should be read as instances of a rhetorical use of the perfect in a visionary context (the prophetic perfect) is indicated by the framework of the surrounding verses (24:1–3, 13), where future tenses predominate.[43] The continuity of 24:4–12 with this framework is made clear in 24:13, which begins: *kî kōh yihyeh bĕqereb hā'āreṣ bĕtôk hā'ammîm / kĕnōqep zayit*, "for thus it will be in the midst of the earth, among the peoples / as the beating of the olive tree." The conjunction *kî*, "for," looks back to the images of disaster in 24:4–12 and links them to the image of the stripped olive tree in 24:13, which is presented as a future reality with the imperfect form *yihyeh*. By means of the perfect forms in 24:4–12, the prospect of desolation is brought near and presented as if it had unfolded before the speaker's eyes.[44]

The response of the earth is described in 24:4 with the verbs *'ābal*, "to mourn," *nābēl*, "to droop" or "to wilt," and *'umlal*, "to languish." The verb *nābēl* occurs most often in the sense of the drooping and wilting of vegetation.[45] In Isa 40:7, 8 it is parallel to *yābēš*, "to dry up." With these associations *nābēl* in this verse brings out the physical nuances of *'ābal* as

---

[43] On the future orientation of the perfect forms in 24:4–12, see Samuel R. Driver, *A Treatise on the Use of the Tenses in Hebrew* (3d ed.; Oxford: Clarendon, 1892), §14; Kaiser, *Isaiah 1–39*, 181. So Rudolph (*Jesaja 24–27*, 27) on 24:4–6.

[44] So S. R. Driver, *Treatise on the Use of the Tenses*, §14, on the effect of the prophetic perfect: "[it] imparts to descriptions of the future a forcible and expressive touch of reality, and reproduces vividly the certainty with which the occurrence of a yet future event is contemplated by the speaker." In an attempt to convey this vivid sense in English I have translated the perfects of 24:4–12 in the present. The three perfect forms that occur after the *kî*, "for," in the second and third bicola of 24:5 are taken as simple past tenses because they explain what has led up to the envisioned devastation. The imperfect forms in 24:9 (*yištû*) and 24:12 (*yukkat*) function as iteratives that add to the sense of immediacy; see S. R. Driver, *Treatise on the Use of the Tenses*, §36. The shift to the perfect in 24:4–12 does not, then, introduce a situation that differs from that described in 24:1–3, 13, and 17–20. So Gray, *Critical and Exegetical Commentary*, 410, contra Duhm, *Das Buch Jesaia*, 144–46. Rudolph (*Jesaja 24–27*, 31) interprets 24:7b–13 as describing a situation in the present. The choice of perfect forms here may also be related to a traditional use of the perfect in this *topos*.

[45] See, e.g., Isa 1:30; 28:1, 4; 34:4; 40:7, 8; Jer 8:13; Ezek 47:12.

"to dry up" and of *'umlal* as "to waste away," so that the response of the earth appears to be a drought. The universality of this drought is suggested by the paralleling of *'ereṣ* with *tēbēl,* "world,"[46] and the languishing of the height of heaven, the source of rain, along with the earth intensifies its severity.[47] The reference in 24:6 to a curse that devours (*'ākělâ*) the earth, with the result that the inhabitants shrink in number (*ḥārû*) and "few are left," is consistent with the phenomenon of drought, which causes famine and death.[48]

At the same time, the verb *nābēl,* "to wilt," takes on a psychological aspect in Ps 18:46:

> As soon as they heard, they obeyed me,
>> foreigners came cringing to me;
> Foreigners wilted [*yibbōlû*]
>> and came trembling[49] out of their fortresses.

Here the meaning of *nābēl* comes closer to "to become discouraged, lose heart."[50] This connotation picks up the tones of lamenting in *'ābal* and *'umlal,* creating a scene of pervasive mourning in which both heaven and

---

[46] The word *tēbel* stands in most, if not all, cases for the earth as a whole or for the inhabited earth; cf. Isa 27:6. So Marie-Joseph Lagrange, "L'Apocalypse d'Isaïe (24–27)," *RB* 3 (1894): 200–31; Auvray, *Isaïe 1–39,* 223; Gray, *Critical and Exegetical Commentary,* 411; Wildberger, *Jesaja 13–27,* 920; Sweeney, "Textual Citations in Isaiah 24–27," 43 n. 19; BDB, 385b; contra Robert Lowth, *Isaiah: A New Translation; with a Preliminary Dissertation, and Notes* (Boston: William Hilliard; Cambridge, Mass.: James Munroe, 1834), 263.

[47] The image of the host of heaven "wilting" (*yibbôl*) like leaves is found in Isa 34:4.

[48] There is inherent irony in this reading: the devouring (*'ākêlâ*) of the earth by the curse has left human beings without anything to eat. See the discussion above of *'ākal* in Jer 12:7–13.

[49] The Hebrew reads *wěyaḥrěgû.* The translation of this verb is difficult. It is a *hapax legomenon;* the parallel passage in 2 Sam 22:46 reads *wěyaḥgěrû,* "and came girding themselves," which is assumed to represent metathesis of *rêš* and *gîmel.* Analogous expressions are found in Mic 7:17 and Hos 11:10, 11 with verbs that clearly mean "to tremble in fear" (*rāgaz* and *ḥārad,* respectively); hence it is possible that *wěyaḥgěrû* is a corruption of *wěyeherdû* (see Hos 11:10, 11). So BDB, 353a. Note, however, that 4 QSam^a has *yḥgrwʿ.* See Eugene C. Ulrich Jr., *The Qumran Text of Samuel and Josephus* (HSM 19; Missoula, Mont.: Scholars Press, 1978), 109–11; and P. Kyle McCarter Jr., *II Samuel* (AB 9; New York: Doubleday, 1984), 462, 472.

[50] Cf. Exod 18:18, where the context concerns physical, but perhaps also psychological, exhaustion.

earth participate. In this light the statement in 24:6 that "few are left" takes on pointed significance: the dead are many.

Alternation between physical and psychological responses continues in 24:7, where the theme of the response of the earth is sustained through a sequence of subsidiary motifs. In 24:7 it is not the earth as a whole that responds to the disaster, but the wine and the vine, basic elements of agriculture in Israel, along with those who traditionally celebrate the harvest (the "glad of heart"). The wine mourns (*'ābal*) and the vine languishes (*'umlĕlâ*), just as the glad of heart sigh (*ne'enḥû*).

The psychological aspect of *'ābal* and *'umlal* is predominant here and is reinforced by the following verses, which elaborate on the absence of joy and rejoicing that should accompany the harvest.[51] In 24:8 the "joy" (*māśôś*) of the timbrel and lyre cease along with the noise of human revellers (*'allîzîm*). Images of the dissociation of music and rejoicing from harvest continue in 24:9: those who drink wine no longer do so with a song (*baššîr*), and beer is bitter (*yēmar*) to those who drink it. Since the verb *mar,* "to be bitter," is most often used figuratively,[52] the bitterness of the drink can be taken on one level to mean that it is no longer cheering.

Despite the overt sense of mourning and sorrow in 24:7–9, the suggestion of aridity underlies these verses as well. "The wine dries up, the vine wastes away" is a natural reading of the first colon of 24:7. The absence of joy, music, cheerful noise, and singing signal a harvest that has failed, with the result that what drink there is, is literally bitter to the taste.[53]

Human and natural responses intermingle in the scene of harvest time in 24:7–9; in 24:10–12 the scene shifts to the city, and the responses to disaster are primarily human.[54] These responses are connected with those that precede by the repetition of key elements. In 24:11 a cry arises outside over the lack of wine (*yayin*), and gladness (*śimḥâ*) has passed away

---

[51] Cf. Isa 16:10.

[52] See, e.g., Lam 1:4; Isa 22:4 (in the *pi'el*); 1 Sam 30:6; 2 Kgs 4:27; Ruth 1:13. See BDB, 600ab.

[53] So BDB, 600a.

[54] I do not see in these verses an allusion to a specific city. The *qiryat tōhû,* "empty city," is emblematic of all cities as they await judgment from YHWH. See LXX, which reads *qiryat tōhû* as πᾶσα πόλις, "every city." So Clements, *Isaiah 1–39,* 202; Kaiser, *Isaiah 1–39,* 181, 184–85; Plöger, *Theocracy and Eschatology,* 56; Lagrange, "L'Apocalypse d'Isaïe (24–27)," 204; Sweeney, "Textual Citations in Isaiah 24–27," 43; John F. A. Sawyer, *Isaiah* (2 vols.; Daily Study Bible; Philadelphia: Westminster, 1984–1986), 1:206; cf. Wildberger, *Jesaja 13–27,* 926–27.

(cf. 24:7), while the rejoicing (*māśôś*) of the earth has gone into exile (cf. 24:8). But the overall picture created in 24:10–12 is more of a city brought to ruin and mourning by military defeat than of one ravaged by drought.[55] The empty city is broken (*nišbĕrâ*); the verb *nišbar* implies, on a literal level, physical destruction. The houses are shut up so that none can enter, suggesting that the inhabitants are huddled behind locked doors for fear of marauders.[56] The outcry in the streets for wine in 24:11 can be heard as a response to the disruption of the agricultural cycle by invasion or the depletion of stores by plunder, while the depiction of the "joy of the earth" as "gone into exile" (*gālâ*) sharpens the impression of military defeat. The desolation (*šammâ*) left in the city in the first colon of 24:12 is illustrated by the beating of the city gates to a ruin (*šĕ'îyâ*) in the second colon, an image that clearly calls to mind a conquered city.[57]

Elements of mourning in 24:11–12 cluster around these images of military defeat. The outcry in the streets is a sign of the loss of rejoicing and well-being symbolized by wine. The noun *ṣĕwāḥâ*, "outcry," occurs in contexts of grief and distress elsewhere in the Hebrew Bible; its use in Ps 144:14 offers a close parallel: *ṣĕwāḥâ birḥōbōtênû*, "outcry in our squares." In 24:11b gladness (*śimḥâ*) has passed on, and the joy of the earth (*mĕśôś hā'āreṣ*) has gone into exile. Similarly, in the noun *šammâ*, "desolation," in 24:12 the psychological sense of appallment and horror can be heard.[58]

A few verbal echoes in these verses recall the depiction of the withered earth and harvest that precede them. Although the *qiryat tōhû*, "empty city," is presented as a ruined city in 24:10, the word *tōhû* might also be heard in the literal sense of "desert, wasteland."[59] The outcry for

---

[55] Contra Kaiser (*Isaiah 1–39*, 185), who sees these verses, also, as describing the effects of drought. Here the word *tōhû* conveys the abstract sense of "desolation, emptiness," in contrast to the literal sense of "desert, wasteland" it carries in, e.g., Deut 32:10 (see BDB, 1062b). The epithet *qiryat tōhû*, "the empty city," need not imply that the city is completely deserted but simply that it is empty of normal traffic and commerce and, perhaps, that the population is greatly diminished. The outcry for wine in the streets is not necessarily a contradiction to this epithet, therefore.

[56] So Gray, *Critical and Exegetical Commentary*, 413. Duhm (*Das Buch Jesaia*, 146) also raises the possibility that the inhabitants of the houses have fled or died. Wildberger (*Jesaja 13–27*, 927) proposes that the houses are blocked by rubble.

[57] So Rudolph, *Jesaja 24–27*, 31.

[58] So Wildberger, *Jesaja 13–27*, 928; Rudolph, *Jesaja 24–27*, 31.

[59] See, e.g., Deut 32:10; Ps 107:40; Job 6:18; 12:24; Isa 34:11; 45:18; and the textual note above on Jer 4:23. So also Clements, *Isaiah 1–39*, 202–3; and Joseph Jensen, *Isaiah 1–39* (OTM 8; Wilmington, Del.: Michael Glazier, 1984), 194.

wine in 24:11 can be attributed to the impact of warfare on viticulture, but it also recalls the drying up (*'ābal*) of the wine and wasting away (*'umlal*) of the vine in 24:7.[60] And *šammâ,* "waste," can be heard in terms of the devastation caused by drought as well as by military defeat.

At the same time, the images of military defeat in 24:10–12 cast a shadow back on 24:4–9, giving the images of mourning in those verses another dimension. The devouring (*'ākal*) of the curse in 24:6 may be interpreted as military rout as well as drought; both are standard curses.[61] Further, the expression "the curse devours" (*'ākĕlâ*) recalls the similar trope "the sword devours" (*'ākĕlâ*) in Jer 12:12.[62] Finally, the repetition of the *nip'al* of *š'r,* "to be left," creates an echo that underscores death-dealing catastrophe. In 24:6 "few are left" (*niš'ar*); in 24:12 "desolation is left [*niš'ar*] in the city."

Human and natural images thus overlap and interact throughout the central section of the poem. They are drawn together in a pair of similes as this section concludes in 24:13:

> For thus it will be in the midst of the earth [*hā'āreṣ*],
>   among the peoples [*hā'ammîm*];
> Like the beating [*nōqep*] of the olive tree,
>   like the gleaning [*kĕ'ôlēlōt*] when the vintage [*bāṣîr*] is completed.

The paralleling of the phrase "in the midst of the earth" by the phrase "among the peoples" suggests that "earth" here represents the inhabited world. At the same time, each phrase retains its own integrity, and both the earth itself and the nations are brought to mind. The disaster that will strike them is compared to the beating of olive trees at harvest time and the gleaning (of vines) after the vintage (*bāṣîr*), a word that recalls the failing wine and vine of 24:7–9. The final images of this section, then, pertain to the earth: the world and its peoples are represented as a stripped olive tree and as plucked vines.

As noted above, 24:14–16 function as a narrative aside with respect to the main flow of imagery in the rest of the poem. Yet there is a hint of the convergence of mourning and drought in the use of the root *rzb,* "to waste away." In 24:16b the narrator responds to the treacherous and their

---

[60] The noun *ṣĕwāḥâ,* "outcry," occurs in Jer 14:2 as part of a communal lament over a massive drought.

[61] See Deut 28. Deut 28:49–51 makes an explicit connection between invasion and the dearth of food: verse 51 states that the enemy "will eat [*wĕ'ākal*] the offspring of your cattle [*bĕhemtĕkā*] and the produce of your ground [*'ădmātĕkā*]."

[62] See also Isa 1:20; Hos 11:6; Jer 2:30; Deut 32:42; 2 Sam 2:26; 11:25; 18:8.

dealings: "But I say, "Leanness to me! Leanness to me! Woe to me!" (*rozî-lî rozî-lî ʾôy lî*). The root *rzh*, "to be or grow lean," occurs here and in Isa 17:4–6, in the context of gleaning:

> And on that day,
> The glory of Jacob will be brought low,
>   and the fat of his flesh be made lean [*yērāzeh*].
> And it will be as the reaper's[63] gathering the grain,
>   when his arm harvests the ears,
> And it will be as one gleaning the ears,
>   in the valley of Rephaim.
> The gleanings [*ʿôlēlōt*] will be left in it
>   as at the beating [*kĕnōqep*] of the olive tree
> Two, three berries at the very top,
>   four, five on the branches of the fruit tree.

In these verses the concept of wasting away and growing lean (*yērāzeh*) is compared to gleaning (*ʿôlēlōt*), which entails the stripping away of the land's fruit.[64] The parallels between this passage and Isa 24:13 are obvious, and the connection between *yērāzeh* and *ʿôlēlōt* established in the former provides a parallel for the connection of wasting away (*rozî*) in 24:16 with the image of gleaning (*ʿôlēlōt*) in 24:13. This image, in turn, looks back to the scene of drought and failed harvest developed in 24:4–9.

At the same time the exclamation *rozî-lî rozî-lî* is linked by a similar parallel pattern to the expression of mourning that follows it: *ʾôy lî*. In this juxtaposition the noun *rozî* is given a figurative context in which pining and languishing is suggested as well as physical diminishment.

In the concluding section of the poem the flight of the inhabitants of the earth in 24:17–18a from the coming judgment is mirrored by the cataclysmic movements of earth and heaven itself in 24:18b–20. The images with which the poem ends correspond roughly to those introduced at the beginning, but they are given an active character. The scrambling of the *yôšēb hāʾāreṣ*, "inhabitant of the earth," in 24:17–18a corresponds to the scattering of the earth's inhabitants (*yōšĕbêhā*) by YHWH in 24:1. The quaking and heaving of the earth in 24:18b–20 recalls the twisting (*ʿiwwâ*) of its surface by YHWH in 24:1.

The response of the earth in 24:18b–20 is also more complex than the simple image of the earthquake in 24:1. In 24:18b the height of heaven is involved, as its "windows" (*ʾărubbôt*) open, releasing the floods of water behind them. The merism of heaven and earth in 24:18b ("the windows of

---

[63] Read *qōṣēr* for *qāṣîr*, "harvest" (MT).

[64] See also Num 13:20, where the adjective *rāzâ*, "lean" is applied to the land.

the height of heaven are opened / and the foundations of the earth quake"), like that in 24:4, evokes the cosmos as a whole.

The shuddering of the earth is vividly conveyed by a sequence of verbs in 24:18b–20: *rāʿaš*, "to quake"; *hitrôʿaʿ*, "to break apart"; *hitpôrēr*, "to split"; *hitmôṭēṭ*, "to totter"; *nûaʿ*, "to tremble"; *hitnôdēd*, "to sway"; and *nāpal*, "to fall." The roots *rʿʿ, prr, mwṭ,* and *nwd* occur in the *hitpaʿel* and convey a sense of oscillating motion. The use of the infinitive absolute with the *hitpaʿel* forms of the first three verbs adds an onomatopoeic dimension to the semantic sense of iterativity and motion.[65] The contortions of the earth in these verses parallel the frantic movements of the inhabitant of the earth (*yôšēb bāʾāreṣ*) in 24:17–18a, who will flee, fall, and climb as the impending terror impells.

In the final verse of the poem (24:20) these parallels converge. The earth is compared to one of its inhabitants, as it staggers (*tānûaʿ*) like a drunkard and falters under the weight of its transgression (*pišʿāh*). Just as the inhabitant of earth who runs from the approaching terror will fall (*yippōl*) into a pit but will not escape even by climbing up out of it (24:18a), so the earth falls (*wĕnāpĕlâ*) and cannot rise up again. In 24:20 the simile of the drunkard and the personification of the earth as flailing under a burden of transgression fuse the predicaments of natural world and human inhabitants, so that the one is seen in the other.

The response of the earth in Isa 24:1–20 resembles the array of reactions to the advent of the divine warrior. The quaking of the earth, the drying up of the land, and the rainstorm ensuing from the opening of the heavens are all natural phenomena that manifest the theophany of YHWH.[66] The correspondences between Isa 24:1–20 and Jer 4:23–28 are

---

[65] See Duhm (*Das Buch Jesaia,* 148) on the way these constructions further the poetry of 24:19–20. As in 24:4–12, the perfect and *wayyiqtol* forms in these verses function to bring a sense of immediacy to the foretelling of catastrophe (so Rudolph, *Jesaja 24–27,* 27).

[66] See Gerhard von Rad, "The Origin of the Concept of the Day of Yahweh," *JSS* 4 (1959): 97–108, esp. 104, and the discussion above of the response of the earth in Jer 4:23–28. Cross (*Canaanite Myth and Hebrew Epic,* 170) points to the imagery of the storm god as divine warrior in Isa 24:19–23. The disparate characteristics of these phenomena are noted by Wildberger, *Jesaja 13–27,* 938; and Gray, *Critical and Exegetical Commentary,* 420. As argued above in the discussion of Amos 1:2, different aspects of the power of the deity are presented together elsewhere in the Hebrew Bible as well as in the Sumerian city laments. See, e.g., the combination of drought and earthquake in Nah 1:2–8, fire and earthquake in Isa 64:1–3, and, by simile, fire and water in Mic 1:4. In Isa 24:1–20 these phenomena coincide with images of warfare and military invasion (24:10–12) that bring the *topos* of the divine warrior into the historical arena, as in Jer 4:23–26.

notable here, specifically the occurrence of the verb *rāʿaš,* "to quake" (Isa 24:1; Jer 4:24), the use of the *hitpaʿel* to depict the shaking of the earth (Isa 24:19–20; Jer 4:24), and the participation of both sky (heavens) and earth in the desolation (Isa 24:4, 18b and Jer 4:23, 28). Further, the scarcity of inhabitants remaining on the earth (*ʾĕnôš mizʿār,* "few are left") in Isa 24:6 parallels the absence of people (*ʾên hāʾādām,* "there was no one") in Jer 4:25. The mourning (*ʾābal*), languishing (*ʾumlal*), and wilting (*nābēl*) of earth as a whole, and of wine and vine in particular, in Isa 24:4, 7 recall the turning of fruitful land to desert in Jer 4:26 and the mourning (*ʾābal* and *qādar*) of the earth in Jer 4:28. Finally, the breaking (*nišbar*) of the empty city and the battering (*ḥukkat*) of its gates in Isa 24:10, 12 are reminiscent of the pulling down (*nittaṣ*) of cities before the anger of YHWH in Jer 4:26.

What is distinctive about Isa 24:1–20, however, is that whereas in other prophetic passages that evoke the *topos* of the divine warrior it is clear that YHWH is acting in battle against a specific enemy (whether Israel, Judah, or a foreign power), no particular nation is indicated here. There is no reference in 24:1–20 to Israel, Judah, or Zion[67] or to Babylon, Edom, or any other foreign entity. Nor does the present context of Isa 24:1–20 suggest such a referent. Rather this scene of devastation follows a sequence of judgment oracles against a range of foreign nations (Isa 13–21; 23) as well as against Judah and Jerusalem (Isa 22). In the rest of Isa 24–27 Israel and Judah are mentioned only in terms of their ultimate restoration. Isaiah 24:1–20, then, can be interpreted as a culminating manifestation of divine power against all on the earth who oppose it.[68]

---

[67] As noted above, the phrases *měśôś hāʾāreṣ,* "the rejoicing of the earth," in 24:11 and *běqereb hāʾāreṣ,* "in the midst of the earth," in 24:13 are cited by Johnson (*From Chaos to Restoration,* 30–33) as allusions to Jerusalem. See, e.g., *měśôś hāʾāreṣ* in Lam 2:15; Ps 48:3; cf. Isa 60:15; 65:18. (On the other hand, see Jer 49:25, where Damascus is given the epithet *qiryat měśôśî,* "the city of my joy.") The resonance in these phrases of the special fate of Jerusalem adds poignancy and immediacy to the depiction of judgment in Isa 24:1–20 without altering the universal scope of judgment established in the passage as a whole. This is especially evident in the personification in 24:11: "the joy of the earth has gone into exile" (*gālâ*), an expression that powerfully recalls the Israelites' experience of exile and brings that memory to bear on the current situation.

[68] Seitz (*Isaiah 1–39,* 175) argues that Isa 13–14 and 24–27, both of which exhibit a focus on world judgment, form an *inclusio* around the oracles against the nations (Isa 13–23). This structuring, he claims, is an indication that the judgment in 24:1–20 pertains ultimately to Babylon (see also Vermeylen, *Du Prophète Isaïe à l'apocalyptique,* 1:354–56). According to Seitz, Babylon in Isa 24 is both an agent of judgment against the whole earth and the object of God's final judgment. It is also

SIN OR PUNISHMENT

The complex relationship between sin, punishment, and the mourning earth found in the passages discussed above finds full expression in Isa 24:1–20. In this passage the mourning and drying up of the earth is explained in terms of a curse that devours the earth, decimating its inhabitants (24:6). The curse is the consequence (*ʿal-kēn*) of the transgressions of these inhabitants, who are also linked, by the conjunction *kî*, to the pollution of the earth. They have transgressed the laws (*tôrōt*), overstepped the decree (*ḥōq*), and broken the eternal covenant (*běrît ʿôlām*). The phrase *běrît ʿôlām*, "eternal covenant," recalls the Priestly account of the covenant with Noah, as representative of all humanity, in Gen 9:16. At the same time this phrase is used in the Priestly narratives of the covenant with Abraham (Gen 17:7, 13, 19) and of the Sabbath command (Exod 31:16) as well as in the Priestly law codes in connection with particular laws.[69]

These other contexts for *běrît ʿôlām* imply that in Isa 24:5, where it is linked with *tôrōt*, "laws," and *ḥōq*, "decree," the phrase carries associations beyond the general promise of divine goodwill toward humanity that it represents in Gen 9:8–17. In Isa 24:5 the eternal covenant entails a range of specific norms for behavior that can be violated.[70] In Deut 28 and Lev 26, as noted above, curses are invoked by YHWH on the Israelites if they fail to follow the norms articulated in the commandments, ordinances, and

---

possible, however, that Isa 13 and 14, which refer to the cosmic impact of Babylon's fall, foreshadow the final, extended drama of world judgment in Isa 24:1–20.

[69] So in Lev 24:8 with the Sabbath offering and in Num 18:19, where the allotment offered to the priests is declared to be a *běrît melaḥ ʿôlām*, "eternal covenant of salt." The terms *ḥōq*, "statute or decree," and *běrît ʿôlām* are paired in Ps 105:10 (= 1 Chr 16:17). Further, the phrase *ḥoq-ʿôlām*, "eternal decree," occurs in connection with *běrît ʿôlām* in Lev 24:8–9, and the synonymous phrase *ḥuqqat ʿôlām* is linked with *běrît melaḥ ʿôlām* in Num 18:19. The phrases *ḥoq-ʿôlām* and *ḥuqqat ʿôlām* occur elsewhere in the Priestly legal writings as well as in Jer 5:22 (see BDB, 349a–350a, 762b).

[70] See the discussion in Wildberger (*Jesaja 13–27*, 921–22) on the phrase "have broken the eternal covenant." Wildberger asserts that in 24:5 the concepts of the Noachic covenant and the Sinaitic covenant have flowed together ["ineinandergeflossen sind"]. Cf. Cross, *Canaanite Myth and Hebrew Epic*, 236. For other views see Johnson (*From Chaos to Restoration*, 27–29), who identifies the *běrît ʿôlām* in Isa 24:5 with the Sinaitic covenant, and Seitz (*Isaiah 1–39*, 180–82), who identifies it with the Noachic covenant. Jon R. Levenson (*Creation and the Persistence of Evil: The Jewish Drama of Divine Omnipotence* [San Francisco: Harper & Row, 1987; repr., Princeton: Princeton University Press, 1994], 27–28) translates *běrît ʿôlām* here as "ancient covenant" and dissociates it from the unconditional Noachic covenant.

statutes (*ḥuqqôt*). In Isa 24:6 such a curse devours the earth.[71] It is evident that the citing of *tôrōt,* "laws," *ḥōq,* "decree," and *bĕrît ʿôlām,* "eternal covenant," together evokes the relationship between Israel and YHWH. The use of these terms to explain worldwide disaster is an example of the way this passage extends judgment (and the criterion for judgment, or covenant) to the whole earth yet underscores the significance of Israel and hints at its central role in the judgment to come.[72]

A direct relationship is drawn in Isa 24:5–6 between human transgression (24:5) and curse (24:6) by means of the linking phrase *ʿal-kēn,* "and so."[73] It can be assumed that divine will empowers the curse, but the curse is set in motion by the violation of established boundaries of social and cultic interaction.[74] That act begets consequence is underscored twice in 24:6. First, the description of the curse in the first colon is followed in the second by the explicit statement: "and its inhabitants bear their guilt" (*wayyeʾšĕmû*). Here the use of a *wayyiqtol* form reinforces the sense of logical consequence established by *ʿal-kēn* in the preceding colon. Second, the phrase *ʿal-kēn* is reiterated at the beginning of the next bicolon: "And so the inhabitants of the earth have dwindled / and few are left."

The direct relationship between transgression and curse, act and consequence evident in 24:4–6 is manifest also in the conclusion of the poem (24:19–20). The final bicolon implies that the earth is breaking down under the weight of its own transgressions. Just as in 24:5 the earth lies polluted under (*taḥat*) its inhabitants and their violations of law, decree, and covenant, so in 24:20 the earth falls (*wĕnāpĕlâ*) under the weight of the transgressions that lie upon it (*ʿālêhā*). The use of the verb *hēpēr,* "to break, violate," to describe the violation of the eternal covenant (24:5) and of *hitpôrēr,* "to split or break apart," to convey the shuddering of the earth (24:19) forms a verbal echo that reinforces the connection between act and consequence.[75]

Curse language and imagery is reflected in the central section of the poem (24:7–12) as well. The motif of the cessation (*šābat*) of joy and of joyful sounds that recurs in 24:7–9 and is echoed in 24:11 reflects a traditional

---

[71] Cf. Zech 5:1–4.

[72] For examples of the judgment of foreign nations according to criteria familiar within the community of Israel, see the standard to which Babylon is held in Jer 50:29 and 51:4–5. See also the use of the term *pešaʿ,* "transgression," in reference both to the foreign nations and to Judah and Israel in Amos 1:3–2:16.

[73] See the similar function of *ʿal-kēn* in Hos 4:1–3.

[74] See the discussion above of the theme of sin or punishment in Jer 23:10.

[75] Although these two verbs may derive from two different roots (so BDB, 830ab; *HAL,* 916b–917), they are linked by phonological similarity.

curse found in ancient Near Eastern treaties as well as in prophetic oracles of divine judgment.[76] The signs of military defeat in 24:10–12 can be
seen as reminiscent of the curses enumerated in Deut 28:25, 48–57. Even
the first verse of the poem echoes a Deuteronomic curse. The announcement that YHWH is about to twist the surface of the earth and scatter
(*wĕhēpîṣ*) its inhabitants in 24:1 is reminiscent of Deut 28:64: "And
YHWH will scatter you [*wehĕpîṣĕkā*] among all the peoples, from one
end of the earth to the other." In both cases the direct agency of YHWH
is evident. The introductory verse of Isa 24:1–20 thus sounds a tone that
evokes the divine warrior, whose appearance causes the earth to con-
vulse and wither and the heavens to languish and then to storm. The
sounding of this tone at the beginning of the poem is a reminder that the
following verses, which suggest a direct relationship between transgression and curse, act and consequence, are to be heard in terms of the
fundamental agency of YHWH.

SOCIAL OR NATURAL DISORDER

A single bicolon in 24:5 names the signs of social disorder: "for they
have transgressed [*'āběrû*] the laws, overstepped [*ḥālĕpû*] the decree /
broken [*hēpērû*] the eternal covenant." The threefold violation here represents the disintegration of the social order mandated by YHWH. The outcry
of the speaker in 24:16 against the "treacherous" (*bōgĕdîm*) reinforces the
sense of social breakdown.

The perfect forms of *'ābar, ḥālap,* and *hēpēr* in 24:5 are read here as
simple past tenses rather than as prophetic perfects because they are
introduced by the conjunction *kî,* "for," an indication that they explain the
cause of the pollution mentioned in the previous colon. The perfects of
the rest of 24:4–12 refer, as noted above, to a future situation. In these
verses signs of social and natural disorder appear, but they are envisioned,
as in Jer 12:7–13, as the result of the judgment falling upon the earth.
Hence the abnormal harvest, in which silence replaces joyful sounds
(24:7–9), and the breakdown of social intercourse and order in the city,
where "every house is shut up so none can enter" and "there is a cry for
wine outside" (24:10).

---

[76] See further Delbert R. Hillers, *Treaty-Curses and the Old Testament Prophets*
(BibOr 16; Rome: Pontifical Biblical Institute, 1964), 57–58, and the use of the
verb *hišbît* in Hos 2:13; Jer 7:34; 16:9; Ezek 26:13 and of the verb *šābat* in Lam
5:15. Cf. Isa 16:10 and Jer 25:10. Note that in Jer 7:34 YHWH will make cease
(*wĕhišbattî*) the sound of joy and rejoicing in the cities of Judah and in the streets
(*mēḥuṣôt*) of Jerusalem, just as the outcry for wine is heard in the streets (*baḥuṣôt*)
in Isa 24:11.

A hint of disorder in the present may exist in the epithet *qiryat tōhû,* "the empty city" (24:10), however. The word *tōhû* occurs in the abstract sense, "nothingness, worthlessness," five times in Second Isaiah,[77] once in Third Isaiah (59:4), and once in what may be another postexilic Isaianic passage (29:21).[78] In Isa 59:4 *tōhû* is yoked with falsehood and wickedness:

> There is none who petitions justly [*bĕṣedeq*]
>   and none who pleads honestly [*be'ĕmûnâ*].
> They trust in emptiness [*tōhû*] and speak what is worthless [*šāw'*];
>   they conceive hardship [*'āmāl*], and they beget trouble [*'āwen*].

It is possible that if, in fact, Isa 24:1–20 is a postexilic composition, the nuance of moral emptiness and worthlessness is present in the epithet *qiryat tōhû.* Given the connotation of *tōhû* in Isa 59:4, this epithet suggests internal disorder within the city, where moral emptiness, worthlessness, hardship, and trouble replace the *ṣedeq,* "righteousness," and *'ĕmûnâ,* "trustworthiness," that should undergird the community.[79] In 24:10 the internally disordered, worthless city is about to be externally broken (*nišbar*) and turned into a wasteland. The echo created here between present social disorder and the disorder to come makes its own point.

POLLUTION

The root *ḥnp,* "to be polluted, profane," signals the theme of pollution in Isa 24:5: "The earth lies polluted [*ḥānĕpâ*] under its inhabitants." The imagery of this verse is consistent with the biblical view that

---

[77] Isa 40:17, 23; 41:29; 44:9; 49:4.

[78] On the dating of 29:17–24, see Clements (*Isaiah 1–39,* 240–41), who sees affinities between this passage and Isa 24–27.

[79] Cf. Hos 4:1–2. Isa 59:4 is part of an oracle addressed to the community of Israel. In Second Isaiah the word *tōhû* is applied to the foreign nations as a whole and their rulers (Isa 40:17, 23), to their gods (41:29, where *'āyin* should be read for *'āwen*), to idolmakers (44:9), to the physical earth as a whole (negatively, 45:18), and even with reference to self by the servant of YHWH (49:4). There is no reason, then, to limit the reference of *qiryat tōhû* to the city of Babylon, as Gray (*Critical and Exegetical Commentary,* 412) and Vermeylen (*Du Prophète Isaïe à l'apocalyptique,* 1:354 n. 2) propose. Their interpretation of the epithet as "the city of idolatry" presumes a specialized context for the word *tōhû* (see 1 Sam 12:21; Isa 41:29; 40:23) that is neither evident in the rest of Isa 24:1–20 nor dominant in the other passages in which the word occurs. The resonance of idolatry may be present along with the other associations of this word, however (so Lagrange, "L'Apocalypse d'Isaïe (24–27)," 204).

bloodshed pollutes the earth.[80] As mentioned above, an image of blood staining the earth is found in the story of Cain and Abel in Gen 4:1–16, where Abel's blood soaks into the ground (4:10–11). A similar image occurs later in the Isaiah Apocalypse, in Isa 26:21: "and the earth will uncover her blood / and will no longer cover over her slain."[81] The phrasing of Isa 24:5, where the earth lies polluted under (*taḥat*) its inhabitants, evokes such images.[82] Although the second and third cola of 24:5 specify the breaking of laws, decree, and covenant as the cause of the earth's pollution, the paradigmatic role of bloodshed, the ultimate violation of social order, may linger in the background here. This is suggested not only by the affinity of this verse with the concept of bloodshed literally polluting the ground but also by the thematic similarity of the verse to Hos 4:1–3, where bloodshed (*dāmîm*) is named as the culminating crime in a series of transgressions.

The articulation of the theme of pollution in 24:5 finds an echo in the concluding image of 24:20, where the transgression (*pešaʿ*) of the earth weighs upon it (*ʿālêhā*), causing it to heave and shake, evoking images of an earthquake. Here again the earth lies under its offenses and is distorted by them.

MOURNING AS STRIPPING

This motif appears in various forms in Isa 24:1–20. In 24:1 the earth is to be stripped and thrust into a state of mourning by the action of YHWH: "Behold, YHWH is about to make empty [*bôqēq*] the earth and lay it waste [*ûbôlĕqāh*]." The semantic affinity between "make empty" and "strip" is evident, but the connection is strengthened by the pairing of *nābaq*, "to be emptied out," with *nābaz*, "to be plundered," in 24:3. The associations of the root *bqq* with stripping are even clearer in Nah 2:3, where the *qal* verb is used with the metaphor of a tree (or vine) stripped of its branches:

> For YHWH is restoring the majesty of Jacob,
>   as the majesty of Israel;
> For annihilators [*bōqĕqîm*] have annihilated them [*bĕqāqûm*],
>   and ruined [*šiḥētû*] their branches.

---

[80] See the use of *ḥnp* in Num 35:33 and Ps 106:38. See the discussion above of the theme of pollution in Hos 4:1–3.

[81] See also Ezek 24:7–8. Cf. Duhm, *Das Buch Jesaia,* 148.

[82] Rudolph (*Jesaja 24–27,* 31) draws attention to the use of the preposition *taḥat,* "under," in relation to bloodshed and the pollution of the earth in this verse.

The image of judgment as stripping in Isa 24:1–20 is fully developed in the similes of the olive tree and the grapevine in 24:13. Here the fate of the earth is compared to the harvesting of olives, when the tree is beaten in order to strip the last fruits off the branches, as well as to the gleaning of vines after the vintage.[83]

These images of stripping are connected with mourning indirectly, through their proximity to the image of the mourning earth in 24:4 and the related scenes of woe in 24:7–12. In 24:1, 3, and 13, moreover, the earth plays a passive role; it is stripped as part of YHWH's punitive action. In 24:4 the stripping of the earth becomes part of earth's mourning over disaster. The withering and loss of vegetation implied by the physical associations of *'ābal* ("to mourn" and "dry up"), *nābēl* ("to wilt" and "to lose heart"), and *'umlal* ("to waste away" and "to languish") is bound to the grieving process implied by their psychological sense. Hence stripping can be seen as part of the mourning rite undertaken by the earth in its distress: a response to judgment (or consequence) as well as a sign of judgment (or consequence).[84]

The association of the mourning and stripping of the earth with its pollution (Isa 24:5) is reminiscent of Jer 23:9–11. A similar thematic configuration occurs in Third Isaiah (64:5):

> All of us have become like one who is unclean [*kaṭṭāmē'*],
>> and all our righteous acts like a stained garment [*ûkĕbeged 'iddîm*].
> All of us wilt [*wannābel*] like leaves,
>> and our wickedness [*wa'ăwōnēnû*] like the wind carries us away.

The repetition of the phrase "all of us" in the first and second bicolon yokes the simile of wilting leaves (conveyed, as in Isa 24:4, by the verb *nābēl*) and the pollution of the community. The juxtaposition of the two images suggests a relationship between them, whereby pollution can be seen as a kind of degeneration in the community that is expressed figuratively as "wilting." The final simile connects wilting, stripping, and judgment or consequence: the wind that carries away the polluted ones like dry leaves is a figure for the wickedness of the community.

---

[83] For the representation of judgment as the stripping of fruit or vegetation elsewhere in Isaiah, see, e.g., 16:8–11; 17:5–6; 18:5–6. Cf. Jer 11:16 and Mic 7:1.

[84] Mourning and stripping are brought together again in 24:7 in the mourning and drying up (*'ābal*) of the wine and the languishing and wasting away (*'umlĕlâ*) of the vine. The dual associations of these verbs are drawn out in 24:8, 9, and 11, where grieving over the failed harvest testifies to the reality of the stripping of the earth. In these verses mourning and drying up are differentiated as the mourners lament over the earth's sterility.

DECREATION

Hints of the theme of decreation appear throughout this passage. Perhaps the most marked representation of this theme occurs in 24:18b: *kî-ʾărubbôt mimmārôm niptāḥû / wayyirʿăšû môsĕdê ʾāreṣ*, "for the windows of the height of heaven are opened / and the foundations of the earth quake." As widely noted, the first colon of this verse resembles the account of the opening (*niptaḥ*) of the windows (*ʾărubbōt*) of heaven in the Priestly version of the flood tradition.[85] The pairing of this image with the quaking of the foundations of the earth in Isa 24:18b, further, parallels the coordination in Gen 7:11 of the opening of the windows of heaven with the breaking open (*nibqaʿ*) of the springs of the great deep *(tĕhôm rabbâ)* that lies under the earth according to ancient Israelite cosmology.[86] The imagery of the breaking (*hitrôʿaʿ*) and splitting apart (*hitpôrēr*) of the earth in 24:19 strengthens this correspondence and adds to the impression of the breakdown of creation. The announcement in 24:1 that YHWH is about to twist the surface of the earth (*pānêhā*) and scatter (*wĕhēpîṣ*) its inhabitants reflects a similar cosmic deconstruction.

Many commentators have seen in 24:18b a portrayal of the coming judgment as a resurgence of the flood, the paradigmatic undoing of the known order.[87] The representation of the earth as "polluted" (*ḥānĕpâ*) from the acts of its inhabitants in 24:5 serves as a thematic parallel to the Priestly account of the flood, which stresses the corruption of the earth by its human inhabitants.[88] The phraseology is different, as Gen 6:11–12 uses the verbs *nišḥat*, "to be corrupt," and *hišḥît*, "to corrupt," to express this corruption rather than *ḥānēp*, "to be polluted, profane," but the verbs convey similar concepts in these contexts.[89]

---

[85] See Gen 7:11; 8:2. The word for heaven used in Isa 24:4 is *mārôm*, rather than *šāmayim*, as in Gen 7; *mārôm* is used with this meaning elsewhere in the Isaian collection (see Isa 24:4; 32:15; 33:5; 57:15; 58:4).

[86] So also Duhm, *Das Buch Jesaia*, 148.

[87] See Plöger, *Theocracy and Eschatology*, 55; Vermeylen, *Du Prophète Isaïe à l'apocalyptique*, 1:350, 355; Lagrange, "L'Apocalypse d'Isaïe (24–27)," 204; Robert Murray, "Prophecy and the Cult," in *Israel's Prophetic Tradition: Essays in Honour of Peter R. Ackroyd* (ed. Richard Coggins, Anthony Phillips, and Michael A. Knibb; Cambridge: Cambridge University Press, 1982), 210–11; Seitz, *Isaiah 1–39*, 180–81; Clements, *Isaiah 1–39*, 205.

[88] See, further, the discussions above of the theme of decreation in Hos 4:1–3 and of pollution in Jer 12:7–13 and 23:9–12.

[89] Some commentators see, further, an allusion to the Yahwist narrative of the tower of Babel in the announcement in Isa 24:1 that YHWH is about to twist the

Within this framework the phrase *běrît ʿôlām* in 24:5 recalls the "eternal covenant" between God and all living beings in Gen 9:16,[90] but in a different, conditional form. Earth's inhabitants have broken this covenant by transgressing laws (*tôrōt*) and overstepping the decree (*ḥōq*). The word *ḥōq* here is often taken as a reference to the many *ḥuqqôt*, or statutes, of the Israelite legal codes. Yet *ḥōq* can mean "boundary, limit" as well as "decree, statute." In the former sense it often represents the boundaries with which YHWH orders the natural world and all of creation.[91] This word, then, embodies the fundamental unity of the social and natural order as well as recalling the statutes of Israelite law. Its use with *běrît ʿôlām* in Isa 24:5 reinforces the impression given in the poem as a whole, that the disintegration of the social order has undermined the laws governing the entire created order. It appears that in this composition the Sinaitic covenant has been universalized so that its scope matches that of the Noachic covenant.

Associations of primeval decreation are raised as well by the expression *qiryat tōhû*, "empty city" (24:10). In light of the images of decreation in Isa 24:1–20 as a whole, the word *tōhû* calls to mind the designation of the earth before creation as *tōhû wābōhû*, "a formless waste," in Gen 1:2.[92] If *tōhû* is interpreted with the literal meaning, "desert, wasteland," an allusion to the dry chaos tradition can also be seen.[93] The whole motif of the coming destruction as a return to primeval chaos is thus condensed in the epithet *qiryat tōhû*. Since *tōhû* can also be heard in reference to the present state of disorder within the city, this epithet captures the notion of poetic justice as well.

The reversion to chaos portrayed in these verses is not, however, to be seen as a final end. The inhabitants of the earth are scattered, not obliterated (24:1); whereas in Jer 4:25 "there is no one," here, "few are

---

surface of the earth (*pānêhā*) and scatter (*wěhēpîṣ*) its inhabitants. So Duhm, *Das Buch Jesaia*, 144; Rudolph, *Jesaja 24–27*, 30; Kaiser, *Isaiah 1–39*, 182; Vermeylen, *Du Prophète Isaïe à l'apocalyptique*, 1:355.

[90] So Duhm, *Das Buch Jesaia*, 145; Rudolph, *Jesaja 24–27*, 31; Kaiser, *Isaiah 1–39*, 183; Seitz, *Isaiah 1–39*, 180.

[91] See BDB, 349ab; cf. Jer 5:22; 31:36 (*ḥuqqōt* in 31:35); Job 14:5, 13; 26:10; 28:26; 38:10; Ps 148:6; Prov 8:29. See also the discussion of the theme of creation in Jer 4:23–28.

[92] Wildberger (*Jesaja 13–27*, 927) cautions that the use of *tōhû* in Isa 24:10 does not prove literary dependence on the Priestly creation account, especially since the word occurs frequently in Second Isaiah. The word could nevertheless refer to common phraseology used in contexts of creation; see, e.g., Isa 45:18. As Wildberger himself notes, it is certainly suitable for the description of chaos in contrast to the created cosmos.

[93] See the discussion above of the theme of decreation in Jer 4:23–28.

left" (24:6). Those who remain sigh (24:7) and cry out over the lack of wine (24:1). There is an apparent finality to the vision of 24:17–20, where no inhabitant of earth will escape, and the earth itself will fall, unable to rise again. Within the context of Isa 24–27 as a whole, however, the apparent death throes of the earth in Isa 24 form part of a larger scenario in which the wicked and arrogant will be brought down and the righteous led to safety.[94]

Summary of Literary Techniques

The literary devices and techniques evident in Isa 24:1–20 are manifold, and it is only possible to discuss here those that most closely pertain to the metaphor of earth mourning. Verbs and other words with dual associations include, in addition to *'ābal, 'umlal* ("to languish" and "to waste away"), *nābēl* ("to wilt" and "to lose heart"), and *šammâ* ("desolation" and "appallment"). The nouns *ḥōq*, "decree" and "boundary," and *tōhû*, "worthlessness" and "desert," bear dual meanings of a different sort. Instances of personification, in addition to the earth mourning, include the languishing of the heavens (24:4), the simile comparing the earth to a drunkard (24:20), and the staggering of the earth under its transgressions (24:20). The personification of the abstract quality "the joy of the earth" as going into exile adds an additional flourish. In terms of the representation of the human realm by natural imagery, the similes of the beating of the olive tree and the gleaning of the grapevine in 24:13 compare agricultural phenomena to the judgment of the earth's peoples as well as of the earth itself.

Links between human and natural responses include the paralleling of the mourning and withering of the earth with the bearing of guilt by, and dwindling of, its inhabitants in 24:4–6; of the mourning and languishing of wine and vine with the sighing of the glad of heart and stilling of joyful sounds in 24:7–9; and of the panic of the inhabitants of the earth with the shaking of the earth itself in 24:17–20. The wordplay linking the roots for the breaking (*hēpēr*) of the eternal covenant and the splitting apart (*hitpôrēr*) of the earth creates a parallel that suggests the association of act and consequence. Throughout Isa 24:1–20 the interweaving of human and natural imagery illustrates the interconnected fate of the earth and its peoples.

---

[94] See, e.g., 26:1–21. Wildberger (*Jesaja 13–27,* 204) assigns 26:7–21 to the basic groundwork, or first stage of composition, of the Isaiah Apocalypse; he considers 26:1–6 to be a later addition that is difficult to date. Clements (*Isaiah 1–39,* 213) concurs while raising some questions about individual verses within 26:7–21.

OVERALL EFFECT OF THE METAPHOR

The metaphor of earth mourning plays a central role in this passage, although it is not as prominent here as it is in some of the other passages considered to this point. Isaiah 24:1–20 is an expansive composition in which the metaphor forms part of a sequence of images of the earth in distress. At the same time, literary techniques such as repetition, paralleling, and *inclusio* bring these images together in patterns that draw attention to the significance of the judgment about to fall.

The metaphor of earth mourning introduces the core section of the poem (24:4–13) and is linked to the explanation of the coming judgment (24:5–6). The metaphor thus serves as a paradigm for all the disasters named. Further, the initial image of earth mourning is rearticulated in the mourning of wine and vine and the human mourning that accompany these in 24:7–9. Through this extended modulation the metaphor becomes a major motif to which other images and motifs in the poem can be related.

The persistent focus on the earth in Isa 24:1–20 contributes to the impression of universal judgment the passage creates. Recurrent images of the earth as an entity serve to define the parameters of judgment, just as does the catalogue of social classes in 24:2 and, in a negative way, the absence of proper names and clear historical allusions. In this composition the cosmic imagery can be taken in its broadest sense. Whereas in Jer 4:23–28 images of sky and earth heighten the vision of the destruction of Judah and underscore the repercussions of the end of the nation, in Isa 24:1–20 the cosmic imagery overshadows any allusion to the fate of a particular nation or city. Rather, by naming in the context of cosmic judgment the triad *tôrōt, ḥōq,* and *běrît ʿôlām,* terms that explicitly summon up the covenant between YHWH and Israel, this passage reveals the universal roots of that covenant. It shows these roots reaching back to a covenant with all humanity, which protects the entire created order, and even to the forging of creation itself.

Finally, it should be noted that in Isa 24:1–20 all the themes and motifs associated with the metaphor of earth mourning in the nine passages as a body are not only suggested but are fully expressed. The elaborate articulation of these themes, as opposed to the succinct or partial evocation of them, may be an indication of the late origin of this passage within the prophetic tradition. It may also be a sign of composition in writing.

Isaiah 33:7–9

Text, Translation, and Textual Notes

מַלְאֲכֵי שָׁלוֹם מַר יִבְכָּיוּן׃   הֵן אֶרְאֶלָּם צָעֲקוּ חֻצָה 7

שָׁבַת עֹבֵר אֹרַח   נָשַׁמּוּ מְסִלּוֹת 8

לֹא חָשַׁב אֱנוֹשׁ׃   הֻפַר בְּרִית מָאַס עָרִים

הֶחְפִּיר לְבָנוֹן קָמֵל   אָבַל אֻמְלְלָה אָרֶץ 9

וְנֹעֵר בָּשָׁן וְכַרְמֶל׃   הָיָה הַשָּׁרוֹן כָּעֲרָבָה

7 Behold [a]the people of Ariel[a] cry out outside,
    the messengers of peace weep bitterly.
8 The highways are desolate,
    the traveler has ceased.
    Covenant is broken, treaty[b] disregarded;
    no one is respected.
9 [c]The earth mourns, languishes[c];
    Lebanon is ashamed, it wastes away.
    Sharon has become like a desert plain,
    and Bashan and Carmel shake off [d]their leaves.[d]

[a–a] Read *’er’ellîm* for *’er’ellām* (MT), with some MSS; so *BHS*. The translation of MT is problematic. 1QIsa[a], LXX, Syr., Aquila, Symmachus, and Theodotion have read *’er’ellām* as two words. LXX assumes the root *yr’*, "to fear," reading the first colon of 33:7 as ἰδοὺ δὴ ἐν τῷ φόβῳ ὑμῶν αὐτοὶ φοβηθήσονται· οὓς ἐφοβεῖσθε, φοβηθήσονται ἀφ’ ὑμῶν, "Behold with the fear of you they will be afraid; those whom you fear will fear you." This salutary affirmation does not fit with the rest of 33:7–9 in MT and is clearly much longer than the corresponding colon in MT.[95] The other versions mentioned presume the root *r’h*, "to see." 1QIsa[a] reads (*’r’ lm*),[96] Syr. (*’tḥz’ lhwn*),[97] Aquila (οραθησομαι αυτοις), and Symmachus and Theodotion

---

[95] Overall, LXX diverges widely from MT in Isa 33:7–8.

[96] Cf. Richard D. Weis, "Angels, Altars, and Angles of Vision: The Case of אראלם in Isaiah 33:7," in *Tradition of the Text: Studies Offered to Dominique Barthélemy in Celebration of his Seventieth Birthday* (ed. Gerard J. Norton and Stephen Pisano; OBO 109; Fribourg: Éditions universitaires; Göttingen: Vandenhoeck & Ruprecht, 1991), 286.

[97] A number of Syr. MSS read *ntḥz’ lhwn*, "he will appear to them."

(οφθησομαι αυτοις), read "I will appear to them." Vulgate also assumes the root *rʾh* but reads *videntes,* "the watchers." These variant readings indicate a complex textual and interpretive history for Isa 33:7.[98]

The above translation, "people of Ariel," presumes a connection between *ʾerʾellîm* (in the emended MT) and the name *ʾărîʾēl,* "Ariel," given to Jerusalem in Isa 29:1–2, 7.[99] The singular noun may also occur as a proper name in 2 Sam 23:20, where LXX reads δύο υἱοὺς αριηλ, "two sons of Ariel," for *šěnê ʾărîʾēl* (MT).[100] In Isa 29:1–2 a further association of *ʾărîʾēl* may be evident. In this verse the word is used to refer both to Jerusalem (29:1–2a) and to something with which Jerusalem is compared (29:2b). Since 29:3–4 concern battle, death, and the underworld, a link with the dead and the underworld is conjectured.[101] Later Jewish interpreters translate *ʾerʾellîm* in Isa 33:7 as "angels."[102] The Vulg. translation of *ʾerʾellām* as *videntes,* "watching" or "watchers," and of *malʾăkê šālôm* in the parallel colon as *angeli pacis,* "angels of peace," may reflect such readings. Among modern interpreters, Murray argues that *ʾerʾellîm* refers to "destructive spirits of the lower world."[103] Other lines of reasoning presume a link

---

[98] For a detailed discussion of this history, see Weis, "Angels, Altars, and Angles of Vision," 285–92; and Samuel Feigin, "The Meaning of Ariel," *JBL* 39 (1920): 131–37.

[99] Commentators who adopt this reading include Hermann Gunkel, "Jesaja 33, eine prophetische Liturgie," *ZAW* NS 1 (1924): 178; Hans Wildberger, *Jesaja 28–39* (BKAT 10/3; Neukirchen-Vluyn: Neukirchener Verlag, 1982), 1294; Vermeylen, *Du Prophète Isaïe à l'apocalyptique,* 1:432; Auvray, *Isaïe 1–39,* 286, 287–89; William A. M. Beuken, "Jesaja 33 als Spiegeltext im Jesajabuch," *ETL* 67 (1991): 17–18; Brevard S. Childs, *Isaiah and the Assyrian Crisis* (SBT 2/3; London: SCM, 1967), 112; NAB.

[100] Cf. *šěnê ʾărîʾēl* in 1 Chr 11:22. McCarter (*II Samuel,* 491) explains the loss of *benê* from MT by haplography. The word *ʾărîʾēl* may in turn be related to *ʾarʾēlî,* which functions both as a proper name (Gen 46:16; Num 26:17) and a gentilic adjective (Num 26:17); see BDB, 72a. Others translate *ʾărîʾēl* in 2 Sam 23:20 as "hero" (so Syr., *gnbrym*) and *ʾerellîm* in Isa 33:7 as "heroes" (so Duhm, *Das Buch Jesaia,* 211; Kaiser, *Isaiah 13–39,* 337). Franz Delitzsch (*Jesaja* [5th ed; Giessen and Basel: Brunnen, 1984], 350–51), following MT, reads the plural suffix rather than the plural ending and translates "their heroes." T. K. Cheyne (*The Book of the Prophet Isaiah: Critical Edition of the Hebrew Text* [Leipzig: Hinrich, 1899], 107) suggests that the meanings "heroes" and "Jerusalemites" are both to be understood in Isa 33:7.

[101] Cf. Akkadian *arallû,* a poetic name for the underworld (*CAD* 2:226b–227a; *AHw,* 64a). For further discussion, see Feigin, "Meaning of Ariel," 133.

[102] See Weis, "Angels," 288; and Feigin, "Meaning of Ariel," 133. Wildberger (*Jesaja 28–39,* 1294) comments, however, that this translation may simply reflect an attempt to provide a parallel for *malʾăkê šālôm* in the next colon.

[103] "Prophecy and the Cult," 212.

between *ʾerʾellîm* and *ʾărîʾēl*,[104] "altar hearth," in Ezek 43:15, 16 and yield the translation "priests,"[105] or find a connection with *ʾrʾl* in the Mesha inscription.[106] Given all the possibilities, any translation must be tentative.[107]

 b Read *ʿādîm* for *ʿārîm*, "cities" (MT); 1QIsaᵃ reads *ʿdym*. The word *ʿādîm* is proposed here and assigned the meaning "treaty" or "treaty stipulations" on the basis of Old Aramaic and Akkadian. The Aramaic absolute plural noun *ʿdn* and determined plural *ʿdyʾ* occur in the Sefire treaties with this meaning; Akkadian *adû* is found in Neo-Assyrian treaty texts.[108]

 c–c Read *ʾābal ʾumlal hāʾāreṣ* for *ʾābal ʾumlĕlâ ʾāreṣ* (MT). The use of the third masculine singular verb (*ʾābal*) with a feminine subject (*ʾereṣ*) is not unknown,[109] but the coupling of a masculine verb (*ʾābal*) and a feminine verb (*ʾumlĕlâ*) where both refer to the same subject is unusual.[110] The present division of words in MT may reflect the influence of Isa 24:7, where *ʾābal* occurs with a masculine subject (*tîrôš*) but is directly followed by *ʾumlĕlâ* joined to a feminine subject (*gepen*).

 d–d The object "their leaves" is implied although not stated explicitly. See the transitive use of the verb *nāʿar,* "to shake, shake off," in Isa 33:15, where the righteous person shakes off bribes from the hand, and in Neh 5:13, where Nehemiah "shakes out" the bosom of his garment. In Ps 109:23 the psalmist is "shaken off" (*ninʿartî*) like a locust.[111]

---

[104] So K; Q reads *ʾărîʾēl*. But note also the form *harʾēl* in Ezek 43:15.

[105] See *HAL,* 80a.

[106] See *KAI* 131:12 [17–18]; *KAI* 30:5. See the discussion in Feigin, "Meaning of Ariel," 134.

[107] For a summary of proposed interpretations and bibliography, cf. Jacob Hoftijzer and K. Jongeling, *Dictionary of the North-West Semitic Inscriptions* (Leiden: Brill, 1995), 100.

[108] See *KAI* 222, 223, 224; and *CAD* 1:131a–134.

[109] See Paul Joüon, *Grammaire de l'Hébreu Biblique* (Rome: Pontifical Biblical Institute, 1923), §150j–k.

[110] Delitzsch (*Jesaja,* 351) and William H. Irwin (*Isaiah 28–33: Translation with Philological Notes* [BibOr 30; Rome: Pontifical Biblical Institute, 1977], 146) argue that this syntactical construction is not problematic. Wildberger (*Jesaja 28–39,* 1295) emends MT as above; Duhm (*Das Buch Jesaia,* 211) and NAB read *ʾābĕlâ ʾumlĕlâ ʾāreṣ,* making both verbs feminine in accord with the feminine subject. The present form of MT is slightly more difficult to explain in this case, although confusion of *ʾālep* and *hê* and subsequent haplography might account for the shortening of *ʾabĕlâ* to *ʾābal.*

[111] Cf. Job 38:13 and see Duhm, *Das Buch Jesaia,* 211; Wildberger, *Jesaja 28–39,* 129; Kaiser, *Isaiah 1–39,* 112.

DELIMITATION OF THE PASSAGE

Since Gunkel's description of Isa 33 as a type of "prophetic liturgy" that moves through a variety of literary forms derived from the cult,[112] the chapter has been seen by many interpreters as one composition, however loosely unified.[113] Within this unity, however, individual sections can be discerned in terms of both form and content, and 33:7–9 can be seen as one of these sections.[114] The chapter opens with a woe oracle in 33:1; 33:2–6 represents a plea to YHWH for help and an expression of confidence in divine salvation.[115] The *bēn* that begins 33:7 marks a new section, a short lament that ends in 33:9. In 33:10 YHWH breaks upon the scene, speaking directly of a decision to intervene. Although the speech in 33:10–13 may be seen as a divine response to the lament uttered in 33:7–9, the lament itself can be considered separately.[116] The rest of the Isa 33 may be divided into a brief Torah liturgy (33:14–16) and a long oracle of salvation (33:17–24).[117]

AUTHORSHIP AND DATING

Opinions on the dating of Isa 33 vary widely. Most interpreters agree that the absence of historical detail and even of proper names renders this composition particularly hard to place in a historical setting.[118] Several commentators have dated the chapter to the time of First Isaiah, assuming

---

[112] "Jesaja 33," 177–208.

[113] See Wildberger, *Jesaja 28–39*, 1284–85, 1322–23. The poem refers to a "destroyer" (*šôdēd*, 33:1) who will eventually be overthrown at the same time that justice is established within Jerusalem.

[114] Wildberger (ibid., 1322–23), e.g., divides Isa 33 into three major sections (33:1–6, 7–16, 17–24), each of which can be subdivided into smaller units. Gunkel's division is somewhat different ("Jesaja 33," 194–208).

[115] Gunkel ("Jesaja 33," 197) claims that 33:2–6 reflect the traditional *Gattung* of the communal lament.

[116] So Wildberger, *Jesaja 28–39*, 1296; Kaiser, *Isaiah 1–39*, 340; Childs, *Isaiah and the Assyrian Crisis*, 115; Vermeylen, *Du Prophète Isaïe à l'apocalyptique*, 1:431–32; Clements, *Isaiah 1–39*, 264.

[117] So Clements, *Isaiah 1–29*, 266; Vermeylen, *Du Prophète Isaïe à l'apocalyptique*, 1:433; Wildberger, *Jesaja 28–39*, 1310. With respect to 33:14–16, cf. the entrance liturgies of Pss 15; 24.

[118] The possibility that some of these units predate, in some form, the present composition is raised by Gunkel, "Jesaja 33," 189, 208; and Vermeylen, *Du Prophète Isaïe à l'apocalyptique,* 1:429. The concern here, however, is to understand the role of the metaphor of the mourning earth contained in 33:9 within the composition of which it is an integral part. This composition includes, beyond 33:7–9, Isa 33 as a whole.

that the situation it depicts represents the impact of Sennacherib's siege of Jerusalem (705–701 B.C.E.).[119] Others, however, place Isa 33 in the post-exilic period.[120] Since this period is relatively open-ended, there is pronounced variation in more precise dating.[121]

The most convincing arguments for dating are based on literary considerations and suggest a general time frame rather than a specific event or sequence of events. Wildberger points to a number of similarities in language, form, and style between Isa 33 and Isa 24–27, which he assigns a postexilic date.[122] He further notes that the allusion to *haššārôn* in 33:9 suggests a late period, as this name for the northern coastal plain occurs primarily in arguably postexilic biblical texts.[123] Gunkel perceives an affinity between the style of Isa 33 and compositions of the postexilic period and on this basis sets the chapter in the time of Third Isaiah.[124] Similarly, Beuken's argument that Isa 33 is a "mirror text" that reflects the themes of the book of Isaiah as a whole, looking backward to First Isaiah as well as ahead to Second and Third Isaiah, implies a date of composition after Third Isaiah.[125]

---

[119] So Delitzsch, *Jesaja,* 348, 350–51; Seitz, *Isaiah 1–39,* 233–35; Lack, *La Symbolique du Livre d'Isaïe,* 69.

[120] Childs (*Isaiah and the Assyrian Crisis,* 114–15) suggests that Isa 33 as a whole may represent a reflection from a later time on the Assyrian invasion of 705–701 B.C.E. Clements (*Isaiah 1–39,* 265) proposes an exilic origin, and John Barton (*Isaiah 1–39* [OTG; Sheffield: Sheffield Academic Press, 1995], 99) acknowledges this as a possibility.

[121] Duhm (*Das Buch Jesaia,* 208–9, 210–11), who sets the chapter in the context of the struggle between Judas Maccabeus and Antiochus Eupator in 162 B.C.E., proposes the latest dating. Kaiser (*Isaiah 1–39,* 341–42) dates Isa 33 to the Hellenistic period; Johannes Lindblom (*Prophecy in Ancient Israel* [Philadelphia: Fortress, 1962], 284 n. 106) to the time of Alexander's advance toward Palestine. Wildberger (*Jesaja 28–39,* 278–88) and Gunkel ("Jesaja 33," 195) favor an early postexilic date. Others accept a postexilic date without further specification: see, e.g, Murray, "Prophecy and the Cult," 207; and Childs, *Isaiah and the Assyrian Crisis,* 114.

[122] *Jesaja 28–39,* 1287–88, 1297–98. See also the discussion above of the dating of Isa 24–27.

[123] Ibid., 1297. See Isa 35:2; 65:10; Cant 2:1; 1 Chr 27:29. The most likely exception to a late dating is the reference to *šārôn* (or *laššārôn*) in Josh 12:18 as part of a list of kings whom the Israelites defeated under Joshua. Cf. also the Eshmunazar inscription (*KAI* 14:19) and *KAI* 181:13; 222A:34.

[124] "Jesaja 33," 195.

[125] "Jesaja 33 als Spiegeltext," 5–35. Vermeylen (*Du Prophète Isaïe à l'apocalyptique,* 1:429) further asserts that both the vocabulary of Isa 33 and the theology it expresses point to the postexilic community.

In general, the ahistorical tenor of this chapter and its eschatological focus are consistent with late Israelite prophecy.[126] So, too, the concept of a judgment upon the wicked within Israel that precedes the restoration and salvation of the nation, a concept implicit in the Torah liturgy of 33:14–16, is familiar in postexilic prophetic literature.[127]

THEMES AND MOTIFS

THE RESPONSE OF THE EARTH

Like Hos 4:1–3, this passage exhibits a two-part structure in which the depiction of a human situation is followed by a description of the response of the earth. The introductory particle *hēn*, "behold!" in 33:7 calls the audience to look upon a scene of danger, grief, and disorder. A note of mourning is sounded in 33:7: the people cry out (*ṣāʿăqû*) and messengers of peace weep (*yibkāyûn*) bitterly. The verb *ṣāʿaq* (or its bi-form *zāʿaq*) frequently occurs in the *qal* in contexts of distress and need. In Isa 65:14 and Jer 49:3 *ṣāʿaq* is parallel to *hêlîl*, "to wail";[128] in Job 31:38 *zāʿaq* is parallel to *bākâ*.

As in the ritual of mourning itself, normal activity has ceased in 33:8. The highways are desolate (*nāšammû*). They are literally empty or deserted, since "the traveler has ceased" (*šābat*), but in the context of the crying out and weeping of 33:7, the second meaning of the root *šmm*, "to be appalled," insinuates itself as well. An implicit personification is thereby created: the highways are appalled or horrified.[129]

The verb *šābat*, "to cease," used in 33:8 to convey the lack of ordinary traffic on the highways, recalls the occurrences of *šābat* and *hišbît* in the prophetic literature in the context of the cessation of joy, a common divine punishment.[130] Not only have normal activities ceased in this

---

[126] For a summary of the nature of late Israelite prophecy see, e.g., as noted above, Petersen, *Late Israelite Prophecy,* 14–15; Clements, "Patterns in the Prophetic Canon," 54; idem, "Prophecy As Literature," 73; and Blenkinsopp (*History of Prophecy,* 226–39).

[127] So Childs, *Isaiah and the Assyrian Crisis,* 116. For a discussion of this concept in Isa 33, see Wildberger, *Jesaja 28–39,* 1322–23.

[128] See also the pairing of *zāʿaq* and *hêlîl* in Isa 14:31; Jer 25:34; 47:2; 48:20; Ezek 21:17.

[129] See also Wildberger, *Jesaja 28–39,* 1299. Cf. the mourning (*ʾăbēlôt*) of the roads to Zion in Lam 1:4.

[130] See Isa 24:7–9 and the discussion above of the theme of sin and punishment in Isa 24:1–20. See also Hos 2:13; Isa 16:10; Jer 7:34; 16:9; Lam 5:15; Ezek 26:13 and Hillers, *Treaty-Curses and the Old Testament Prophets,* 57–58.

sad scene, but aberrant behavior is prevalent. The second bicolon of 33:8 focuses on human relationships: covenants or agreements are broken and disregarded, and no one is respected. Attitudes as well as actions are faulted with the use of the verbs *mā'as,* "to despise, hold in contempt" as well as "to reject," and *ḥāšab,* "to esteem, value, regard."[131]

The situation sketched in 33:7–8 is reflected in the response of the earth in 33:9. Here the verb *'ābal* is paired with *'umlal,* as in Hos 4:3 and Isa 24:4, 7. The impression of human distress created in 33:7–8 draws out the psychological aspect of mourning and grieving in both verbs: *ṣā'aq,* "to cry out," and *bākâ,* "to weep," in 33:7 are complemented by *'ābal,* "to mourn," and *'umlal,* "to languish," in 33:9. The impression of siege and of the aftermath of battle in 33:7 brings out the role of the earth (*'ereṣ*) as both the dwelling place of the dead and mourner over the dead.

This initial image of the mourning earth is extended by the naming of four geographical regions in turn: Lebanon, Sharon, Bashan, and Carmel. These four regions locate the scene in Israel and its vicinity, but they are also symbols of lush vegetation. In the Hebrew Bible Carmel occurs both as a proper name referring to the wooded mountain or mountain range in northern Palestine, as in Amos 1:2, and as a noun meaning "fruitful land," as in Jer 4:26.[132] References to the forests and cedars of Lebanon are also frequent in the Hebrew Bible,[133] as are mentions of the oaks and cattle of Bashan or simply of Bashan as a fertile place.[134] These three terms appear together in various combinations elsewhere in the prophetic literature to create a composite image of prosperity and fertility.[135] The figurative use of Sharon occurs in exilic or postexilic texts.[136] In Isa 35:2, for example, Lebanon, Carmel, and Sharon are brought together to represent the blossoming that will occur in the desert when those redeemed by YHWH return to Zion.

In Isa 33:9, however, this constellation of richly fertile places fades and withers. Lebanon is confounded (*heḥpîr*) and wastes away (*qāmēl*). The verb *heḥpîr,* "to show shame," takes on here the same sense that *bôš,* "to

---

[131] See BDB, 549ab, 362b–63a.

[132] BDB, 502a.

[133] See, e.g., Isa 2:13; 10:34; 14:8; 60:13; Jer 22:6.

[134] See, e.g., Isa 2:13; Ezek 27:6; Deut 32:14; Ps 22:13; Amos 4:1; Jer 50:19.

[135] Lebanon and Bashan are paired in Isa 2:13 (see also Jer 22:20–23), Carmel and Bashan in Mic 7:14 and Jer 50:19, and Lebanon, Carmel, and Bashan in Nah 1:4.

[136] See, as noted above, Isa 35:2; 65:10; Cant 2:1; 1 Chr 27:29. William L. Reed ("Sharon," *IDB* 4:309) suggests that in some of these texts Sharon represents thick woods as well as a fertile plain. Cf. Harry R. Weeks, "Sharon," *ABD* 5:1161.

be ashamed," does in Jer 12:13, where shame reflects defeat and disappointment as well as guilt.[137] The psychological dimensions of *heḥpîr* reinforce the aspect of mourning in *ʾābal,* and the personification of Lebanon echoes that of the earth. At the same time Lebanon's shame is connected with the experience of drought through the pairing of *heḥpîr* and *qāmēl,* "to decay, waste away."[138] The latter verb occurs in the Hebrew Bible only here and in Isa 19:6, which forms part of an oracle against Egypt. This oracle predicts the drying up of the Nile, when "reeds and rushes will waste away" (*qāneh wāsûp qāmēlû*).

The imagery of drought is explicit in the following bicolon. Sharon has become like the *ʿărābâ,* "desert plain," and the leaves of Bashan and Carmel drop off (*wĕnōʿēr*). The latter image is consonant with the picture of a dry landscape, where leaves shrivel and drop off.

In the expansion of an initial image of mourning and languishing, then, the lushest areas of Israel metamorphose into arid regions with no vegetation at all. These images of drought represent the mourning of the earth in 33:9 as withering and decay. Conversely, the drying up of these fertile regions is presented as a response of mourning related to the human misery sketched in 33:7–8.[139]

In Isa 33:9 the human situation and the response of the earth remain essentially distinct. The images of 33:7–8 pertain to human activity (people, messengers, highways, travelers, covenant, and treaty); those of 33:9 primarily to the earth itself (decay, desertification, and the loss of vegetation). The first two verses describe the effects of war and social anarchy, the last verse the effects of drought.

Yet echoes reverberate between the two halves of the poem. In the first bicolon of 33:9, the dual associations of the verbs *ʾābal, ʾumlal,* and *heḥpîr* and the resultant personification of the earth and of Lebanon create a bridge between the human and natural worlds: the earth mourns over human distress and is brought to shame because of it.[140] The use of the verb *nāšam,* "to be desolate, appalled," to describe the highways in 33:8 forms another link between 33:7–8 and 33:9, as the desolation of the highways and the

---

[137] Cf. the use of the *qal* verb *ḥāpēr,* "to be ashamed," in Jer 15:9.

[138] Irwin (*Isaiah 28–33,* 147) suggests that *heḥpîr* may also mean "to turn pale."

[139] All of the verbs used in 33:9 to describe the transformation of Lebanon, Sharon, Bashan, and Carmel are either in the *qal* or the *hipʿil*. The verbs *heḥpîr* and *hāyâ* are stative, as is *qāmēl,* but still convey the notion of an independent response, with no mention of an agent.

[140] It can be argued that Bashan and Carmel are also personified in 33:9, since the verb *nāʿar,* "to shake off," is used elsewhere only with a human or divine subject. See BDB, 654b.

absence of travelers and human commerce in 33:8 is consistent with the picture of desertification created in 33:9.[141] The parallel syntax of 33:8–9, which comprises a sequence of verb-initial clauses, further yokes the two sections of the passage, as does the near rhyme of the "breaking" (*ḥēpēr*) of covenant (33:8) and the "shame" (*ḥeḥpîr*) of Lebanon (33:9).

Another link between 33:8 and 33:9 is possible. If *ʾerʾellîm* in 33:7 is heard as an indirect reference to the inhabitants of the underworld,[142] the mourning of the earth (*ʾereṣ*) in 33:9 takes on an additional resonance. As noted above, the noun *ʾereṣ* can serve as a synonym for Sheol.[143] If an allusion to the underworld is heard in both the first and second sections of 33:7–9, both sections fuse into a single image of death in which the crying out of the inhabitants of the underworld and the mourning of the earth that is their doman conjoin. From this perspective the aspect of mourning in the verb *ʾābal* remains predominant throughout.

It should be noted that the coalescence in 33:9 of the mention of Lebanon, Bashan, and Carmel as a double subject, the verb *ʾumlal,* the implicit imagery of leaves and vegetation, and the overall impression of drought finds close parallels in the hymn to YHWH the divine warrior in Nah 1:2–8, cited above. In Nah 1:4 YHWH is praised as the one

> Who rebukes the sea and makes it dry [*wayyabbĕšēhû*],
>   and has dried up [*heḥĕrîb*] all the rivers;
> Bashan and Carmel languish [*ʾumlal*],
>   and the bud of Lebanon languishes [*ʾumlal*].

In light of the resemblances between this verse and Isa 33:9, it may be that the persona of the divine warrior lingers in the background of the latter. The image of the divine warrior is clearly visible in the plea to YHWH in 33:2–3 ("At the roaring sound the peoples flee / at your rising up, the nations are scattered") and in YHWH's declaration in 33:10: ("Now I will arise, says YHWH / now I will be raised high, now I will lift myself up").

---

[141] Kaiser (*Isaiah 1–39,* 345) raises the possibility of another connection between 33:7–8 and 33:9: the drought described in 33:9 is a result of enemy invasion (cf. Jer 4:23–28; 12:7–13; see also Isa 14:16–17; 16:8–11; Jer 48:32–33). Kaiser finds in Isa 33:9 an allusion to the motif of the enemy from the north by seeing in 33:7–9 a reflection of the activities of the "destroyer" (*šôdēd*) mentioned in 33:1. There are no definitive indications in Isa 33 that the *šôdēd* represents a foreign enemy as opposed to an internal or even symbolic force, however.

[142] See the discussion above of *ʾerʾellîm* and Isa 29:2–4.

[143] See the discussion above of the response of the earth in Hos 4:1–3.

SIN OR PUNISHMENT

In this brief text the state of the earth reflects the state of the human community. The author seems more concerned to illustrate the prevailing dysfunction than to relate its causes, and the passage has a stative quality. These verses illustrate the effects of distress without exploring its genesis. Yet the juxtaposition of human and natural states suggests some connection between them.

The first two bicola of this poem portray the external signs of a crisis; in this they resemble Jeremiah's vision in Jer 4:23–26, where the prophet looks upon a ruined landscape.[144] The third bicolon (33:8b), however, probes the internal social fabric of the community and presents a triad of actions and attitudes: covenant is broken (*hēpēr*), treaty is despised (*mā'as*), and there is no respect (*ḥāšab*) for others. That this behavior represents transgression is borne out later in Isa 33 in the Torah liturgy of 33:14–15. Here a reference to the sinners (*ḥaṭṭā'îm*) and the godless (*ḥānēpîm*) in Zion is followed by a characterization of the righteous that stands in contrast to the sketch given in 33:8. The relation between 33:7–9 and 33:14–15 is underscored by the recurrence of similar vocabulary. In 33:15 the righteous one despises (*mō'ēs*) what is gained by oppression; in 33:8 treaty is despised (*mā'as*). In 33:15 the righteous shakes off (*nō'ēr*) his hands to keep them from grasping at bribes; in 33:9 Bashan and Carmel shake off (*nō'ēr*) their leaves.

Still, the reference to the breaking of covenant in 33:8 is not wholly clear: Is a particular covenant meant or the concept of covenant in general? And what type of covenant is alluded to? Neither 33:7–9 nor Isa 33 as a whole offer specific details that point to any historical context for the breaking of a covenant. Despite the attempts of some commentators to trace the covenant in 33:8 to such a context, it seems that this verse refers to a recurrent pattern of behavior rather than to a particular instance.[145]

Further, the almost telegraphic nature of the imagery in these verses make it difficult to determine what kind of covenant is in question. Wildberger proposes that the covenant broken in Isa 33:8 is the eternal covenant (*bĕrît 'ôlām*) with YHWH mentioned in 24:5. In 33:7–9 as in

---

[144] The *hēn*, "behold," that begins Isa 33:7 corresponds to the *hinnēh*, "look," of Jer 4:23–26.

[145] So Wildberger, *Jesaja 28–39*, 1298; Childs, *Isaiah and the Assyrian Crisis*, 115; Clements, *Isaiah 1–39*, 267; and Kaiser, *Isaiah 1–39*, 345; contra Delitzsch, *Jesaja*, 351; Duhm, *Das Buch Jesaia*, 211; and Gunkel, "Jesaja 33," 200. Note the comment of Ackroyd ("Book of Isaiah," 351a) that the images of 33:7–9 as a whole may well be "metaphors for general distress" rather than representative of a specific historical situation.

24:5–6, he argues, the rupturing of this covenant entails the disintegration of the basic norms of human life and the falling of divine disfavor on the earth in the form of a curse.[146] Yet although the coupling of the verb *hēpēr,* "to break," with *běrît,* "covenant," occurs in both 33:8 and 24:5, as does the yoking of *'ereṣ,* "earth," with *'ābal,* "to mourn," and *'umlal,* "to languish," in both 33:9 and 24:4, many of the details articulated in 24:4–6 are absent in 33:7–9. In 24:5 not only is the covenant specified as a *běrît 'ôlām,* "eternal covenant," but it is linked to *tôrōt,* "laws," and *ḥōq,* "decree." These three terms together convey the concept of the covenant between YHWH and the people of Israel.

In 33:7–9, however, specific indications of this divine covenant are lacking. The impression of general social disorder created in 33:7–8a and the reference to lack of respect for others in 33:8b suggest the breaking of human agreements as much as they do the covenant with YHWH.[147]

Other references to divine agency in 33:7–9 are similarly elusive. The first two bicola suggest the effects of war on civil society, but there is no sign of the divine warrior here, although the ceasing (*šābat*) of travelers in 33:8 is reminiscent of the cessation (*šābat*) of joy and rejoicing in Isa 24:8 and threatened by YHWH as a curse elsewhere in the prophetic literature.[148] Comparison with Nah 1:4, noted above, reveals a trace of the divine warrior in the languishing of the earth and the withering of Lebanon, Sharon, Bashan, and Carmel in 33:9. But this trace only serves to emphasize the very different focus of this passage, where social breakdown (33:7–8) is juxtaposed directly with the mourning and withering of the earth (33:9). The echoing of sounds that links the breaking (*hēpēr*) of covenant with the shame (*heḥpîr*) of Lebanon also suggests a direct relationship between the two.

Further, although the phraseology of these verses resembles that of Isa 24:4–6, both the language and structure of Isa 33:7–9 also echo Hos 4:1–3, where the earth mourns (*te'ĕbal*) and all its inhabitants languish (*wĕ'umlal*) in response to the transgressions of Israel. Yet even this analogy is imperfect: the phrase *'al-kēn,* "and so," which introduces the response of the earth in Hos 4:3 and relates this response to the offenses of the Israelites,

---

[146] Wildberger, *Jesaja 28–39,* 1299–3000.

[147] Cf. Hos 10:4. The picture created by this disregard of human commitments can, of course, also recall the violation of the covenant with YHWH. See, especially, the Torah or entrance liturgy in 33:14–15, which refers to a range of laws. On the interpretation of *běrît* in 33:8 as a human agreement, see Clements, *Isaiah 1–39,* 267; Jensen, *Isaiah 1–39,* 257.

[148] See Hillers, *Treaty-Curses and the Old Testament Prophets,* 57–58, and the use of the verb *hišbît* in Hos 2:13; Jer 7:34; 16:9; Ezek 26:13 and of *šābat* in Lam 5:15.

is lacking in Isa 33:9. If a sequence of cause and effect is adumbrated in Isa 33:7–9, it consists in the direct response of the earth to a human situation; only the lightest shadowing of divine agency is revealed. But this schema may well be overdrawn: what is clearly presented is the parallel condition of the nation and its land.

SOCIAL OR NATURAL DISORDER

An impression of social disorder, in which normal activities and behavior are suspended, is created in 33:7–8. The focus on the lack of activity on the highways and roads and the hint of war and danger recall Judg 5:6–8, which describe the beleaguered condition of Israel before Deborah leads the tribes to victory.[149] But it is also reminiscent of Lam 1:4:

> The roads to Zion mourn [*ʾăbēlôt*]
> > because none come to the appointed feasts;
> All her gates are desolate [*šômēmîm*];
> > her priests sigh;
> Her virgins grieve,
> > and it is bitter [*mar*] for her.[150]

The occurrence of the roots *ʾbl*, "to mourn," and *šmm*, "to be desolate, appalled," and the adjective *mar*, "bitter," here and in Isa 33:7–9 link the two passages.[151] The common vocabulary and imagery invite a reading of these passages together despite the fact that their compositional settings are different.[152] In addition to depicting the desolation of the highways and the failure of peace (33:7), however, the Isaian passage also alludes to the lapse of trust and respect among members of the community (33:8). This lapse is symbolized in the breaking of covenant, which represents a fundamental structure of communal life.

POLLUTION

Only a slender thread connects this picture of social anarchy with the theme of pollution. In 33:14 there is a reference to the "godless" or "impure" in Zion: "The sinners [*ḥaṭṭāʾîm*] in Zion are in dread / trembling has seized

---

[149] This parallel has been often noted; see, e.g., Childs, *Isaiah and the Assyrian Crisis,* 115.

[150] Cf., further, the parallels between Isa 33:7–8 and 59:7–9.

[151] For a full discussion of the connections of Lam 1:4 with the nine passages considered in this study, see Delbert R. Hillers, "The Roads to Zion Mourn," *Perspective* 12:1–2 (1971): 121–34.

[152] See the discussion in chapter 7 of the way recurrent phrases and themes convey meaning in traditional poetry.

the impure [ḥănēpîm]." Within the larger composition Isa 33, 33:14 seems to look back to the transgressions sketched in 33:8: the breaking of covenant, rejection of treaty, and disrespect of neighbor. It is perhaps those who pursue such activities who are referred to as the "sinners" and the "impure" in 33:14. The root ḥnp, from which the adjective ḥānēp is derived, means "to be polluted" and, with reference to human beings, "to be profane or godless."[153] In Isa 9:16 the profane one (ḥānēp) is linked with the doer of evil (mēraᶜ). In the light of 33:14, the social disorder portrayed in 33:7–8 can be seen as perpetrated by those who are both sinners and profane, or polluted (ḥānēp). The accompanying picture of the earth itself sick and dying (33:9), suggests—but only suggests—that 33:7–9 as a whole be read in terms of the scenario sketched in Isa 24:4–6. Because of (kî) the violation of laws, statute, and covenant, these verses declare, the earth lies polluted (ḥānĕpâ), and it mourns (ᵓābĕlâ), wilts (nābĕlâ), and languishes (ᵓumlĕlâ).[154]

MOURNING AS STRIPPING

The motif of mourning as stripping is evoked by the imagery of 33:9: those regions with the richest growth of trees, grass, and plants turn barren. The ᶜărābâ, "desert plain," that Sharon becomes serves as a symbol of aridity, devoid of all life.[155] The fates of Lebanon, Bashan, and Carmel illustrate the process by which this transformation occurs. Lebanon, a symbol for dense woods, wastes away (qāmēl). Bashan and Carmel exhibit the physical action of stripping: they "shake off" (wĕnōᶜēr) their leaves or covering.

The connection between stripping, mourning, and the devastation of the earth in this verse is heightened by the present placement of Isa 33. Isaiah 32:11–12 contains a call to the "women at ease" to strip (pĕšōṭâ), become naked (wĕᶜōrâ), gird on sackcloth (waḥăgôrâ), lamenting (sōpĕdîm) over the ruination of the pleasant fields (śĕdê-ḥemed), the fruitful vine (gepen pōrîyâ), and the soil (ᵓădāmâ).[156]

DECREATION

The imagery and phraseology of decreation present in many of the other passages examined in this study are absent in Isa 33:7–9. Yet the

---

153 See the discussions above of pollution in Jer 23:9–12 and Isa 24:1–20.

154 See also Jer 3:1–3 and the discussion above of the theme of pollution in 23:9–12.

155 See, e.g., Jer 2:6; 17:6; Isa 35:1, 6–7; 41:19; 51:3. See, further, the discussion below on the theme of decreation in Isa 33:7–9.

156 Here, as in other instances of the call to mourn in the prophetic literature, it is human mourners who strip themselves in mourning over the earth, rather than the earth itself that mourns.

word *ʿărābâ,* "desert plain," in 33:9 is reminiscent of *midbār* and the chaos traditions associated with barren and sparsely settled regions.[157] The noun *ʿărābâ* occurs in Jer 2:6 and 17:6, passages that evoke the notion of a dry chaos by presenting the desert as a place of darkness and aridity, hostile to life. In other exilic or postexilic Isaian passages the *ʿărābâ* appears in opposition to the blossoming and fertility YHWH will bring about with the re-creation of the nation of Israel.[158] In Isa 51:3 the affiliation with creation traditions is particularly clear:

> For YHWH will comfort Zion,
> he will comfort all her waste places [*ḥorbōtêhā*];
> And make her desert [*midbārāh*] like Eden,
> and her desert steppe [*wěʿarbātāh*] like the garden of YHWH.[159]

The link between *hāyâ haššārôn kaʿărābâ,* "Sharon has become like a desert plain," in Isa 33:9 and such traditions is tightened by the use of this word with Lebanon, Carmel, and Sharon in Isa 35:1–2:

> The desert [*midbār*] and parched land [*wěṣiyyâ*] will exult,[160]
> and the desert plain [*ʿărābâ*] will rejoice and blossom.
> Like the crocus[161] it will surely blossom
> and rejoice, yes, there will be rejoicing[162] and singing out with joy.
> The glory of Lebanon [*hallěbānôn*] will be given to it,
> the splendor of Carmel and Sharon [*hakkarmel wěhaššārôn*].

SUMMARY OF LITERARY TECHNIQUES

The parallel drawn between the human realm (33:7–8) and the natural realm (33:9) in this passage is reflected in the presence of verbs with

---

[157] See the discussion above of the theme of decreation in Hos 4:1–3.

[158] See Isa 35:1–2; 41:18–19; Isa 51:3.

[159] I read the two perfect forms and the one *wayyiqtol* form in this verse as representing the use of perfect forms in a visionary context, i.e., the prophetic perfect.

[160] Read *yāśūśû* for *yěśūśûm* (MT) with one MS; so *BHS*. MT may represent a dittography, the following word being *midbār* (see BDB, 965a). Wildberger (*Jesaja 28–39,* 1353) follows Delitzsch in suggesting that the final *mêm* may represent a paragogic *nûn* that has been assimilated to the following *mêm*. It is also possible that MT may represent an instance of enclitic *mêm*.

[161] Read *kaḥăbaṣṣālet,* "like the crocus," with 35:2 rather than with 35:1 (MT); so *BHS*.

[162] Read *gîlâ* for *gîlat* (MT); so *BHS*, Wildberger (*Jesaja 28–39,* 1353). Wildberger concludes that the absolute noun substitutes here for the infinitive construct.

both a physical and a psychological meaning. These include, in addition to *ʾābal, ʾumlal* ("to languish" and "to waste away") and *nāšam* ("to be desolate" and "to be appalled"). The personification of the earth, which mourns and languishes; of Lebanon, which is ashamed; and of Bashan and Carmel, which shake off their leaves, further underscores the parallel states of the nation and the earth. These poetic devices integrate distinct images of human and natural distress into one expression of mourning, in which the earth is a major participant. The close rhyme of *ḥēpēr* in 33:8 with *ḥeḥpîr* in 33:9 hints at a causal connection between the breaking of covenant and the shame of Lebanon associated with its wasting away, a connection that is suggested by the two-part structure of these verses.

Overall Effect of the Metaphor

The effect of the metaphor of earth mourning in Isa 33:7–9 should be considered not just within the confines of these three verses but in light of Isa 33 as a whole. The metaphor functions in a relatively straightforward fashion within 33:7–9. The state of the earth mirrors the state of the nation; the connection between the two states is suggested but not explored. The passage offers a glimpse of the condition of Israel, a condition that is portrayed, at least on a figurative level, in terms of an external threat but also in terms of internal dissolution.

As in Jer 4:23–26, the speaker looks upon and describes a devastated land. Within the broader context of Jer 4, devastation is clearly the result of military invasion, and it is confirmed as part of a divine plan in 4:27–28. What precedes and follows the vision in Jer 4:23–28 are sequences of prophecies concerning the enemy from the north and the destruction YHWH intends this enemy to bring upon Judah. Isaiah 33:7–9, on the other hand, describes the condition from which the faithful appeal to YHWH to deliver them (33:2–6) and from which they are assured he will deliver them (33:10–24), although 33:14–16 specify that it is the righteous, not the sinners or the impure in Zion, who will be saved. The focus of the "prophetic liturgy" of Isa 33 is the restoration of Zion to peace and stability and the power of YHWH to accomplish this for those who follow God's ways. Its focus is not the judgment of the nation, the reasons for this judgment, or the executors of judgment.[163]

The somewhat static scene presented in 33:7–9 in fact serves as part of the prelude to the main action of Isa 33, which begins in 33:10 ("'Now I

---

[163] The nation "whose language you do not know" (Jer 5:15) is a major player in Jer 4:5–6:30; in Isa 33:19: "the people of a speech too difficult to understand" are mentioned only in passing, with the main emphasis resting on an inviolable Jerusalem ruled by YHWH.

will arise,' says YHWH / now I will be raised high; now I will lift myself up") and ends with the assurance of well-being and forgiveness in 33:24. This may explain why in Isa 33:7–9, unlike Jer 4:23–28, there is only a trace of the theme of decreation. In what precedes and follows these verses the interest lies in YHWH's making whole again what has already disintegrated and scattered.

While Isa 33:7–9 is reminiscent of Jer 4:23–28, it also shares striking phraseological parallels with Isa 24:1–20. In 33:7 the people cry out (*ṣāʿăqû*) outside (*ḥûṣâ*); in 24:11 there is an outcry (*ṣĕwāḥâ*) for wine in the streets (*baḥûṣôt*). In 33:7 the messengers of peace weep bitterly (*mar*), and in 24:9 drink tastes bitter (*yēmar*). As the highways are desolate (*nāšammû*) in 33:7, so only desolation (*šammâ*) is left in the city in 24:12. As the traveler ceases (*šābat*) on the road in 33:8, so the sound of timbrel and lyre ceases (*šābat*) in 24:8. Covenant is broken (*hēpēr bĕrît*) in 33:8; the eternal covenant is broken (*hēpērû bĕrît ʿôlām*) in 24:5. Moreover, the triad "covenant is broken, treaty disregarded, and no one is respected" of Isa 33:8 corresponds to the threefold "they have transgressed the laws, overstepped the decree, broken the eternal covenant" of 24:5. No person (*ʾĕnôš*) is respected in 33:8; few people (*ʾĕnôš*) are left in 24:6. The earth mourns (*ʾābal*) and languishes (*ʾumlĕlâ*) in 33:9; the earth mourns (*ʾābĕlâ*) and wilts and the world languishes (*ʾumlĕlâ*) and wilts in 24:4.

Despite these correspondences, it is clear that many of these words and phrases are used in different contexts in the two passages (with the exception of the central metaphor of the earth mourning). This is true for the immediate contexts of these words and phrases and also for the overall context created by each composition. The breaking of covenant (*hēpēr bĕrît*) provides an example. In 33:8 violation of covenant is associated primarily with the breakdown of social coherence and with the infertility of the land. In 24:5 the violation of the *bĕrît ʿôlām* and of particular stipulations (*tôrōt,* "laws," and *ḥōq,* "decree") takes on wider dimensions in light of the world judgment envisioned in Isa 24:1–20. The created order itself is threatened as this period of judgment looms, filling the compositional horizon. In contrast, although Isa 33:7–9 offers a look back at a dark period, Isa 33 as a whole looks forward to the beauty and nobility of YHWH's salvation. In Isa 24:1–20 images and phrases associated in the prophetic tradition with the judgment of Israel communicate the imminent reality of worldwide upheaval. In Isa 33:7–9 images of war, disruption, and mourning convey the suffering and uncertainty of those who hope for deliverance.

6
JOEL 1:5-20

TEXT, TRANSLATION, AND TEXTUAL NOTES

5 הָקִיצוּ שִׁכּוֹרִים וּבְכוּ   וְהֵילִלוּ כָּל־שֹׁתֵי יָיִן
עַל־עָסִיס   כִּי נִכְרַת מִפִּיכֶם:

6 כִּי־גוֹי עָלָה עַל־אַרְצִי   עָצוּם וְאֵין מִסְפָּר
שִׁנָּיו שִׁנֵּי אַרְיֵה   וּמְתַלְּעוֹת לָבִיא לוֹ:

7 שָׂם גַּפְנִי לְשַׁמָּה   וּתְאֵנָתִי לִקְצָפָה
חָשֹׂף חֲשָׂפָהּ וְהִשְׁלִיךְ   הִלְבִּינוּ שָׂרִיגֶיהָ:

8 אֱלִי כִּבְתוּלָה חֲגֻרַת־שַׂק   עַל־בַּעַל נְעוּרֶיהָ:

9 הָכְרַת מִנְחָה וָנֶסֶךְ   מִבֵּית יְהוָה
אָבְלוּ הַכֹּהֲנִים   מְשָׁרְתֵי יְהוָה:

10 שֻׁדַּד שָׂדֶה   אָבְלָה אֲדָמָה
כִּי שֻׁדַּד דָּגָן   הוֹבִישׁ תִּירוֹשׁ   אֻמְלַל יִצְהָר:

11 הֹבִישׁוּ אִכָּרִים   הֵילִילוּ כֹּרְמִים
עַל־חִטָּה וְעַל־שְׂעֹרָה   כִּי אָבַד קְצִיר שָׂדֶה:

12 הַגֶּפֶן הוֹבִישָׁה   וְהַתְּאֵנָה אֻמְלָלָה
רִמּוֹן גַּם־תָּמָר וְתַפּוּחַ   כָּל־עֲצֵי הַשָּׂדֶה יָבֵשׁוּ
כִּי־הֹבִישׁ שָׂשׂוֹן מִן־בְּנֵי אָדָם: ס

13 חִגְרוּ וְסִפְדוּ הַכֹּהֲנִים   הֵילִילוּ מְשָׁרְתֵי מִזְבֵּחַ
בֹּאוּ לִינוּ בַשַּׂקִּים   מְשָׁרְתֵי אֱלֹהָי
כִּי נִמְנַע מִבֵּית אֱלֹהֵיכֶם   מִנְחָה וָנָסֶךְ:

14 קַדְּשׁוּ־צוֹם   קִרְאוּ עֲצָרָה
אִסְפוּ זְקֵנִים   כֹּל יֹשְׁבֵי הָאָרֶץ
בֵּית יְהוָה אֱלֹהֵיכֶם   וְזַעֲקוּ אֶל־יְהוָה:

15 אֲהָהּ לַיּוֹם

כִּי קָרוֹב יוֹם יְהוָה   וּכְשֹׁד מִשַּׁדַּי יָבוֹא׃

16 הֲלוֹא נֶגֶד עֵינֵינוּ   אֹכֶל נִכְרָת

מִבֵּית אֱלֹהֵינוּ   שִׂמְחָה וָגִיל׃

17 עָבְשׁוּ פְרֻדוֹת   תַּחַת מֶגְרְפֹתֵיהֶם

נָשַׁמּוּ אֹצָרוֹת   נֶהֶרְסוּ מַמְּגֻרוֹת   כִּי הֹבִישׁ דָּגָן׃

18 מַה־נֶּאֶנְחָה בְהֵמָה   נָבֹכוּ עֶדְרֵי בָקָר

כִּי אֵין מִרְעֶה לָהֶם   גַּם־עֶדְרֵי הַצֹּאן נֶאְשָׁמוּ׃

19 אֵלֶיךָ יְהוָה אֶקְרָא

כִּי אֵשׁ אָכְלָה נְאוֹת מִדְבָּר   וְלֶהָבָה לִהֲטָה כָּל־עֲצֵי הַשָּׂדֶה׃

20 גַּם־בַּהֲמוֹת שָׂדֶה תַּעֲרוֹג אֵלֶיךָ   כִּי יָבְשׁוּ אֲפִיקֵי מָיִם

וְאֵשׁ אָכְלָה נְאוֹת הַמִּדְבָּר׃ פ

5 Awake, you drunkards, and weep,
   and wail, all you drinkers of wine,
Over the sweet wine,
   for it is cut off from your mouth.
6 For a nation has come up against my land
   strong, and without number.
Its teeth are lion's teeth,
   and its jaws are those of a lioness.
7 It has made my vine a desolation,
   and my fig tree splinters.[a]
It has stripped it and thrown it down;
   its branches have turned white.

8 Wail[b] like a virgin girded with sackcloth
   for the husband of her youth!
9 Cut off are cereal offering and drink offering
   from the house of YHWH.
The priests mourn,[c]
   the ministers of YHWH;
10 The field is destroyed,
   the ground mourns;[d]
For the grain is destroyed,
   the new wine is ashamed,[e]
   the oil languishes.

11 ᶠBe ashamed,ᶠ you farmers!
    Wail,ᶠ you vinedressers!
  Over the wheat and the barley;
    for the harvest of the field is lost.
12 The vine is ashamed,
    and the fig tree languishes;
  The pomegranate, also the date and apple,
    all the trees of the field are withered;
    forᵍ joy ʰis shamed awayʰ from humankind.

13 Gird yourselves and lament, O priests!
    Wail, ministers of the altar!
  Enter, keep vigil in sackcloth,
    ministers of my God!
  For held back from the house of your God
    are cereal offering and drink offering.
14 Sanctify a fast,
    call an assembly!
  Gather the elders,
    all who dwell in the land,
  Into the house of YHWH your God,
    and cry out to YHWH!

15 Alas for the day!
  For the day of YHWH is near,
    and as destruction from the Almighty it comes.
16 Is not before our eyes,
    food cut off?
  From the house of our God,
    gladness and exultation?

17 ⁱThe seeds shrivel
    the threshing floors are dismayed;ⁱ
  The storehouses are desolate,
    the binsʲ have broken down,
    because the grain is ashamed.
18 How the beasts sigh,
    the herds of cattle are confused!
  Because they have no pasture;
    even the flocks of sheep ᵏsuffer punishment.ᵏ

19 To you, YHWH, I cry;
  For fire has devoured the pastures of the wilderness;
  And flame ignited all the trees of the field.

20 Even the beasts of the field thirst for you;
   for the streams have dried up,
   and fire has devoured the pastures of the wilderness.

[a] *HAL* (1050b) suggests the meaning "stump" for the *hapax legomenon qĕṣāpâ.*

[b] The feminine form of the imperative here may reflect either the implied collective subject, namely, the community, which is compared to a virgin (*kibtûlâ*), or the feminine gender of *gapnî*, "my vine," and *tĕʾēnātî*, "my fig tree," in 1:7. Syriac (*ʾly*) and Vulg. (*plange*) follow MT; LXX reads θρήνησον πρός με, "lament to me," which could reflect either a dittography (*ʾĕlî ʾēlî*)[1] or a longer Hebrew text, possibly *hêlîlî ʾēlî*, "wail to me,"[2] which was subsequently shortened through haplography. The verb *ʾālâ* is a *hapax legomenon* corresponding to Aramaic *ʾl*, "to wail." Its presence here has raised questions in light of the repeated use in this passage of the verb *hêlîl*, "to wail, howl" (1:5, 11, 13). It has been suggested, for example, that *ʾĕlî* is a corruption of *hêlîlî*, "wail!" or, as Sellin suggests, of *ʾiblî*, "mourn!"[3] Alternatively, as an Aramaism this particular verb form may have been part of a traditional expression: "Wail like a virgin over the husband of her youth."

[c] So Vulg. (*luxerunt*). LXX (πενθεῖτε, "mourn!") reflects the imperative *ʾiblû*. Syriac (*ytbw mlkʾ bʾblʾ*, "the kings sit in mourning") diverges from MT but probably reflects *ʾābĕlû* (cf. Syr. of Amos 1:2; Hos 4:3; Isa 24:7).

[d] So Vulg. (*luxit*). LXX (πενθείτω ἡ γῆ, "let the earth mourn!") again reads an imperative; Syr. uses the expression *wytbt bʾblʾ*, "and sits in mourning."

[e] So Vulg. (*confusum est*). LXX (ἐξηράνθη) and Syr. (*wybš*) have interpreted *hôbîš* as a *hipʿil* of the root *ybš*, "to dry up," used in a stative or noncausative sense (cf. Zech 10:11). The plural form *hōbîšû* in 1:11, however, clearly stems from the root *bwš*, "to be ashamed," since its subject there is *ʾikkārîm*, "farmers," and it is parallel to the *hipʿil* imperative of the root *yll*, "to wail." Further, the unambiguous form *yābēšû*, "are dried up," is used in 1:12 to convey the withering of trees. There is deliberate play on the homonymic *hipʿils* of the roots *bwš* and *ybš* in this passage, given that

---

[1] So Julius A. Bewer, *A Critical and Exegetical Commentary on Obadiah and Joel* (ICC; Edinburgh: T&T Clark, 1911), 83; Arvid S. Kapelrud, *Joel Studies* (UUA 1948:4; Uppsala: Lundequist, 1948), 31; Wilhelm Rudolph, *Joel- Amos-Obadja-Jona* (KAT 13/2; Gütersloh: Mohn, 1971), 39; Ernst Sellin, *Das Zwölfprophetenbuch* (2d ed.; 2 vols.; KAT 12/1–2; Leipzig: Deichertsche, 1929–1930), 1:152.

[2] So Hans W. Wolff, *Joel and Amos* (Hermeneia. Philadelphia: Fortress, 1977), 18.

[3] *Zwölfprophetenbuch,* 1:153. Cf. Bewer (*Critical and Exegetical Commentary,* 83), who relates it to *ʾēbel.*

hôbîš, "to be ashamed," occurs in contexts that immediately call to mind the root *ybš* (so here and in 1:12 [2x] and 17). In order to retain a sense of this wordplay, I have read *hôbîš* consistently in these verses as a *hipᶜil* of the root *bwš.*[4]

f–f The form *hôbîšû,* translated here as an imperative, could also be read as a third masculine plural finite verb. So Vulg. (*confusi sunt*); Syr. (*bhtw*), like MT, is ambiguous. LXX (ἐξηράνθησαν, "has dried up") reads the 3 m. pl. *hipᶜil* of the root *ybš,* "to dry up." The parallel verb *hêlîlû* in the next colon can also be taken as a third masculine plural form; so Vulg. (*ululaverunt*); Syr. (*wᵓyllw*) is ambiguous. LXX (θρηνεῖτε, "wail!") translates an imperative. The call to lament in 1:5–14 is punctuated by a series of imperatives (see 1:5, 8, 11, 13, 14); in particular, *hêlîlû* in 1:11 echoes *hêlîlû* in 1:5 and *ᵓĕlî* in 1:8, both of which are clearly imperatives.[5] It could be argued, however, that since 1:9–10, which precedes this bicolon, and 1:11b–12, which follows, describe the miserable condition of the land and its inhabitants, *hôbîšû* and *hêlîlû* in this verse are best seen as third masculine plural forms that convey the reactions of the farmers and vinedressers.[6]

g I have translated the particle *kî* here in a causal sense. As Thérèse Frankfort points out, *kî* occurs throughout Joel 1:5–20 (1:5, 6, 10, 11, 13, 15, 17, 18, 19 20) with causative import.[7] In 1:12 causality takes on an explicative aspect, as *kî* functions to expand on the phenomenon of the shame and withering of vine and trees described in the first two bicola of 1:12. Cf. 1:16, where the cutting off of food is yoked to the cutting off of gladness and exultation.[8]

---

[4] So Samuel R. Driver (*The Books of Joel and Amos* [Cambridge: Cambridge University Press, 1897], 41, 43, 46), who argues on the basis of the parallel personification evident in Isa 24:7 and 33:9; Carl-A. Keller, *Joël, Abdias, Jonas* (CAT 11a; Geneva: Labor et Fides, 1992), 112 n. 3; BDB, 386b; RSV. Rudolph (*Joel-Amos-Obadja-Jona,* 39) asserts that both meanings are possible in 1:10, 11, 12, and 17; see also Sellin, *Zwölfprophetenbuch,* 1:153. NRSV translates *hôbîš* as a *hipᶜil* of the root *ybš* in every verse but 1:11; NAB does so only in 1:12.

[5] See Rudolph, *Joel-Amos-Obadja-Jona,* 39.

[6] So Kapelrud, *Joel Studies,* 41–42; Keller, *Joël, Abdias, Jonas,* 109, 113–14; Bewer, *Critical and Exegetical Commentary,* 84.

[7] "Le כִּי de Joel I 12," *VT* 10 (1960): 447. Contra Frankfort, Wolff (*Joel and Amos,* 32) argues that *kî* is asseverative in 1:10b as well as here.

[8] See BDB, 473b: "the causal relation expressed by *kî* is sometimes subtle, especially in poetry, ... sometimes it is explicative, justifying a statement by unfolding the particulars which establish or exemplify it" (cf. 2 Sam 23:5a; Isa 7:8; 9:4; 10:8). This explanation diverges from that of Frankfort ("Le כִּי de Joel I 12," 445–48), who argues for the causative import of *kî* in terms of strict consequentiality. Many commentators interpret *kî* here in an asseverative sense, as "surely, indeed."

h–h So LXX (ἤσχυναν); Vulg. (*confusum est*). Syriac [*d*]*btlt* ("has ceased") probably reflects an attempt to simplify the imagery of MT. With Driver, I have taken the phrase "joy is ashamed" as a pregnant construction: joy is confounded or defeated and has disappeared.[9]

i–i Read *ḥattû gornōtêhem*, "their threshing floors are dismayed," for *taḥat megrĕpōtêhem* (MT).[10] The noun *megrāpâ*, "shovel," as well as the verb ʿābĕšû, "shrivel," and noun *pĕrūdâ*, "grain, seed," in the first colon of 1:17a are *hapax legomena*.[11] The versions diverge both from MT and from each other. LXX reads ἐσκίρτησαν δαμάλεις ἐπὶ ταῖς φάνταις αὐτῶν, "the heifers are restive at their mangers"; Syr., *wṭwy mwšḥʾ ʾl ʾwrwthyn*, "and the heifers are parched at their mangers." The Vulg. translates *conputruerunt iumenta in stercore suo*, "the beasts rot in their dung." All these readings probably represent attempts to interpret a difficult text;[12] hence, for example, *pĕrūdôt* is read as *pārôt*, "heifers"; ʿābĕšû as *pāšû*, "spring about," (cf. Jer 50:11) or as ʿāpĕšû, "have rotted," from the Aramaic verb ʿpš;[13] and *megrĕpōtêhem* as *riptêhem*, "their stalls" (cf. Hab 3:17).[14]

The translation proposed here is consistent with the series of personifications evident in 1:17–18: the grain is "ashamed" (*hôbîš*), the beasts "sigh" (*neʾenḥâ*), the cattle "are confused" (*nābōkû*), and the flocks of sheep "suffer

---

[9] *Joel and Amos*, 43; see also Keller, *Joël, Abdias, Jonas*, 113; and Bewer, *Critical and Exegetical Commentary*, 82.

[10] So Theodore H. Robinson and Friedrich Horst, *Die zwölf kleinen Propheten* (2d ed.; HAT 14; Tübingen: Mohr, 1954), 60.

[11] The noun *perdtāʾ*, "grain, seed, berry," is attested in Syriac; see J. Payne Smith, ed., *A Compendious Syriac Dictionary* (Oxford: Clarendon, 1903), 458a. The noun *pĕrîdāʾ* occurs in *Tg. Isa.* 48:19, where it refers to "grains of sand"; in the later targums with similar meanings; and in the Babylonian Talmud with the meaning "jujube berry"; see Marcus Jastrow, ed., *A Dictionary of the Targumim, the Talmud Babli and Yerushalmi, and the Midrashic Literature* (New York: Judaica, 1971), 1225b. Rudolph (*Joel-Amos-Obadja-Jona*, 40) interprets *pĕrūdôt* as the feminine plural passive participle of *pārad*, "to separate," and translates "what has been set aside" or "reserved for later" ["was man beiseite getan hat, was man sich für später aufhebt"], i.e., "stored." The feminine plural passive particle could, in fact, mean "seed." The Syriac noun *magraptāʾ* is attested as "shovel, ladle"; cf. Payne Smith, *Compendious Syriac Dictionary*, 251b. In *Tg. Onq.* and *Tg. Ps.-J. magrôpîtāʾ* means "fire shovel"; *magrēpâ, magrêpâ*, "spade, shovel," occur in Mishnaic and rabbinic Hebrew. Cf. Jastrow, *Dictionary*, 730ab.

[12] M. Sprengling, "Joel 1, 17a," *JBL* 38 (1919): 130–31. Cf. Kapelrud, *Joel Studies*, 65.

[13] See Jastrow, *Dictionary*, 1100b.

[14] For a full discussion of these variants along with alternative translations, see Sprengling, "Joel 1, 17a," 129–41; Rudolph, *Joel-Amos-Obadja-Jona*, 39–40. On ʿābĕšû and *megrĕpōtêhem*, see S. R. Driver, *Books of Joel and Amos*, 45 n. 2.

punishment" (*ne'šāmû*). Further, reading "threshing floors" in 1:17 adds to the phraseological correspondences between the picture of distress in 1:5–20 and the vision of restoration in 2:21–27 (note the "beasts of the field" in 1:20 and 2:22; the "pastures of the wilderness" in 1:19, 20 and 2:22; the list of fruit trees in 1:12 and the phrase "the tree bears its fruit" in 2:22; the fig tree and vine in 1:7, 12 and 2:22; the wine and oil in 1:10 and 2:24). In 2:24 the phrase *ûmālĕ'û haggŏronôt bār,* "and the threshing floors will be full of grain," balances *ḥattû gornōtêhem,* "their threshing floors are dismayed," in 1:17.

j–j Read *mĕgūrôt* for *mammĕgūrôt* (MT); so Vulg. (*apothecae,* "storehouses"). MT probably represents a dittography (so *BHS*), although Rudolph interprets the first *mêm* as representing a partitive *min* and would revocalize *mimmĕgūrôt.*[15] In LXX, ληνοί, "wine vats" (so Syr., *m'ṣrt'*), may be a contextual interpretation of the rare word *mĕgûrâ,* found elsewhere in MT only in Hag 2:19, where it is not reflected in LXX.

k–k LXX (ἠφανίσθησαν), Syr. (*spw*), and Vulg. (*disperierunt*) have probably read *nāšammû,* "are laid waste," rather than *ne'šāmû* (MT). Rudolph defends MT by pointing out that LXX elsewhere translates the root *'šm* with ἀφανίζω, "to destroy" (see Hos 5:15; 10:2; 14:1),[16] contra Sellin, who considers the occurrence of the verb *'āšam* in Hos 10:2 and 14:1 (as well as of *ne'ĕšam* in Joel 1:18) a "later mistake."[17]

DELIMITATION OF THE PASSAGE

The first chapter of Joel consists of a sequence of related segments that is punctuated by imperatives (1:2, 3, 5, 8, 11, 13, 14) and cries of lament (1:15, 18, 19). This sequence does not take the form of a classic lament,[18] although it is clearly related to this genre.[19] The chapter, or a major part of it, has been labeled, rather, a call to lament.[20]

---

[15] *Joel-Amos-Obadja-Jona,* 40.

[16] Ibid., 41.

[17] *Zwölfprophetenbuch,* 1:156 ("spätere Verschreibung"). S. R. Driver (*Books of Joel and Amos,* 46) contends that the root *'šm* was understood in the sense of the root *šmm,* "to be desolate, appalled," by "the Jews." He may mean here the translators of LXX.

[18] So most commentators, with the exception of Kapelrud (*Joel Studies,* 4), who finds a lament in 1:2–12 and considers 1:13–20 a continuation in the lament style.

[19] Gösta W. Ahlström (*Joel and the Temple Cult of Jerusalem* [VTSup 21; Leiden: Brill, 1971], 130–31) asserts that 1:2–2:17 is composed in the style of a lament.

[20] See the discussion of this genre in Wolff, *Joel and Amos,* 20–22. Wolff considers 1:5–14 a call to lament; so also Keller, *Joël, Abdias, Jonas,* 115. Jörg Jeremias ("Joel/Joelbuch," *TRE* 17:92–93) identifies all of 1:2–2:17 as such a call.

Whether or not a precise form-critical designation fits this poem, some clear parameters set off the text considered here (1:5–20).[21] Joel 1:1 functions as the superscription to the entire book; 1:2–3 serves as a call to attention; and 1:4 provides background for the call to lament that begins in 1:5 with three imperatives: *hāqîṣû*, "awake!"; *ûbĕkû*, "and weep!"; *wĕhêlîlû*, "and wail!" The sequence of imperatives is resumed in subsequent verses: *ʾĕlî* ("wail!") in 1:8; *hōbîšû* ("be ashamed!") and *hêlîlû* ("wail!") in 1:11;[22] *ḥigrû wĕsipdû* ("gird on sackcloth and lament!"), *hêlîlû* ("wail!"), and *bōʾû lînû baśśaqîm* ("keep vigil in sackcloth!") in 1:13; *qaddĕšu-ṣôm* ("sanctify a fast!"), *qirʾû ʿăṣārâ* ("call an assembly!"), *ʾispû zĕqēnîm* ("gather the elders!"), and *wĕzaʿăqû ʾel-yhwh* ("and cry out to YHWH!") in 1:14.

In 1:15–18 expressions of woe over an imminent Day of YHWH and descriptions of disaster add urgency to the foregoing commands. The poem concludes in 1:19–20 as the prophet raises his own cry to YHWH. The repetition of phrases in these verses slows the forward movement of the poem, adding sonority and creating a solemn conclusion.[23] The imperative in 2:1 thus breaks on the ear much like the trumpet blast it enjoins: *tiqʿû šôpār bĕṣîyôn*, "Blow the horn in Zion!" In 2:1–17 the call to lament is resumed, but the locust plague is presented in a wholly different manner: the locusts assume supernatural proportions as storm troops of the divine warrior, who routs his enemies on the Day of YHWH. The connection between locust plague, drought, and divine manifestation adumbrated in 1:15 is fully developed in this section.

That Joel 1 and 2 are closely linked is clear, considering the persistence of the call to lament, fast, and cry to YHWH in both sections.[24] Yet 1:5–20 may be considered a separate poetic section, a summons to lament to YHWH over natural phenomena that have devastated the land and that are seen as signs of human alienation from the divine.

---

[21] Jeremias ("Joel/Joelbuch," 93) notes the literary character of the text regardless of any external signs of dependence on a liturgy, where one might expect more typical forms.

[22] As noted above, these forms can also be read as perfects.

[23] Thus "To you, YHWH, I cry" (1:19) is echoed by "even the beasts of the field pant for you" (1:20), and "the trees of the field" (1:19) by "the beasts of the field" (1:20). The phrase "fire has devoured the pastures of the wilderness" (1:19) is repeated in 1:20. For a similar division of 1:5–20, see Wolff, *Joel and Amos,* 21–22; Keller, *Joël, Abdias, Jonas,* 115–19; Rudolph, *Joel-Amos-Obadja-Jona,* 47–49.

[24] See Jeremias ("Joel/Joelbuch," 93) on the repetition of the first half of the imitated liturgy (i.e., the call to lament that elicits a divine response) in these chapters.

Authorship and Dating

The dating of Joel 1:5–20 is linked to questions concerning the compositional history of Joel as a whole. As in Isa 24 and 33, the lack of concrete historical references in Joel 1–4 expands the role of conjecture in situating the prophetic speeches of this book. Most scholars have noted, however, a distinction between the first two chapters and the last two. The literary focus of Joel 1–2 is on a plague of locusts and an accompanying drought that have ravaged the land. Although the description of the locusts becomes highly figurative in Joel 2, and scenes of an ultimate catastrophe, or Day of YHWH, predominate, the imagery of a locust invasion and the repeated call to lament and fast link these two chapters.[25] This extended composition comes to a conclusion in 2:18–27 with YHWH's promise to remove the invaders, restore fertility to the land, and reestablish harmony between God and the human community.[26]

In contrast, there is no allusion to a locust plague in Joel 3–4. Here the battle imagery refers to the nations, at least two of which are mentioned by name.[27] These will be put to shame for the wrong they have done Judah and Jerusalem. Further, whereas Joel 1–2 raises the possibility that the day of disaster that threatens Israel can be averted through prayer and repentance (2:12–27), in Joel 4 the Day of YHWH is presented as a final reckoning on the nations, so as to deliver Israel. In Joel 3 a further distinction is made: only those who call on the name of YHWH, and whom YHWH calls, will be saved (3:5).[28] These differences between Joel 1–2, on the one hand, and 3–4, on the other, appear fundamental, despite the many parallels in language, imagery, and structure between these two units.[29] The provenance of Joel 1–2, then, should be considered separately from that of Joel 3–4.[30]

---

[25] Contra Wolff (*Joel and Amos*, 7) and Jeremias ("Joel/Joelbuch," 93–94), I do not take the battle imagery of Joel 2 literally, since in 2:4–9 the locusts are explicitly compared to an army rather than vice versa; see S. R. Driver, *Books of Joel and Amos*, 28–29.

[26] So Robinson and Horst, *Die zwölf kleinen Propheten*, 55.

[27] The destruction of Egypt and of Edom is mentioned in 4:19; the list of foreign peoples in 4:4–8 is a later addition, according to most commentators. See, e.g., Wolff, *Joel and Amos*, 8.

[28] See Otto Plöger, *Theocracy and Eschatology* (Oxford: Basil Blackwell, 1968), 102–3.

[29] For a discussion of these parallels, see Wolff, *Joel and Amos*, 7–8; J. Bourke, "Le jour de Yahvé dans Joel," *RB* 66 (1959): 5–31.

[30] So Robinson and Horst, *Die zwölf kleinen Propheten*, 55; Sellin, *Zwölf- prophetenbuch*, 1:144–47; Plöger, *Theocracy and Eschatology*, 96–105; Otto Eissfeldt,

Arguments presented in favor of the postexilic dating of Joel 1–2 are inconclusive, as those who argue for a preexilic date have pointed out.[31] Thus the absence of any mention of a king and the central role of priests in these chapters may simply indicate the genre of a call to lament a natural disaster.[32] Likewise the reference to cereal and drink offerings (1:9, 13) do not in themselves point to cultic rituals of the postexilic period.[33]

It is true, however, that whereas the preexilic prophets frequently condemn the priestly class for failed leadership, decry cultic abuse, and denigrate the role of cultic rituals alone in winning divine favor, no such criticisms are voiced in Joel 1–2.[34] Rather, the prophet raises the hope of

_____

The Old Testament: An Introduction (New York: Harper & Row, 1965), 392–94; B. S. Childs, *Introduction to the Old Testament As Scripture* (Philadelphia: Fortress, 1965), 390–92; Theodore Hiebert, "Joel, Book of," *ABD* 3:878–79. Bernhard Duhm ("Anmerkungen zu den Zwölf Propheten," *ZAW* 31 [1911]: 187) identifies a major division between 1:1–2:17 and 2:18–4:21; he considers the latter unit a prose expansion of apocalyptic character. Artur Weiser (*Das Buch der zwölf kleinen Propheten* [ATD 24/1; Göttingen: Vandenhoeck & Ruprecht, 1949], 89), Bourke ("Le jour de Yahvé dans Joel," 78), and Bewer (*Critical and Exegetical Commentary,* 51–56) acknowledge a basic distinction between Joel 1–2 and 3–4 but argue that the prophet himself expanded the former with the latter (although Bewer excises a number of segments throughout Joel 1–2 as later interpolations). Others who assume the overall unity of Joel and thus date the bulk of it to a single period include Wolff, *Joel and Amos,* 6–8; Kapelrud, *Joel Studies,* 181–82, 191; Ahlström, *Joel and the Temple Cult of Jerusalem,* 21–11; Jeremias, "Joel/Joelbuch," 92–94; Rudolph, *Joel-Amos-Obadja-Jona,* 23–24; S. R. Driver, *Books of Joel and Amos,* 10–11; and James L. Crenshaw, *Joel* (AB 24C; New York: Doubleday, 1995), 29–34, 133–37.

[31] See, e.g., Kapelrud, *Joel Studies,* 181–89, 191; Rudolph, *Joel-Amos-Obadja-Jona,* 25, 27–28.

[32] See the communal lament over the drought in Jer 14:1–10, in which no king is mentioned. Richard Coggins ("An Alternative Prophetic Tradition?" in *Israel's Prophetic Tradition: Essays in Honour of Peter R. Ackroyd* [ed. Richard Coggins, Anthony Phillips, and Michael A. Knibb; Cambridge: Cambridge University Press, 1982], 88–89) notes the liturgical as opposed to the historical emphasis of Joel in relation to the difficulty of dating the collection.

[33] So Ahlström, *Joel and the Temple Cult of Jerusalem,* 14–16; Kapelrud, *Joel Studies,* 35–36; and Rudolph, *Joel-Amos-Obadja-Jona,* 28.

[34] Kapelrud (*Joel Studies,* 184–85) concedes this point; see also Robinson and Horst, *Die zwölf kleinen Propheten,* 55; S. R. Driver, *Books of Joel and Amos,* 12. Cf. Jer 14:11, the divine response to the lament over the drought in 14:1–10, where YHWH rejects the lamenting, fasting, and offerings of the people as well as the prophet's intercession for them. Note also the condemnation of "prophet and priest" in 14:18, part of the related lament in 14:17–18 (on the connections between

divine mercy if the people will express their penitence by rites of fasting and mourning (2:12–14).[35] The lack of reference to the Assyrians, the Babylonians, or any other military aggressor, except by way of simile (2:4–5) or metaphor (2:20), is also suggestive.[36]

These absences from the text of Joel 1–2 constitute arguments from silence. On the positive side are several considerations. First, there are similarities between Joel 1–2 and parts of Haggai, First Zechariah, and Malachi.[37] The first two of these collections are dated with relative certainty to the postexilic period; the book of Malachi is generally considered to be roughly contemporaneous, although its dating is less uncertain. In all three collections the themes of economic hardship, agricultural scarcity, and hunger are sounded and related to failure in the cultic sphere: to the lack of wholehearted participation either in the rebuilding of the temple (Haggai and First Zechariah) or in the temple cult (Malachi).[38] In Mal 3:11, further, there is a reference to the "devourer" ([*bā*]*'ōkēl*), most probably the locust, that threatens the land.[39] The rare word *mĕgûrâ*, "barn, storage bin," in Hag 2:19 occurs elsewhere in the MT only in Joel 1:17.[40]

Other linguistic usages support a postexilic date for Joel 1–2. Among those in Joel 1 discussed at length by Ahlström[41] are the imperative *'ĕlî*, an apparent Aramaism,[42] and the phrase *min-bĕnê* (with unassimilated *min*), common in 1 and 2 Chronicles.[43] To these might be added the noun *'āsîs,*

---

the various laments in 14:1–15:9, see William L. Holladay, *Jeremiah 1* [Hermeneia; Philadelphia: Fortress, 1986], 421–25).

[35] See Holladay, *Jeremiah 1,* 422.

[36] So also Crenshaw, *Joel,* 24.

[37] See Ahlström, *Joel and the Temple Cult of Jerusalem,* 112; and John D. W. Watts, *The Books of Joel, Obadiah, Jonah, Nahum, Habakkuk, and Zephaniah* (Cambridge: Cambridge University Press, 1975), 14.

[38] See Hag 1:2–11; 2:15–20; cf. Zech 8:9–12; Mal 3:9–12. In these passages the community is threatened not with military disaster but with agricultural catastrophe. See also Joseph Blenkinsopp, *A History of Prophecy in Israel* (rev. ed.; Louisville: Westminster John Knox, 1996), 200–22.

[39] Cf. Joel 1:4, where the activity of the four types of locusts mentioned is consistently conveyed with the verb *'ākal,* "to eat, devour."

[40] See the textual note above.

[41] *Joel,* 1–22.

[42] Joel 1:8. But see the discussion in the textual note above of possible textual corruption.

[43] Joel 1:12. In his discussion of this phrase Ahlström (*Joel and the Temple Cult of Jerusalem,* 21) cites Hans Bauer and Pontus Leander, *Historische Grammatik der*

"sweet wine" (1:5),[44] and the participle *kōrĕmîm,* "vinedressers," in parallelism with *'ikkārîm,* "farmers" (1:11).[45] The occurrence of the *hip'il* of the root *ybš,* "to dry up," with the stative meaning, "to show dryness," elsewhere in MT only in Zech 10:11 suggests a late date for the wordplay evident in Joel 1:10, 12 (2x), and 17 between *hōbîš,* the *hip'il* of the root *buš,* "to be ashamed," and *hôbîš,* the *hip'il* of *ybš.*

A series of explicit parallels in Joel 1–2 with other prophetic passages is also cited as evidence of the kind of literary dependence characteristic of late prophecy.[46] This assumption is bolstered by the fact that a number of these parallels are with other late prophetic texts, in particular Ezekiel, Second Isaiah, and Isa 13.[47] In addition to precise correspondences are the more general similarities between the yoking of the fates of animals and pastures (*nĕ'ôt midbār*) in Joel 1:18–20 and Jer 9:9 and the mourning (*'ābal*) of the priests in Joel 1:9 and their sighing (*'ānah*) in Lam 1:4.[48]

Moreover, there are numerous verbal links, beyond the metaphor of earth mourning, between Joel 1:5–20 and the late composition Isa 24:1–20. These include the devouring (*'ākal*) of the locusts in Joel 1:4 and the devouring of the curse (*'ākĕlâ*) in Isa 24:6; the call to lament to the drunkards (*šikkôrîm*) and drinkers of wine (*šōtê yāyin*) in Joel 1:5 and the sorrow of those who drink wine (*yištû-yāyin*) and beer (*šēkār*) in Isa 24:9; the shame (*hōbîš*) and languishing (*'umlal*) of wine, oil, vine and fig tree in Joel 1:10, 12 and the mourning (*'ābal*) and languishing (*'umlal*) of wine and vine in Isa 24:7; the personification of joy (*śāśôn*) in Joel 1:12 and in Isa 24:11 (*māśôś*); and the bearing of punishment by the flocks of sheep in Joel 1:18 (*ne'šāmû*) and by the inhabitants of the earth in Isa 24:6 (*wayye'šĕmû*).[49]

---

hebräischen Sprache des alten Testaments (Halle: Niemeyer, 1918–1922; repr., Hildesheim: Olms, 1962), §15.

[44] This word occurs in MT elsewhere only in Amos 9:13; Isa 49:26; Cant 8:2; and Joel 4:18. The verb *'āsas,* "to press," occurs only in Mal 3:21. Cf. BDB, 779a.

[45] These terms are parallel in 2 Chr 26:10 and, with suffixes, in Isa 61:5; the participle *kōrĕmîm* occurs alone in Jer 52:16 = 2 Kgs 25:12.

[46] See the discussion above of the authorship and dating of Isa 24:1–20.

[47] See, e.g., (1) Joel 1:15 and Ezek 30:2–3; Isa 13:6; Zeph 1:7; Obad 15; (2) Joel 2:1–2 and Zeph 1:14–15; (3) Joel 2:3 and Ezek 36:35; Isa 51:3; (4) Joel 2:6 and Nah 2:11; (5) Joel 2:27 and Ezek 36:11; Isa 45:5, 6. See the list in S. R. Driver, *Books of Joel and Amos,* 19–20, and the discussion in George B. Gray, "The Parallel Passages in 'Joel,' in Their Bearing on the Question of Date," *Exp* 4:8 (1893): 212–25.

[48] Note also that in Joel 1:18 the beasts sigh (*ne'enhâ*).

[49] As noted above in the discussion of the dating of Isa 24:1–20, literary dependence is not always easily distinguished from dependence on traditional phraseology, but the extent of the parallels in a given text to other texts is significant, as is the

Finally, the complex and architectonic style of Joel 1, in which repetition shapes a sequence of related scenes and images and there is a dense clustering of poetic devices, suggests composition in writing and hence possibly a late date.[50] All these factors lend credence to the postexilic dating of Joel 1:5–20. Some have made a case for more precise dating to the early restoration period before the reforms of Ezra and Nehemiah (hence to the era of Haggai and First Zechariah, or possibly Malachi),[51] but certainty is elusive given the few textual clues. A separate question concerns the place of 1:15, which announces the imminence of the Day of YHWH, within the larger unit. Duhm asserts that the reference to this day in 1:15 (like those in 1:2, 10, 11) is an interpolation intended to link a preexisting lament over a locust plague with the late eschatological prophecies of Joel 3–4.[52] Eissfeldt's judgment that explicit and implicit references to the Day of YHWH in Joel 1 are "firmly anchored in their contexts" and that lament over a locust plague and alarm over a coming Day of YHWH are not mutually exclusive is accepted here.[53] The verbal link formed by the use of the root *šdd* in 1:10 and 15 is noteworthy in this regard. In 1:10, "the field is destroyed" (*šuddad śādeh*) and "the grain is destroyed" (*šuddad dāgān*); in 1:15 the Day of YHWH is near and will come like destruction from the Almighty (*ûkĕšōd mišadday yābô'*).

THEMES AND MOTIFS

THE RESPONSE OF THE EARTH

In Joel 1:5–20 not only do human and natural images reflect each other throughout; in the end, they blend into one. Within this call to

---

nature of these parallels. Close or verbatim correspondences that recall only one other text (or a limited set of texts) may be more indicative of literary dependence than of traditional usage.

[50] See S. R. Driver (*Books of Joel and Amos,* 24), who cites A. B. Davidson on the "cultured and polished style" of the book. See, further, the discussion below.

[51] So Ahlström, *Joel and the Temple Cult of Jerusalem,* 112–29; Watts, *Joel,* 13; cf. Plöger, *Theocracy and Eschatology,* 105; S. R. Driver, *Books of Joel and Amos,* 25; Sellin, *Zwölfprophetenbuch,* 1:148. Those who date either Joel 1–2 or the book as a whole to the period following the reforms of Ezra and Nehemiah include Wolff, *Joel and Amos,* 5; Robinson and Horst, *Die zwölf kleinen Propheten,* 55; Bewer, *Critical and Exegetical Commentary,* 58–59; and Jeremias, "Joel/Joelbuch," 92.

[52] "Anmerkungen zu den Zwölf Propheten," 185; so also Robinson and Horst, *Die zwölf kleinen Propheten,* 61; Sellin, *Zwölfprophetenbuch,* 1:155; Bewer, *Critical and Exegetical Commentary,* 50.

[53] *Old Testament,* 392–93. See also Wolff, *Joel and Amos,* 22–23.

liturgical lament, elements of the natural and human worlds join in a single ritual of mourning. This union is accomplished in part by recurrent wordplay that pairs verbs bearing both physical and psychological senses with a variety of subjects, so that meanings slip and shift rapidly as the poem progresses, blurring the distinction between human (psychological) and natural (physical).

The frequent repetition of certain words and phrases in 1:5–20 further points to the confluence of agricultural disaster, human woe, and cultic rites.[54] The two words that recur most often in this passage are *śādeh*, "field" (5x), and *hôbîš* (5x). As noted above, *hôbîš* can be understood as both the *hipʿil* of the root *bwš*, with the meaning "to show shame," and the *hipʿil* of the root *ybš*, with the meaning "to show dryness." The recurrence of *śādeh* sharpens the poem's focus on the condition of the land;[55] the repetition of *hôbîš* underscores the fusion of physical and psychological responses.[56] The role of mourning is evident in the repetition of the imperative *hêlîlû*, "wail!" (3x), along with the related command *ʾĕlî*, "wail!" (once).[57] Finally, the phrases *bêt yhwh*, "house of YHWH," and *bêt ʾĕlōhêkem*, "house of your God," occur a total of four times, while the phrase *mĕšārĕtê*, "ministers of," is repeated three times, indicating the centrality of cultic rituals.[58]

Repetition also creates an overall structure that testifies to the major themes of this passage. Five calls to lament (1:5, 8, 11, 13, 14) and two cries of lament (1:15, 19) are issued in the poem, marking off a series of segments. The prophetic speaker calls the community (including drunkards, priests, farmers, vinedressers, elders, and "all the inhabitants of the land") to lament over the devastation of the earth and its crops. Yet as the

---

[54] Keller (*Joël, Abdias, Amos*, 110) groups the words in these verses around the following three foci: agriculture, devastation, and the cult.

[55] This focus is evident in a number of other repetitions in 1:5–20: *gepen*, "vine" (3x); *dāgān*, "grain" (2x); *tĕʾēnâ*, "fig tree" (2x); *bĕhēmâ* or *bahămôt*, "beasts" (2x); *nĕʾôt midbār*, "pastures of the wilderness" (2x). See also the use of the root *krt*, "to cut off" (either *nikrat* or *hokrat*), with a series of agricultural products: *ʿāsîs*, "sweet wine"; *minḥâ wānesek*, "cereal offering and drink offering"; and *ʾōkel*, "food."

[56] The dual reference of *hôbîš* is drawn out by the repetition of *ʾābal*, with its dual associations of mourning and drying up (2x), and *ʾumlal*, "to languish" and "to waste away" (2x).

[57] The stress on mourning is reinforced by the repetition of *ʾābal* (2x) and *ʾumlal* (2x) and by the twofold reference to the girding on of sackcloth (*ḥāgar* with *śaq* or *śaqqîm*).

[58] The repetition of *hakkōhănîm*, "priests" (2x) and of the phrase *minḥâ wānesek*, "cereal offering and drink offering" (2x), reinforces this impression.

prophet's own laments in 1:15, 19 and his elaboration of the present devastation in 1:9b–10, 12, 17–18, 20 clearly show, land, priest, people, and
prophet are already in mourning for what has been lost. Throughout the
poem the response of the earth to its loss matches both the manifest grief
of the people and the ritual expression of sorrow to which they are called.

Within the framework of lament, then, there is an alternating pattern,
in which the human community is on the one hand called to mourn over
the natural world (and is thereby distinguished from it) and on the other
hand joins with it in mourning (and thus is identified with it). As this pattern develops, the focus of the poem moves back and forth between
human mourning and the mourning of field, trees, crops, and beasts. The
overall literary structure of the poem holds both foci together.

The call to lament begins in 1:5 with an appeal to the drunkards and
drinkers of wine to wake up to the reality around them: the wine in which
they revel has been cut off.[59] It is easy to hear in this address an echo of
the cessation of revelling in Isa 24:9 among those who drink wine at the
celebration of the harvest.[60]

---

[59] That the call to lament in 1:5–20 is directed toward a present reality rather
than an imminent (future) reality is indicated by the prevalence of perfect forms
throughout. (The exceptions are *taʿărôg*, "thirst for," in 1:20, which may be read
in a durative sense, and *yābôʾ*, "is coming," in 1:15, where the reference is to the
Day of YHWH, a day that is prefigured in the present disasters.) These perfect
forms cannot easily be read as belonging to a visionary rhetorical mode that
makes the future more immediate (the prophetic perfect). Contrast, e.g., the call
to lament in Jer 9:9–10, in which the perfect forms that describe the devastation
of the land in 9:9 are succeeded by a clear future reference in 9:10: "I will make
[*wĕnātattî*] Jerusalem into heaps, ... and Judah I will make [*ʾettēn*] a desolation."
It seems more likely that in Joel 1:5–20 the people are being urged to lament on
the basis of an already desperate situation, which intimates the possibility of
worse to come. So Rudolph, *Joel-Amos-Obadja-Jona,* 41; S. R. Driver, *Books of
Joel and Amos,* 25–26; Jeremias, "Joel/Joelbuch," 91–97. In contrast, imperfect
forms predominate in 2:1–11, which describes the full horror of the approaching
Day of YHWH.

[60] Cf. Isa 16:10. At the same time the pejorative term *šikkôrîm,* "drunkards," conveys a sense of inappropriate indulgence that has stupefied those who imbibe so
that they are unaware of what is happening around them. So Keller, *Joël, Abidas,
Jonas,* 111. Cf. the use of *šikkôr* (or *šikkōr*) in Isa 19:14; 28:1, 3; 1 Sam 1:13; 1 Kgs
16:9; Prov 26:9; Ps 107:27; Job 12:25. Sellin (*Zwölfprophetenbuch,* 1:152) and
Rudolph (*Joel-Amos-Obadja-Jona,* 43), in contrast, see no hint of reproach in this
term, arguing that it is parallel here to the neutral *šōtê yāyin,* "drinkers of wine,"
and refers only to a normal expression of joy and celebration. The usages of *šikkôr*
cited above, however, add at least a shadow of negative association to this epithet,
especially given its combination with the command *hāqîṣû,* "wake up!"

The reality to which the drunkards of 1:5 are recalled is the destruction caused by a locust swarm to the land, which is given three distinct appellations: *ʾarṣî*, "my land"; *gapnî*, "my vine"; and *tĕʾēnātî*, "my fig tree" (1:6–7). Each of these expressions has a dual reference: each can be taken literally, as referring to the devastation of the earth and its most valued crops, or figuratively, as alluding to the nation or community of Judah.[61] The first colon of 1:7 emphasizes this dual reference: *śām gapnî lĕšammâ*, "it has laid waste my vine." The noun *šammâ* means both "waste" and "appallment,"[62] and the use of this word to denote an occasion for horror and appallment appropriate to grief complements the figurative dimensions of "my vine," integrating the destruction of the earth with the concept of human mourning. In this the colon evokes Jer 12:10–11, discussed above:

> Many shepherds have ruined my vineyard [*karmî*];
>   they have trampled my field [*ʾet-ḥelqātî*].
> They have made the field of my delight [*ʾet-ḥelqat ḥemdātî*]
>   into a desolate desert [*lĕmidbar šĕmāmâ*].
> It has been made a desolation [*śāmāh lišmāmâ*];
>   it mourns [*ʾābĕlâ*] to my sorrow, desolate [*šĕmēmâ*].[63]

In the three opening verses of Joel 1:5–20 the earth is simply the object of destruction by locusts. In the following verses (1:8–10), earth and community respond to the disaster, and the phraseology suggests drought as well as a locust plague.[64] It has been proposed that the appeal in 1:8 to "lament [*ʾĕlî*] like a virgin girded with sackcloth for the bridegroom of her

---

[61] On the dual aspect of *ʾereṣ* as land and nation, see the discussion above of the response of the earth in Hos 4:1–3. The use of *kerem*, "vineyard," as a figure for Israel was noted above in relation to Jer 12:7–13. Israel (or Judah) is compared to a vine (*gepen*) in Hos 10:1; Jer 2:21; 6:9; 8:13; Ezek 19:10; and to a fig tree or figs (*tĕʾēnâ*) in Hos 9:10; Jer 8:13; 24:1, 2, 3, 5, 8; 29:17. Cf. BDB, 172b, 1061a.

[62] BDB, 1031b; see also the discussion above of the response of the earth in Jer 4:23–28 and Isa 24:12.

[63] In this verse *šĕmāmâ*, "desolation," is used rather than the related noun *šammâ*.

[64] On the natural relationship between locust plague and drought, see Watts, *Joel*, 19–20; Sellin, *Zwölfprophetenbuch*, 1:153. *CAD* (1:30) cites the use of *abālu*, "to dry up," in a religious text that refers to the activity of the locust: "the evil locust which dries up the orchards." Ronald A. Simkins ("God, History, and the Natural World in the Book of Joel," *CBQ* 55 [1993]: 441–42) argues that the images of drought in 1:10–20 merely depict the visual effects on the landscape of the locust swarm in combination with a normal dry season. Kathleen S. Nash ("The Cycle of Seasons in Joel," *TBT* 27 [1989]: 74–80), on the other hand, sees in Joel 1 two separate phenomena: a locust plague and a drought.

youth" is a reflection of the Ugaritic myth of Anat mourning over Baal's defeat at the hands of Mot, a defeat that results in the withering and languishing of the earth.[65] In terms of the text itself, the linking in 1:10 of the verbs *'ābal*, "to mourn"; *hôbîš*, "to show shame" and "to show dryness"; and *'umlal*, "to languish" and "to waste away," with the ground (*'ădāmâ*), new wine (*tîrôš*), and oil (*yiṣhār*), respectively, suggests drought, at least as a nuance.

The wordplay in these verses puts human and natural responses on the same plane. The priests mourn (*'ābĕlû*, 1:9) and so does the ground (*'ābĕlâ*, 1:10), while the new wine is ashamed (*hôbîš*) and the oil languishes (*'umlal*) in 1:10. All these verbs can be heard as one response of distress on the part of different subjects.[66] Yet the nuance of drying up and wasting away in the response of the earth hints at a distinct mode of mourning. The priests perform their rites of mourning; the ground, the wine, and the oil mourn by drying up and wasting away.[67]

The structure of 1:10 facilitates the understanding of the mourning or shame of the earth as a response to destruction. The first bicolon of the verse begins with a passive construction: *šuddad śādeh*, "the field is destroyed," which is followed by an indication of active response: *'ābĕlâ 'ădāmâ*, "the ground mourns." The second bicolon repeats this pattern, reinforcing it with the particle *kî*, "for, because." The phrase *kî šuddad dāgān*, "for the grain is destroyed," is followed by another response: the new wine is ashamed (*hôbîš*), and the oil languishes (*'umlal*).

The impression of active response on the part of the earth is strengthened by the opening bicolon of the next verse (1:11), in which farmers and vinedressers are called upon to show shame (*hôbîšû*) and to wail (*hêlîlû*). Again, human actors and elements of the earth are placed on the same plane: both new wine (1:10) and farmers (1:11) are ashamed (*hôbîš*), while the ground (1:10) mourns (*'ābal*) and the vinedressers (1:11) wail (*hêlîl*). The theme of mourning is sustained in the second

---

[65] See Kapelrud, *Joel Studies,* 32–24; Delbert R. Hillers, "The Roads to Zion Mourn," *Perspective* 12:1–2 (1971): 127–30. Hillers (130–33) notes, however, that it is very likely that this expression does not represent a conscious reference to Ugaritic myth but rather traditional usage.

[66] For the response of shame (*bwš*) in contexts of disaster and mourning, see the discussion above of the response of the earth in Jer 12:7–13. In relation to the occurrences of *hôbîš* in Joel 1, see especially S. R. Driver, *Books of Joel and Amos,* 41. In Joel 1:5–20 *hôbîš* can be read as "ashamed" in the sense of "put to shame," "overcome," "cast down," or, simply, "defeated," "failed" (see, e.g., the RSV translation of 1:10, 12, 17 and the rendering by NAB of 1:10 and 17).

[67] D. J. A. Clines ("Was There an *'BL* II 'Be Dry' in Classical Hebrew?" *VT* 42 [1992]: 9) attributes all nuances of drying up in *'ābal* to such a conceit.

bicolon of 1:11: the harvest of the field (qĕṣîr śādeh) is lost (ʾābad). The verb ʾābad occurs frequently in contexts of the destruction of nations and, in later texts, of the death of individuals.[68] Hence the response of both human beings and nature is presented as mourning over the death of the harvest.

The devastation of vines and trees is drawn into this scenario in 1:12. In this verse the introduction of the unequivocal verb yābēš, "to dry up," in the phrase kol-ʿăṣê haśśādeh yābēšû, "all the trees of the field are withered," brings to the surface the implicit wordplay of the preceding verses. This phrase occurs in the second bicolon of a verse comprising three bicola. In the first bicolon, the vine is ashamed (hôbîšâ), and the fig tree languishes (ʾumlĕlâ); in the second, all the trees of the field wither (yābēšû); in the third gladness is shamed (hôbîš) away from humankind.

The progression in these three bicola deftly effects the crossover between human and natural responses characteristic of the poem as a whole. In the first bicolon vine and fig tree take on the role of human mourners: they are ashamed, and they languish. The presence of yābēšû, "have dried up," in the following bicolon, however, encourages the identification of hôbîš as a hipʿil of the root ybš and the reading of ʾumlal as "to waste away" in what precedes. The verb yābēšû thus strengthens the inclination to see here the natural phenomenon of withering and wasting away. In the third bicolon the subject of hôbîš is the human quality of gladness. In this case the influence of yābēšû in the preceding colon encourages the reading "gladness dries up" (that is, disappears) as well as "gladness is ashamed." The traditional associations between harvest and rejoicing, already evoked in 1:5, further bind the separate images in this verse into a single scene of desiccation and despair.[69]

In 1:13–16 the focus shifts to human lamenting. In 1:13 the priests are called to gird on sackcloth, lament, and wail over the holding back of cereal offering and drink offering from "the house of your God." In 1:14 they are exhorted to summon the leaders and "all the inhabitants of the land" (kōl yōšĕbê hāʾāreṣ) to the "house of YHWH your God" so that they, too, may fast and cry out to YHWH.

In 1:15 the prophet gives voice to his own rendition of that cry: "Alas, for the Day of YHWH is near!" This lament is related in 1:16 to the cutting off of food (ʾōkel) as well as of joy and gladness (śimḥâ wāgîl) "from the house of our God." Here the disappearance of crops

---

[68] See BDB, 19b.

[69] Cf. the cutting off of food along with "joy and gladness" in 1:16. On the disappearance of harvest joy in 1:12, see Keller, Joël, Abdias, Jonas, 114; Bewer, Critical and Exegetical Commentary, 83; Watts, Joel, 20.

and gladness sketched in 1:12 is linked to the temple, the center of human ritual activity.

The threefold repetition of "the house of God" in 1:13–16 binds these verses, with their stress on ritual mourning, together. In 1:17–20 the focus shifts again to the response of the earth, and the vocabulary of both physical and psychological distress reappears. In 1:17 the seeds are shrivelled (*'ābĕšû*); the near rhyme of *'ābĕšû* and *yābĕšû* (1:12) underscores the continuity of the motif of drought. Perhaps in response to the loss of the seeds, the threshing floors, where grain is collected, are "dismayed" (*ḥattû*). The statement that the storehouses are "desolate" (*nāšammû*) means, most obviously, that they are physically empty. Yet the secondary meaning of *nāšam*, "to be appalled, horrified," is latent. The storage bins are pulled down (*nehersû*), which speaks of physical ruin; yet the grain is ashamed (*hōbîš*).[70] If *hōbîš* is heard as a *hipʿil* of the root *ybš*, "to dry up," on the other hand, the phrase *hōbîš dāgān*, "the grain withers," also represents a physical phenomenon that matches the shrivelling of the seed in the first colon of the verse.

In 1:18 a sequence of personifications of animal subjects unfolds. In the first bicolon the beasts sigh (*ne'enḥâ*) and the herds of cattle are confused (*nābōkû*). The verb *ne'enḥâ* occurs elsewhere in the Hebrew Bible in contexts of human distress and mourning,[71] while *nābôk* conveys the confusion and consternation associated with crisis.[72] The verse ends with a final image of flocks of sheep suffering punishment (*ne'šāmû*). The root *'šm* is found elsewhere in the Hebrew Bible in contexts of human wrongdoing and often carries associations of an internal state of guilt. Particularly pertinent to its occurrence here is the instance in Isa 24:6, where the inhabitants of the earth suffer punishment (*wayye'šĕmû*) and dwindle (*ḥārû*) under a curse that devours (*'ākĕlâ*) the earth. In Joel 1:18–19 the sheep suffer punishment, and fire and flame devour (*'ākĕlâ*) the pastures of the wilderness. In light of these parallels it is all the more apparent that in Joel 1:18 the sheep are placed on the same plane as human beings and suffer punishment from the twin plagues (or curses) of locust swarm and drought, just as do the human inhabitants of the land, those called to mourn.

The final verses of the poem (1:19–20) sustain the balancing of human and natural despair. The prophet laments in 1:19:

---

[70] The verbs *ḥat* and *bôš* occur together in Jer 14:4, part of a communal lament over drought: the ground is dismayed (*ḥattâ*) and the farmers are ashamed (*bōšû*).

[71] See, e.g., Isa 24:7; Lam 1:4, 8, 11, 21; Ezek 9:4; 21:11, 12. Cf. BDB, 58b.

[72] See Exod 14:3; Esth 3:15. Cf. BDB, 100b.

To you, YHWH I cry,
For fire has devoured the pastures of the wilderness,
and flame ignited all the trees of the field.

This verse is echoed almost exactly in 1:20, except that the thirsting of the beasts of the field for YHWH stands in place of the prophet's cry:

Even the beasts of the field thirst for you,
    for the streams are dried up,
    and fire devours the pastures of the wilderness.

The distinction between the verbs *qārāʾ*, "call," and *ʿārag*, "thirst for, long for," reflects the difference between the voiced appeal of the human speaker and the mute longing of the animals.[73] At the same time the parallels between the two verses, in particular the chiming of the last line of 1:20 with the opening lines of 1:19 ("and fire devours the pastures of the wilderness"), bring the poem to an end on a final note of unison.[74]

SIN OR PUNISHMENT

It is notable that in Joel 1:5–20, as in Joel 1–2 as a whole, there is no explicit mention of the wrongdoing or failings of the community.[75] Yet both textual and extratextual factors lead the reader (or hearer) to understand the crisis the community faces as a consequence of or punishment for unspecified failings. Locusts as well as drought are invoked in Deut 28 as curses upon Israel for failure to uphold the law,[76] and the notion of curse manifest there reflects traditional identification of natural disaster with divine disfavor. Further, the reference to the Day of YHWH in 1:15 as a day of destruction (*šōd*) introduces associations of the divine warrior, who summons the powers of nature against those who oppose him. The

---

[73] The verb *ʿārag* occurs elsewhere in MT only in Ps 42:2, where the longing or thirsting (*taʿărōg*) of the psalmist for God is compared to the longing or thirsting (*taʿărōg*) of a hart for streams of water (*ʾăpîqê māyim*). Here the beasts thirst (*taʿărōg*) for God because the *ʾăpîqê māyim* are dried up.

[74] It is further possible to see an *inclusio* around the poem as a whole that balances human and nonhuman reactions to the crises of locust plague and drought. The wailing to which the drinkers of wine are called in 1:5 because of the cutting off of sweet wine is echoed in 1:20 by the thirsting of the beasts because the streams of water have dried up.

[75] See also the comments of Wolff, *Joel and Amos,* 13; S. R. Driver, *Books of Joel and Amos,* 12.

[76] See Deut 28:38–42; cf. Amos 4:7–9, esp. 4:9. See also Bourke, "Le Jour de Yahvé dans Joel," 15; Ahlström, *Joel and the Temple Cult of Jerusalem,* 29.

topos of the Day of YHWH is developed more fully in Joel 2, but it is interesting to compare the use in 1:7 of the verb *ḥāśap*, "to strip bare," which conveys the devouring action of the locusts in Joel 1:7, and the imagery of fire (*ʾēš*) and flame (*lehābâ*) in Joel 1:19–20 with the theophany of YHWH in Ps 29:7–9, where the voice of YHWH flashes forth like flames of fire (*lahăbôt ʾēš*) and strips bare (*wayyeḥĕśōp*) the forests.[77]

In addition, if Joel 1 is seen as integrally related to Joel 2,[78] then the call in 2:12–13 to return (*šûbû*) to YHWH "with all your heart" (*bĕkol-lĕbabkem*) echoes the summons to lament in 1:5, 8, 11, 13, and 14, making explicit an implied separation between the community and YHWH.[79] Although the exact nature of this separation is not detailed in Joel 1–2 (nor, for that matter, in Joel 3–4), reference in postexilic prophetic texts outside the book of Joel to divine judgment in the form of agricultural catastrophe may illumine the way the locust plague and accompanying drought are envisaged here. In Hag 1:6–11 the reality of a scant harvest is depicted in terms that resemble the account in Joel 1:5–20 at several points. In Hag 1:11 YHWH states:

> I have called for a drought upon the earth [*hāʾāreṣ*] and upon the mountains and upon the grain [*haddāgān*] and upon the new wine [*hattîrôš*] and upon the oil [*hayyiṣhār*] and upon that which the ground [*hāʾădāmâ*] brings forth, and upon people [*hāʾādām*] and upon the beasts [*habbĕhēmâ*].

The elements named in this verse resemble those featured in Joel 1:10, 12, and 17–18. In Hag 2:17 YHWH recalls striking the people with blight, mildew, and hail and then, in 2:19, asks, "Is the seed still in the bin [*bammĕgûrâ*]? And do the vine [*haggepen*] and the fig tree [*wĕhattĕʾēnâ*] and the pomegranate [*wĕhārimmôn*] and the olive tree [*wĕʿēṣ hazzayit*] still not bear?" The occurrence of the rare word *mĕgûrâ* here and in Joel

---

[77] Wolff (*Joel and Amos*, 35) notes that the fire and flame of Joel 1:19–20 are reminiscent of theophany traditions found in Pss 29:7; 50:3; 97:3 as well as in descriptions of the Day of YHWH in Zeph 1:18 and Joel 2:3.

[78] See the discussion above of the delimitation of Joel 1:5–20.

[79] When the call to lament in Joel 1:5–20 is read together with 2:12–13, repentance is seen as a major aspect of the mourning enjoined on the community. On the connection between mourning and penitential rites, see Ernst Kutsch, "'Trauerbräuche' und 'Selbstminderungsriten' im Alten Testament," in *Drei Wiener Antrittsreden* (TS 78; Zurich: EVZ, 1965), 25–37; Gary A. Anderson, *A Time to Mourn, A Time to Dance: The Expression of Grief and Joy in Israelite Religion* (University Park: Pennsylvania State University Press, 1991), 51–52. See also Isa 58:5; Job 42:6; Jonah 3:5.

1:17 is striking, as is the correspondence between the grouping of vine and fruit trees in this verse and in Joel 1:12.

The troubles of the land in these passages from Haggai are attributed to the meager efforts of the returned exiles in the rebuilding of the temple.[80] In Joel 1:5–20 agricultural disaster cannot necessarily be understood as imputed to the same cause. The similarities between this passage and Hag 1:6–11; 2:17–19 may nevertheless indicate that the destruction of the harvest in Joel 1 was related by the author of this text and its audience to failings on the part of the community toward YHWH.

In Mal 3, similarly, the people of Jerusalem are warned against a full range of offenses, including sorcery, adultery, swearing falsely, oppressing hired servants, mistreating widows and orphans, turning away sojourners, and not fearing God (3:5). They are also condemned for cheating in the bringing of tithes and offerings to the temple (3:8–9). If the people do bring full tithes, YHWH will release rain from the heavens and will rebuke the "devourer" ([*bā*]*ʾōkēl*), or locust,[81] so that it does not destroy the fruit of the ground (*hāʾădāmâ*) and so that the vine of the field (*haggepen baśśādeh*) does not fail to bear (3:11). Again, the parallels between the destruction of the locust envisioned in Mal 3:11 and that depicted in Joel 1:5–20 do not indicate precise correspondence in every aspect. But the passage from Malachi does provide another example of the way natural disasters are linked to human misdeeds in late prophetic writings.

The absence of any mention of specific offenses in Joel 1:5–20 is perhaps easier to understand in light of the general formulation of 2 Chr 7:13–14:

> If I shut up the heavens and there is no rain, and if I command the locust to devour the land [*leʾĕkôl hāʾāreṣ*], and if I unleash pestilence on my people; if my people who are called by my name humble themselves and pray and seek my face and turn [*wĕyāšūbû*] from their wicked ways [*middarkêhem hārāʿîm*], then I will hear from the heavens and I will forgive their sins [*lĕhaṭṭāʾtām*] and I will heal their land [*ʾarṣām*].

In this passage YHWH promises to heal the destruction caused by drought, locust plague, and disease if the people turn (*šûb*) from their "wicked ways." Perhaps such general rubrics for human behavior as "wicked ways" and "sins" are to be understood as lying behind the locust plague and drought in Joel 1:5–20. Certainly the repeated summons in these verses to lament, wail, and cry to YHWH "in the house of YHWH your God" (1:14)

---

[80] Cf. Zech 8:9–13.

[81] Locusts are represented as devouring (*ʾākal*) in Joel 1:4 and 2:25 as well as in Amos 4:9 and 2 Chr 7:13.

is consistent with YHWH's direction in 2 Chr 7:14 that the people humble themselves, pray, and "seek my face" in the newly built temple.

MOURNING AS STRIPPING

The imagery of locust plague and drought in Joel 1:5–20 evokes the motif of mourning as stripping, as do a number of verbal allusions. Joel 1:4, which directly precedes the call to lament in 1:5–20, emphasizes the denuded swath cut by the locusts as they move in a series of four waves across the earth: what one type of locust has left, the next group devours (*ʾākal*).[82] The devouring action of the swarm is elaborated on in 1:7:

> It has made my vine a desolation,
>   and my fig tree splinters.
> It has stripped it bare [*ḥāśōp ḥăśāpāh*] and thrown it down;
>   its branches have turned white.

On a literal level the verb *ḥāśap*, "to strip off, strip bare," conveys the removal of fruit, leaves, and even bark. But this verb also suits the figurative dimensions of "my vine" and "my fig tree" as representing Judah, since *ḥāśap* occurs elsewhere in the prophetic literature in the context of the punishment and defeat of peoples (either of Israel/Judah or of the nations).[83] In Jer 13:26, for example, the motif of the stripping of Judah as a prostitute appears. In this and other instances the stripping of peoples can be seen as an imposed state of mourning. The link between stripping, punishment, and mourning is explicit in Isa 47:1–3a:

> Come down and sit in the dust [*ʿāpār*],
>   virgin daughter of Babylon;
> Sit on the ground [*lāʾāreṣ*] without a throne,
>   daughter of the Chaldeans.
> For you will not again be called
>   delicate and exquisite.
> Take millstones and grind flour,
>   uncover your veil
> Strip off [*ḥeśpî*] your long skirt, uncover your leg,
>   Cross through rivers.
> Your nakedness will be exposed;
>   yes, your shame [*ḥerpātēk*] will be seen.

---

[82] Cf. the sequence of actions in Isa 24:18 and in Amos 5:19 in reference to the Day of YHWH.

[83] See Isa 20:4; 47:2–3; Jer 13:26; 49:10. In Jer 49:9–10 YHWH's stripping of Esau (Edom) is compared to the gleaning of grapevines. The element of shame and disgrace is present in Isa 20:4; 47:2–3; Jer 13:26.

Here Babylon, in the figure of a young woman, is compelled to engage in the mourning rite: to sit in the dust and to strip herself of her normal clothing. Here, too, images of the mourning ritual merge with the depiction of enslavement, defeat, and shame.

In similar fashion, the stripping of vine and fig tree in Joel 1:7 and the shame of wine (1:10), vine (1:12), and grain (1:17), as well as of farmers (1:11) and of gladness (1:12), represent a rite of mourning that the land has been forced to undergo by the ravages of the locusts. As would befit an image of military defeat, the locusts are described as a hostile nation (*gôy*) in 1:6.

The placement of this scene of the stripping of the land just before the call to "lament like a virgin girded with sackcloth" in 1:8 supports this correlation of mourning and stripping. A young woman who is girded in sackcloth has stripped off her clothes and put on the traditional garment of mourning. The association between stripping and ritual mourning is echoed again in 1:12–13. In 1:12, the various fruit trees and all the trees of the field wither (*yābēšû*), thereby losing their fruit and leaves, just as gladness disappears from humankind. If gladness is understood as an antonym of mourning, then mourning is implied by the stripping of vegetation and harvest joy here.[84] In 1:13 the prophet calls again, this time to the priests: "Gird yourselves in sackcloth and lament!" and "Keep a vigil in sackcloth!" Here the priests are enjoined to mimic the stripping that has already taken place in the fields around them.

Other images complement the motif of mourning as stripping in 1:5–20. The repeated use of the root *krt*, "to cut off," with reference to a range of subjects is notable. The sweet wine (*ʿāsîs*), with which the harvest is celebrated, is cut off (*nikrat*) in 1:5; cereal offering and drink offering (*minḥâ wānesek*), basic elements of the cult, are cut off (*hokrat*) in 1:9; and both food (*ʾōkel*), the material basis of human life, and gladness and exultation (*śimḥâ wāgîl*) in the temple, which signify a positive relationship with YHWH, are cut off (*nikrat*) in 1:16.[85] The mention of the broken-down (*nehersû*) storage bins in 1:17 evokes a flattened landscape, lacking the structures that represent agricultural well-being.[86] Finally, the

---

[84] See the link between the commands to be glad (*gîlî/gîlû*) and to rejoice (*ûśĕmāḥî/wĕśimḥû*) and rain and fertility in Joel 2:21–24. On mourning and gladness as antonyms, see Anderson, *A Time to Mourn*, 49–54.

[85] Cf. the recurrent use of the *hipʿil* of *krt* in Mic 5:9–13.

[86] The verb *nehersû* (*nipʿal*), means, in the *qal*, "to throw down, tear down," and may evoke scenarios of stripping; cf. the use of *hāras* with *hikrît*, "to cut off," in Mic 5:10. I have translated *nehersû* here in the middle voice, "have broken down," as more consistent than the passive with the depiction of Joel 1; so Rudolph, *Joel-Amos-Obadja-Jona*, 40.

devouring (*ʾākĕlâ*) by fire of the pastures of the wilderness in 1:19–20, which parallels the devouring (*ʾākal*) by the locusts of all that is in their path in 1:4, stands as the final image of the poem: earth utterly bare.[87]

DECREATION

There is an echo of creation language in this poem in the phrases *kol-ʿǎṣê haśśādeh,* "all the trees of the field" (1:12), and *bahǎmôt śādeh,* "the beasts of the field" (1:20). The latter expression is reminiscent of the phrase *ḥayyat haśśādeh,* "the animals of the field," found in contexts of creation.[88] The former expression (or a close variant) is used in a variety of contexts to represent all the trees of the earth.[89]

In Joel 1:12 a whole range of trees falls under the rubric *kol-ʿǎṣê haśśādeh:* fig (*tĕʾēnâ*), pomegranate (*rimmôn*), date (*tāmār*), and apple (*tappûaḥ*). Similarly, the reference to the "beasts" (*bĕhēmâ*) at the beginning of 1:18 is followed by further specifications that recall the range of living creatures on earth: cattle (*ʿedrê bāqār*) and sheep (*ʿedrê haṣṣōʾn*) as well as, in 1:20, the "beasts of the field" (*bahǎmôt śādeh*).[90] The enumeration of grain (*dāgān*), new wine (*tîrôš*), oil (*yiṣhār*) in 1:10 and wheat (*ḥiṭṭâ*) and barley (*śĕʿōrâ*) in 1:11 fills out the catalogue of creation.

This catalogue does not feature the elemental constituents of creation as much as it does the continuity of creation in the ongoing cultivation of the earth and herding of animals, that is, in agriculture. These verses are more reminiscent of the continuum of creation depicted in Ps 104 than of the origins of creation in Gen 1–2.[91] Psalm 104:14–16 serves as an example as it praises

---

[87] The parallel between the devouring of fire and locusts is even closer if one considers the metaphor comparing the invading locusts to fire in Joel 2:3–4, and it is possible that fire serves as a symbol for the locusts here. See S. R. Driver, *Books of Joel and Amos,* 47; Simkins, "God, History, and the Natural World," 440, 442. In Amos 7:4, however, fire apparently represents drought. Rudolph (*Joel-Amos-Obadja-Jona,* 49) argues that fire and flame are images for the scorching east wind, or sirocco.

[88] See Gen 2:19, 20; 3:1, 14 and the discussion above of the theme of decreation in Hos 4:1–3.

[89] See, e.g., Exod 9:25; Lev 26:4; Isa 55:12.

[90] These are generally thought to represent wild animals (so, e.g., Wolff, *Joel and Amos,* 20; Sellin, *Zwölfprophetenbuch,* 156; Rudolph, *Joel-Amos-Obadja-Jona,* 49).

[91] The bases of agricultural life are established in these chapters, however, and the man created in Gen 2 becomes the first farmer (2:15). On the agricultural orientation of the Yahwist source in Gen 1–11, see Theodore Hiebert, *The Yahwist's Landscape: Nature and Religion in Early Israel* (New York: Oxford University Press, 1996), 30–82.

The one who causes grass to grow for the beasts,
    and plants for humanity to cultivate,
So that they may bring forth food for the earth,
    and wine to gladden the human heart.
So that they may make their faces shine with oil
    And so that bread sustains the human heart.
The trees of YHWH are well watered,
    the cedars of Lebanon that he planted.

By naming the particulars of agricultural life, Joel 1:5–20 shows how the plagues of locust and drought have touched its full range, from the field to the grain, wine, and oil; from the vine to the fig tree and pomegranate, date, and apple; from the seed to the threshing floor and storage bin; from the drinker of sweet wine, to the priests who sanctify offerings of cereal and drink in the temple, to the farmers and vinedressers who work the land; from the herds of cattle to the flocks of sheep. It is this spectrum of life on earth that is threatened with eradication as the concluding refrain makes clear: "and fire has devoured the pastures of the wilderness" (1:20). Here the "pastures of the wilderness" (*ně'ôt hammidbār*) have become desert (*midbār*), and Joel 1:5–20 depicts, in its own way, the reversion of creation into an empty wasteland.

SUMMARY OF LITERARY TECHNIQUES

Joel 1:5–20 achieves solemn simplicity of style through a complex coalescence of literary techniques. The central technique is personification, which occurs eleven times in the passage. Of these instances, ten attribute human responses to subjects related to the cultivation of the earth.[92] Hence the ground mourns (*'ābělâ*), the new wine is ashamed (*hôbîš*), and the oil languishes (*'umlal*) in 1:10; the vine is ashamed (*hôbîšâ*) in 1:12; the threshing floors are dismayed (*hattû*), the storehouses appalled (*nāšammû*), and the grain ashamed (*hōbîš*) in 1:17; the beasts sigh (*ne'enhâ*), the herds of cattle are confused (*nābōkû*), and the flocks of sheep suffer punishment (*ne'šāmû*) in 1:18; and the beasts of the field thirst or long for (*ta'ărôg*) YHWH in 1:20.[93] Many of these instances of personification entail the use of verbs with dual meanings and associations and thus can be heard in a physical, as well as a psychological, sense. Thus the ground dries up (*'ābělâ*), the new wine dries up (*hôbîš*), the oil dwindles away (*'umlal*), the vine dries up (*hôbîšâ*), the storehouses are

---

[92] If the joy that is shamed away from humankind in 1:12 is seen as harvest joy, then this personification is drawn into an agricultural context as well.

[93] The eleventh element personified is joy (*śāśôn*), in 1:12.

deserted (*nāšammû*), and the grain dries up (*hôbîš*). At the same time the poem's use of *'ābal* and *hôbîš* with human subjects (priests in 1:9, farmers in 1:11) and the balancing of human and natural subjects through the creation of parallel structures bespeaks the convergence of the two realms. The rapid shifting between natural and human perspectives accomplished with the aid of these techniques brings together the mourning of human actors over the devastated land and the devastation of the land itself, so that people and earth raise one cry of grief and longing to YHWH.

OVERALL EFFECT OF THE METAPHOR

The metaphor of the ground (*'ădāmâ*) mourning in Joel 1:5–20 forms part of a detailed picture of distress in the face of natural disaster. This metaphor constitutes one figure in a mosaic of figures and images that range from the seeds shrivelling to the priests girding themselves with sackcloth. All the scenes in this mosaic illustrate aspects of the theme of the mourning of land and people. What is more, individual elements within these scenes overlap and merge, creating a holographic effect that adds depth and resonance to the overall picture of lamentation.

It is notable that a number of the themes expressed in some of the passages discussed above remain unvoiced here. There are, for example, no allusions to social disorder or to pollution and only scant reference to the role of sin and punishment in the experienced devastation. Rather than presenting a full constellation of interrelated themes and motifs, Joel 1:5–20 focuses on the response of land and people to disaster, developing this in detail. Hence, for example, not only does the ground (*'ădāmâ*) mourn and dry up, but grain, wine, oil, wheat, barley, harvest, vine, fig tree, and various fruit trees are named and described as actors. This elaboration serves, as noted above, to evoke the fullness of created life on earth. But it may also be seen as characteristic of a more literary, as opposed to oral, style.[94]

In Joel 1:5–20, as in Isa 33:7–9, the metaphor of earth mourning is emblematic of a present state of distress. In the light of Joel 1–2 as a whole, this present state is itself a portent of even greater catastrophe: the Day of YHWH. The depiction of widespread mourning in the land in 1:5–20 is intended to rouse those who are stricken to raise a lament to YHWH in the proper communal rituals of mourning and repentance. In Isa 33:7–9 the

---

[94] See the discussion above of Isa 24:1–20. Coggins ("An Alternative Prophetic Tradition?" 84) asserts, in a comment on Nahum, that the tendency to dwell on a particular aspect of the prophetic message and to focus on details is characteristic of later prophetic collections (i.e., post–eighth century).

description of desolation forms part of a series of laments uttered with confidence in ultimate deliverance for those who "walk righteously" (33:15). Just so, the call to lament in Joel 1:5–20 is issued not as a warning of inexorable judgment but in hopes of restoration, if priests and people will only "return" (*šūbû*) to YHWH with their whole hearts (2:12).

It is appropriate that the consummate intertwining of the human and natural realms in this passage occurs within a literary context grounded in agricultural life, since agriculture is the result of a fundamental interaction between human society and the natural world.[95] Among the nine passages considered here, Joel 1:5–20 brings to its most supple and realistic expression the interdependence of these two facets of creation in the continuance of creation as a whole.

---

[95] On the relation between the agricultural basis of Israel and themes of creation and cosmic order in the Hebrew Bible, see Rolf P. Knierim, "Cosmos and History in Israel's Theology," *HBT* 3 (1981): 59–123.

7

THE AESTHETICS OF ORAL TRADITIONAL
POETRY AND THE BIBLICAL TEXT

The discussion of prophetic texts in this study has focused on the inter-relationships among them. These nine texts share a metaphor conveyed by the verb *'ābal* and the noun *'ereṣ* or a semantically related noun or noun phrase. They share other vocabulary, phraseology, imagery, and poetic devices. They also show similarities in theme and motif. The correspondences between the passages, save for the shared use of the verb *'ābal*, are not exact, however. Vocabulary and theme do not recur uniformly in each of the nine passages; rather, clusters of words and themes appear in varying configurations and in distinctive literary contexts.

The question arises, then, On what basis can these passages be compared beyond the pairing of *'ābal* with *'ereṣ* or a related subject? Does comparing them elucidate the meaning of their shared metaphor? How do other biblical passages with similar phraseology and kindred themes relate to the nine texts under discussion?

Scholars of literary traditions outside the Hebrew Bible have noted similar phenomena and raised similar questions in their consideration of the characteristic forms of oral traditional poetry and the way these forms convey meaning. Two recent comparative studies by John M. Foley summarize and extend the research done on oral epic poetry since the seminal work of Milman Parry and Albert B. Lord.[1]

These studies are described in some detail in this chapter, with analogies provided from the discussion of the nine biblical prophetic passages

---

[1] The two primary studies by Foley referred to here are *Traditional Oral Epic: The Odyssey, Beowulf, and the Serbo-Croatian Return Song* (Berkeley and Los Angeles: University of California Press, 1990) and *Immanent Art: From Structure to Meaning in Traditional Oral Epic* (Bloomington: University of Indiana Press, 1991). Lord's and Parry's work achieved wide circulation with the publication of Lord's *The Singer of Tales* (Harvard Studies in Comparative Literature 24; Cambridge, Mass.: Harvard University Press, 1960). See also the writings of Milman Parry in *The Making of Homeric Verse: The Collected Papers of Milman Parry* (ed. Adam Parry; New York: Oxford University Press, 1987).

above. This initial marking of points of similarity is followed by an analysis of the bases for comparison between oral epic poetry and the prophetic speeches of the Hebrew Bible.[2]

In presenting the main points of Foley's work as it relates to the study at hand, it is best to begin where he does, with a discussion of the parameters of traditional oral poetry. In *The Singer of Tales* Lord maintains a strict distinction between works composed orally and those composed in writing and rules out the idea of a transitional stage reflecting a mix of the two compositional techniques.[3] Oral composition, he argues, relies almost exclusively on the use of formulas, or set phrases; formulaic expressions, which follow set syntactic and semantic patterns; and traditional themes, or narrative units. Written composition, alternatively, generates original expressions and structures. Yet Lord acknowledges that the presence of formulas in written or literary style points to its origins in oral style and further notes that the existence of nonformulaic expressions in oral texts, especially those produced by gifted oral poets, proves that "the seeds of 'literary' style are already present in oral style."[4] He thus hints at a continuum between oral and written style.

Foley, along with others, argues that measures of formulaic density in a work are not valid assessments of oral composition. Different poetic traditions operate according to different prosodic and linguistic constraints, which may or may not lead to the production of the same degree or kind of formulas.[5] In the case of ancient texts extant only in written form, a long and complicated history of editing and transmission adds another set of factors. Further, many written texts, despite their distance from putative oral origins, exhibit a range of features associated with oral traditional works, including formulaic phraseology and typical narrative structures. Such texts include, for example, the Homeric epics, much Old English poetry, and the Epic of Gilgamesh; all are "manuscript or tablet works of finally uncertain provenance that nevertheless show oral traditional

---

[2] On the application of research on oral traditional literature in extrabiblical contexts to the study of the Hebrew Bible, see Susan Niditch, *Oral World and Written Word: Ancient Israelite Literature* (Library of Ancient Israel; Louisville: Westminster John Knox, 1996), esp. 1–38, 108–34.

[3] Lord would consider any mixed or transitional style as part of the development of written style.

[4] *Singer of Tales,* 130–31.

[5] *Traditional Oral Epic,* 3–5; see 121–239 for his elaboration of this thesis. See also Jack Goody on the *tyrannie de la formule* (*The Interface between the Written and the Oral* [Cambridge: Cambridge University Press, 1987], 98–99).

characteristics."[6] Foley characterizes such texts as *oral-derived texts,* as opposed to *unambiguously oral texts.* Oral-derived texts, may, in their present form, have been composed in writing, yet they draw on "deep roots in oral tradition" and reflect an oral aesthetic.[7]

THE COMPOSITION OF TRADITIONAL ORAL AND ORAL-DERIVED POETRY

Foley's discussion of the composition of traditional oral or oral-derived epic in *Traditional Oral Epic* touches on the three aspects of phraseology, theme, and story pattern,[8] echoing Lord's distinction of formula, theme, and song. Foley diverges from Lord, however, in declining to subsume phraseology under the label of formula.[9]

Foley sees, rather, a "spectrum of phraseology" in traditional oral epic poetry. This spectrum includes formulas (verbatim repetitions), such as the noun-epithet phrases in Homer, and formulaic expressions, which exhibit syntactic, metric, and semantic correspondence. But it also includes phrases that correspond to each other only partially or obliquely. Partial

---

[6] *Traditional Oral Epic,* 5. There are several known recensions of the Gilgamesh Epic, a work that offers many parallels to biblical traditions. See Jeffrey Tigay, *The Evolution of the Gilgamesh Epic* (Philadelphia: University of Pennsylvania Press, 1982).

[7] "Word-Power, Performance, and Tradition," *Journal of American Folklore* 105 (1992): 291–92. For a broad view of what constitutes an oral work as well as of the continuum between oral and written literature, see Ruth Finnegan, *Oral Poetry: Its Nature, Significance and Social Context* (Cambridge: Cambridge University Press, 1977), 16–23, 28–29, 127–33; see also Walter J. Ong, *Orality and Literacy: The Technologizing of the Word* (London: Methuen, 1982), 26–27; and Goody, *Interface,* 78–109.

[8] The last aspect is not discussed here, since the focus of this study is on discrete passages that contain the metaphor of earth mourning rather than on the equivalent of a whole narrative sequence of passages. The fact that the prophetic writings are nonnarrative is a basic distinction between the tradition they represent and the literary traditions studied by Foley. See further the discussion of this distinction below.

[9] Milman Parry ("Studies in the Epic Technique of Oral Verse Making I: Homer and Homeric Style," in *The Making of Homeric Verse,* 301–4) analyzes sets of lines from the *Iliad* and the *Odyssey* and finds them to be almost entirely formulaic. Lord (*Singer of Tales,* 47) examines a passage from the repertoire of a Yugoslavian epic singer and concludes that 25 percent of the whole lines and 50 percent of the half-lines in the sample are formulas and that "there is no line or part of a line that did not fit into some formulaic pattern." A formulaic line, as opposed to a formula, is defined by Parry and Lord as exhibiting basic syntactic, metric, and semantic correspondences with other lines without constituting a verbatim repetition. See Parry, "Studies in the Epic Technique," 301; Lord, *Singer of Tales,* 47.

correspondences result from the fact that poetic phrases are formed according to the prosodic and linguistic rules of the given oral tradition. Established formulaic patterns also exert an influence, but their influence is shaped by the underlying conventional strictures of the poetic line.[10]

In examining the occurrences of the phrase ἔπεα πτερόεντα, "winged words," in the *Odyssey,* for example, Foley discovers a wide range of patterning. Over half of the sixty-one instances of this phrase occur in the whole-line formula καὶ μιν φωνήσας ἔπεα πτερόεντα προσηύδα, "and speaking, he addressed [him] with winged words." But the phrase also occurs in the second half-line (hemistich) formula ἔπεα πτερόεντα προσηύδα, which combines with various patterns in the first hemistich, most, but not all, of which, correspond syntactically to the first hemistich of the whole-line formula cited above. And ἔπεα πτερόεντα is also found attached to the verb ἀγορεύω, "to proclaim," in the second hemistich. There is thus a mix of formulas and formulaic patterns containing the phrase ἔπεα πτερόεντα, and no one pattern adequately describes the modulations and permutations of phraseology that occur at both the whole-line and hemistich levels.[11]

One might compare the variety described here to that evident in the phraseology of the nine biblical prophetic passages that contain the metaphor of earth mourning. A prime example would be the formulation of the bicolon in which the metaphor occurs. In terms of the articulation of the metaphor itself, although the verb *ʾābal* is constant throughout, and although it is most frequently linked with the subject *ʾereṣ,* "earth" (7x), it is also yoked with *nĕʾôt rōʿîm,* "the pastures of the shepherds," in Amos 1:2; *ʾădāmâ,* "the ground," in Joel 1:10; and *ḥelqat ḥemdātî,* "my pleasant field" (by implication), in Jer 12:11. In Isa 24:4 *ʾereṣ,* "earth," is the subject of *ʾābal,* but in 24:7 *tîrôš,* "the wine," mourns (*ʾābal*).

Further, the position of the metaphor in the poetic line and the phrases with which it is linked in parallelism vary widely. In six cases the metaphor occurs in the first colon of the line and is paralleled by an echoing phrase in the second (Amos 1:2; Hos 4:1–3; Jer 4:28; 12:4; Isa 24:7; 33:9). In Jer 23:10 it constitutes the second colon of a tricolon and is parallel to the third colon; in Isa 24:4 it begins a tricolon and is paralleled in the following two cola. In Jer 12:11 it occurs in the second colon of a bicolon but is not synonymously parallel to what precedes, whereas in Joel 1:10 it occurs in

---

[10] *Traditional Oral Epic,* 127–29, 136–37, 172–76.

[11] Foley (*Traditional Oral Epic,* 144) reiterates his position in discussing the occurrence of θυμόν, "heart," in various colonic, hemistichal, and whole-line patterns in the *Odyssey:* "The point is that none of the lines treated is in any sense 'archetypal' or 'seminal,' and yet the similarities are unmistakable."

synonymous parallelism in the second colon of a bicolon that itself parallels the following tricolon.[12]

Among the instances of synonymous parallelism just listed, *ʾābal* is paralleled by a number of different verbs: by *yābēš*, "to be dry" (Amos 1:2; Jer 12:4; 23:10) and *ʾumlal*, "to languish" (Hos 4:3; Isa 24:7); by *šuddad*, "to be destroyed," *ʾumlal*, and *hôbîš*, "to show shame" (Joel 1:10);[13] and by *qādar*, "to mourn, grow dark" (Jer 4:28). In Isa 24:4 *ʾābal* and *nābēl*, "to droop," are paired with *ʾumlal* and *nābēl*; in Isa 33:9 *ʾābal* and *ʾumlal* with *hehpîr*, "to show shame," and *qāmēl*, "to waste away." The subjects of these parallel phrases vary similarly. In Amos 1:2 the subject is "the top of Carmel"; in Hos 4:3, "all who dwell in it [the earth]"; in Jer 4:28, "the sky"; in Jer 12:4, "the grass of every field"; in Jer 23:10, "the pastures of the wilderness"; in Isa 24:4, "the world" and "the sky"; in Isa 33:9, "Lebanon"; and in Joel 1:10, "the field," "the grain," "the wine," and "the oil."

Another example can be found in what appear to be traces of, or variations on, the merism *běhayyat haśśādeh ûběʿôp haššāmayim*, "[with] the animals of the field and the birds of the air," which occurs in Hos 4:3. Jeremiah 4:25 refers to "all the birds of the air" (*wěkol-ʿôp haššāmayim*); 12:4, to the "beasts and the birds" (*běhēmôt wāʿôp*); 12:9, to "all the animals of the field" (*kol-hayyat haśśādeh*); Joel 1:18, 20 to the "beasts" (*běhēmâ*) and the "beasts of the field" (*bahămôt śādeh*). The similarities between "the grass of every field" (*wěʿēśeb kol-haśśādeh*) in Jer 12:4 and "all the trees of the field" (*kol-ʿăṣê haśśādeh*) in Joel 1:12, 19 are also notable. In another example, the phrase "the pastures of the shepherds" (*něʾôt rōʿîm*) substitutes in Amos 1:2 for the more common expression "the pastures of the wilderness" (*něʾôt midbār*), which occurs in Jer 23:10 and Joel 1:19–20.[14]

Even the variations on the single word *karmel* in the nine passages may represent a pattern of phraseological variation. In Amos 1:2 and Isa 33:9 *karmel* functions as a proper noun referring in the first instance to Mount Carmel, in the second to a region known for exceptional fertility. Jeremiah 4:26 refers to the *karmel*, "fruitful land," and the appellation *karmî*, "my vineyard," given to Judah in Jer 12:10 is reminiscent of this noun. In all contexts what has been fruitful is turned to desert and devastation.

The precise prosodic constraints of Homeric epic tend to produce recurrent verbatim formulas and formulaic patterns. The poetic line of

---

[12] It should be acknowledged that the scansion of particular lines may be disputed.

[13] Or "to show dryness."

[14] Cf. Jer 9:9; Joel 2:22; Ps 65:13.

Serbo-Croatian oral epic, less constrained but in some ways cognate to Greek hexameter, is also conducive to recurrent phrases. The prosody of Old English epic is quite different, being more loosely defined and in some aspects still eluding definition.[15] Old English stress-based meter allows significant variation in the syllable count of the line. The basic prosodic structure is the half-line, which contains two word stresses. These half-lines are bound by alliteration into lines, though only one word in each half-line need show alliteration.[16] Half-lines can combine in a number of metrical configurations. Further, the integrity of the half-line allows a phrase to be completed at either the middle or the end of the line or to extend over more than a single line.

These features of Old English poetry, Foley suggests, produce a phraseology that is not limited to the "encapsulated phrase" that varies only in "strictly defined ways"[17] but one in which the single word or root element, highlighted as it is by both alliteration and stress, also plays a prominent role. Formulas and formulaic patterns do occur in Old English epic, but with a wide range of syntactic, metric, and semantic correspondences that include, for example, the regular association of a given half-line with a single alliterating word in the other half-line.

Foley notes as well the existence of clusters of words or root syllables that extend beyond the half or whole line. Such three- or four-verse patterns, he proposes, represent more than the habitual associations of lines found in Serbo-Croatian poetry[18] but may in fact constitute "integral structures" in themselves.[19] Two different passages from *Beowulf,* for example, each show a cluster of roots conveying the coming of night, shadows, and fear. The form taken by this cluster differs in each instance: the order of the key words varies, alternate words for "shadow" are used, and the phraseological contexts of the key words are not parallel.[20]

This example provides another, perhaps even closer, analogue to the variant phraseological patterns in the nine biblical prophetic passages considered above, especially with respect to the prominent role of the single word or root. In the biblical texts the phrase "the earth mourns" is associated with other key words as well as with whole phrases. As noted above, *'umlal,* "to languish" (Hos 4:3; Isa 24:4 [2x], 7; 33:9; Joel 1:10), and *yābēš,*

---

[15] Foley, *Traditional Oral Epic,* 201–4. In this way Old English poetry may provide a closer analogue to Hebrew poetry than do the Greek or Serbo-Croatian epics.

[16] The first line may have up to two alliterating elements, or staves.

[17] *Traditional Oral Epic,* 202.

[18] See Lord, *Singer of Tales,* 58–60.

[19] Foley, *Traditional Oral Epic,* 204–7.

[20] Ibid., 207–12.

"to dry up" (Amos 1:2; Jer 12:4; 23:10), are often linked with *ʾābal* in parallel phrases, but *yābēš* also occurs outside of such a phraseological parallel (Joel 1:12, 20). The verb *nāšam,* "to be desolate or appalled" (Joel 1:17; Isa 33:8; Jer 12:11), appears in these passages, as do the related nouns *šěmāmâ,* "desolation" (Jer 4:27; 12:10, 11), and *šammâ,* "desolation" (Isa 24:12; Joel 1:7), and the adjective *šěmēmâ,* "desolate" (Jer 12:11). Other recurrent roots and words include the verb *ʾākal,* "to devour" (Jer 12:9, 12; Isa 24:6; Joel 1:19–20); the noun *rāʿâ,* "evil" (Jer 12:4; 23:10, 11), and the semantically related adjective *rāšāʿ,* "wicked" (Jer 12:1); the root *bwš,* "to be ashamed" (Jer 12:13; Joel 1:10, 11, 12, 17),[21] and the semantically similar verb *ḥeḥpîr,* "to be ashamed" (Isa 33:9); the noun *karmel,* "Carmel, fruitful land" (Amos 1:2; Jer 4:26; Isa 33:9), and the related noun *kerem,* "vineyard" (Jer 12:10).[22]

The correspondence of these recurrences to the clustering of roots in *Beowulf* described above is not exact, since the configuration of word and root clusters in the nine prophetic passages changes significantly in each passage.[23] Yet the repetition of words and roots over the body of the nine passages is noteworthy.

Foley's description of Old English poetic epic illustrates that the forms of traditional phraseology vary not just within, but among, poetic traditions. He posits a similar spectrum of traditional narrative structure, or theme.[24] In doing so he affirms Lord's stress on the multiformity of theme

---

[21] In addition, this root may be called to mind by the imperfect form of the verb *yābēš,* "to dry up," in Amos 1:2, as noted in the discussion above of that passage.

[22] See the chart of recurrent words and roots in the appendix. The list above does not include the recurrences in either Isa 24:1–20 or Joel 1:5–20 of words found in only one other text, as this phenomenon may reflect the tendency toward literary citation characteristic of these two passages, and hence dependence on a written text. See, for example, the appearance of the verb *rāʿaš,* "to quake," in Jer 4:24 and Isa 24:18; the root *šdd,* "to destroy," in Jer 12:12 and Joel 1:10 (2x); the verb *bāgad,* "to be treacherous," and the noun *beged,* "treachery," in Jer 12:1 and Isa 24:16; the verb *ḥānēp,* "to be polluted, ungodly," in Jer 23:11 and Isa 24:6; the noun *ʾālâ,* "curse," in Jer 23:10 and Isa 24:5; the root *ʾšm,* "to bear punishment," in Isa 24:6 and Joel 1:18; the verb *ḥēpēr,* "to break," in Isa 24:5 and 33:8; and the verb *šābat,* "to cease," in Isa 24:8 (2x) and 33:8. At the same time, literary dependence can also be seen as a sign of the reliance of what Foley might call *oral-derived* texts on familiar phraseology.

[23] Note, however, the recurrence of *ʾābal, yābēš,* and *něʾôt* in Amos 1:2; Jer 12:4; 23:10 and of *ʾābal, ʾākal,* and the root *šmm* in Jer 12:7–13; Isa 24:1–20; Joel 1:5–20. Cf. the appendix.

[24] See *Traditional Oral Epic,* 240–358. Foley adopts Lord's concept of theme as one of the recurrent narrative units or typical scenes that make up an epic poem.

in oral poetry. Lord found that the essential ideas constituting a theme were expressed variously in different performances of individual singers as well as in the performances of different singers; in performances of the same song as well as in performances of different songs. Variations reflect the style and artistic conception of the singer, the compositional necessities of the song, and the contingencies of the performance. They include differences in phraseology and in the details, order, and number of thematic elements.[25]

Foley's study traces the range of variation in recurrent themes with respect to phraseological correspondence and constituent actions or elements. Even within one poem—the *Odyssey*—he discerns a spectrum of multiformity as he examines the three typical themes of bath, greeting, and feast.

In his discussion of the bath theme, for example, he considers seven occurrences that show a consistent narrative core of "washing, anointing, and donning new clothes."[26] Common phraseology is apparent in the description of these actions: whole-line phrases, hemistich phrases, and even couplets are repeated, if not verbatim, then in closely related forms. Yet the phraseological correspondence between instances of the theme is not uniform. Hemistich formulas combine with different hemistich partners in different passages, and whole lines in one passage that match those in another passage are followed by whole lines that match lines in a different passage. Further, the sequence of recurrent phrases is interrupted by lines that are unique, paticularizing a given bath scene in light of its narrative context. Overall, the length of the bath scenes ranges from four to eleven lines.

The parallels between this description of variation in the bath theme and thematic variation in the nine prophetic passages considered here must be carefully drawn. First, the term *theme* is used differently in studies of oral literature and folklore than it is in this study or in literary

---

Theme is thus defined as "a self-contained unit describing a single event" (*Traditional Oral Epic*, 245–46).

[25] *Singer of Tales*, 16–17, 68–94, 102–23. At the same time Lord (*Singer of Tales*, 69–71, 92) stresses a degree of verbal correspondence between renditions of a given theme as well as a customary order of elements. See also Albert B. Lord, "Perspectives on Recent Work in Oral Literature," in *Oral Literature: Seven Essays* (ed. J. Duggan; Edinburgh: Scottish Academic; New York: Barnes & Noble, 1975), 20; Albert B. Lord, "Formula and Non-Narrative Theme in South Slavic Oral Epic and the OT," *Semeia* 5 (1976): 101–2.

[26] This schema, Foley notes, was first discerned by Walter Arend in *Die typischen Scenen bei Homer* (Problemata, Forschungen zur classischen Philologie 7; Berlin: Weidmann, 1933), 124–26. For a biblical parallel, see 2 Sam 12:20.

criticism generally, where *theme* represents a topic or general concept.[27] A basic distinction to be noted in this study is that whereas in the epic traditions studied by Foley and Lord, theme is defined as a narrative unit, the prophetic texts are nonnarrative. Yet the nine passages discussed above have been delimited as discrete units of prophetic speech in which the metaphor of earth mourning is presented and developed and in which certain themes (using the term in its more common usage) consistently recur. The themes of the response of the earth, sin and punishment, social and natural disorder, the pollution of the earth, and the dissolution of the created order, as well as the motif of mourning as stripping, correspond roughly to the narrative elements of, for example, the bath theme described above (washing, anointing, and donning new clothes).[28]

The variation in phraseological correspondence among the different presentations of the bath theme in the *Odyssey* is comparable to the even greater phraseological variation noted above in the presentation and development of the metaphor of earth mourning. Comparing the nine passages as a whole, it is readily apparent that although certain phrases show points of correspondence, whether at the level of colon or bicolon and tricolon, multiformity is prevalent. The evocations of the dissolution of creation in Jer 4:23–26; 12:4; and Hos 4:3 show only broad resemblances: "I looked and there was no one / and all the birds of the air had fled" (*rā'îtî wĕhinnēh 'ên hā'ādām / wĕkol-ʿôp haššāmayim nādādû*) in Jer 4:25 corresponds roughly to "all who dwell in it languish / with the beasts of the field, and the birds of the air" (*wĕ'umlal kol-yôšēb bāh / bĕḥayyat haśśādeh ûbĕʿôp haššāmayim*) in Hos 4:3. This last colon is echoed by *suppêtâ bĕhēmôt wāʿôp*, "the beasts and the birds are swept away"[29] in Jer 12:4 (although *bĕhēmôt*, "beasts," replaces the phrase *ḥayyat haśśādeh*). Yet the phrase *yōšĕbê-bāh* in 12:4, which might be

---

[27] See "Theme," *The New Princeton Encyclopedia of Poetry and Poetics* (ed. Alex Preminger and T. V. F. Brogen; Princeton, N.J.: Princeton University Press, 1993), 1281; M. H. Abrams, *A Glossary of Literary Terms* (6th ed.; Fort Worth, Tex.: Harcourt Brace, 1993), 121; Theodor Wolpers, "Motif and Theme As Structural Content Units," in *The Return of Thematic Criticism* (ed. W. Sollors; Cambridge, Mass.: Harvard University Press, 1993), 89–91; Menachem Brinker, "Theme and Interpretation," in Sollors, *Return of Thematic Criticism,* 21–26. Cf. R. Scholes and R. Kellogg, *The Nature of Narrative* (London: Oxford University Press, 1966), 26.

[28] See the discussion of nonnarrative theme in Lord, "Formula and Non-Narrative Theme," 98–99; and Robert C. Culley, "Oral Tradition and the OT: Some Recent Discussion," *Semeia* 5 (1976): 18–19. The distinction between narrative and nonnarrative theme is examined at greater length below.

[29] This emended reading of MT is proposed above; see the textual note on this verse.

thought to correspond to *kol-yôšēb bāh* in Hos 4:3, occurs in a different context: not in connection with the description of the disintegration of the earth but with the explanation of its demise (the wickedness of "those who dwell in it").[30]

Similarly, the turning of earth into desert is represented in Jer 4:26 with the colon *rā'îtî wĕhinnēh hakkarmel hammidbār*, "I looked, and behold the fruitful land had become desert." In Jer 12:10, this idea is conveyed by a lengthier description:

> *rō'îm rabbîm šiḫătû karmî*
> *bōsĕsû 'et-ḥelqātî*
> *nātĕnû 'et-ḥelqat ḥemdātî*
> *lĕmidbar šĕmāmâ.*

> Many shepherds have ruined my vineyard,
>   they have trampled my field.
> They have made the field of my delight
>   into a desolate desert.

Clearly there are points of similarity in the two renditions, notably, the correspondence between *karmel* and *karmî* and between *midbar* and *lĕmidbar šĕmāmâ*, but they are significantly different. The word *šĕmāmâ* is lacking in Jer 4:26, for example, but occurs later in the same passage in 4:28 in the context of YHWH's proclamation of destruction. As Jer 4:26–28 and 12:10 illustrate, instances of correspondence between the articulations of common thematic elements are often separated by phrases unique to the individual passages. In some instances there are no phraseological correspondences; the depiction of social disorder in Hos 4:2, for example, shares no phraseology with that in Isa 33:8.

Further, the lines of phraseological correspondence between passages are often crisscrossed. With respect to the description of the response of the earth, Isa 33:9 shares with Hos 4:3 the pairing of *'ābal*, "to mourn," and *'umlal*, "to languish," but not the reference to Carmel, which the former text has in common with Amos 1:2, where *'ābal* is paired with *yābēš*, "to dry up."

The examination of other traditional themes in the *Odyssey* brings out further points of comparison with the texts of concern in this study. The feast theme, as Foley defines it, comprises a longer set of sequential actions: washing, the setting out of a table, the serving of bread, the serving

---

[30] Even within Hos 4:1–3 similar phrases appear in different contexts, as noted above. In 4:1 *yôšĕbê hā'āreṣ* refers to the inhabitants of Israel, whom YHWH is indicting; in 4:3 *kol-yôšēb bāh* refers to all life affected by the mourning of the earth.

of meat and wine, eating, and satiety. Yet one of these actions—the serving of meat and wine—does not occur in every instance. The set of elements in a typical narrative unit in the Homeric epic is defined over the body of tradition as a whole, but the entire set is not replicated in every instance. Similarly, in the nine prophetic passages considered here, the theme of the dissolution of creation, though prominent in passages such as Jer 4:23–28 and Isa 24:1–20, is not explicit in Amos 1:2; Jer 12:7–13; 23:9–12; and Isa 33:7–9. A depiction of social disorder is lacking in Jer 4:23–28 and Joel 1:5–20, and the theme of the pollution of the earth is absent in Isa 33:7–9 and Jer 1:5–20.[31]

The greeting theme in the *Odyssey* has a much looser narrative core. It can comprise words of welcome, of farewell, or of honor and may include both the words of the speaker and the response of the addressee. It shows no common phraseology aside from the greeting χαῖρε and the verb δειδίσκομαι, "to hail," and no series of distinct actions.[32] This theme shows an even more flexible set of elements and phrases than do the shifting constellations of phraseology, imagery, motif, and theme found in the nine prophetic passages considered here.

The variation in narrative structure and verbal correspondence evident in these three themes from the *Odyssey* is also evident in the Serbo-Croatian and Old English epic tradition. In the case of Serbo-Croatian epic it is possible to compare the treatment of themes in different performances and by different singers.[33] In four performances of two songs by a single singer, Foley notes, again, a range of verbal correspondence between parallel thematic elements and flexibility in the order and number of elements. The diverging patterns of phraseology and thematic clustering in the four passages from Jeremiah might be placed beside those found in this example.

Performances by two different singers from the same local region, or dialect, reveal a greater diversity in phraseology, with few related phrases, even where both singers are communicating essentially the same narrative scenario. Performances by singers of different regions diverge even more widely, with almost no correspondence between expressions of the same theme and greater discrepancy in narrative content, though the overall

---

[31] The basis of comparison in these cases is attenuated by the fact that one would not expect to find the same set cluster of elements in nonnarrative texts that one finds in epic narratives.

[32] In this sense it is difficult to conceive of this type of theme in the same category as a type scene. See the description and discussion of the greeting theme in Foley, *Traditional Oral Epic,* 257–65.

[33] See Lord, *Singer of Tales,* 68–94, 102–23; and Foley, *Traditional Oral Epic,* 288–328.

grouping of basic ideas persists.[34] Such differences between singers can be compared to differences in the way the metaphor of earth mourning is developed in, for example, Amos 1:2 and Hos 4:1–3, especially since the historical provenance of these two passages may overlap.

In the Old English tradition, theme, like phraseology, is even more loosely shaped. A consistent narrative sequence is discernible in the examples Foley considers, despite flexibility in the order and content of the constituent motifs. But verbal correspondence is significantly sparser and, where it exists, more often involves words and word roots than it does formulaic phrases. In one striking example, the sea-voyage theme in *Beowulf* occurs in the context of a sea burial, or funeral, involving obvious changes in presentation.[35] In fact, Foley suggests, the concept of recurrence may not adequately represent the degree of variability between phraseology and narrative idea found in *Beowulf*. What is evident is a "deep structure" of narrative pattern reflected in a "surface structure of diction that can shift widely in its formulaic and morphemic make-up while staying within theme's ideational boundaries."[36] Again, the Old English pattern may provide the closest parallel to the degree of variation found in the prophetic passages discussed above.

THE RECEPTION OF TRADITIONAL ORAL AND ORAL-DERIVED POETRY

The way the patterns and structures of traditional oral poetry convey meaning to an audience is the subject of Foley's study *Immanent Art*. The mode of conveying meaning in traditional oral texts, Foley argues, differs in degree and kind from that operative in purely written works. The recurrent phraseology, themes, and story patterns of oral literature may appear predictable and primitive, if not clichéd and uninventive, to the literate mind. Yet these traditional elements actually give depth and breadth to a particular performance or text by evoking the entire poetic tradition held in the mind of the audience or reader. Literary allusions, whether direct or oblique, that connect one work to another work (or works) do not elicit the presence of other contexts to the same extent or with the same

---

[34] Foley, *Traditional Oral Epic,* 278–328. These conclusions echo Lord's in his chapters "Theme" and "Songs and the Song" in *Singer of Tales,* although Lord assumes some basis of verbal correspondence between instances of theme, as Foley notes (*Traditional Oral Epic,* 280–81). Foley's interest lies in tracing the spectrum of variation from virtually no verbal correspondence to a relatively high degree of correspondence (*Traditional Oral Epic,* 327–28).

[35] Foley, *Traditional Oral Epic,* 342–44.

[36] Ibid., 357.

intensity that the recurrent phrases, scenes, and tales of oral literature do. In Foley's words:

> The key difference lies in the nature of tradition itself. Structural elements are not simply compositionally useful, nor are they doomed to a "limited" area of designation; rather they command fields of reference much larger than the single line, passage, or even text in which they occur. Traditional elements reach out of the immediate instance in which they appear to the fecund totality of the entire tradition, defined synchronically and diachronically, and they bear meanings as wide and deep as the tradition they encode.[37]

The elements of traditional art include a significant extratextual dimension that must be considered in interpretation. These elements function as "foci for meaning," linking the nominal or denotative sense of a passage to the tradition that surrounds and lies behind it and giving it an immanent or connotative meaning. Foley calls this mode of conveying meaning *metonymy* because in oral works a phrase or scene evokes many other instances of that phrase or scene and their contexts, and thereby the tradition as a whole. This tradition transcends the sum of its parts and is never fully manifest in one performance or version. The noun epithets of Homeric and Serbo-Croatian epic, for example, stand for the fullness of the character to whom they are applied—for the character as she or he appears throughout the particular poem and in other poems within that tradition.[38]

---

[37] *Immanent Art,* 7. Lord (*Singer of Tales,* 148; see also 65–66) makes a similar observation: "Each theme, small or large—one might even say, each formula—has around it an aura of meaning which has been put there by all the contexts in which it has occurred in the past. It is the meaning that has been given it by the tradition in its creativeness. To any poet at any given time, this meaning involves all the occasions on which he has used the theme, especially those contexts in which he uses it most frequently; it involves also all the occasions on which he has heard it used by others, particularly by those singers whom he first heard in his youth, or by great singers later by whom he was impressed. To the audience the meaning of the theme involves its own experience of it as well. The communication of this supra-meaning is possible because of the community of experience of poet and audience."

[38] Foley, *Immanent Art,* 18–21. Cf. Gregory Nagy, "Formula and Meter: The Oral Poetics of Homer," in *Greek Mythology and Poetics* (Myth and Poetics; Ithaca, N.Y.: Cornell University Press, 1990), 23. Foley provides a particularly graphic example from a contemporary culture of the way tradition overlays a particular oral performance. In rural Rajisthan (India) stories are performed in song and dance in front of a tapestry that illustrates scenes from the larger epic to which they belong.

The related concepts of implicit reference to a tradition and of metonymic meaning are fundamental to oral-derived, as well as to unambiguously oral, works. In both types of composition there is a balance between meaning that bears the imprint of the individual poet and the particular compositional context and meaning that reflects traditional patterns.[39] In oral-derived works the balance may shift in the direction of an individually stamped mode of meaning, but the reliance of the poet on traditional phraseology and structures is still fundamental to "aesthetic creativity."[40]

In approaching the question of meaning, Foley operates on the assumption that to limit the sphere of reference of traditional structures to the individual passage or even to the individual work is to misread a traditional work. To ignore the wider, immanent context of these structures in favor of the immediate context alone is, paradoxically, to remove them from their natural settings. Such a procedure "might well parallel the dysfunction occasioned by forcing a novel into another generic category or into another unrelated literary tradition."[41]

The dimension of extratextual referentiality is not, of course, limited to oral or oral-derived literature, and it is receiving renewed attention in recent studies of intertextuality in written corpora. Literary citations and allusions, the use of literary genres and conventions, and the presence of the inherited literary tradition itself create a context for individual written works.[42] But the parameters of oral and oral-derived literature

---

The tapestry is actually brought into the performance when the performer uses a special wand to point to the episode he will perform, and a lamp is held up to the appropriate scene.

[39] In fact, Foley defines tradition as "a dynamic, multivalent body of meaning that preserves much that a group has invented and transmitted but that also includes as necessary defining features both an inherent indeterminacy and a predisposition to various kinds of changes or modifications" ("Word-Power, Performance, and Tradition," 276).

[40] Foley, *Immanent Art,* 9; see also 13–38, 246–47.

[41] "Word-Power, Performance, and Tradition," 276; see also *Immanent Art,* 36–37. Lord (*Singer of Tales,* 97) observes with respect to the habitual associations of themes in Serbo-Croatian epic: "to be numb to an awareness of this kind of association is to miss the meaning not only of the oral method of composition and transmission, but even of epic itself." See the description by Richard J. Clifford (*Fair Spoken and Persuading: An Interpretation of Second Isaiah* [Theological Inquiries; New York: Paulist, 1984], 38) of the art of Second Isaiah: "The core of his thought he often only alludes to: he counts on the tradition to be so deeply ingrained in the audience's heart and head that mere hints suffice for the whole to be called up."

[42] For a summary of the general lines of the literary approach known as intertextuality, see Abrams, *Glossary of Literary Terms,* 9, 285.

are conceived here in terms of the extent to which meaning is conveyed primarily by bringing the body of tradition to bear on the compositional moment (as opposed to recreating the immediacy of that moment). It should be acknowledged that in some written works the concentration of traditional literary forms, motifs, and scenarios as well as of literary allusions or citations presents a parallel phenomenon to that found in oral and oral-derived literature.[43] Once again, sharp boundaries between the oral and written spheres are inappropriate. It is better to speak of the general tendencies particular to these two modes of composition and reception.

Foley's approach to the study of traditional oral poetry is based on his assessment of these general tendencies. In the absence of a live oral tradition, in which numerous performances by various performers of different works can be heard and recorded over time, the traditional background of oral-derived works must be reconstructed from texts. By collecting from available texts all instances of a given phrase or theme and comparing their phraseological and narrative contexts, some sense of the span of tradition lying behind each instance can be gained. When available texts within a given tradition are few—as is the case with the Homeric and Old English (as well as the biblical) traditions—the resulting sense of the tradition is necessarily sketchy to the modern reader.

Yet the process of collection and comparison can bring readers closer to an appreciation of the full import and resonance of a passage while transcending debates about authorial intention that cannot be resolved on a purely textual basis.[44] Although this method, as noted, is not dissimilar to methods taken up in literary studies, the importance of reference to a wider tradition is heightened in oral and oral-derived works.

Foley's discussion of book 24 of the *Iliad* provides examples of the way Homer uses traditional phrases and narrative structures to evoke associations developed throughout the *Iliad* and the *Odyssey*.[45] Homer's art

---

[43] In terms of the Hebrew Bible, Michael Fishbane (*Biblical Interpretation in Ancient Israel* [Oxford: Clarendon, 1985]) traces indications of an innerbiblical exegesis that presumes the literary dependence of one biblical text upon another within the Hebrew Bible. This phenomenon can also be seen, however, in terms of the recurrence of traditional typologies and phrases in variant forms, a view consistent with the aesthetic of oral-derived literature. See Fishbane's discussion on pp. 287–89.

[44] See, e.g., Foley, *Immanent Art,* 247–52, 161–62.

[45] Ibid., 135–89. For an extended study of the complex interplay of traditional allusions and narrative context in the *Iliad,* see Laura M. Slatkin, *The Power of Thetis: Allusion and Interpretation in the Iliad* (Berkeley and Los Angeles: University of California Press, 1991); see also idem, "The Wrath of Thetis," *Transactions of the American Philological Association* 116 (1986): 1–24.

consists in the way he "harnesses" these associations to suit his compositional context.[46] The phrase φάος ἠελίοιο, "the light of the sun," for example, occurs in book 24 and in five other instances in the *Iliad* (as well as nine times in the *Odyssey*), often in narrative contexts where death threatens but is held in suspension while a preventative action is taken. This background shades the instance in book 24 where Priam, as he approaches Achilles to request Hector's body, states that he himself has been allowed "to go on living myself and continue to look on the sunlight."[47] Achilles' assent to this request allows Priam (as well as the rest of the Trojans) to continue to look on the sunlight—but only until Hector's funeral rites are completed and the battle resumes.

Similarly, the phrase πυκινόν ἔπος, "shrewd or wise word," occurs five times in the *Iliad* outside of book 24, in each case representing a message of great import intended to change the course of the ongoing battle. This wider context brings poignancy to the use of this phrase by Andromache in book 24, where she laments that she did not hear from Hector a last πυκινόν ἔπος that she could remember afterwards in her widowhood. In this case the traditional associations act as a foil for what is unique and nontraditional in the particular instance.

In like manner, the epic themes of self-defilement and lamentation, which follow an expected narrative pattern, intensify the presentation of the grieving of Achilles over Patroklos and of Andromache over Hector while at the same time throwing into relief details that reveal the particular depth of their sorrow. The extremity of Achilles' anger and grief is further highlighted by the repeated breaking off of the feast theme throughout books 23 and 24, a theme that traditionally represents community and the prelude to a resolution.

In these cases the recurrence of a phrase or theme brings resonance and heightened awareness to an important narrative moment. At the same time, the familiar pattern raises expectations that increase sensitivity to modifications within the narrative context.

A similar aesthetic can be seen at work in the group of nine prophetic passages considered above, where phraseological and thematic patterns enhance and define meaning. Thus the background theme of the undoing of creation, as it is conveyed by characteristic phraseology and imagery in Hos 4:1–3; Jer 4:23–28; 12:1–4; and Isa 24:1–20, allows one to see in the agricultural crisis of Joel 1:5–20 the disintegration of the created order. The withering of vegetation in response to the utterance of YHWH in Amos 1:2 and the denuding of fertile regions in Isa 33:9 are

---

[46] See, e.g., *Immanent Art,* 23–24, 29, 159, 252.

[47] Homer, *Iliad* 24.558 (trans. Richmond Lattimore).

similarly drawn into this context. The recurrent linking of the mourning earth with images of the undoing of creation also contributes to the power of Isa 24:1–20 as a culminating vision of world judgment and return to cosmic chaos.

The motif of mourning as stripping, evoked in Hos 4:3; Isa 33:9; and Joel 1:7 (and in other prophetic passages in which this motif is articulated more explicitly),[48] gives heightened import to the overrunning and destruction of vineyard and field by the shepherds in Jer 12:10, to the beating of the olive tree and gleaning of vines in Isa 24:13, and even to the pulling down of cities in Jer 4:26, binding these images to the metaphor of the mourning earth. The role of tradition as a contrasting foil is illustrated in Jer 12:1–4, where the intensity of the prophetic lament is increased by the distinction in this text between the flourishing of the wicked and the mourning of the earth.

In all these instances, individual images and phrases are placed within an integrated context of meaning and hence gain fuller meaning. The recurrent patterns of phraseology, imagery, and theme draw the reader beyond the bounds of the particular text, even where the given expression of a theme or phrase is partial or merely suggested.[49]

IMPLICATIONS FOR THE STUDY OF BIBLICAL POETIC TEXTS

The apparent parallels between compositional patterns in the three extrabiblical poetic traditions discussed above and in the nine biblical prophetic passages of this study are suggestive. Yet how solid is the basis of comparison between these different traditions? Conclusions about the role of tradition in composition and in conveying meaning must take into account factors that delineate similarities and differences among the traditions compared. Foley offers five parameters for the study and comparison of oral traditional works: (1) the textual (manuscript) tradition of a composition; (2) its oral basis; (3) its genre (*genre dependence*); (4) the traditions that underlie it (*tradition dependence*); and (5) the interplay between its synchronic and diachronic contexts.[50]

The first parameter, which concerns the textual tradition of a composition, is clearly pertinent to the Hebrew Bible and has been taken up frequently in the discussion of the passages above. The second question to be considered in comparing the literature of the Hebrew

---

[48] See, e.g., as noted above, Hos 2:4–15; Isa 3:18–26; 16:8–10; 32:9–14; Jer 48:31–33.

[49] See, in relation to the Homeric tradition, Slatkin, *Power of Thetis,* 1–16.

[50] *Traditional Oral Epic,* 5–11; see also *Immanent Art,* 14–16.

Bible to oral and oral-derived works from other traditions concerns the oral component of the Hebrew Bible and of the prophetic texts, in particular.[51]

That oral traditions lie behind much of the Hebrew Bible has been widely assumed since the work of Gunkel,[52] but the role of such traditions in the evolution of the biblical texts in their present form is an ongoing subject of inquiry. It is generally thought that considerable distance separates the Hebrew Bible in its present textual form from any oral roots. Though biblical texts show signs of what is considered to be oral style—recurrent phrases, word and phrase clusters, motifs, and narrative schemata—these texts, in their present form, cannot be assumed to have been composed, performed, or transmitted orally. As Rolf P. Knierim has observed:

> While oral language does or may stand behind the written texts generally, the written texts are phenomena *sui generis*. They reflect a significant distance from the realm of oral language and cannot be considered as intending primary reproductions of oral texts.[53]

Studies of oral features in biblical poetic texts have concluded in a number of cases, however, that although an original basis in oral composition cannot be proved or disproved, many texts draw on patterns that

---

[51] In deliberating this question it is helpful to keep in mind Finnegan's definition of oral poetry, which includes the aspects of transmission and performance as well as of composition, and her claim, based on cross-cultural studies, that oral composition includes composition before, as well as during, a performance (*Oral Poetry*, 17–19). See also Goody, *Interface*, 80, 91–92.

[52] In explaining his theory of the oral basis of much of the Hebrew Bible, Gunkel ("Problems of Hebrew Literary History," in *What Remains of the Old Testament* [New York: Macmillan, 1928], 58–59) points to the recurrent themes and expressions found throughout: "In the Psalms, for instance, we find an extraordinary sameness of content—in different Psalms we find the same thoughts, moods, forms of expression, metaphors, rhetorical figures, phrases. Even the very greatest writers in Israel, the prophets, frequently exhibit the most striking uniformity." See also Dan Ben-Amos, "Folklore in the Ancient Near East," *ABD* 2:823. The work of John Van Seters, which stresses the shaping role of literary and scribal conventions in the biblical narrative genres, provides a contrasting perspective. See, e.g., his "Oral Patterns or Literary Conventions in Biblical Narrative," *Semeia* 5 (1976): 139–54.

[53] "Criticism of Literary Features, Form, Tradition, and Redaction," in *The Hebrew Bible and Its Modern Interpreters* (ed. D. A. Knight and G. M. Tucker; Philadelphia: Fortress, 1985), 145.

probably stem from an oral tradition.[54] In these studies the concept of a transitional text, or at least a transitional stage between primarily oral and primarily written composition, is entertained.[55] The notion of oral-derived literature, composed in writing but attuned to the forms and modes of oral composition, is pertinent as well.

With respect to the prophetic literature in particular there is still general acceptance of the assumption that many of the figures spoken of as classical prophets delivered messages orally, framing or composing them in their own words.[56] How these original messages were modified and

---

[54] See Robert C. Culley, *Oral Formulaic Language in the Biblical Psalms* (Toronto: University of Toronto Press, 1967), especially 113–19; Culley, "Oral Tradition and the OT," 1–33; William J. Urbrock, "Oral Antecedents to Job: A Survey of Formulas and Formulaic Systems," *Semeia* 5 (1976): 111–35; William Whallon, "Formulaic Language in the Old Testament," *Comparative Literature* 15 (1963): 13–14; Robert B. Coote, "The Application of the Oral Theory to Biblical Hebrew Literature," *Semeia* 5 (1976): 51–64. See also Ben-Amos, "Folklore in the Ancient Near East," 2:819a, 822b–23a. On the role of traditional language and structures in prose narrative, see, e.g., Robert C. Culley, *Themes and Variations: A Study of Action in Biblical Narrative* (SemeiaSt; Atlanta: Scholars Press, 1992); Susan Niditch, *Folklore and the Hebrew Bible* (GBS; Minneapolis: Fortress, 1993); Geo Widengren, "Oral Tradition and Written Literature among the Hebrews in the Light of the Arabic Evidence, with special regard to Prose Narratives," *AcOr* 23 (1959): 201–62; David M. Gunn, "On Oral Tradition: A Response to John Van Seters," *Semeia* 5 (1976): 155–61; and Weston W. Fields, "The Motif 'Night As Danger' Associated with Three Biblical Destruction Narratives," in *"Shaʿarei Talmon": Studies in the Bible, Qumran, and the Ancient Near East Presented to Shemaryahu Talmon* (ed. M. Fishbane and E. Tov; Winona Lake, Ind.: Eisenbrauns, 1992), 17–19.

[55] Coote states: "the focus shifts to the process of composition in writing as it is affected by the formulas, themes, patterns, and modality of oral tradition" ("Application of the Oral Theory," 57). Cf. the discussion by Ellen F. Davis, (*Swallowing the Scroll: Textuality and the Dynamics of Discourse in Ezekiel's Prophecy* [Bible and Literature 21; Sheffield: Almond, 1989], 36–38), who places Ezekiel as a transitional figure in the evolution of Israelite prophecy from oral to written composition. See also Niditch, *Oral World and Written Word,* 60–107; and idem, "Biblical Composition and Oral Literature: A Reappraisal" (paper presented at the annual meeting of the AAR/SBL, Washington, D.C., 21 November 1993); Culley, *Oral Formulaic Language,* 25–27, 113–14; Gunn, "On Oral Tradition," 160–61; Whallon, "Formulaic Poetry in the Old Testament," 13–14; and Gunkel, "Problems of Hebrew Literary History," 65–66. On the influence of the existence of writing on oral literature generally, see Goody, *Interface,* 78–109.

[56] It should be noted that this consensus is based on reasonable assumptions rather than on definitive evidence. On challenges to these assumptions, see, e.g.,

developed in the later processes of writing and redaction is a subject of ongoing investigation. The question of whether later prophetic compositions (such as Isa 24:1–20 and Joel 1:5–20) were initially composed in writing is also debated.[57] Whatever the continuing insights provided by research in these areas, it appears reasonable to apply the term *oral-derived* to many prophetic compositions, as works that reflect features of oral compositional style and speak within an orally shaped aesthetic.

A third preliminary concern has to do with the comparison of different genres. This concern is especially pertinent in relation to the concept of theme. Prophetic poetry, like almost all biblical poetry, is essentially nonnarrative. Since Lord originally defined *theme* in terms of his work on Serbo-Croatian epic poetry, the question arises as to what bearing his and later studies have on nonnarrative poetry. Lord mentions this issue in an article in which he suggests that, in general, theme in oral poetry entails "groups of formulas" and the assembling of "prefabricated materials" or "units."[58] In a sample of nonnarrative Serbo-Croatian poetry he discerns two thematic units: merriment and long ago. Each is marked by word repetition; each exists as a structural group in the singer's mind. Foley contributes a similar example from *Beowulf:* the joy-in-the-hall theme is marked by the key words *joy, song* or *sing,* and *sound,* among others, rather than by a set of actions.[59]

Hans M. Barstad, "No Prophets? Recent Developments in Biblical Prophetic Research and Ancient Near Eastern Prophecy," *JSOT* 57 (1993): 39–60. Barstad bases his own arguments for a historical phenomenon of oral prophecy in Israel on the evidence of ancient Near Eastern parallels. On the biblical portrayal of the prophet's active role in composition, see James L. Kugel, "Poets and Prophets: An Overview," in *Poetry and Prophecy: The Beginnings of a Literary Tradition* (ed. J. L. Kugel; Ithaca, N.Y.: Cornell University Press, 1990), 6–8. See also Ben-Amos, "Folklore in the Ancient Near East," 2:824b; and Gene M. Tucker, "Prophecy and Prophetic Literature," in *The Hebrew Bible and Its Modern Interpreters* (ed. D. A. Knight and G. M. Tucker; Philadelphia: Fortress, 1985), 336.

[57] See the discussion of the dating of these passages above and, on Ezekiel, Davis, *Swallowing the Scroll,* 37–39. See also Niditch, *Oral World and Written Word,* 117–20; and, for a definition of oral that includes prior composition in writing, Finnegan (*Oral Poetry,* 16–23).

[58] "Formula and Non-Narrative Theme," 98–99. Culley also raises this issue in "Oral Tradition and the OT," 18–19.

[59] *Immanent Art,* 35. See also the discussion of Donald K. Fry's distinction in Old English poetry between type-scene, which involves the description of a narrative event, and theme, which is not restricted to a narrative event (Foley, *Traditional Oral Epic,* 333–34). One might note here the parallels between the joy-in-the-hall theme and the prophetic motif or *topos* of the disappearance of joyful

Theme in these cases approaches an abstract idea, evoked by semantic clusters describing generic qualities or acts rather than by a specified sequence of actions. On an abstract level, of course, narrative and non-narrative themes can function in similar ways. The Homeric "feast" theme, though represented in a series of concrete actions, still conveys the general qualities of community and hospitality.[60] There is no reason, moreover, to assume that the phraseology of nonnarrative theme does not exhibit at least as wide a range—if not a wider range—of verbal correspondence in different contexts as does narrative theme.

There is some basis of comparison, then, between the treatment of theme in narrative and nonnarrative works, as long as the distinctions between the two categories are respected. The analogue in nonnnarrative compositions to Lord's narrative theme might be a *topos* that entails constitutive elements—though not necessarily actions—and that is expressed by semantically related—though not necessarily identical—vocabulary and phraseology. In this sense the metaphor of the mourning earth, in its association with a set of themes and motifs, might be considered a *topos* comparable to a theme or type-scene in traditional oral epic poetry.[61]

A fourth factor to be considered in applying research on traditional oral poetry to the Hebrew Bible concerns the relationship of biblical Hebrew poetry, particularly prophetic poetry, to the literary conventions and traditions that underlie it. Of primary concern here are the rules of biblical Hebrew poetry and the way they shape diction. A systematic understanding of Hebrew prosody has eluded scholars (or at least scholarly consensus), but a descriptive summary of the main features of Hebrew verse is possible, and the implications of those features for phraseology can be considered.

The Hebrew poetic line divides into cola. The usual pattern is a bicolon (though tricola also regularly occur): two cola separated by a pause, which is often syntactically defined. Characteristic of the poetic line is the phenomenon of parallelism, which, as Kugel has pointed out, functions to bind the two cola together and to integrate the line.[62] Sometimes parallelism

---

sounds, identified by Delbert R. Hillers (*Treaty-Curses and the Old Testament Prophets* [BibOr 16; Rome: Pontifical Biblical Institute, 1964], 57–58) and described above in relation to Isa 24:7–9.

[60] In fact, Foley refers to the joy-in-the-hall theme as "the Anglo-Saxon analogue of the ancient Greek feast theme in metonymic implication" (*Immanent Art,* 35).

[61] Scholes and Kellogg (*Nature of Narrative,* 26–28) use the term *topos* for Lord's *theme* in their discussion of oral poetry, arguing that this term has wider applicability.

[62] "Poets and Prophets," 4.

involves a restatement or echoing in the second (B) colon of what is said in the first (A) colon; sometimes a contrast along opposing, though still parallel, lines. But as Kugel observes, the parallelism of biblical poetry is misnamed because it covers a much wider range of relations between the A and B cola. It includes syntactic, morphological, and semantic correspondence but is not limited to such parallel relations. Differentiation between cola, the subordination of one colon to another, and ellipsis in the second colon also create a sense of connection between the two halves of a line.[63] In particular, parallelism consistently entails a sharpening or exceeding in the B colon of what is stated in the A colon.[64]

The role (or even existence) of meter in Hebrew poetry is obscure, though line and colon length seem to be controlled to some extent.[65] The normal length of a colon is between two and five stressed words.[66] The pattern of a long colon followed by a shorter colon (the so-called *qinah* meter) is evident in much of Lamentations and arguably elsewhere in the Hebrew Bible, but such consistent patterns are not the rule in most biblical poetry, and certainly not in prophetic poetry.[67] Some scholars question the application of the concept of meter to Hebrew poetry at all; Kugel speaks simply of features of poetic diction, such as ellipsis, that keep the poetic line "terse" or compressed—that is, both short and stylistically "heightened."[68]

Yet length and heightened style are variable in Hebrew poetry, as Kugel points out,[69] and parallelism, as noted, entails more differentiation between cola than the standard categories of synonymous, antithetical, and

---

[63] *The Idea of Biblical Poetry: Parallelism and Its History* (New Haven, Conn.: Yale University Press, 1981), 1–58. See also Aloysius Fitzgerald ("Hebrew Poetry," *NJBC* 201–8) on the range of patterns that constitute parallelism, or what he calls "balance between the cola," and Adele Berlin, *The Dynamics of Biblical Parallelism* (Bloomington: Indiana University Press, 1985).

[64] Kugel, *Idea of Biblical Poetry*, 7–12, 29. Kugel summarizes this pattern as B "going-beyond" A.

[65] Michael O'Connor (*Hebrew Verse Structure* [Winona Lake, Ind.: Eisenbrauns, 1980]) has proposed a system of prosodic constraints operating on syntactic categories to explain the structure of Hebrew verse. His list of such constraints confirms the existing variety of poetic forms.

[66] Particles and other unaccented words are generally not counted. Fitzgerald ("Hebrew Poetry," 207) states: "The rule of thumb is to regard as unaccented, small or relatively unimportant words." Clearly, this is a loose definition of meter.

[67] Cf., however, the fairly balanced poetic lines in Job and Proverbs.

[68] *Idea of Biblical Poetry*, 87–95.

[69] Ibid., 88; see also idem, "Poets and Prophets," 4–5.

synthetic allow. The recognized features of Hebrew poetry are loosely defined and variable, allowing for a wide range of phraseological patterning.[70] Phrases take shape at the colon and line level; similarities between phrases range from verbatim repetition to common or related elements. The various manifestations of parallelism produce patterns of word and phrase repetition;[71] synonymous and antithetical parallelism, in particular, encourage the use of characteristic word pairs.[72] The existence of word and phrase repetitions linking lines has also been noted.[73] The variant patterns of phraseological correspondence noted in the discussion above of the nine prophetic passages would seem, then, to be typical of patterns evident in biblical Hebrew poetry as a whole.[74]

The influence of the conventions of Hebrew poetry and prosody constitutes one aspect of tradition dependence, but the broader dimensions of the role of literary tradition in the prophetic corpus must also be assessed. The prophetic speeches stand in a somewhat different relation to literary tradition than do the Homeric, Serbo-Croatian, and Old English epic compositions described above. The opposition between the prophetic message as inspired by a personal visionary experience and as informed by common traditions is a familiar conundrum. That this is a false opposition is widely acknowledged,[75] yet the issue of the degree to which the prophetic

---

[70] Prosodic constraints may be more or less tight depending on the genre. As suggested above, the prophetic genre tends to be looser than other poetic genres.

[71] See Kugel, *Idea of Biblical Poetry*, 5.

[72] The theory that word pairs were created by the demands of parallelism is questioned by Kugel, who points out that such pairs often occur in single (merismatic) phrases and that it is more likely that such phrases were subsequently broken up in the creation of parallel poetic cola (*Idea of Biblical Poetry*, 33). Some scholars have argued that recurrent word pairs constitute the biblical Hebrew version of formula, others retain the notion of formula as a line or half-line phrase, and others accept a mix of formulaic diction. See the discussion in Culley, "Oral Tradition and the OT," 15–17. If a spectrum of phraseology is presumed, traditional patterns need not be limited either to the phrase or to the word pair.

[73] See Fitzgerald, "Hebrew Poetry," 205; O'Connor, *Hebrew Verse Structure*, 109–11, 366–68 (from O'Connor's perspective a colon is a line, a bicolon a couplet, and a tricolon a triplet); James Muilenburg, "A Study in Hebrew Rhetoric: Repetition and Style," in *Congress Volume Copenhagen, 1953* (VTSup 1; Leiden: Brill, 1953), 106–7; idem, "Form Criticism and Beyond," *JBL* 88 (1969): 10–11.

[74] The influence of the regular components of Hebrew verse on poetic diction is as applicable to written poetry as it is to oral poetry. The point is that the commonly identified features of Hebrew poetry foster both recurrence and variation in phraseology.

[75] Foley, *Immanent Art*, 3–9, 23–24, 137–38, 247–52; Ronald E. Clements, *One Hundred Years of Old Testament Interpretation* (Philadelphia: Westminster, 1976),

or poetic work articulates something new, on the one hand, and reformulates the traditional, on the other, remains valid.

In the oral and oral-derived works discussed by Lord and by Foley, a poet or performer brings together traditional formulas and phrases, themes, and story patterns in order to communicate familiar epic tales. Such tales may be adapted to different regional, religious, and historical realities; the details of a story, and the names of characters and places may be changed, for example, and the songs may evolve over time.[76] Further, the imprint of the composer is evident to a greater or lesser degree.[77] But the imprint of the traditional is primary.[78]

The biblical prophetic books, on the other hand, are often seen as conveying innovative messages for Israel, messages depending primarily not on interpretations of past traditions but on a direct insight from God that reveals a new view of past events. Amos's reversal of the traditional meaning of the Day of YHWH is a familiar example.[79] One might also see in the

---

51–58, 70–73; Gerhard von Rad, *The Message of the Prophets* (New York: Harper & Row, 1972), 11–14. From a different perspective, see Georg Fohrer, "Modern Interpretation of the Prophets," *JBL* 80 (1961): 309–19; Muilenburg, "Form Criticism and Beyond," 4–5; and Rolf P. Knierim, "Old Testament Form Criticism Reconsidered," *Int* 27 (1973): 458. See also the discussion in Joseph Blenkinsopp, *A History of Prophecy in Israel* (rev. ed.; Louisville: Westminster John Knox, 1996), 16–26.

[76] Lord (*Singer of Tales*, 118), e.g., reports the deletion from one traditional song of an incident involving an assembly at a mosque because at that time Muslims were forbidden to meet at mosques. See also his discussion on change and stability in the Serbo-Croatian oral poetic tradition (*Singer of Tales*, 102–23) and Foley, *Traditional Oral Epic*, 386. Further, similar song types exist in both Muslim and Christian traditions within the pan-Serbo-Croatian tradition, with corresponding changes in the religion and names of the characters as well as in place names (*Traditional Oral Epic*, 40). For a representative list of studies on modification within the "established contours" of Homeric composition, see Slatkin, *Power of Thetis*, 1 n. 1.

[77] Note the comparison of performances of different singers and of different performances by the same singer in Lord (*Singer of Tales*, 102–18; appendixes 1 and 2).

[78] For a strong statement on the dependence of the Homeric poems on tradition, both in terms of diction and theme, see Gregory Nagy (*The Best of the Achaeans: Concepts of the Hero in Archaic Greek Poetry* [Baltimore: Johns Hopkins University Press, 1979], 3): "To my mind there is no question, then, about the poet's freedom to say accurately what he means. What he means, however, is strictly regulated by tradition. The poet has no intention of saying anything untraditional." The distinction between narrative and nonnarrative poetry may have some bearing on the amount of variation and innovation in an oral or oral-derived work.

[79] To speak of a reversal presupposes, of course, recognition of a preexisting tradition.

image of YHWH as a lion in Amos 1:2 the reversal of a traditional motif in which YHWH serves as a guardian or defender of Israel and preys on the foreign nations. Such a motif is reflected in, for example, Isa 31:4–5 and Joel 4:16.[80]

The primacy of unique elements in the prophetic speeches has been forcefully stated by Georg Fohrer:

> Probably no part of the Old Testament, least of all the prophets, can be viewed exclusively from the standpoint of its traditional content or the duality of tradition and interpretation. Almost always there is a more or less imposing mass of individual ideas and expressions, spontaneous or derived, that do not derive from this tradition. The prophets in particular were primarily charismatics, claiming to preach not a tradition, but the living word of Yahweh that had been delivered to them.[81]

At the same time, the participation of the prophetic speeches in common traditions is clear, giving rise to the question posed by Ronald E. Clements:

> The use made by the prophets of certain traditional forms of speech, and the presence of particular common ideas and motifs in their preaching raises issues relating to the essential nature of prophetic inspiration and revelation.[82]

---

[80] Cf. Jer 25:30–31. For a discussion of lion imagery in the prophetic literature in relation to ancient Near Eastern traditions of guardian animals, see Michael T. Davis and Brent A. Strawn, "Isaiah 31:4–5 in the Light of Lion Iconography in the Ancient Near East" (paper presented at the annual meeting of the AAR/SBL, New Orleans, 25 November 1996).

[81] *Introduction to the Old Testament* (New York: Abingdon, 1968) 29–30. See also the brief summary of other scholars who stress the independence of the prophets from previous Israelite traditions in Tucker, "Prophecy and the Prophetic Literature," 334–35. There may be other oral or oral-derived traditions in which the poet or speaker plays a similar role, but these traditions are not among those discussed by Lord or Foley in the works mentioned above. The question of the composition of new songs along the lines of the old, as opposed to the reenactment of traditional songs, is mentioned briefly, but not developed, by Lord (*Singer of Tales,* 26). He does, however, refer to the concept of generic songs that take many different forms in the Serbo-Croatian oral epic tradition and thereby leaves open a role for the singer in creating new songs, however dependent on traditional pattern (Lord, *Singer of Tales,* 101, 119–23).

[82] *Prophecy and Tradition* (Atlanta: John Knox, 1975), 24. See also Walter E. Rast, *Tradition History and the Old Testament* (GBS; Philadelphia: Fortress, 1972), 59–71; Tucker, "Prophecy and the Prophetic Literature," 326–35; Joseph Blenkinsopp, *Prophecy and Canon: A Contribution to the Study of Jewish Origins*

In fact there are at least four different contexts of tradition at issue in this study. The broadest context is that of ancient Near Eastern literature and culture as a whole. Within this corpus laments such as the lamentations over the cities of Sumer and Ur, noted above, are particularly important, as are the traditional curses reflected in many of the nine prophetic texts examined. A second context of tradition is the body of sociocultural and literary traditions of Israel, which often parallel broader ancient Near Eastern patterns. Within this context Israelite traditions of creation, of divinely wrought flood and storm, of divine curses, of legal or ethical norms, and of ritual practices, among others, bear on the nine passages considered above. The prophetic literature employs a variety of traditional literary forms or subgenres, from the lament (Jer 12:1–4; 14:1–9; Isa 33:7–9; cf. Joel 1:5–20), to the riddle (Amos 3:3–8; Jer 12:5), to the hymnic refrain (Amos 4:13; 5:8–9; 9:5–6). Each form may exhibit characteristic features of phraseology, structure, or theme.

A third context of tradition is that prevalent in the prophetic literature itself.[83] Again, the influence of tradition extends to the forms of prophetic speech, such as the judgment oracle, the *rîb,* and the vision report; to phraseology such as the messenger formula; to motifs such as the harlotry of Israel or the comparison of Israel to a vine or vineyard; to broad themes such as the judgment of Israel, the punishment of the nations, or the new age of salvation.[84] The apparent quoting in later prophetic books of earlier collections of prophecy, though it may signal the existence of a written tradition, also witnesses to the reality of a prophetic tradition.[85] The recurrent

---

(University of Notre Dame Center for the Study of Judaism and Christianity in Antiquity 3; Notre Dame, Ind.: Notre Dame University Press, 1977), 143–44.

[83] See Clements, *Prophecy and Tradition,* 3–5, 24–40; Joseph Blenkinsopp, *Sage, Priest, Prophet: Religion and Intellectual Leadership in Ancient Israel* (Louisville: Westminster John Knox, 1995), 143–44; Otto H. Steck, "Theological Streams of Tradition," in *Tradition and Theology in the Old Testament* (ed. D. A. Knight; Sheffield: JSOT Press, 1977), 201–5. It is easier to establish this context of tradition than it is the previous two contexts because it exists within one overall genre, that of the prophetic literature.

[84] Scholars further discern particular branches of prophetic tradition, claiming, for example, that Jeremiah refers back to Hosea or that First Isaiah is particularly influenced by Amos. See, e.g., Blenkinsopp, *History of Prophecy,* 104–5; Clements, *Prophecy and Tradition,* 91. For regional and theological distinctions (dialectical differences in Foley's terms [*Traditional Oral Epic,* 9 n. 21]), see, e.g., Robert R. Wilson, *Prophecy and Society in Ancient Israel* (Philadelphia: Westminster, 1980).

[85] See, e.g., the reference to the prophet Micah and the citation of Mic 3:12 in Jer 26:18 as well as the extensive citations noted above in Isa 24:1–20 and Joel 1:5–20.

metaphor of the mourning earth, found only in the prophetic literature, clearly belongs in this context.

Within this third level of tradition, as within the second, individual prophetic texts show great flexibility and independence with respect to inherited patterns, as seen, for example in the variation in the structure of the judgment oracle,[86] in the development of oracles of salvation in Second Isaiah, and in the individual styles and thematic foci of each prophetic collection. A prime example of literary flexibility in the nine passages of this study is the reversal in Jer 12:8 of the image of YHWH as a lion found in Amos 1:2. In the latter verse, YHWH roars from Zion and lifts up his voice (*yittēn qôlô*) against the nations and the people of Judah and Israel.[87] In Jer 12:8 it is Judah that "lifts up her voice against me [YHWH]" (*nātĕnâ ʿalay bĕqôlāh*).

Finally, a fourth context of tradition in the biblical prophetic literature is that established within the particular prophetic collection, not only, perhaps, by the prophet and his immediate followers but also by later redactors.[88] The pairing of *qādar*, "to mourn" and "to be dark," with *ʾābal* in Jer 4:28, for example, was considered above in terms of this level of tradition. The verb *qādar* occurs elsewhere in Jeremiah, as does the motif of darkness, especially in association with desert and aridity. Even within a given prophetic collection, however, the possibility of great variety in poetic conception and expression is evident in the distinctive development of the metaphor of earth mourning in each of the four passages from Jeremiah.

A standard caveat must be raised with respect to reconstructing the traditional context of the prophetic books, however. Fohrer points out that many of the traditions extant during the prophetic period would have been "fragmentary" and "inchoate" in relation to the form in which they are presented in the final redaction of Hebrew Bible;[89] Clements argues, further, that these traditions were also quite diverse.[90] Hence the themes evoked

---

[86] See Claus Westermann, *Basic Forms of Prophetic Speech* (Louisville: Westminster John Knox, 1991), 169–209. See also Gene M. Tucker, "Prophetic Speech," *Int* 32 (1978): 40–43.

[87] See the discussion above of Amos 1:2.

[88] The fourth, third, and second contexts of tradition described here correspond roughly to the three levels of tradition distinguished by Foley (*Traditional Oral Epic*, 9 n. 21, 279): the idiolectal (of a single singer), the dialectal (of a local tradition), and the national or tradition-wide (of a language).

[89] Georg Fohrer, *History of Israelite Religion* (Nashville: Abingdon, 1972), 283.

[90] See the discussion of covenant, wisdom, and cult traditions in Clements, *Prophecy and Tradition*, especially 87–89.

by the characteristic phraseology, vocabulary, motifs, and structures in the prophetic books do not necessarily add up to a uniform perspective, even within the final redaction of the prophetic corpus.

Further, the fluidity and diversity of Israelite religious and literary traditions means, as Clements notes, that it is often difficult to tell whether a prophetic composition has modified a tradition or is working with an already-modified tradition. It can be just as difficult, he suggests, to determine whether a later prophetic book is deliberately referring to an earlier work or whether each has drawn on elements of common tradition.[91] Given the assumption of an oral aesthetic, on the one hand, and the evidence of individual poetic vision and style, on the other, it is not possible to trace precisely the transmission and development of literary traditions in the prophetic collections. Any analysis of the interrelationships between texts must therefore remain to some extent impressionistic.

These complications apply as well to Foley's fifth parameter for the study of traditional oral and oral-derived texts: the interplay between their diachronic and synchronic contexts.[92] His definition of the synchronic context encompasses the composition itself, the entire repertoire of the given poet or singer/performer, and the repertoire of the community of poets or singer/performers of which he is a part. The diachronic context represents the previous history of the tradition manifested in a text.[93]

This definition might be applied to the biblical prophetic literature as follows. The synchronic context of a prophetic passage consists, in the first place, of the passage itself, then of other passages within the particular prophetic collection that stem from roughly the same period, and, finally, of passages of roughly the same period in other prophetic collections. The diachronic context comprises texts from different periods.

The synchronic and diachronic dimensions interact continually in a traditional text because the state of the tradition at a given time encompasses its previous expressions, which reach backward in time.[94] In attempting to

---

[91] See also Fishbane, *Biblical Interpretation,* 288–89.

[92] *Traditional Oral Epic,* 2–3, 10.

[93] Niditch (*Oral World and Written Word,* 6, 25) applies the categories of synchronic and diachronic somewhat differently. She defines the synchronic dimension as the overarching traditional oral poetic common to Israelite literature of various times and places. The diachronic dimension consists in the variations of this poetic in individual compositions.

[94] See the discussion of synchronic and diachronic factors with respect to Homeric epic in Nagy, "Formula and Meter," 18–35. At the same time, the articulation of a tradition at a given moment contributes to its future shape and thus points forward in time.

date the nine passages of this study and in discussing them in roughly chronological sequence, the diachronic aspect of the traditions they express has been respected. In exploring the development of those traditions within individual texts and collections from a similar period, the synchronic aspect has been considered. The two cannot ultimately be separated, however, since the diachronic span of the tradition imbues the individual expression, and the individual expression informs its continued evolution. Again, it is difficult to define just how the diachronic dimension shapes, and is shaped by, the synchronic dimensions of the metaphor of earth mourning.

This clarification of the bases for comparison of the nine biblical prophetic passages of this study to the extrabiblical poetic traditions described above lends credence to the apparent compositional parallels between them. At the same time, it exposes areas of dissimilarity, especially with respect to genre and the relationship to tradition. What strikes one on the whole in the consideration of the nine prophetic passages is the utter distinctiveness of each, despite common strands. This distinctiveness is marked even within the group of four texts from the same prophetic collection (Jeremiah).

In many ways the passages appear more unlike than like; it is only on examination of their basic components—their bare bones, as it were—that a network of similarities emerges. Perhaps this process is illustrative of the way literary tradition shapes conception and expression in the biblical prophetic literature. Such shaping appears, at least in the case of the nine examples studied here, to occur at a deep level that allows much free play to the prophetic vision and poetic imagination in the moments of experience and communication.

8

CONCLUSIONS

Within the nine passages considered in this study, the metaphor of earth mourning serves as a figure of distress. It reflects a state of disaster that has befallen, or is about to befall, the human community and at the same time introduces a contrasting perspective, as the state of the earth itself is held up as a silent witness against the state of its inhabitants. Close reading of the nine passages shows further that the metaphor attracts a cluster of accompanying phrases, motifs, themes, and literary techniques that move with it in the varying expressions of disaster in which it occurs. Not every phrase, motif, theme, or literary device is represented in each passage, yet there are lines of continuity over the body of passages.

The recurrent phraseology and thematic foci linked to the metaphor have been labeled formulaic or typical by some commentators and taken as signs of redactional insertion. It has been argued above, however, that the verses in which the metaphor occurs are integrated into their literary contexts and that they originate, for the most part, with the speeches and poems to which they now belong. It has been further suggested that these compositions range in date from the eighth century or a little later (Amos 1:2; Hos 4:13) through the postexilic period, with four late preexilic passages from Jeremiah in between (Jer 4:23–28; 12:1–4, 7–13; 23:9–12). The literary contexts of the metaphor vary widely in these nine passages, but the metaphor itself remains a constant.

The work of Foley and other scholars on oral and oral-derived poetic traditions outside the Hebrew Bible supports the attempt to map a common field of reference for the recurrent phraseology and thematic configurations associated with this metaphor.[1] Through the reading of all nine

---

[1] See also the model suggested by Claude Bremond ("Concept and Theme," in *The Return of Thematic Criticism* [ed. Werner Sollors; Cambridge: Mass.: Harvard University Press, 1993], 49–55) of the "thematic field," which he illustrates by comparing a set of folktales with striking parallels but also significant variations or mutations. This model facilitates the description of the relations among a group of texts that exhibit divergent as well as analogous patterns. The texts may have thematic connections with at least one other text but fewer connections with some

prophetic passages (and of other related biblical texts), patterns have emerged that cannot be identified as such when individual texts are considered separately. Such patterns may be only faintly suggested in individual instances and thus easily overlooked or minimized. Yet when the related texts are read together, common strands stand out and coalesce.

The continuous strands thus displayed bring, according to Foley's concept of metonymy, an extratextual dimension of meaning to bear on the individual prophetic expression, giving it significance and communicative power it does not possess alone. To borrow the expression Hillers uses in relation to these passages, the tradition lying behind them appears to act as a third partner in the creative process, along with the author and the event or situation described.[2]

This notion of the literary tradition as a tapestry in which individual compositions participate, and in view of which they should be read, need not imply the dependence of one prophetic text on the written text of another. Rather, the continuity of expression and conception in such passages may reflect a common stream of poetic language and imagination in the prophetic tradition, on which individual prophetic speeches and poems draw. The distinction between what one might call literary dependence and tradition dependence is difficult to define.[3] The postexilic compositions Isa 24:1–20 and Joel 1:5–20 show multiple signs of precise literary citation or allusion; earlier texts exhibit broader similarities of phraseology and imagery. The concept of "oral-derived" literature is helpful in accommodating the ambiguity of literary influence here. Works composed in writing that show extensive dependence on other written texts may still be exhibiting the penchant for recurrent phraseology, imagery, and themes that characterize an oral aesthetic.[4]

-----

than with others and none at all with still others. According to Bremond, "the continuity of this field is intuitively perceptible, even though it is not possible to abstract a conceptual nucleus present in all manifestations of the theme" ("Concept and Theme," 53). The field consists in the view of any one manifestation of the theme as a transformation of another.

[2] "The Roads to Zion Mourn," *Perspective* 12:1–2 (1971): 121–22. As noted above, however, Hillers's focus is on the Ugaritic myth lying behind the imagery of these passages.

[3] See, e.g., Fishbane (*Biblical Interpretation in Ancient Israel* [Oxford: Clarendon, 1985], 285–91), who addresses a similar issue in his definition of innerbiblical exegesis; Hillers, "Roads to Zion Mourn," 130–32; and the discussion by Hans Wildberger (*Jesaja 13–27* [BKAT 10/2; Neukirchen-Vluyn: Neukirchener Verlag, 1978], 920) over whether Isa 24:1–20 is literarily dependent on Jer 4:23–28.

[4] Cf. the critique by David O. Ross Jr. ("Commentaries on the *Aeneid:* S. J. Harrison, *Vergil: Aeneid 10;* K. W. Grandsen, *Virgil. Aeneid Book XI,*" *CJ* 90 [1994]:

The point is, perhaps, not so much that the nine texts of this study were composed in relation to one another, nor that they cannot help but be read in relation to one another, as a reader sensitive to the possibilities of innerbiblical exegesis, intertextuality, or even conventional literary analysis might do. Rather, the point is that the passages were most likely both composed and heard in reference to shared modes of expression, above and beyond any written literary dependence, and that understanding these modes is key to appreciating both the meaning of these texts and the way meaning is communicated in them.

The breadth and depth of the associations embodied in traditional modes of expression are diminished when recurrent phrases and themes are regarded as flatly typical by modern readers. Traditional phrases are often short and may seem to stand out, or even jar, in particular contexts.[5] Yet to disregard them is to lose much of the power of the prophetic word. In this respect, Albert Lord's statement, with which Nagy concludes his own discussion of the diachronic and synchronic aspects of formula and meter in the Homeric corpus, is worth repeating here. Speaking about traditional oral poetry, Lord says:

> It cannot be treated as a flat surface. All the elements in traditional poetry have depth, and our task is to plumb their sometimes hidden recesses; for there meaning will be found. We must be willing to use the new tools for investigation of multiforms of themes and patterns, and we must be willing to learn from the experience of other oral traditional poetics.[6]

81–86, esp. 82–83) directed at presumptions of literary dependence in Vergil. Ross assumes that familiarity with previous literary works among the Augustan poets had an oral basis: "Poetry was oral in ways we don't easily appreciate: words and phrases of older verse were as constantly audible to a Roman poet as the tags and themes of all sorts of music that fill the head of a musician today" ("Commentaries on the *Aeneid*," 83).

[5] Cf. the discussion by Wildberger (*Jesaja 13–27*, 925, 928, 938) on the apparent inconsistency with which traditional expressions of disaster are applied in Isa 24:1–20, yet the overall unity achieved in the depiction of a frightful future. See also the discussion of John M. Foley (*Immanent Art: From Structure to Meaning in Traditional Oral Epic* [Bloomington: University of Indiana Press, 1991], 252) on the way traditional phrases "echo against their most immediate surroundings, acting as firm anchors for the rapidly shifting action they help to rationalize."

[6] "Homer As an Oral Poet," *Harvard Studies in Classical Philology* 72 (1968): 46, cited in Gregory Nagy, "Formula and Meter: The Oral Poetics of Homer," in *Greek Mythology and Poetics* (Myth and Poetics; Ithaca, N.Y.: Cornell University Press, 1990), 35.

This study has attempted to plumb the associations evoked by certain phrases, images, motifs, and themes in a set of prophetic texts. It has undertaken this task by focusing closely on individual passages, tracing the connections between the compositional elements found in them and comparable elements in other passages, and keeping in mind differences as well as similarities in historical provenance. The patterns established create a context for meaning that transcends the bounds of the individual speech or poem, the individual prophetic collection, or even the prophetic corpus itself, as the parallels between the nine passages considered here with certain psalms or with the creation accounts of Gen 1–11 illustrate.[7]

At the same time, this context is malleable; hence the flexibility and idiosyncraticity of phraseology, imagery, and thematic conception in each of these passages. Characteristic features of the particular prophetic collection are often reflected in the treatment of the metaphor of earth mourning in an individual text. This is evident in the pairing of *'ābal* with *qādar,* "to mourn" or "to grow dark," in Jer 4:28; in the representation of YHWH's voice like a lion's in Amos 1:2; or in the linking of the mourning of the earth with liturgical lament in Joel 1:5–20. The stress on the role of human transgression in the mourning of the earth is prominent in Hos 4:1–3, while the presentation of the earth's mourning as a counterpoint to the wickedness of its inhabitants, who are indifferent to it, is especially evident in Jer 12:1–4; 12:7–13; and, perhaps, 23:9–12. The

---

[7] Cf. the conclusions of Claire R. Mathews ("Apportioning Desolation: Contexts for Interpreting Edom's Fate and Function in Isaiah," *Society of Biblical Literature 1995 Seminar Papers* [ed. Eugene H. Lovering Jr.; SBLSP 34; Atlanta: Scholars Press, 1995], 250–66, esp. 255–60, 265) on the need to establish a broad, interprophetic context for the interpretation of Isa 34–35. In contrast, note, e.g., the discussion by James L. Crenshaw (*Joel* [AB 24C; New York: Doubleday, 1995], 100) of the word *'ikkārîm,* "farmer," which is paired with *kōrĕmîm,* "vinedresser," in Joel 1:11. Crenshaw identifies the former as simply a "rare loan word." Although he cites its occurrence in Isa 61:5 and 2 Chr 26:10 as well as in Amos 5:16b in connection with *'ēbel,* "mourning," he does not comment on the coupling of *'ikkārîm* with *kōrĕmîm* in 2 Chr 26:10 or with *kōrĕmêkem,* "their vinedressers," in Isa 61:5. Nor does he mention the link between the mourning of the *'ikkār,* "farmer," in Amos 5:16 and lamentation (*mispēd*) in the vineyards (*kĕrāmîm*) in Amos 5:17a. These pairings of *'ikkārîm* or *'ikkār* and *kōrĕmîm* point to a traditional merism for all who work the land or for the realm of agriculture itself, and the link with lamentation in Amos foreshadows Joel. Further, *'ikkārîm* occurs in Jer 14:4 in the context of a communal lament over a massive drought, a lament that can be seen in many ways as parallel to the call to lament in Joel 1:5–20. In Jer 14:4–6, e.g., the dismay of the ground (*'ădāmâ*) and the shame (*bōš*) of the farmers (*'ikkārîm*) is followed by a description of the distress of the animals (cf. Joel 1:10, 11, 18–20).

interweaving of images of military invasion with images of drought is notable in Jer 4:23–28 and 12:7–13.

Yet there is wide variation even within the passages that form part of the Jeremianic collection. The vision of the aftermath of destruction in Jer 4:23–28 contrasts with the ongoing suffering of creation in Jer 12:4. The imagery of Jer 12:1–3, which centers around the wicked as a defined group, contrasts with the image of God's heritage turned hostile predator in Jer 12:8–9. The battle imagery surrounding Jer 4:23–28, explicit in 12:10–12, evoked in Isa 24:10–12 and 33:7–8a, and introduced figuratively in Joel 1:6, is absent in Jer 12:1–4 and 23:9–12. The emphasis on act and consequence reflected in Jer 12:1–4, 13 and 23:12 is wholly lacking in 4:23–28, where the punitive act of the divine warrior predominates. The linking of the metaphor of earth mourning to the specific condemnation of prophet and priest and the corruption of the temple is found only in Jer 23:11.

Differences in historical setting clearly play a role in the development of the metaphor in different literary contexts. In the six passages that can be considered preexilic, for example, the metaphor is tied to an impending definitive judgment on the people of Israel or Judah. In the three postexilic texts (Isa 24:1–20; 33:7–9; Joel 1:5–20), the metaphor serves as part of a depiction of devastation that, in the wider context of these passages (Isa 24–27; 33; Joel 1–2), yields to the hope of restoration and blessing for the faithful. Historical differences may also explain differences in literary style, the earlier passages relying more on brief metonymic references and Isa 24:1–20 and Joel 1:5–20 showing the more elaborate and extended style associated with composition in writing.

Finally, the character of the individual prophetic and poetic vision undoubtedly plays a role in shaping differing expressions of the traditional motif of earth mourning. The almost quiescent scene of devastation in Jer 4:23–28, where the land has already relapsed into desert, and the static quality of Isa 33:7–9, where disintegration is portrayed as an ongoing reality but there is no explicit mention of its cause, seem to reflect distinct individual poetic conceptions rather than simply representing typical expressions of a given theme. Similarly indicative of artistic discretion are both a two-part literary structure, in which human transgression is followed directly by the distress of the earth (as seen in Hos 4:1–3; Jer 12:1–4; Isa 33:7–9), and the deft intertwining of human responses and the response of the earth (Jer 4:23–28; 12:7–13; Isa 24:1–20; Joel 1:5–20).

The implications of the recurrent features of the nine passages for the significance of the metaphor of earth mourning are manifold. One such feature, the persistent linking of the mourning of the earth with the theme of the undoing of creation, is notable in view of current discussions about the role of creation traditions in the prophetic literature and in the Hebrew

Bible in general. In the nine passages, the envisioned collapse of the nation or community is tied to the wasting away of the earth itself and, the poetic language frequently suggests, to the breakdown of the primary elements of creation. In these instances the devastation of the earth is conveyed with language and imagery evocative of traditions of creation and decreation reflected in the biblical creation accounts as well as in other biblical and extrabiblical texts.

Some scholars connect themes of creation and the undoing of creation in the prophetic literature with developments in Israelite theology arising out of the exile. Gerhard von Rad, for example, asserts that the prophetic literature does not draw on traditions of creation before Second Isaiah, where these traditions play a significant, even central role.[8] Von Rad attributes the "sudden incorporation of the creation tradition" in the preaching of Second Isaiah to the confrontation of Israel with the massive world empire of the Babylonians, a situation that inspired an appeal to YHWH as the creator of the world. Stahl, following similar lines of thought, relates the portrayal of the reversal of creation in Zeph 1:2 and Hos 4:3 to the "radical change" ("Umbruch") brought about by the Babylonian invasion of 597.[9]

This study affirms, in contrast, that neither the use of creation traditions in the prophetic literature nor the connection made there between the stumbling of Israel and Judah as nations and the subversion of the created order can be traced exclusively to the impact of the exile. The assertion that among the prophetic passages considered here, both pre-exilic and postexilic texts rely on the imagery and phraseology of creation and decreation supports the views of those who assign a significant role to creation traditions in the prophetic tradition before Second Isaiah.[10]

---

[8] *Old Testament Theology* (2 vols.; New York: Harper & Row, 1965), 2:240–41.

[9] Rainer Stahl, "'Deshalb trocknet die Erde aus und verschmachten alle, die auf ihr wohnen...' Der Versuch einer theologiegeschichtlichen Einordnung von Hos 4, 3," in *Alttestamentlicher Glaube und Biblische Theologie: Festschrift für Horst Dietrich Preuss zum 65. Geburtstag* (ed. Jutta Hausmann and Hans-Jürgen Zobel; Stuttgart: Kohlhammer, 1992), 171–72.

[10] See, e.g., Helga Weippert, *Schöpfer des Himmels und der Erde: Ein Beitrag zur Theologie des Jeremiabuches* (SBS 102; Stuttgart: Katholisches Bibelwerk, 1981), 14–15, 89; Laurent Wisser, "La création dans le livre de Jérémie," in *La création dans l'orient ancien* (ed. Louis Derousseaux; Congrès de L'ACFEB, Lille (1985); LD 127; Paris: Cerf, 1987), 258; John D. W. Watts, *Vision and Prophecy in Amos* (Leiden: Brill, 1958), 64; Karl Eberlin, *Gott der Schöpfer—Israels Gott: Eine exegetisch-hermeneutische Studie zur theologischen Funktion alttestamentlicher Schöpfungsaussagen* (BEATAJ 5; Frankfurt: Lang, 1986), 229–39; and A. Penna, "Il cosmo nella letteratura profetica," in *Il cosmo nella Bibbia* (ed. Giuseppe De Gennaro; Naples: Edizioni Dehoniane, 1982), 201–93.

In fact, it may be that the prophetic literature, along with the Psalms, the wisdom writings, and even some of the legal material[11] of the Hebrew Bible, reflect traditions about creation that formed an integral part of the thinking of the Israelites about their life, their history, and their God.

Von Rad has characterized the role of creation theology in the Hebrew Bible as ancillary to the role of redemption theology,[12] but this study lends weight to Knierim's statement that the Hebrew Bible does refer much more than is commonly assumed to YHWH's "relationship to and presence in the order of the world."[13] The various "cosmologically oriented texts" found throughout the Hebrew Bible are part of the expression of Israel's faith, Knierim asserts.[14] Moreover, the shape of this faith is consonant with the rooting of Israelite society in agriculture, with its elemental interface between human need and labor and the cyclic workings of the cosmos.[15]

Without entering into discussion about whether creation traditions or redemption traditions are primary in Israelite belief,[16] it can be asserted, on the basis of the texts studied here, that both play a part. It is difficult to counter von Rad's argument that creation beliefs rarely appear in the Hebrew Bible independently from allusions to YHWH's redemptive acts or, to put it more broadly, to YHWH's intervention in human history. Von Rad, for example, refers to the doxologies in the book of Amos (4:13; 5:8–9; 9:5–6), which praise the creative and sustaining power of YHWH in the cosmos, as having "no specific message of their own," but as functioning to universalize the prophetic message.[17] In the nine prophetic passages of this study, YHWH's dismantling of the created order is clearly connected to the history of the relationship between YHWH and Israel: to the giving of laws and land, to the transgression of the former and the forfeiture of the latter. An interrelationship between different facets of

---

[11] See Jon R. Levenson, "The Theologies of Commandment in Biblical Israel," *HTR* 73 (1980): 28–32.

[12] "The Theological Problem of the Old Testament Doctrine of Creation," in *The Problem of the Hexateuch* (London: SCM, 1966), 131–43.

[13] Rolf P. Knierim, "Cosmos and History in Israel's Theology," *HBT* 3 (1981): 63.

[14] Ibid., 66.

[15] Ibid., 64, 84–85.

[16] Knierim (ibid.) and Hans H. Schmidt ("Creation, Righteousness, and Salvation: 'Creation Theology' As the Broad Horizon of Biblical Theology," in *Creation in the Old Testament* [ed. Bernhard W. Anderson; IRT 6; Philadelphia: Fortress, 1984], 102–17) argue for the former; von Rad ("Theological Problem") for the latter.

[17] "Theological Problem," 135.

Israelite belief need not be interpreted as subordinating one tradition to the other, however.[18]

Within the context of the allusions to creation in the body of passages considered here, the active response of the earth embodied in the metaphor of earth mourning takes on special significance. The interplay of human, natural, and divine personae presented in the nine prophetic passages images the relationship between God, human beings, and the earth in the accounts of the origins of the cosmos and of human life in Gen 1–11. The nine passages thus exhibit in skeletal form the broad schema of creation and decreation developed in detail in the narratives that make up the primeval history.[19]

It is interesting to note that whereas these narratives now stand as a thematic introduction to the Pentateuch and to the Hebrew Bible as a whole, arguably four of the nine prophetic passages serve as thematic headings or introductions in their own contexts. Amos 1:2 introduces both the set of oracles against the nations that follow it in 1:3–2:16 as well as the book of Amos as a whole. A similar role is assigned Hos 4:1–3, which precedes the specific oracles against priest, prophet, and king in 4:4–5:7,[20] as well, perhaps, as the longer section Hos 4–11. Jeremiah 23:9–12 begins a sequence of judgment speeches against the prophets of Judah in 23:13–40. Finally, the depiction of cosmic judgment in Isa 24:1–20 initiates a series of prophecies in Isa 25–27 that concern the eventual restoration of the righteous.[21]

---

[18] Note that Knierim ("Cosmos and History," 81–101) diverges from von Rad in asserting that the cosmic order sets the standard for human history in the biblical literature. On the intertwining of themes of creation and redemption in the Psalms, e.g., see Richard J. Clifford, "The Hebrew Scriptures and the Theology of Creation," *TS* 46 (1985): 512–16.

[19] In light of the parallels between the phraseology of the Priestly account of the flood in Gen 6:11–13 and characteristic vocabulary in Ezekiel, Joseph Blenkinsopp (*The Pentateuch: An Introduction to the First Five Books of the Bible* [ABRL; New York: Doubleday, 1992], 79) suggests that "the prophetic understanding of Israelite history as leading inexorably to disaster and exile, especially as it comes to expression in Ezekiel, forms the subtext to P's deluge narrative." Considering the phraseology and imagery in the nine prophetic passages examined here, one might conjecture that the scattered allusions to creation traditions in the prophetic literature form a background for their fuller articulation in continuous narrative form in the Priestly and Yahwist strands of the primeval history.

[20] Jörg Jeremias (*Der Prophet Hosea* [ATD 24/1; Göttingen: Vandenhoeck & Ruprecht, 1983], 59) argues that Hos 4:1–3 serves as a preface for the entire middle section of Hos (Hos 4–11).

[21] Cf. the literary roles of Zeph 1:2–4 and Nah 1:2–6, passages that share phraseology and motifs with the nine texts of this study.

If the metaphor of earth mourning can be seen as conveying a theological message about the interrelationship of human beings, God, and the cosmos, it must also be viewed in its literary role in the nine passages in which it occurs. The introduction of the earth as a persona provides an alternative arena in which the human audience can view the disorder that either pervades it or is about to engulf it. The focus on the earth in these passages builds distance into the prophetic pronouncement. It enables listeners to see with greater sharpness the situation in which they are immersed, either because the mourning of the earth mirrors their own devastation or because it is held up as a silent witness against them.

The inclusion of the earth as an actor thus widens the scope of the prophetic vision, lifting the eyes of those who receive it beyond the immediate human situation to the broad horizon of the created world. In this, the role of the metaphor parallels that of the similes in the *Iliad*. It is also reminiscent of the technique of *ekphrasis,* the description of a work of visual art. This technique is exemplified in the *Iliad* in the account of the shield of Achilles (18.478–608), with its scenes of the heavens, of peaceful and warring cities, of agriculture and festival.[22] In the case of the metaphor of earth mourning, however, the result is not to shrink the view of human endeavor, as the Homeric similes often do, by contrasting it with the ongoing cycles of the natural world. Nor is it simply to create an alternative world that evokes and illumines the real world, as the description of the shield of Achilles does. Rather it is to expand the significance of human actions by showing their impact upon realities that, far from being impervious to human life, are responsive to it, hanging in dynamic balance with it through the relationship with YHWH that defines them both.[23]

---

[22] See Andrew S. Becker, *The Shield of Achilles and the Poetics of Ekphrasis* (Greek Studies: Interdisciplinary Approaches; Lanham, Md.: Rowman & Littlefield, 1995), 1–50, esp. 49–50. Becker notes that the ancient definition of *ekphrasis* is a "description of any kind" (2).

[23] The interrelationship between human beings and nature presumed here calls to mind and can inform contemporary ecological discussions, but distinctions must be drawn. In the biblical texts considered in this study, human beings do not necessarily harm or pollute the natural environment through direct abuse or overuse of the land (although the effects of war on the land may be reflected in Jer 4:23–28 and 12:7–13; cf. Deut 20:19–20). None of the passages link, for example, the mourning of the earth with abandonment of provisions for a sabbatical year of rest from working the land, as specified in Lev 25:1–7. Rather, it is social abuse and disorder that harm the earth indirectly, by incurring the punitive anger of YHWH. This is the basic scenario presented in these texts, even though it is telescoped when primary stress is placed on the causative role of human transgression. In a broad

In these passages earth assumes a human posture, and the result is to amplify human existence. The specter of drought raised by the use of the verb *'ābal* is a threat attached to human transgression throughout the Hebrew Bible, but it attains cosmic proportions in many of these texts as it reaches to the fundamental elements of creation. The metaphor of earth mourning thereby universalizes not only the power of YHWH, as images of natural phenomena do in the *topos* of the divine warrior, the doxologies of Amos, the proclamations of Second Isaiah, or the divine speeches in the book of Job, but the consequences of human action as well.

---

sense the passages evidence the interdependence of human beings and the earth common to agrarian societies. But the relationship to YHWH, from which all things, both good and bad, flow, is primary. See Penna, "Il cosmo nella letteratura profetica," 235–36. In contrast, see, e.g., Christoph Uehlinger, "The Cry of the Earth: Biblical Perspectives on Ecology and Violence," in *Ecology and Poverty: Cry of the Earth, Cry of the Poor* (ed. Leonardo Boff and V. Elizondo; Concilium 1995/5; London: SCM; Maryknoll, N.Y.: Orbis, 1995), 46–48. Uehlinger acknowledges the distinction between ancient and modern views but claims that Hos 4:1–3, as well as Isa 24:1–6 and 33:7–9, reflect "concrete historical experiences" and that "in antiquity political, military, and social conflicts usually also had effects in the ecological sphere." He thus implies that these texts describe the literal damage inflicted by social disorder on the natural environment.

Appendix
Recurrent Words and Roots in the Nine Passages*

	Amos	Hos	Jer 4	Jer 12A	Jer 12B	Jer 23	Isa 24	Isa 33	Joel
ʾbl	X	X	X	X	X	X	X	X	X
ʾereṣ / ʾădāmâ		X	X			X	X	X	X
ʾumlal		X	X				X	X	X
šmm		X			X		X	X	X
ybš	X			X		X			
karmel / kerem	X		X		X			X	
ʾādām / ʾîs / ʾĕnôš		X			X		X	X	
yōšēb		X		X			X		X
ḥayyâ / bĕhēmâ		X		X	X				X
śādeh		X		X					X
ʿôp		X	X	X					
nĕʾôt	X					X			X
midbār / ʿărābâ		X			X			X	
buš / ḥpr					X			X	X
ʾkl					X		X		X
bêtî / bêt ʾĕlōhîm					X	X			X

*Jer12A = 12:1–4; Jer 12B = 12:7–13. Roots and words occurring 3x or more are noted. The word *midbār* is not counted when it occurs in the phrase *nĕʾôt midbār* (Jer 23:10; Joel 1:19, 20).

BIBLIOGRAPHY

Abrams, M. H. *A Glossary of Literary Terms*. 6th ed. Fort Worth, Tex.: Harcourt Brace, 1993.

Acker, Paul. *Revising Oral Theory: Formulaic Composition in Old English and Old Icelandic Verse*. New York: Garland, 1998.

Ackroyd, Peter R. "The Book of Isaiah." Pages 329–71 in *The Interpreter's One-Volume Commentary on the Bible*. Edited by Charles M. Laymon. Nashville: Abingdon, 1971.

Ahlström, Gösta W. *Joel and the Temple Cult of Jerusalem*. VTSup 21. Leiden: Brill, 1971.

Andersen, Francis I., and David N. Freedman. *Amos*. AB 24A. New York: Doubleday, 1989.

———. *Hosea*. AB 24. Garden City, N.Y.: Doubleday, 1980.

Anderson, Gary A. *A Time to Mourn, A Time to Dance: The Expression of Grief and Joy in Israelite Religion*. University Park: Pennsylvania State University Press, 1991.

Arend, Walter. *Die typischen Scenen bei Homer*. Problemata, Forschungen zur classischen Philologie no. 7. Berlin: Weidmann, 1933.

Auden, W. H. *Collected Poems*. Edited by Edward Mendelson. New York: Random House, 1976.

Auvray, Paul. *Isaïe 1–39*. SB. Paris: Gabalda, 1972.

Bakker, Egbert J. *Poetry in Speech: Orality and Homeric Discourse*. Ithaca, N.Y.: Cornell University Press, 1997.

Bakker, Egbert, and Ahuvia Kahane, eds. *Written Voices: Spoken Signs: Tradition, Performance, and the Epic Text*. Cambridge, Mass.: Harvard University Press, 1997.

Barstad, Hans M. "No Prophets? Recent Developments in Biblical Prophetic Research and Ancient Near Eastern Prophecy." *JSOT* 57 (1993): 39–60.

Barton, John. *Isaiah 1–39*. OTG. Sheffield: Sheffield Academic Press, 1995.

Bauer, Hans, and Pontus Leander. *Historische Grammatik der hebräischen Sprache des alten Testaments*. Halle: Niemeyer, 1918–1922. Repr., Hildesheim: Olms, 1962.

Baumann, Arnulf. "אָבַל *'ābhal;* אָבֵל *'ābhēl;* אָבֶל *'ēbhel.*" *TDOT* 1:44–48.

Baumgartner, Walter. *Jeremiah's Poems of Lament*. Translated by D. E. Orton. Sheffield: Almond, 1988.

Becker, Andrew S. *The Shield of Achilles and the Poetics of Ekphrasis*. Greek Studies: Interdisciplinary Approaches. Lanham, Md.: Rowman & Littlefield, 1995.

Ben-Amos, David. "Folklore in the Ancient Near East." *ABD* 2:818–28.

Bentzen, Aage. "The Ritual Background of Amos i 2–ii 16." *OtSt* 8 (1950): 85–99.

Berlin, Adele. *The Dynamics of Biblical Parallelism*. Bloomington: Indiana University Press, 1985.

———. *Zephaniah*. AB 25A. New York: Doubleday, 1994.

Beuken, Willem A. M. "Jesaja 33 als Spiegeltext im Jesajabuch." *ETL* 67 (1991): 5–35.

Bewer, Julius A. *A Critical and Exegetical Commentary on Obadiah and Joel*. ICC. Edinburgh: T&T Clark, 1911.

Blass, Friedrich, and Albert Debrunner. *A Greek Grammar of the New Testament and Other Early Christian Literature*. Translated and revised by Robert W. Funk. Chicago: University of Chicago Press, 1961.

Blenkinsopp, Joseph. *Ezekiel*. IBC. Louisville: John Knox, 1990.

———. *A History of Prophecy in Israel*. Rev. ed. Louisville: Westminster John Knox, 1996.

———. *Isaiah 1–39*. AB 19. New York: Doubleday, 2000.

———. *The Pentateuch: An Introduction to the First Five Books of the Bible*. ABRL. New York: Doubleday, 1992.

———. *Prophecy and Canon: A Contribution to the Study of Jewish Origins*. University of Notre Dame Center for the Study of Judaism and Christianity in Antiquity 3. Notre Dame, Ind.: Notre Dame University Press, 1977.

———. *Sage, Priest, Prophet: Religious and Intellectual Leadership in Ancient Israel*. Library of Ancient Israel. Louisville: Westminster John Knox, 1995.

Bourke, J. "Le Jour de Yahvé dans Joel." *RB* 66 (1959): 5–31.

Bremond, Claude. "Concept and Theme." Pages 46–59 in *The Return of Thematic Criticism*. Edited by Werner Sollors. Cambridge, Mass.: Harvard University Press, 1993.

Brinker, Menachem. "Theme and Interpretation." Pages 21–37 in *The Return of Thematic Criticism*. Edited by Werner Sollors. Cambridge, Mass.: Harvard University Press, 1993.

Bright, John. *Jeremiah*. AB 21. Garden City, N.Y.: Doubleday, 1965.

Brock, Sebastian P., ed. *Isaiah*. The Old Testament in Syriac according to the Peshitta Version 3/1. Peshitta Institute. Leiden: Brill, 1987.

Brueggemann, Walter. "Amos IV 4–13 and Israel's Covenant Worship." *VT* 15 (1965): 1–15.

———. "The Kerygma of the Priestly Writers." *ZAW* 84 (1972): 397–414.

Cassuto, Umberto. *Bible and Ancient Oriental Texts*. Vol. 2 of *Biblical and Oriental Studies*. Jerusalem: Magnes, 1975.

Castellino, Giorgio R. "Observations on the Literary Structure of Some Passages in Jeremiah." *VT* 30 (1980): 398–408.

Cheyne, T. K. *The Book of the Prophet Isaiah: Critical Edition of the Hebrew Text*. Leipzig: Hinrichstsche, 1899.

Childs, Brevard S. "The Enemy from the North and the Chaos Tradition." *JBL* 78 (1959): 187–98.

———. *Introduction to the Old Testament As Scripture*. Philadelphia: Fortress, 1979.

———. *Isaiah*. OTL. Louisville: Westminster John Knox, 2001.

———. *Isaiah and the Assyrian Crisis*. SBT 2/3. London: SCM, 1967.

Clay, Jenny S. Review of Laura M. Slatkin, *The Power of Thetis: Allusion and Interpretation in the Iliad*. *Classical Journal* 89 (1994): 207–9.

Clements, Ronald E. *Isaiah 1–39*. NCB. Grand Rapids, Mich.: Eerdmans, 1987.

———. "Israel in Its Historical and Cultural Setting." Pages 3–17 in *The World of Ancient Israel: Sociological, Anthropological and Political Perspectives*. Edited by Ronald E. Clements. Cambridge: Cambridge University Press, 1989.

———. *Jeremiah*. IBC. Atlanta: John Knox, 1988.

———. *One Hundred Years of Old Testament Interpretation*. Philadelphia: Westminster, 1976.

———. "Patterns in the Prophetic Canon." Pages 42–55 in *Canon and Authority: Essays in Old Testament Religion and Theology*. Edited by George W. Coats and Burke O. Long. Philadelphia: Fortress, 1977.

———. *Prophecy and Tradition*. Atlanta: John Knox, 1975.

———. "Prophecy As Literature: A Re-appraisal." Pages 59–76 in *The Hermeneutical Quest: Essays in Honor of James Luther Mays on his Sixty-Fifth Birthday*. Edited by D. G. Miller. Allison Park, Pa.: Pickwick, 1986.

Clifford, Richard J. *Fair Spoken and Persuading: An Interpretation of Second Isaiah*. Theological Inquiries. New York: Paulist, 1984.

———. "The Hebrew Scriptures and the Theology of Creation." *TS* 46 (1985): 507–23.

Clines, D. J. A. "Was There an *'BL* II 'Be Dry' in Classical Hebrew?" *VT* 42 (1992): 1–10.

Coggins, Richard. "An Alternative Prophetic Tradition?" Pages 77–94 in *Israel's Prophetic Tradition: Essays in Honour of Peter R. Ackroyd*. Edited by Richard Coggins, Anthony Phillips, and Michael A. Knibb. Cambridge: Cambridge University Press, 1982.

Collins, John J. "Old Testament Apocalypticism and Eschatology." Pages 298–304 in *The New Jerome Biblical Commentary*. Edited by Raymond E. Brown, Joseph A. Fitzmyer, and Roland E. Murphy. Englewood Cliffs, N.J.: Prentice Hall, 1990.

Condamin, Albert. *Le Livre de Jérémie*. EBib. Paris: Gabalda, 1936.

Coote, Robert B. "The Application of the Oral Theory to Biblical Hebrew Literature." *Semeia* 5 (1976): 51–64.

Cornill, Carl H. *Das Buch Jeremia*. Leipzig: Tauchnitz, 1905.

Crenshaw, James L. "Amos and the Theophanic Tradition." *ZAW* 80 (1968): 203–215.

———. *Joel.* AB 24C. New York: Doubleday, 1995.

Cross, Frank M. *Canaanite Myth and Hebrew Epic.* Cambridge, Mass.: Harvard University Press, 1973.

———. "The Development of the Jewish Scripts." Pages 133–202 in *The Bible and the Ancient Near East: Essays in Honor of William Foxwell Albright.* Edited by G. Ernest Wright. Garden City, N.Y.: Doubleday, 1965.

Culley, Robert C. "The Confessions of Jeremiah and Traditional Discourse." Pages 69–81 in *"A Wise and Discerning Mind": Essays in Honor of Burke O. Long.* BJS 325. Providence, R.I.: Brown Judaic Studies, 2000.

———. *Oral Formulaic Language in the Biblical Psalms.* Toronto: University of Toronto Press, 1967.

———. "Oral Tradition and the OT: Some Recent Discussion." *Semeia* 5 (1976): 1–33.

———. "Orality and Writtenness in the Prophetic Texts." Pages 45–64 in *Writings and Speech in Israelite and Ancient Near Eastern Prophecy.* Edited by Ehud Ben Zvi and Michael H. Floyd. SBLSymS 10. Atlanta: Society of Biblical Literature, 2000.

———. *Themes and Variations: A Study of Action in Biblical Narrative.* SemeiaSt. Atlanta: Scholars Press, 1992.

Damrosch, David. *The Narrative Covenant: Transformations of Genre in the Growth of Biblical Literature.* San Francisco: Harper & Row, 1987.

Davidson, Robert. "Covenant Ideology in Ancient Israel." Pages 323–47 in *The World of Ancient Israel: Sociological, Anthropological, and Political Perspective.* Edited by Ronald E. Clements. Cambridge: Cambridge University Press, 1989.

Davis, Ellen F. *Swallowing the Scroll: Textuality and the Dynamics of Discourse in Ezekiel's Prophecy.* Bible and Literature 21. Sheffield: Almond, 1989.

Davis, Michael T., and Brent A. Strawn. "Isaiah 31:4–5 in the Light of Lion Iconography in the Ancient Near East." Paper presented at the annual meeting of the AAR/SBL, New Orleans, 25 November 1996.

Deissler, Alfons. *Zwölf Propheten.* NEchtB. Würzburg: Echter, 1981.

Delekat, Lienhard. "Zum Hebräischen Wörterbuch." *VT* 14 (1964): 7–74.

Delitzsch, Franz. *Jesaja.* 5th ed. Giessen and Basel: Brunnen, 1984.

De Roche, Michael. "The Reversal of Creation in Hosea." *VT* 31 (1981): 400–409.

———. "Zephaniah I 2–3: The 'Sweeping' of Creation." *VT* 30 (1980): 104–9.

Diamond, A. R. *The Confessions of Jeremiah in Context: Sources of Prophetic Drama.* JSOTSup 45. Sheffield: Sheffield Academic Press, 1987.

Dobbs-Allsopp, Frederick W. *Weep, O Daughter of Zion: A Study of the City Lament Genre in the Hebrew Bible*. BibOr 44. Rome: Pontifical Biblical Institute, 1993.

Driver, Godfrey R. "Confused Hebrew Roots." Pages 73–82 in *Occident and Orient: Being Studies in Semitic Philology and Literature, Jewish History and Philosophy and Folklore in the Widest Sense, in Honor of Haham Dr. M. Gaster's Eightieth Birthday; Gaster Anniversary Volume*. Edited by Bruno Schindler with A. Marmorstein. London: Taylor, 1936.

Driver, Samuel R. *The Book of the Prophet Jeremiah*. New York: Charles Scribner's, 1907.

———. *The Books of Joel and Amos*. Cambridge Bible for Schools and Colleges. Cambridge: Cambridge University Press, 1897.

———. *Deuteronomy*. 3d ed. ICC. Edinburgh: T&T Clark, 1901.

———. *A Treatise on the Use of the Tenses*. 3d ed. Oxford: Clarendon, 1892.

Duhm, Bernhard. "Anmerkungen zu den Zwölf Propheten." *ZAW* 31 (1911): 1–43, 81–110, 161–204.

———. *Das Buch Jeremia*. KHC 11. Tübingen: Mohr, 1901.

———. *Das Buch Jesaia*. HAT 3/1. Göttingen: Vandenhoeck & Ruprecht, 1902.

Eberlin, Karl. *Gott der Schöpfer—Israels Gott: Eine exegetisch-hermeneutische Studie zur theologischen Funktion alttestamentlicher Schöpfungs-aussagen*. BEATAJ 5. Frankfurt: Lang, 1986.

Edmunds, Lowell, and Robert W. Wallace. *Poet, Public, and Performance in Ancient Greece*. Baltimore: Johns Hopkins University Press, 1997.

Eissfeldt, Otto. *The Old Testament: An Introduction*. New York: Harper & Row, 1965.

Eliade, Mircea. *The Sacred and the Profane*. New York: Harcourt, Brace & World, 1959.

Emerton, John A. "Notes on Jeremiah 12 9 and on Some Suggestions of J. D. Michaelis about the Hebrew words *naḥā, ʿaᵉbrā,* and *jadăᶜ.*" *ZAW* 81 (1969): 182–91.

Eppstein, Victor. "The Day of Yahweh in Jer 4:23–28." *JBL* 87 (1968): 93–97.

Feigin, Samuel. "The Meaning of Ariel." *JBL* 39 (1920): 131–37.

Fields, Weston W. "The Motif 'Night As Danger' Associated with Three Biblical Destruction Narratives." Pages 17–32 in *"Shaʿarei Talmon": Studies in the Bible, Qumran, and the Ancient Near East Presented to Shemaryahu Talmon*. Edited by Michael Fishbane and Emmanuel Tov. Winona Lake, Ind.: Eisenbrauns, 1992.

———. *Sodom and Gomorrah: History and Motif in Biblical Narrative*. JSOTSup 231. Sheffield: Sheffield Academic Press, 1997.

Finnegan, Ruth. *Oral Poetry: Its Nature, Significance and Social Context*. Cambridge: Cambridge University Press, 1977.

Fischer, Bonifatius, H. I. Frede, Johanne Gribomont, H. F. D. Sparks, and W. Thiele, eds. *Biblia Sacra.* Iuxta Vulgatem Versionem. 3d ed. 2 vols. Stuttgart: Deutsche Bibelgesellschaft, 1983.

Fishbane, Michael. *Biblical Interpretation in Ancient Israel.* Oxford: Clarendon, 1985.

———. "Jeremiah IV 23–26 and Job III 3–13: A Recovered Use of the Creation Pattern." *VT* 21 (1971): 151–67.

Fitzgerald, Aloysius. "Hebrew Poetry." Pages 201–8 in *The New Jerome Biblical Commentary.* Edited by Raymond E. Brown, Joseph A. Fitzmyer, and Roland E. Murphy. Englewood Cliffs, N.J.: Prentice-Hall, 1990.

Fohrer, Georg. *History of Israelite Religion.* Nashville: Abingdon, 1972.

———. *Introduction to the Old Testament.* New York: Abingdon, 1968.

———. "Modern Interpretation of the Prophets." *JBL* 80 (1961): 309–19.

Foley, John Miles. *Homer's Traditional Art.* University Park: Pennsylvania State University Press, 1999.

———. *Immanent Art: From Structure to Meaning in Traditional Oral Epic.* Bloomington: Indiana University Press, 1991.

———. *Traditional Oral Epic: The Odyssey, Beowulf, and the Serbo-Croatian Return Song.* Berkeley and Los Angeles: University of California Press, 1990.

———. "Word-Power, Performance, and Tradition." *Journal of American Folklore* 105 (1992): 275–301.

———. "What's in a Sign?" Pages 1–28 in *Signs of Orality: The Oral Tradition and Its Influence in the Greek and Roman World.* Edited by E. Anne MacKay. Mnemosyne: bibliotheca classica Batava; Supplementum 188. Leiden: Brill, 1998.

———, ed. *Teaching Oral Traditions.* New York: Modern Language Association, 1998.

Frankfort, Thérèse. "Le כי de Joel I 12." *VT* 10 (1960): 445–48.

Frymer-Kensky, Tikva. "Pollution, Purification, and Purgation in Biblical Israel." Pages 399–414 in *The Word of the Lord Shall Go Forth: Essays in Honor of David Noel Freedman in Celebration of His Sixtieth Birthday.* Edited by Carol L. Meyers and Michael P. O'Connor. Winona Lake, Ind.: Eisenbrauns, 1982.

Gailey, James H., Jr. "The Sword and the Heart: Evil from the North—and within, an Exposition of Jeremiah 4:5–6:30." *Int* 9 (1955): 294–309.

Gaster, Theodor H. *Myth, Legend, and Custom in the Old Testament.* New York: Harper & Row, 1969.

———. *Thespis: Ritual, Myth, and Drama in the Ancient Near East.* New York: Henry Schuman, 1950.

Gelson, A., ed. *Dodekapropheton.* The Old Testament in Syriac according to the Peshitta Version 3/4. Peshitta Institute. Leiden: Brill, 1980.

Gese, Hartmut. "Amos 8, 4–8: Der kosmische Frevel händlerischer Habgier." Pages 59–72 in *Prophet und Prophetenbuch: Festschrift für Otto Kaiser zum 65. Geburtstag*. Edited by Volkmar Fritz, Karl-Friedrich Pohlmann, and Hans-Christoph Schmitt. BZAW 185. Berlin: de Gruyter, 1989.

Giesebrecht, Friedrich. *Das Buch Jeremia*. 2d ed. HAT 3, 2/1. Göttingen: Vandenhoeck & Ruprecht, 1907.

Goody, Jack. *The Interface between the Written and the Oral*. Cambridge: Cambridge University Press, 1987.

Gray, George B. *A Critical and Exegetical Commentary on the Book of Isaiah*. ICC. New York: Charles Scribner's, 1912.

———. "The Parallel Passages in 'Joel,' in Their Bearing on the Question of Date." *Exp* 4:8 (1893): 208–25.

Gunkel, Hermann. "Jesaja 33, eine prophetische Liturgie." *ZAW* NS 1 (1924): 177–208.

———. "Problems of Hebrew Literary History." Pages 57–68 in *What Remains of the Old Testament*. New York: Macmillan, 1928.

———. *Schöpfung und Chaos in Urzeit und Endzeit*. Göttingen: Vandenhoeck and Ruprecht, 1895.

Gunn, David M. "On Oral Tradition: A Response to John Van Seters." *Semeia* 5 (1976): 155–61.

Hiebert, Theodore. "Joel, Book of." *ABD* 3:878–79.

———. *The Yahwist's Landscape: Nature and Religion in Early Israel*. New York: Oxford University Press, 1996.

Hillers, Delbert R. "Dust: Some Aspects of Old Testament Imagery." Pages 105–9 in *Love and Death in the Ancient Near East: Essays in Honor of Marvin H. Pope*. Edited by John H. Marks and Robert M. Good. Guilford, Conn.: Four Quarters, 1987.

———. "The Roads to Zion Mourn." *Perspective* 12:1–2 (1971): 121–34.

———. *Treaty-Curses and the Old Testament Prophets*. BibOr 16. Rome: Pontifical Biblical Institute, 1964.

Hoftijzer, Jacob, and K. Jongeling. *Dictionary of the North-West Semitic Inscriptions*. Leiden: Brill, 1995.

Holladay, William L. *Jeremiah 1*. Hermeneia. Philadelphia: Fortress, 1986.

———. *Jeremiah 2*. Hermeneia. Philadelphia: Fortress, 1989.

———. "Jeremiah's Lawsuit with God." *Int* 17 (1963): 280–87.

———. "The Recovery of Poetic Passages of Jeremiah." *JBL* 85 (1966): 401–35.

———. "Style, Irony, and Authenticity in Jeremiah." *JBL* 81 (1962): 44–54.

Hubmann, Franz D. *Untersuchungen zu den Konfessionen Jer 11,18–12,6 und Jer 15,10–21*. FB 30. Würzburg: Echter, 1978.

Irwin, William H. *Isaiah 28–33: Translation with Philological Notes*. BibOr 30. Rome: Pontifical Biblical Institute, 1977.

Jacob, Edmond. *Osée*. 3d ed. CAT 11a. Geneva: Labor et Fides, 1992.

Jacobsen, Thorkild. "Mesopotamia: The Cosmos As a State." Pages 125–84 in *The Intellectual Adventure of Ancient Man*. Edited by Henri Frankfort. Chicago: University of Chicago Press, 1946. Repr. with revised bibliographies, 1977.

Janzen, Waldemar. *Mourning Cry and Woe Oracle*. BZAW 125. Berlin: de Gruyter, 1972.

Jastrow, Marcus, ed. *A Dictionary of the Targumim, the Talmud Babli and Yerushalmi, and the Midrashic Literature*. New York: Judaica, 1971.

Jensen, Joseph. *Isaiah 1–39*. OTM 8. Wilmington, Del.: Michael Glazier, 1984.

Jeremias, Jörg. *The Book of Amos*. OTL. Louisville: Westminster John Knox, 1998.

———. "Joel/Joelbuch." *TRE* 17:91–97.

———. *Der Prophet Hosea*. ATD 24/1. Göttingen: Vandenhoeck & Ruprecht, 1983.

Johnson, Dan G. *From Chaos to Restoration: An Integrative Reading of Isaiah 24–27*. JSOTSup 61. Sheffield: Sheffield Academic Press, 1988.

Joüon, Paul. *Grammaire de l'Hébreu Biblique*. Rome: Pontifical Biblical Institute, 1923.

Junker, Hubert. "Textkritische, formkritische und traditionsgeschichtliche Untersuchung zu Os 4,1–10." *BZ* 4 (1960): 165–73.

Kaiser, Otto. *Isaiah 1–39*. OTL. Philadelphia: Westminster, 1974.

———. "The Law As Center of the Hebrew Bible." Pages 93–103 in *"Sha'arei Talmon": Studies in the Bible, Qumran, and the Ancient Near East Presented to Shemaryahu Talmon*. Edited by Michael Fishbane and Emmanuel Tov. Winona Lake, Ind.: Eisenbrauns, 1992.

Kapelrud, Arvid S. *Joel Studies*. UUÅ 1948:4. Uppsala: Lundequist, 1948.

Kaufman, Stephen A. *The Akkadian Influence on Aramaic*. AS 19. Chicago: University of Chicago Press, 1974.

Keller, Carl-A. *Joël, Abdias, Jonas*. CAT 11a. Geneva: Labor et Fides, 1992.

Knierim, Rolf P. "Cosmos and History in Israel's Theology." *HBT* 3 (1981): 59–123.

———. "Criticism of Literary Features, Form, Tradition, and Redaction." Pages 123–65 in *The Hebrew Bible and Its Modern Interpreters*. Edited by Douglas A. Knight and Gene M. Tucker. Philadelphia: Fortress, 1985.

———. "Old Testament Form Criticism Reconsidered." *Int* 27 (1973): 435–68.

Knight, Douglas A. "Cosmogony and Order in the Hebrew Tradition." Pages 133–57 in *Cosmogony and Ethical Order: New Studies in Comparative Ethics*. Edited by Robin W. Lovin and Frank E. Reynolds. Chicago: University of Chicago Press, 1985.

———. *The Traditions of Israel*. SBLDS 9. Missoula, Mont.: Society of Biblical Literature, 1973.

Koch, Klaus. "Is There a Doctrine of Retribution in the Old Testament?" Pages 57–87 in *Theodicy in the Old Testament*. Edited by James L. Crenshaw. Philadelphia: Fortress, 1983.

Kramer, Samuel N. *The Sumerians: Their History, Culture, and Character.* Chicago: University of Chicago Press, 1963.

Kugel, James L. *The Idea of Biblical Poetry: Parallelism and Its History.* New Haven, Conn.: Yale University Press, 1981.

———. "Poets and Prophets: An Overview." Pages 1–25 in *Poetry and Prophecy: The Beginnings of a Literary Tradition*. Edited by James L. Kugel. Ithaca, N.Y.: Cornell University Press, 1990.

Kutsch, Ernst. "'Trauerbräuche' und 'Selbstminderungsriten' im Alten Testament." Pages 25–37 in *Drei Wiener Antrittsreden*. ThSt 78. Zurich: EVZ, 1965.

Lack, Rémi. *La Symbolique du Livre d'Isaïe: Essai sur l'image littéraire comme élément de structuration*. AnBib 59. Rome: Pontifical Biblical Institute, 1973.

Lagrange, Marie-Joseph. "L'Apocalypse d'Isaïe (24–27)." *RB* 3 (1894): 200–231.

Lattimore, Richmond, trans. *The Iliad of Homer*. Chicago: University of Chicago Press, 1951.

Lee, S. *Vetus Testamentum Syriace*. London: British and Foreign Bible Society, 1823. Repr. with the Apocrypha, Reading: United Bible Society, 1979.

Leslau, Wolf. *Comparative Dictionary of Geʿez*. Wiesbaden: Harrassowitz, 1991.

Levenson, Jon D. *Creation and the Persistence of Evil: The Jewish Drama of Divine Omnipotence*. San Francisco: Harper & Row, 1987. Repr., Princeton, N.J.: Princeton University Press, 1994.

———. "The Theologies of Commandment in Biblical Israel." *HTR* 73 (1980): 17–33.

Lindblom, Johannes. *Prophecy in Ancient Israel*. Philadelphia: Fortress, 1962.

Lohfink, Norbert. "Enthielten die im Alten Testament bezeugten Klageriten eine Phase des Schweigens?" *VT* 12 (1962): 260–77.

Lord, Albert B. "Formula and Non-narrative Theme in South Slavic Oral Epic and the OT." *Semeia* 5 (1976): 93–105.

———. "Homer As an Oral Poet." *Harvard Studies in Classical Philology* 72 (1968): 1–46.

———. "Perspectives on Recent Work on Oral Literature." Pages 41–61 in *Oral Literature: Seven Essays*. Edited by Joseph J. Duggan. Edinburgh: Scottish Academic; New York: Barnes & Noble, 1975. Also published in *Forum for Modern Language Studies* 10 (1974): 1–21.

———. *The Singer of Tales*. Harvard Studies in Comparative Literature 24. Cambridge, Mass.: Harvard University Press, 1960.

Lowth, Robert. *Isaiah: A New Translation; with a Preliminary Dissertation, and Notes.* Boston: William Hilliard; Cambridge, Mass.: James Munroe, 1834.

MacKay, E. Anne, ed. *Signs of Orality: The Oral Tradition and Its Influence in the Greek and Roman World.* Mnemosyne: bibliotheca classica Batava; Supplementum 188. Leiden: Brill, 1998.

Martin-Achard, Robert. *Amos: L'homme, le message, l'influence.* Geneva: Labor et Fides, 1984.

Mathews, Claire R. "Apportioning Desolation: Contexts for Interpreting Edom's Fate and Function in Isaiah." Pages 250–66 in *Society of Biblical Literature 1995 Seminar Papers.* Edited by Eugene H. Lovering Jr. SBLSP 34. Atlanta: Scholars Press, 1995.

Mays, James L. *Hosea.* OTL. Philadelphia: Westminster, 1969.

McCarter, P. Kyle, Jr. *II Samuel.* AB 9. New York: Doubleday, 1984.

———. *Textual Criticism: Recovering the Text of the Hebrew Bible.* GBS. Philadelphia: Fortress, 1986.

McKane, William. *Jeremiah.* 2 vols. ICC. Edinburgh: T&T Clark, 1986–1996.

Millar, William R. *Isaiah 24–27 and the Origin of Apocalyptic.* HSM 11. Missoula, Mont.: Scholars Press, 1976.

Miller, Patrick D., Jr. *Sin and Judgment in the Prophets: A Stylistic and Theological Analysis.* SBLMS 27. Chico, Calif.: Scholars Press, 1982.

Mowinckel, Sigmund. *The Psalms in Israel's Worship.* 2 vols. Nashville: Abingdon, 1962.

Muilenburg, James. "Form Criticism and Beyond." *JBL* 88 (1969): 1–18.

———. "Hebrew Rhetoric: Repetition and Style." Pages 193–207 in *Congress Volume Copenhagen, 1953.* VTSup 1. Leiden: Brill, 1953.

Murray, Robert. "Prophecy and the Cult." Pages 200–216 in *Israel's Prophetic Tradition: Essays in Honour of Peter R. Ackroyd.* Edited by Richard Coggins, Anthony Phillips, and Michael A. Knibb. Cambridge: Cambridge University Press, 1982.

Nagy, Gregory. *The Best of the Acheans: Concepts of the Hero in Archaic Greek Poetry.* Baltimore: Johns Hopkins University Press, 1979.

———. "Formula and Meter: The Oral Poetics of Homer." Pages 18–35 in *Greek Mythology and Poetics.* Myth and Poetics. Ithaca, N.Y.: Cornell University Press, 1990.

———. *Poetry As Performance: Homer and Beyond.* Cambridge: Cambridge University Press, 1996.

Nash, Kathleen S. "The Cycle of Seasons in Joel." *TBT* 27 (1989): 74–80.

Neef, Heinz-Dieter. *Die Heilstraditionen Israels in der Verkündigung des Propheten Hosea.* BZAW 169. Berlin: de Gruyter, 1987.

Neher, André. *Amos: Contribution à l'étude du prophétisme.* Paris: Vrin, 1950.

Nicholson, Ernst W. *God and His People: Covenant and Theology in the Old Testament.* Oxford: Clarendon, 1986.

Niditch, Susan. "Biblical Composition and Oral Literature: A Reappraisal." Paper presented at the annual meeting of the AAR/SBL, Washington, D.C., 21 November 1993.

———. *Folklore and the Hebrew Bible*. GBS. Minneapolis: Fortress, 1993.

———. *Oral World and Written Word: Ancient Israelite Literature*. Library of Ancient Israel. Louisville: Westminster John Knox, 1996.

Niles, John D. *Homo Narrans: The Poetics and Anthropology of Oral Literature*. Philadelphia: University of Pennsylvania Press, 1999.

O'Connor, Michael P. *Hebrew Verse Structure*. Winona Lake, Ind.: Eisenbrauns, 1980.

Oden, Robert A., Jr. "The Place of Covenant in the Religion of Israel." Pages 429–47 in *Ancient Israelite Religion: Essays in Honor of Frank Moore Cross*. Edited by Patrick D. Miller Jr., Paul D. Hanson, and Sean Dean McBride. Philadelphia: Fortress, 1987.

Ong, Walter J. *Orality and Literacy: The Technologizing of the Word*. London: Methuen, 1982.

Osiek, Carolyn. "The Oral World of Early Christianity in Rome: The Case of Hermas." Pages 151–72 in *Judaism and Christianity in First-Century Rome*. Edited by Karl P. Donfried and Peter Richardson. Grand Rapids, Mich.: Eerdmans, 1998.

Parry, Adam, ed. *The Making of Homeric Verse: The Collected Papers of Milman Parry*. New York: Oxford University Press, 1987.

Paul, Shalom M. *Amos*. Hermeneia. Minneapolis: Fortress, 1991.

Payne Smith, J., ed. *A Compendious Syriac Dictionary*. Oxford: Clarendon, 1903.

Penna, A. "Il cosmo nella letteratura profetica." Pages 201–93 in *Il cosmo nella Bibbia*. Edited by Giuseppe De Gennaro. Naples: Edizioni Dehoniane, 1982.

Perlitt, Lothar. *Bundestheologie im Alten Testament*. WMANT 36. Neukirchen-Vluyn: Neukirchener Verlag, 1969.

Petersen, David L. *Late Israelite Prophecy: Studies in Deutero-Prophetic Literature and in Chronicles*. SBLMS 23. Chico, Calif.: Scholars Press, 1977.

Phillips, Anthony. "Prophecy and Law." Pages 217–32 in *Israel's Prophetic Tradition: Essays in Honour of Peter R. Ackroyd*. Edited by Richard Coggins, Anthony Phillips, and Michael A. Knibb. Cambridge: Cambridge University Press, 1982.

Plöger, Otto. *Theocracy and Eschatology*. Oxford: Basil Blackwell, 1968.

Polak, Frank H. "The Oral and the Written: Syntax, Stylistics and the Development of Biblical Prose Narrative." *JANESCU* 26 (1998): 59–105.

Preminger, Alex, and T. V. F. Brogen, eds. *The New Princeton Encyclopedia of Poetry and Poetics*. Princeton, N.J.: Princeton University Press, 1993.

Rad, Gerhard von. *The Message of the Prophets.* New York: Harper & Row, 1967.

———. "The Origin of the Concept of the Day of Yahweh." *JSS* 4 (1959): 97–108.

Rast, Walter E. *Tradition History and the Old Testament.* Philadelphia: Fortress, 1972.

Reed, William L. "Sharon." *IDB* 4:308–9.

Reimer, David J. "The 'Foe' and the 'North' in Jeremiah." *ZAW* 101 (1989): 223–32.

Roberts, J. J. M. *Nahum, Habakkuk, and Zephaniah.* OTL. Louisville: Westminster John Knox, 1991.

Robinson, Theodore H., and Friedrich Horst. *Die zwölf kleinen Propheten.* 2d ed. HAT 14. Tübingen: Mohr, 1954.

Ross, David O., Jr. "Commentaries on the *Aeneid:* S. J. Harrison, *Vergil: Aeneid 10;* K. W. Grandsen, *Virgil: Aeneid Book XI.*" *Classical Journal* 90 (1994): 81–86.

Rudolph, Wilhelm. *Hosea.* KAT 13/1. Gütersloh: Mohn, 1966.

———. *Jeremia.* 2d ed. HAT 12. Tübingen: Mohr, 1958.

———. *Jesaja 24–27.* BWANT 4/10. Stuttgart: Kohlhammer, 1933.

———. *Joel-Amos-Obadja-Jona.* KAT 13/2. Gütersloh: Mohn, 1971.

Sawyer, John F. A. *Isaiah.* 2 vols. Daily Study Bible. Philadelphia: Westminster, 1984–1986.

Schmid, Hans H. "Creation, Righteousness, and Salvation: 'Creation Theology' As the Broad Horizon of Biblical Theology." Pages 102–17 in *Creation in the Old Testament.* Edited by Bernhard W. Anderson. IRT 6. Philadelphia: Fortress, 1984.

Scholes, Robert, and Robert Kellogg. *The Nature of Narrative.* London: Oxford University Press, 1966.

Seitz, Christopher R. *Isaiah 1–39.* IBC. Louisville: John Knox, 1993.

Sellin, Ernst. *Das Zwölfprophetenbuch.* 2d ed. 2 vols. KAT 12/1–2. Leipzig: Deichertsche, 1929–1930.

Simkins, Ronald A. "God, History, and the Natural World in the Book of Joel." *CBQ* 55 (1993): 435–52.

Slatkin, Laura M. *The Power of Thetis: Allusion and Interpretation in the Iliad.* Berkeley and Los Angeles: University of California Press, 1991.

———. "The Wrath of Thetis." *Transactions of the American Philological Association* 116 (1986): 1–24.

Smith, Mark S. "Jeremiah IX 9—A Divine Lament." *VT* 37 (1987): 97–99.

Soden, Wolfram von. *Grundriss der akkadischen Grammatik.* AnOr 33/47. Rome: Pontifical Biblical Institute, 1969.

Sprengling, M. "Joel 1, 17a." *JBL* 38 (1919): 129–41.

Stahl, Rainer. "'Deshalb trocknet die Erde aus und verschmachten alle, die auf ihr wohnen...' Der Versuch einer theologiegeschichtlichen

Einordnung von Hos 4, 3." Pages 166–73 in *Alttestamentlicher Glaube und Biblische Theologie: Festschrift für Horst Dietrich Preuss zum 65. Geburtstag*. Edited by Jutta Hausmann and Hans-Jürgen Zobel. Stuttgart: Kohlhammer, 1992.

————. "Gottesgericht oder Selbstzerstörung? Wie ist ein verbindliches Zeugnis ökumenischer Theologie angesichts der ökologischen Herausforderung zu begründen? Eine Reflexion an Hand von Hosea 4, 1–3." Pages 321–21 in *Veritas et Communicatio: Ökumenische Theologie auf der Suche nach einem verbindlichen Zeugnis: Festschrift zum 60. Geburtstag von Ulrich Kühn*. Edited by Heiko Franke et al. Göttingen: Vandenhoeck & Ruprecht, 1992.

Steck, Otto H. "Theological Streams of Tradition." Pages 183–214 in *Tradition and Theology in the Old Testament*. Edited by Douglas A. Knight. Biblical Seminar. Sheffield: JSOT Press, 1977.

Stolz, Fritz. *Strukturen und Figuren im Kult von Jerusalem: Studien zur altorientalischen, vor-und-frühisraelitischen Religion*. BZAW 118. Berlin: de Gruyter, 1970.

Sweeney, Marvin A. *Isaiah 1–39 with an Introduction to Prophetic Literature*. FOTL 16. Grand Rapids, Mich.: Eerdmans, 1996.

————. "Textual Citations in Isaiah 24–27: Toward an Understanding of the Redactional Function of Chapters 24–27 in the Book of Isaiah." *JBL* 107 (1988): 39–52.

Talmon, Shemaryahu. "The 'Desert Motif' in the Bible and in Qumran Literature." Pages 31–63 in *Biblical Motifs: Origins and Transformations*. Edited by A. Altmann. Cambridge, Mass.: Harvard University Press, 1966.

Tromp, Nicholas J. *Primitive Conceptions of Death and the Nether World in the Old Testament*. BibOr 21. Rome Pontifical Biblical Institute, 1969.

Tucker, Gene M. "Prophecy and the Prophetic Literature." Pages 235–68 in *The Hebrew Bible and Its Modern Interpreters*. Edited by Douglas A. Knight and Gene M. Tucker. Philadelphia: Fortress, 1985.

————. "Prophetic Speech." *Int* 32 (1978): 31–45.

Uehlinger, Christoph. "The Cry of the Earth: Biblical Perspectives on Ecology and Violence." Pages 41–57 in *Ecology and Poverty: Cry of the Earth, Cry of the Poor*. Edited by Leonardo Boff and V. Elizondo. Concilium 1995/5. London: SCM, 1995.

Ulrich, Eugene C., Jr. *The Qumran Text of Samuel and Josephus*. HSM 19. Missoula, Mont.: Scholars Press, 1978.

Urbrock, William J. "Oral Antecedents to Job: A Survey of Formulas and Formulaic Systems." *Semeia* 5 (1976): 111–35.

Vall, Gregory R. "From Womb to Tomb: Poetic Imagery and the Book of Job." Ph.D. diss. The Catholic University of America, 1993.

Van Seters, John. "Oral Patterns or Literary Conventions in Biblical Narrative." *Semeia* 5 (1976): 139–54.

Vaux, Roland de. *Social Institutions*. Vol. 2 of *Ancient Israel*. New York: McGraw-Hill, 1965.

Vermeylen, Jacques. *Du Prophète Isaïe à l'apocalyptique*. 2 vols. EBib. Paris: Gabalda, 1977.

Volz, Paul. *Der Prophet Jeremia*. 2d ed. KAT 10. Leipzig: Deichertsche, 1928.

Watson, Janet, ed. *Speaking Volumes: Orality and Literacy in the Greek and Roman World*. Mnemosyne: bibliotheca classica Batava; Supplemntum 218. Leiden: Brill, 2001.

Watts, John D. W. *The Books of Joel, Obadiah, Jonah, Nahum, Habakkuk, and Zephaniah*. Cambridge: Cambridge University Press, 1975.

———. *Vision and Prophecy in Amos*. Leiden: Brill, 1958.

Weeks, Harry R. "Sharon." *ABD* 5:1161–63.

Wehr, Hans. *A Dictionary of Modern Written Arabic*. Edited by J. Milton Cowan. 3d ed. Ithaca, N.Y.: Spoken Language Series, 1976.

Weippert, Helga. *Schöpfer des Himmels und der Erde: Ein Beitrag zur Theologie des Jeremiabuches*. SBS 102. Stuttgart: Katholisches Bibelwerk, 1981.

Weiser, Artur. *Das Buch der zwölf kleinen Propheten*. ATD 24/1. Göttingen: Vandenhoeck & Ruprecht, 1949.

Weis, Richard D. "Angels, Altars, and Angles of Vision: The Case of אֶרְאֶלָּם in Isaiah 33:7." Pages 285–92 in *Tradition of the Text: Studies Offered to Dominique Barthélemy in Celebration of His Seventieth Birthday*. Edited by Gerard J. Norton and Stephen Pisano. OBO 109. Fribourg: Éditions universitaires; Göttingen: Vandenhoeck & Ruprecht, 1991.

Weiss, Meir. "Methodologisches über die Behandlung der Metapher dargelegt an Am. 1,2." *TZ* 23 (1967): 1–25.

Westermann, Claus. *Basic Forms of Prophetic Speech*. Louisville: Westminster John Knox, 1991.

Whallon, William. "Formulaic Language in the Old Testament." *Comparative Literature* 15 (1963): 1–14.

Whitelock, Dorothy, ed. *The Anglo Saxon Chronicle*. London: Eyre & Spottiswoode, 1961.

Widengren, Geo. "Oral Tradition and Written Literature among the Hebrews in the Light of the Arabic Evidence, with Special Regard to Prose Narratives." *AcOr* 23 (1959): 201–62.

Wildberger, Hans. *Jesaja 13–27*. BKAT 10/2. Neukirchen-Vluyn: Neukirchener Verlag, 1978.

———. *Jesaja 28–39*. BKAT 10/3. Neukirchen-Vluyn: Neukirchener Verlag, 1982.

Wilson, Robert R. *Prophecy and Society in Ancient Israel*. Philadelphia: Westminster, 1980.

Wisser, Laurent. "La création dans le livre de Jérémie." Pages 241–60 in *La création dans l'orient ancien*. Edited by Louis Derousseaux. Congrès de L'ACFEB, Lille (1985). LD 127. Paris: Cerf, 1987.

Wolff, Hans W. *Amos the Prophet: The Man and His Background.* Philadelphia: Fortress, 1973.

———. *Hosea.* Hermeneia. Philadelphia: Fortress, 1974.

———. *Joel and Amos.* Hermeneia. Philadelphia: Fortress, 1977.

Wolpers, Theodor. "Motif and Theme As Structural Content Units." Pages 80–91 in *The Return of Thematic Criticism.* Edited by Werner Sollors. Cambridge, Mass.: Harvard University Press, 1993.

Worthington, Ian, ed. *Voice into Text: Orality and Literacy in Ancient Greece.* Mnemosyne: bibliotheca classica Batava; Supplementum 157. Leiden: Brill, 1996.

Worthington, Ian, and John Miles Foley, eds. *Epea and grammata: Oral and Written Communication in Ancient Greece.* Mnemosyne: bibliotheca classica Batava; Supplementum 230. Leiden: Brill, 2002.Woude, Adams S. van der. "Three Classical Prophets: Amos, Hosea, and Micah." Pages 32–57 in *Israel's Prophetic Tradition: Essays in Honour of Peter R. Ackroyd.* Edited by Richard Coggins, Anthony Phillips, and Michael A. Knibb. Cambridge: Cambridge University Press, 1982.

Ziegler, Joseph, ed. *Duodecim prophetae.* Septuaginta. Vetus Testamentum Graecum 12. Göttingen: Vandenhoeck & Ruprecht, 1943.

———. *Isaias.* Septuaginta. Vetus Testamentum Graecum 14. Göttingen: Vandenhoeck & Ruprecht, 1967.

———. *Jeremias. Baruch. Threni. Epistula Jeremiae.* Septuaginta. Vetus Testamentum Graecum 15. Göttingen: Vandenhoeck & Ruprecht, 1957.

Zimmerli, Walther. *Ezekiel 1.* Hermeneia. Philadelphia: Fortress, 1983.

———. "Visionary Experience in Jeremiah." Pages 95–117 in *Israel's Prophetic Tradition: Essays in Honour of Peter R. Ackroyd.* Edited by Richard Coggins, Anthony Phillips, and Michael A. Knibb. Cambridge: Cambridge University Press, 1982.

INDEX OF BIBLICAL REFERENCES

INDEX OF MODERN AUTHORS

277

INDEX OF SUBJECTS